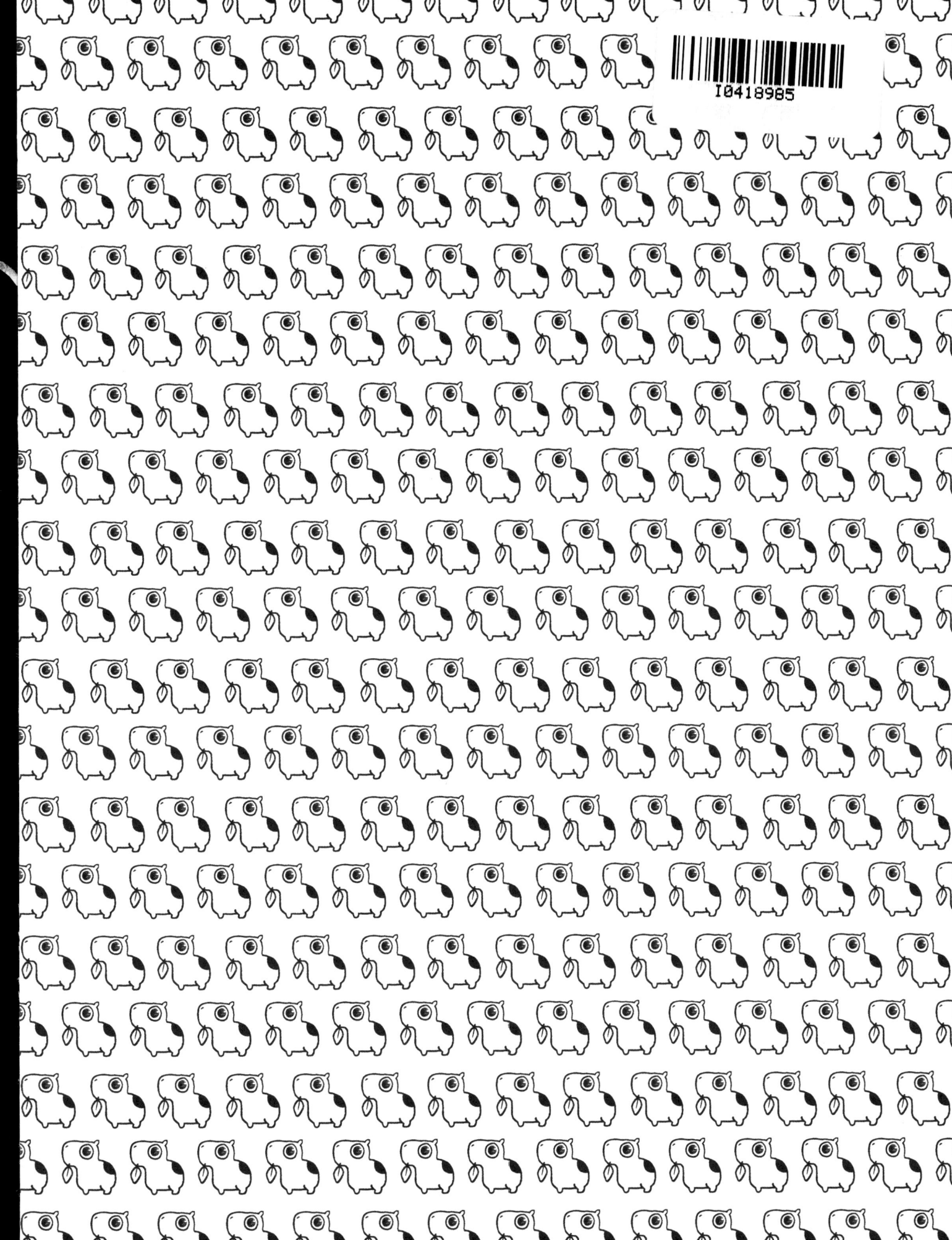

I0418985

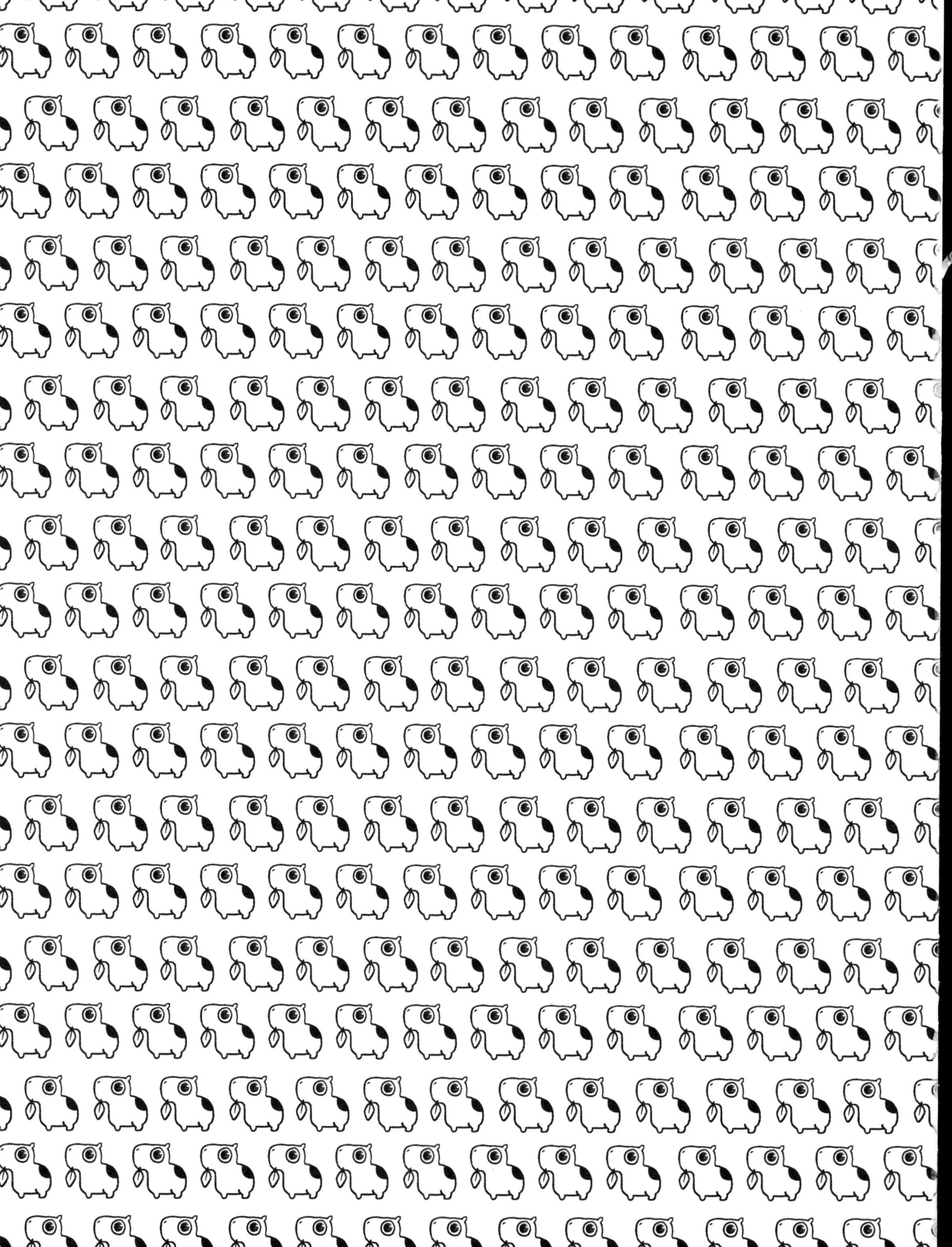

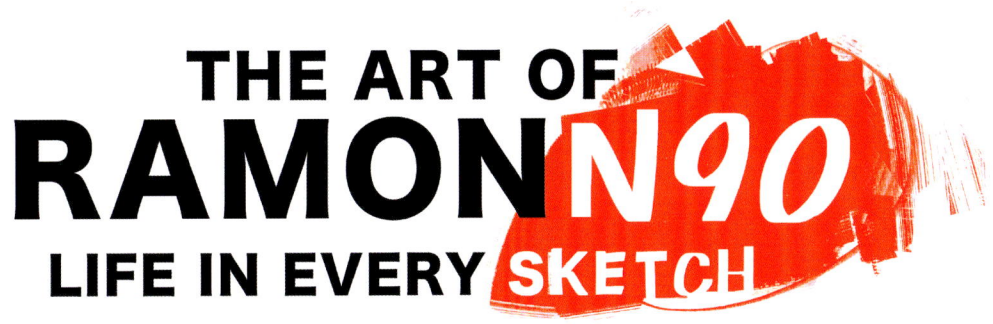

THE ART OF
RAMON N90
LIFE IN EVERY SKETCH

3dtotal Publishing

3dtotalPublishing

Correspondence: **publishing@3dtotal.com**
Website: **store.3dtotal.com**

***The Art of RamonN90: Life in Every Sketch* ©
2026, 3dtotal Publishing.** All rights reserved.
No part of this book can be reproduced in
any form or by any means, without the prior
written consent of the publisher. All artwork,
unless stated otherwise, is copyright of Ramón
Nuñez. All artwork that is not copyright of the
featured artist is marked accordingly.

Every effort has been made to ensure the
credits and contact information listed are
present and correct. In the case of any errors
that have occurred, the publisher respectfully
directs readers to **store.3dtotal.com/pages/
information** for any updated information
and corrections.

Thoughts and opinions expressed in this book
belong to the author and not the publisher.

First published in the United Kingdom, 2026,
by 3dtotal Publishing.

Address: 3dtotal.com Ltd,
29 Foregate Street, Worcester,
WR1 1DS, United Kingdom.

Hard cover ISBN: 978-1-915992-22-2

Printed and bound in China
by C&C Offset Printing Co., Ltd

Visit **store.3dtotal.com** for a complete list
of available book titles.

Editorial Project Manager: Rhiannon Joseph
Lead Editor: Samantha Rigby
Lead Designer: Joseph Cartwright
Studio Manager: Simon Morse
Managing Director: Tom Greenway

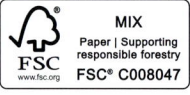

50%
of net profits donated
TO CHARITY

In 2022, 3dtotal Publishing became
successful enough to make a pledge to
donate **50% of its net profits to charity.**
This continues to be possible due to the
incredible support from all our customers,
employees, and partners. At the time
of printing, we have donated over $1.62
million (USD) to charity.

We focus our giving on three charitable
areas: **environmental**, **humanitarian**,
and **animal welfare**. We use organizations
such as Effective Altruism and Founders
Pledge to guide who we help within these
causes. Some ways of doing good are
over 100 times more effective than others,
so donating this way hugely increases the
impact of our contributions.

**SEE 3DTOTAL.COM/CHARITY
FOR FULL DETAILS.**

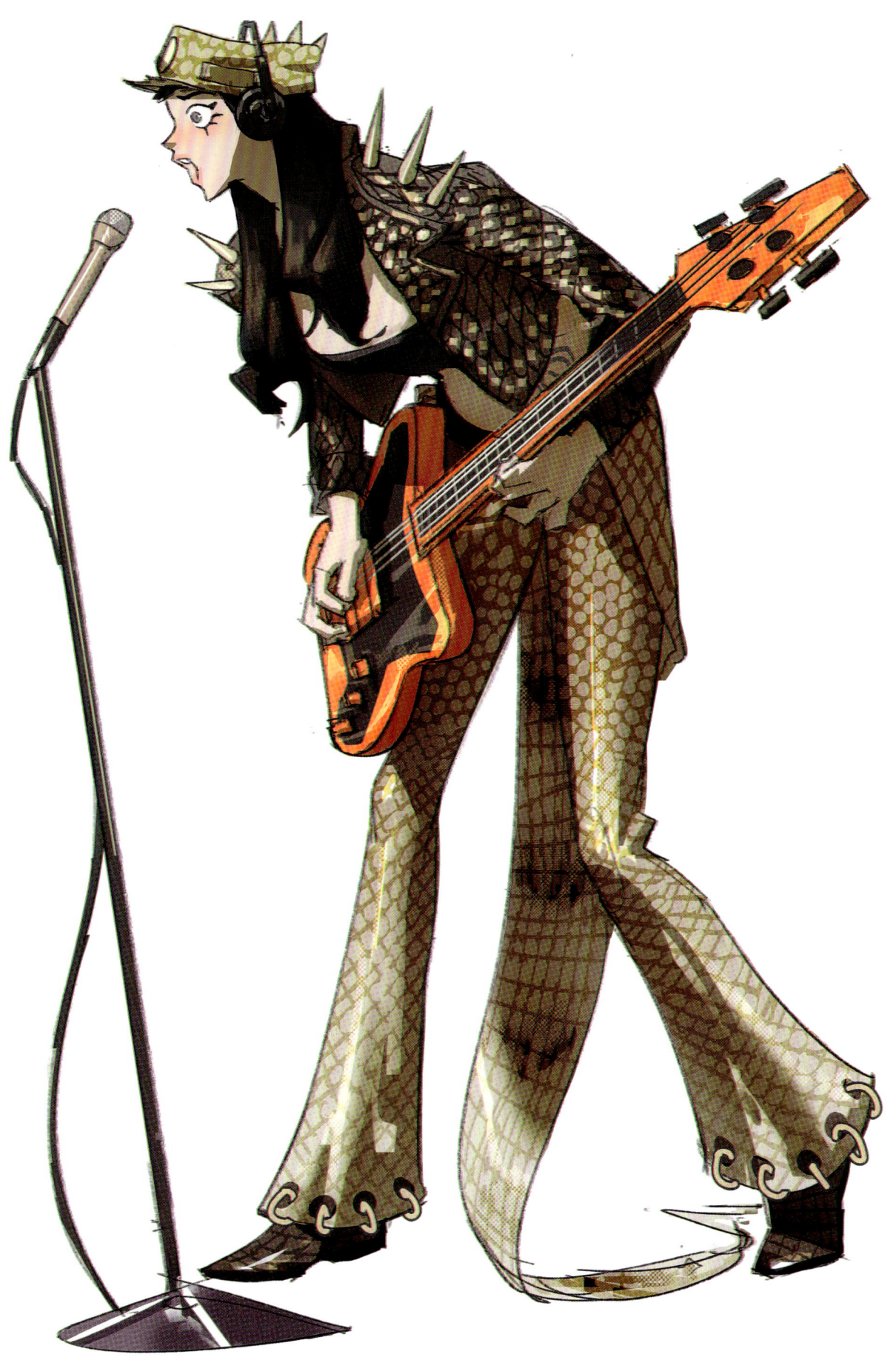

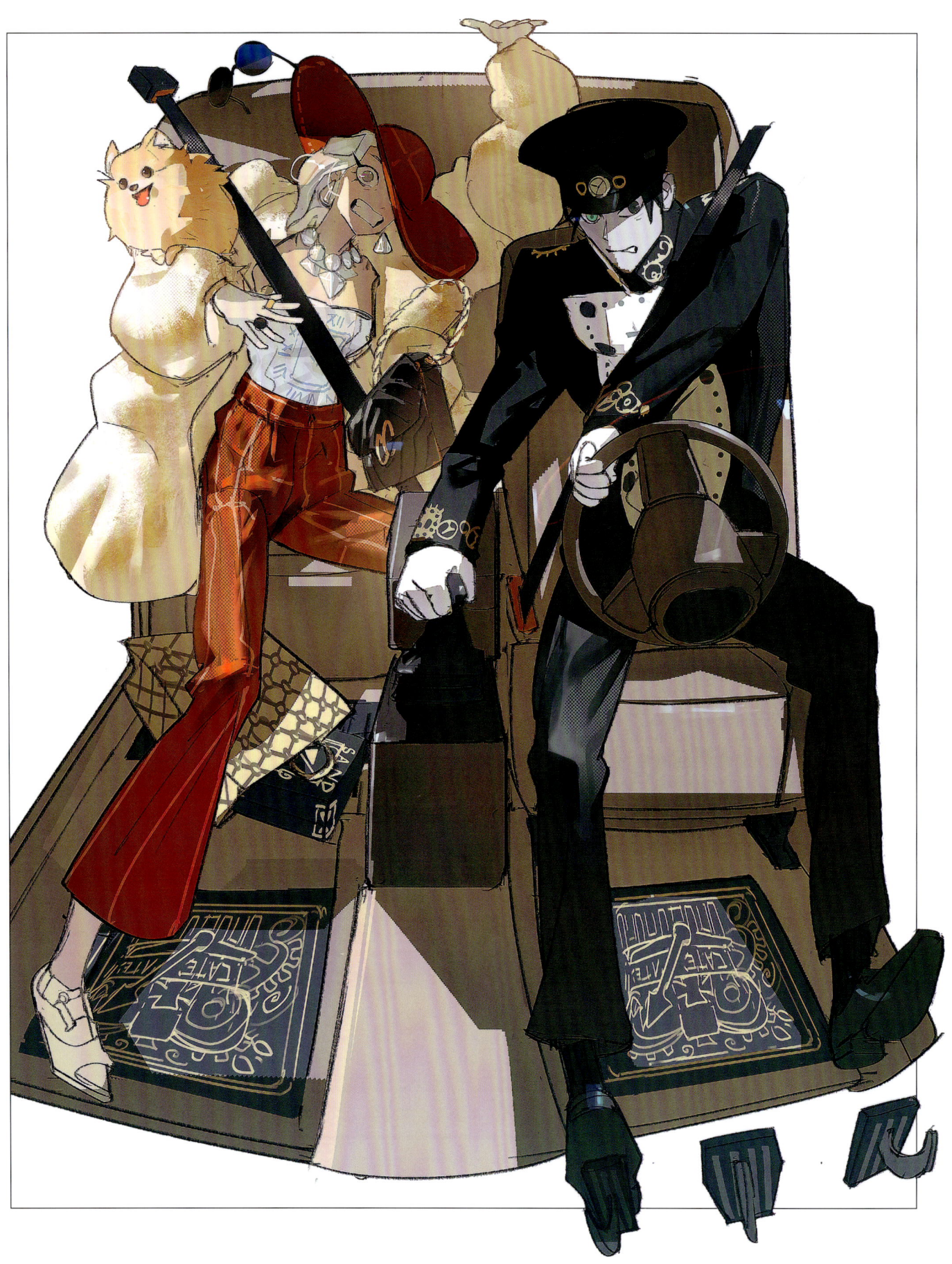

CONTENTS

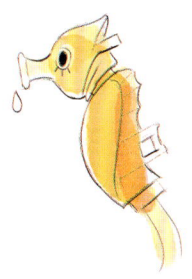

FOREWORD

Ramón is one of those people whose work makes you stop and think, *Damn, this guy is so talented!*

Watching Ramón grow as an artist has been one hell of a ride. When I first saw his work, I could tell he was in full exploration mode, focused and determined. It was clear he wasn't just figuring out how to do things, but *why* to do them. First, I thought, *Maybe he's trying to find what was popular? Maybe he is trying to please clients?* But he didn't seem like that type of person. He was, in fact, on a hunt for what he liked, for what felt real and true to him, for what moved him.

I watched him jump through phases, not only in art but in life, too. He experimented wildly, crashing and burning a few times, and came out the other side with a kind of raw, untamed 'skill' that only develops from throwing yourself at the craft over and over again. And let me tell you, being around him makes you question yourself – how you work, how you tackle projects, and most importantly, how you live – because there's something about him. He pushes you.

If you're in a good place, he motivates you to push harder and chase your goals with everything you've got. If you're not in a good place, though, it feels as if you're going in the opposite direction. Hell, he might even make you jealous: *How can someone be this good?*

The answer is work. All the work. And live as much as you can. Look for the answers by diving head first into everything – every style, every idea, every crazy experiment – without fear, without asking for permission, just for you.

Own each choice and take it with pride. Take the pain. As crazy as it may feel, be like Ramón, because one thing's for sure: even if you don't agree with him, he definitely has something to say, and you'd do well to listen. Buckle up. You're definitely in for a ride.

JESUS CONDE

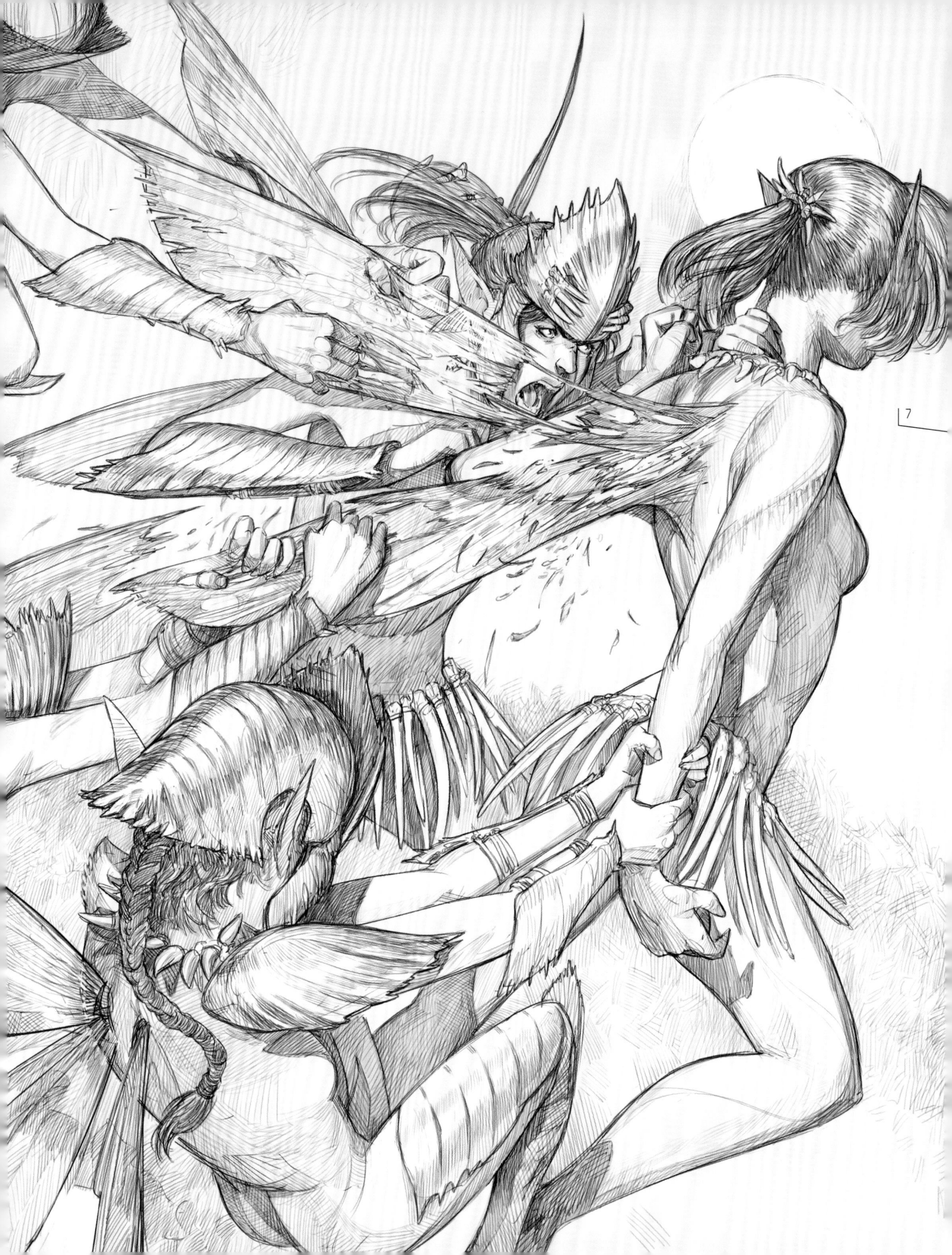

INTRODUCTION

In the context of this book, 'life' refers to the conceptual and technical decisions that I believe are present in my art. *Life in Every Sketch* is nothing but my attempt to describe those decisions in words.

I've never seen things through that lens. 'Life' is not what I aim to capture when making art, but it seems like that's what strikes people the most, especially artists who ask me how to make their own art feel alive. They often use words like 'dead', 'boring', and 'flat' to describe their problem, which tells me there's not only confusion regarding the terms, but also that 'alive' seems to mean something slightly different to everyone.

It's not just one technical trick like curved lines, or one specific kind of concept like two characters talking, but a broad range of ideas all stacked on top of each other, creating a connection with the viewer. I discovered these ideas by accident throughout my journey and I'll be sharing them with you in these pages.

Life in Every Sketch is also about balance. I don't aim to give you a set of rules to strictly follow, but rather provide roads of exploration – places where you can fail. That's right, I am encouraging you to fail in search of your truth, because that's how I did it. An uncomfortable truth about creating art is that it will be painful. Why is that? Because, often, when you create, you don't know exactly what you want. You have vague ideas inspired by your limited understanding of reality, and through your exploration to capture those ideas, you will fail – more times than you would like to accept. Maybe your very first lines will be misplaced, or the way you pictured the image from your imagination will feel wrong. Even the colour you will see in front of you might not match the one you just chose ... But then imagine, after a thousand annoying attempts, you get it right, making you feel accomplished and capable of making the next set of mistakes.

THAT'S THE BEAUTY OF

CREATING: THE PROCESS AND

THE REWARD THAT COMES AFTER

FAILURE. YOU KNOW, LIKE LIFE

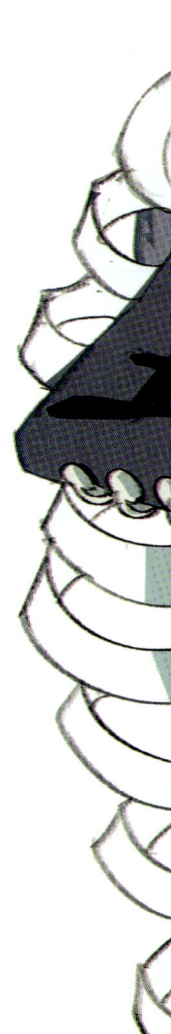

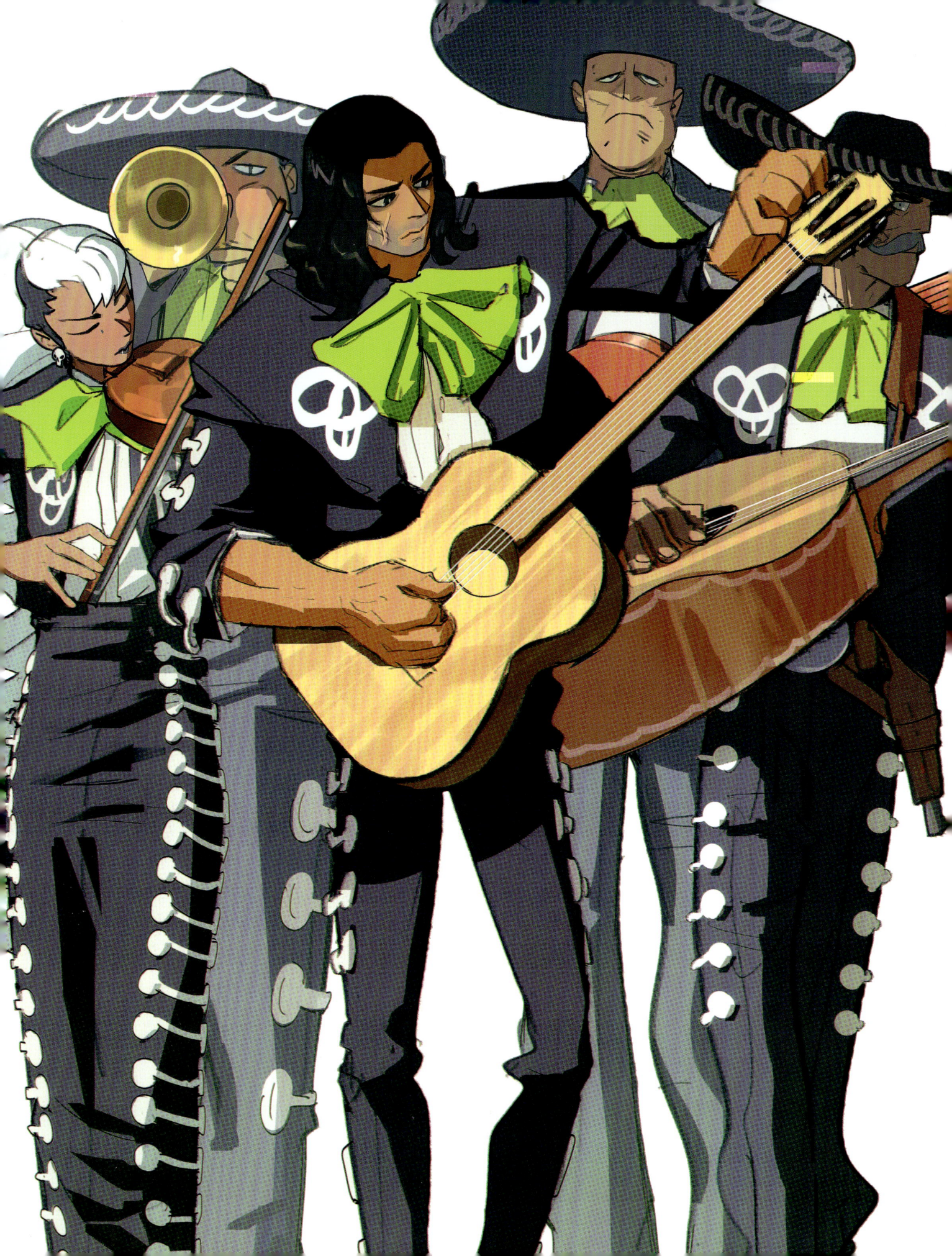

MY CREATIVE JOURNEY

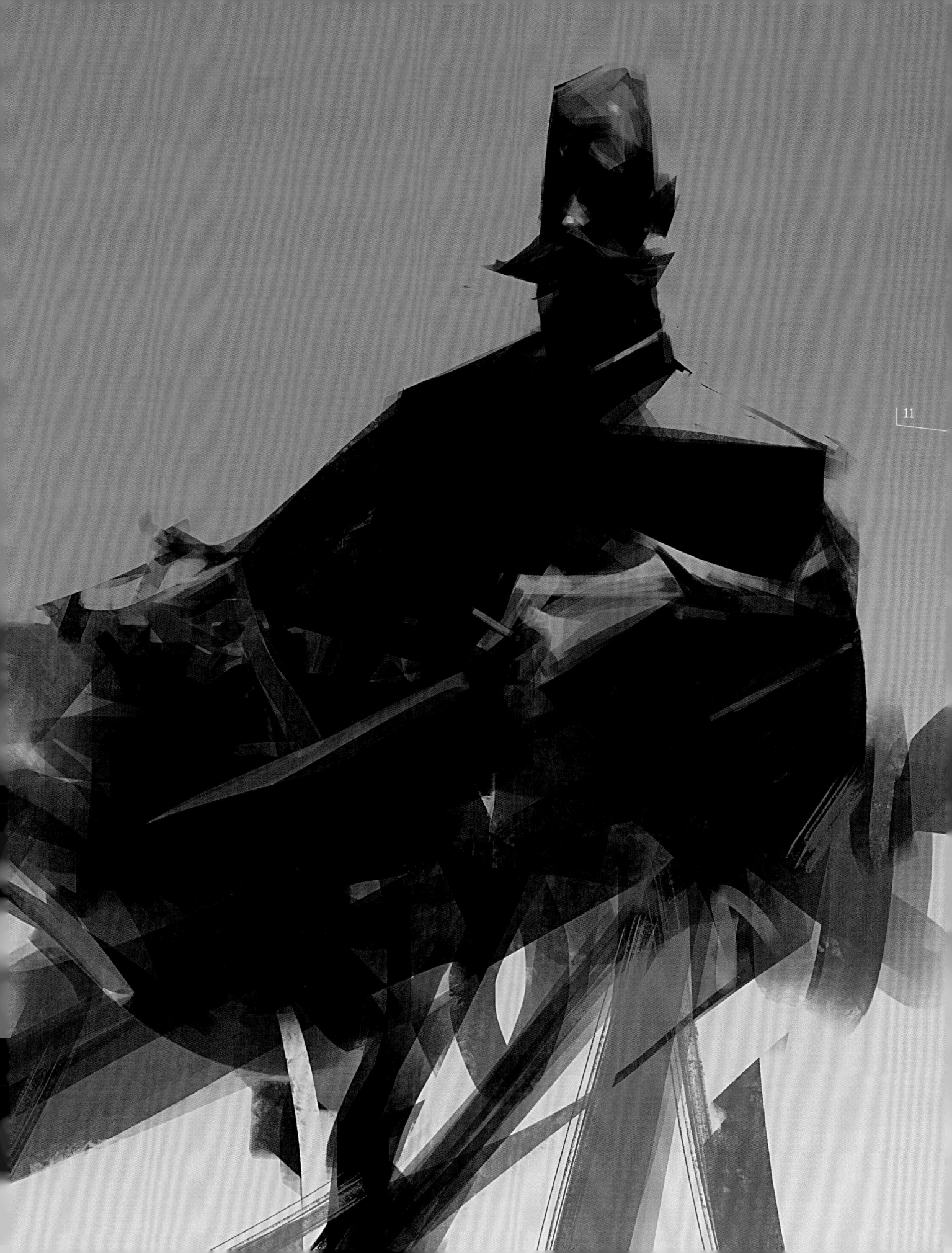

Childhood

As with any other kid back in the nineties, my childhood was filled with cartoons, comics, and video games. I used to draw characters from *Dragon Ball Z* and *Pokémon* while watching the episodes and then sell them at school.

Then, by pure luck, my grandmother saw some comic books at a newsstand – not the popular ones you can find anywhere now, but titles like *Conan the Barbarian* with more adult themes. After a while, my family searched

across town for other publications due to my increasing interest, leading to titles from Marvel and DC, among others. Comics were not a thing in Venezuela, but the moment I was exposed to that medium of storytelling, I was immediately motivated to create my own.

Picture a child trying to achieve the same rendering quality as those professional pieces of art with just a pen and paper, not knowing anything about anatomy,

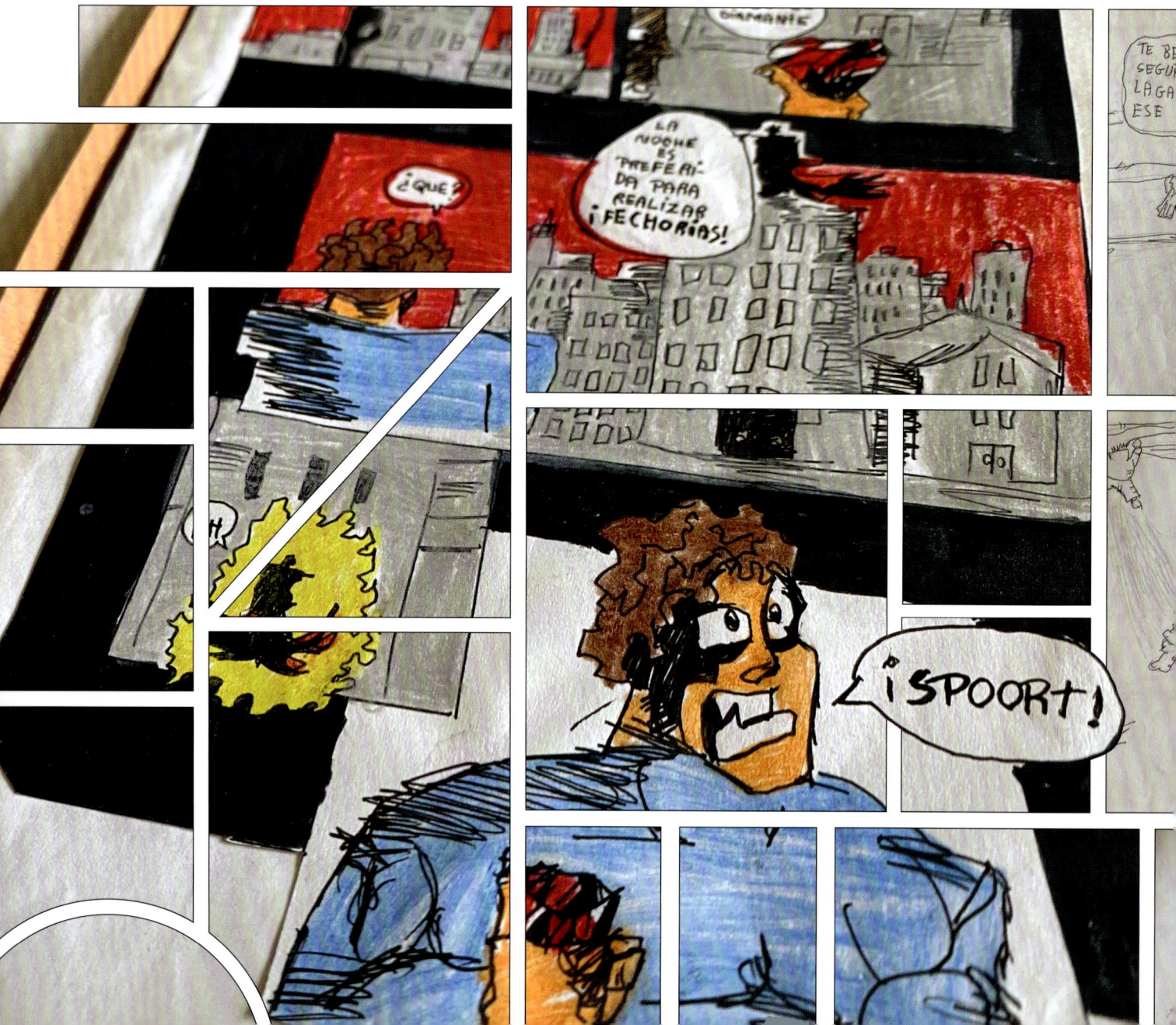

composition, or any other fundamentals. All I had was a strong drive to capture something that fascinated me, that I couldn't quite put into words.

I used to test the effectiveness of my little comic projects by showing them to people who had never been familiar with that type of medium before, like my mother, for instance. If I didn't get that 'reaction' after a set of frames, I knew something was wrong. I got frustrated like every child or artist does, and eventually tried again. I guess that was my way of testing fundamentals I wasn't yet aware of – trial and error.

Was I talented? I'd say stubborn.

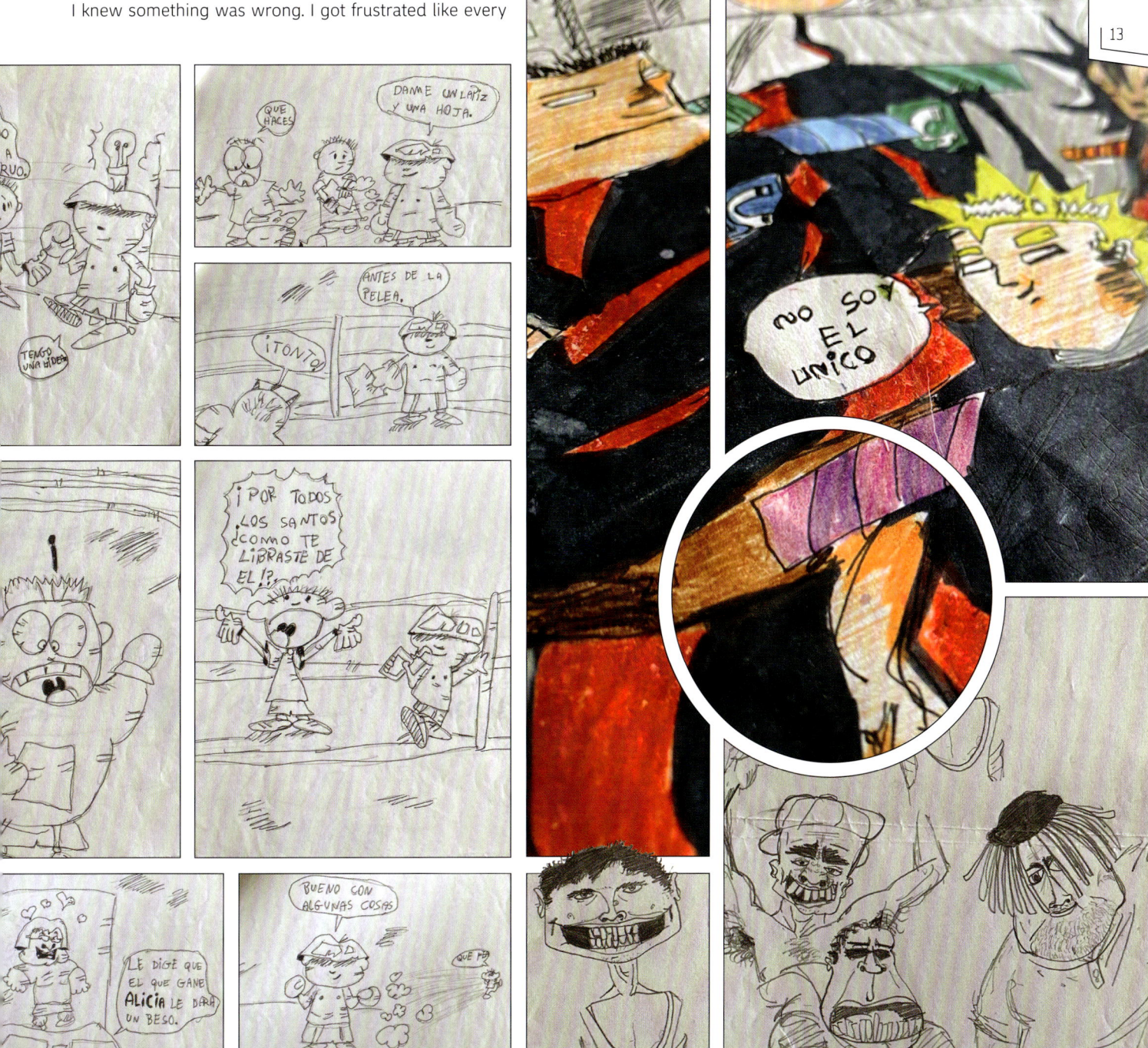

A degree in graphic design

After graduating from high school in Venezuela, I thought the only viable way to make money with my skills was through graphic design. I spent a few years learning the basics of art, as well as programs like Adobe Photoshop and other aspects of the profession, such as branding, and a bit of traditional art. But to be honest, I was very immature back then, and didn't really pay attention in class.

Nevertheless, I was fascinated by the work of professionals on platforms like Behance, where many combined traditional media with branding to create campaigns for companies. After graduating in 2012, I eventually got a job making drawings for clothing brands, while posting personal projects on Behance – not just to gain some online presence, but to build a portfolio for big companies like Coca-Cola, Nike, and others.

Looking back, I was far from landing a job with those companies, but I still tried. Being overly optimistic at times has helped me to keep moving forwards, no matter the odds.

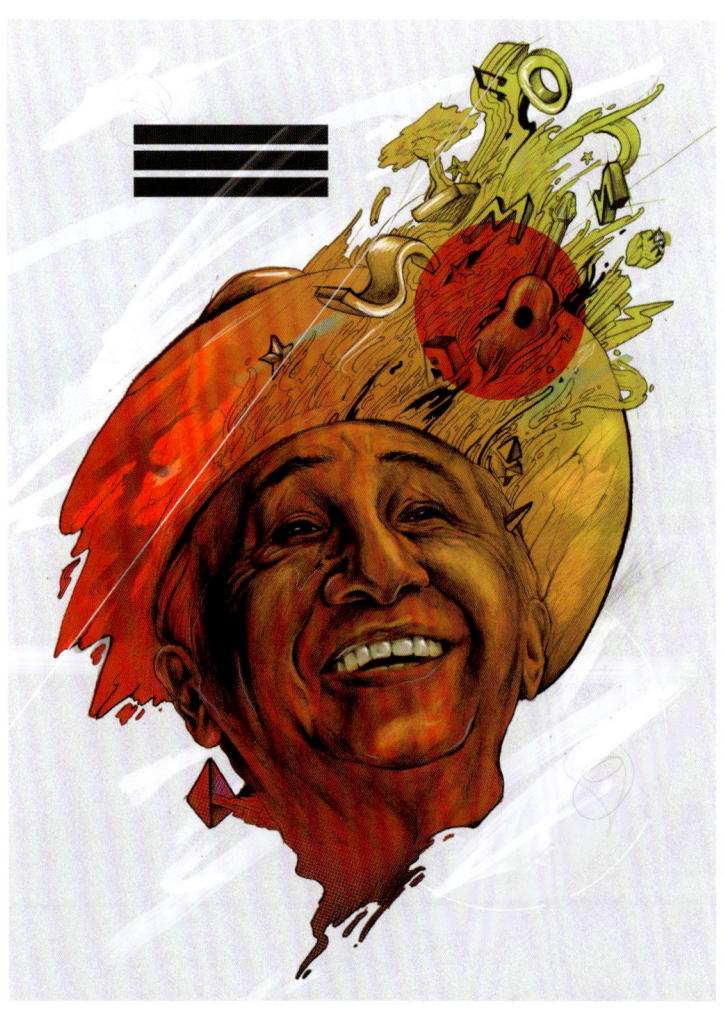

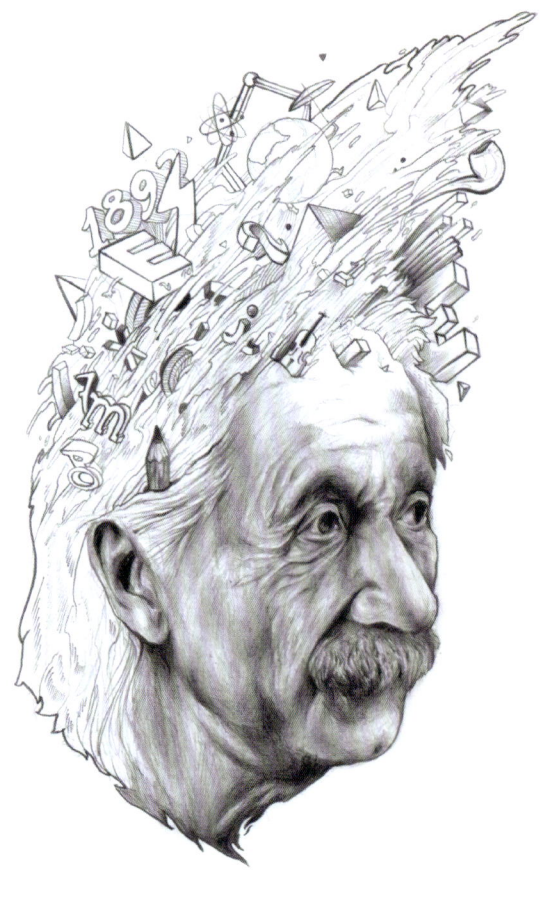

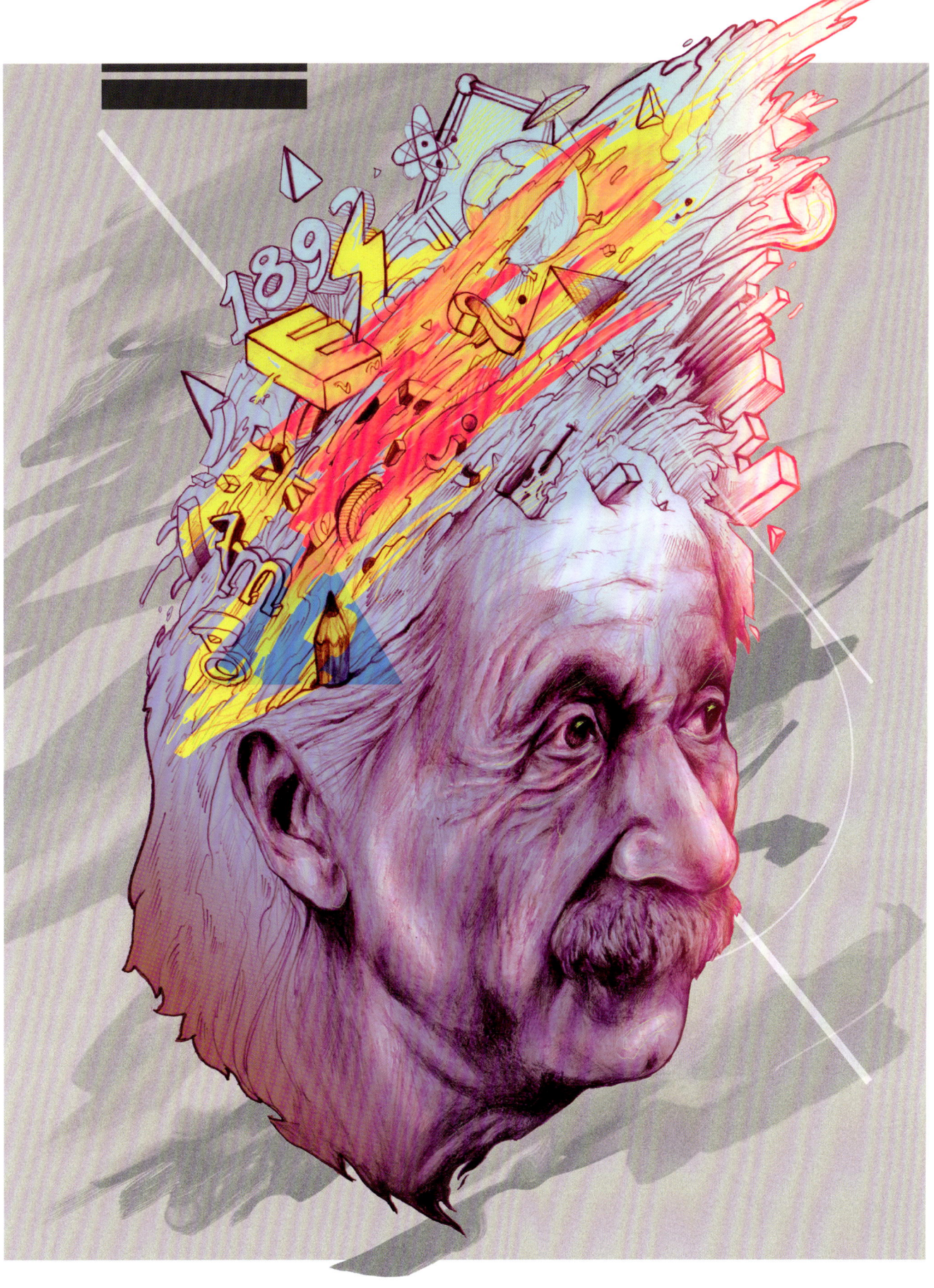

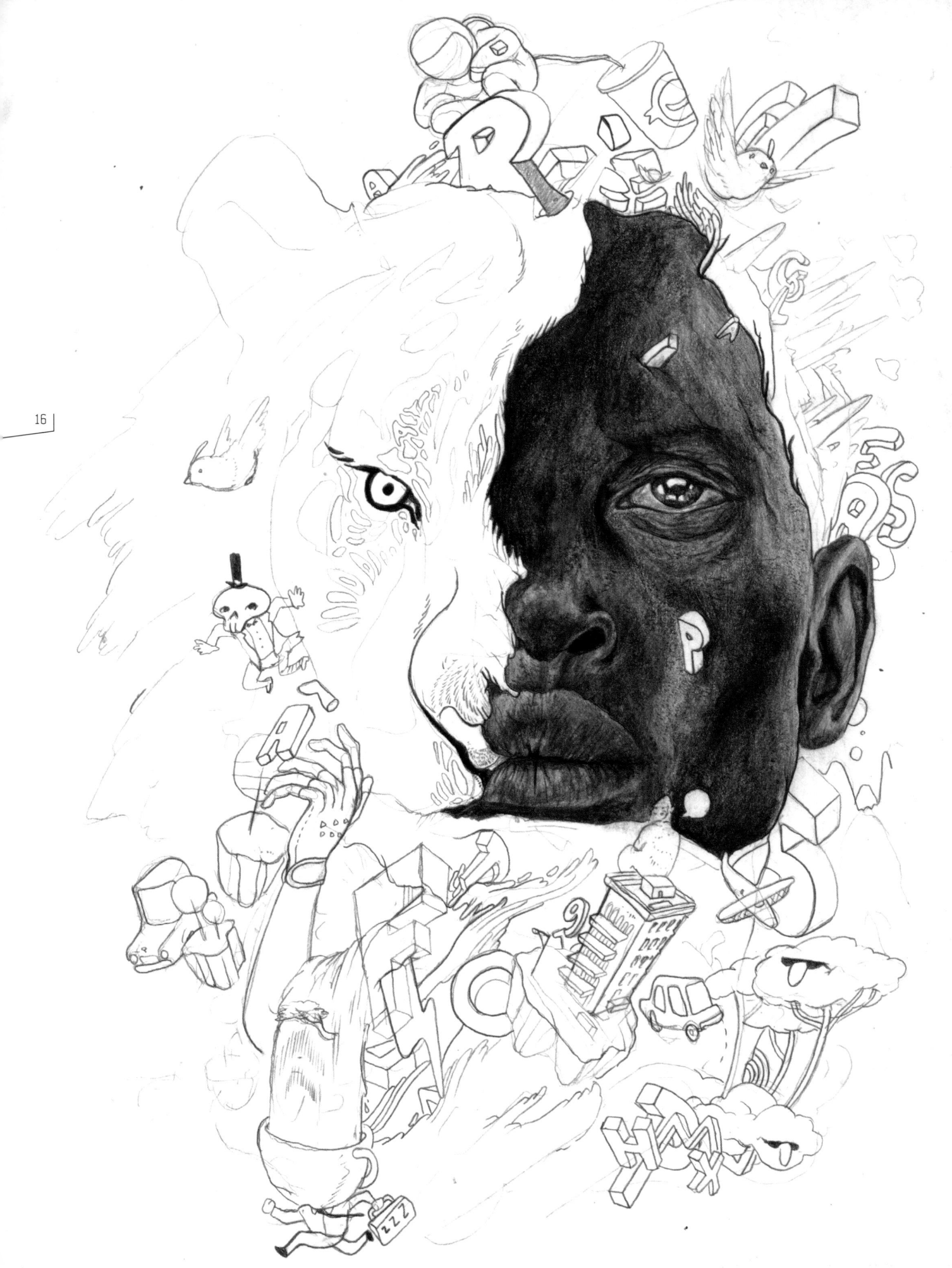

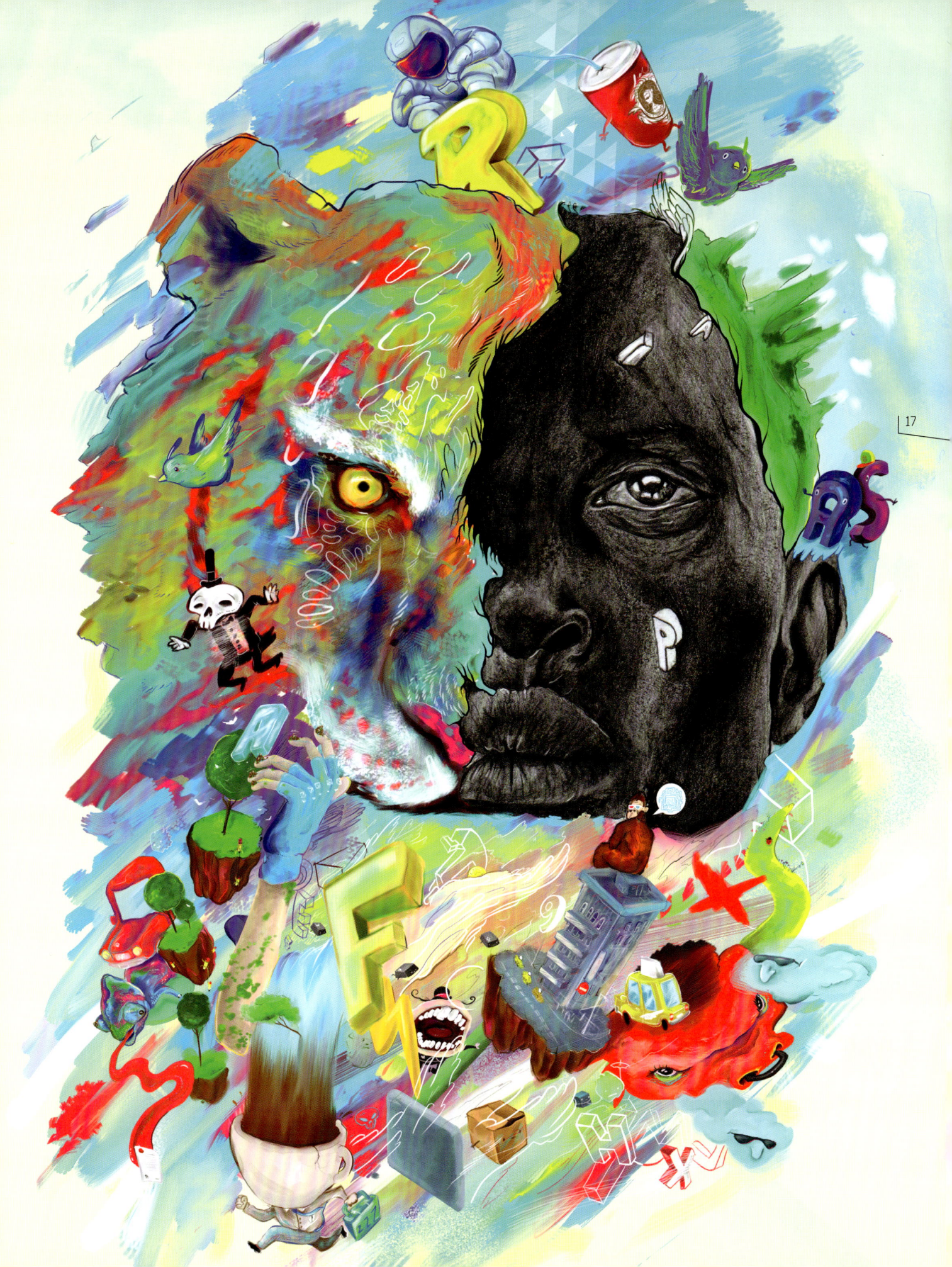

Rediscovering digital art

I used to research artists extensively beyond their portfolios. This led me to the artists they followed, and to discovering techniques that stretched further than traditional and mixed-media art. At this point in my career, I wasn't into digital painting. That changed when I found a site called CGHub, where many concept artists shared their portfolios. It was there that I became aware of this industry that was full of new possibilities.

These artists were creating art for movies and video games, something I had always been drawn to but never fully realized was an actual profession, or at least an option for me. I was shocked by how they could capture reality in such a detailed way using digital painting and computers. It wasn't just the technique – I also reconnected with the things that had inspired me as a kid, telling stories with frames, concepts, and characters. It felt like a whole new horizon of possibilities opened up for me.

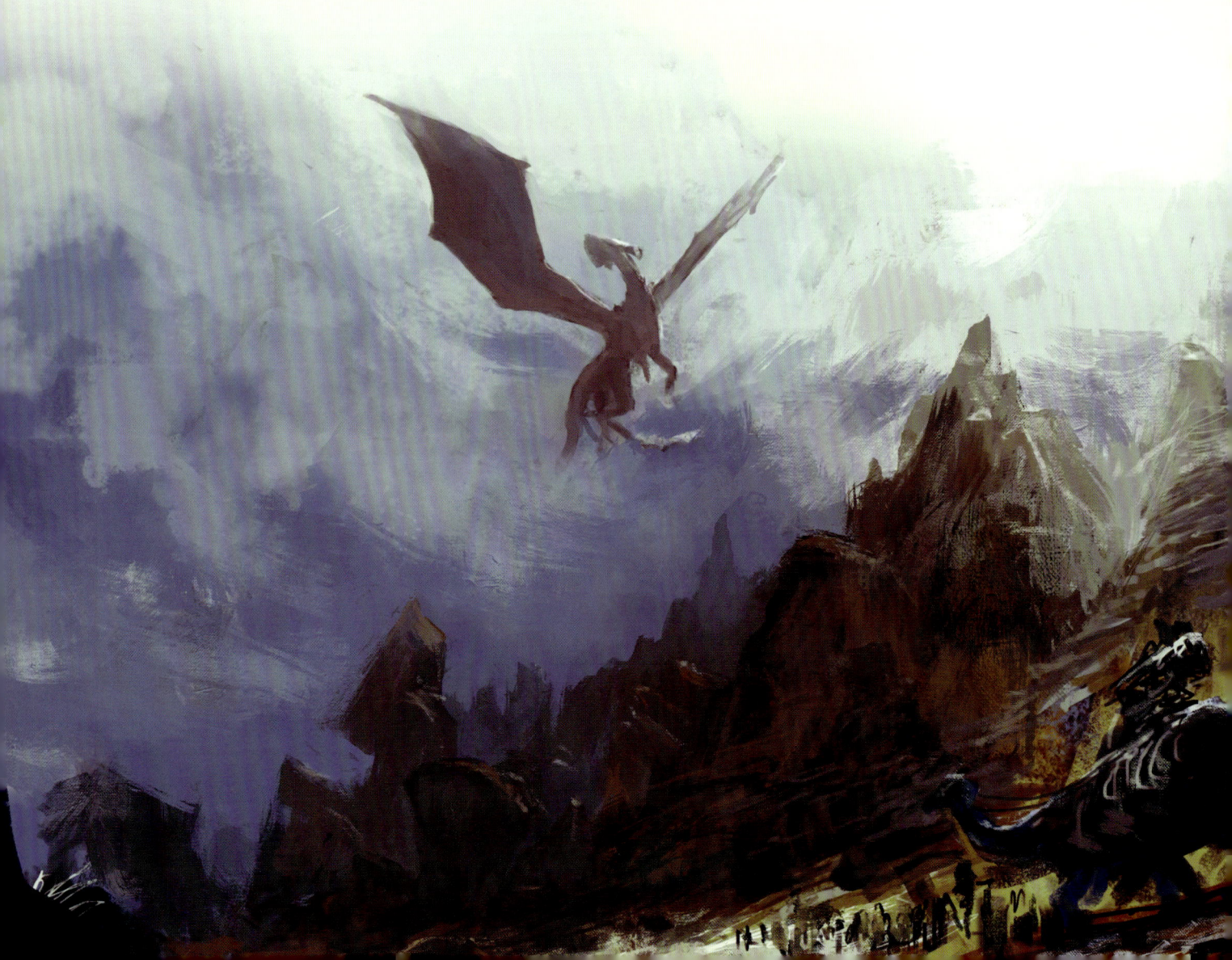

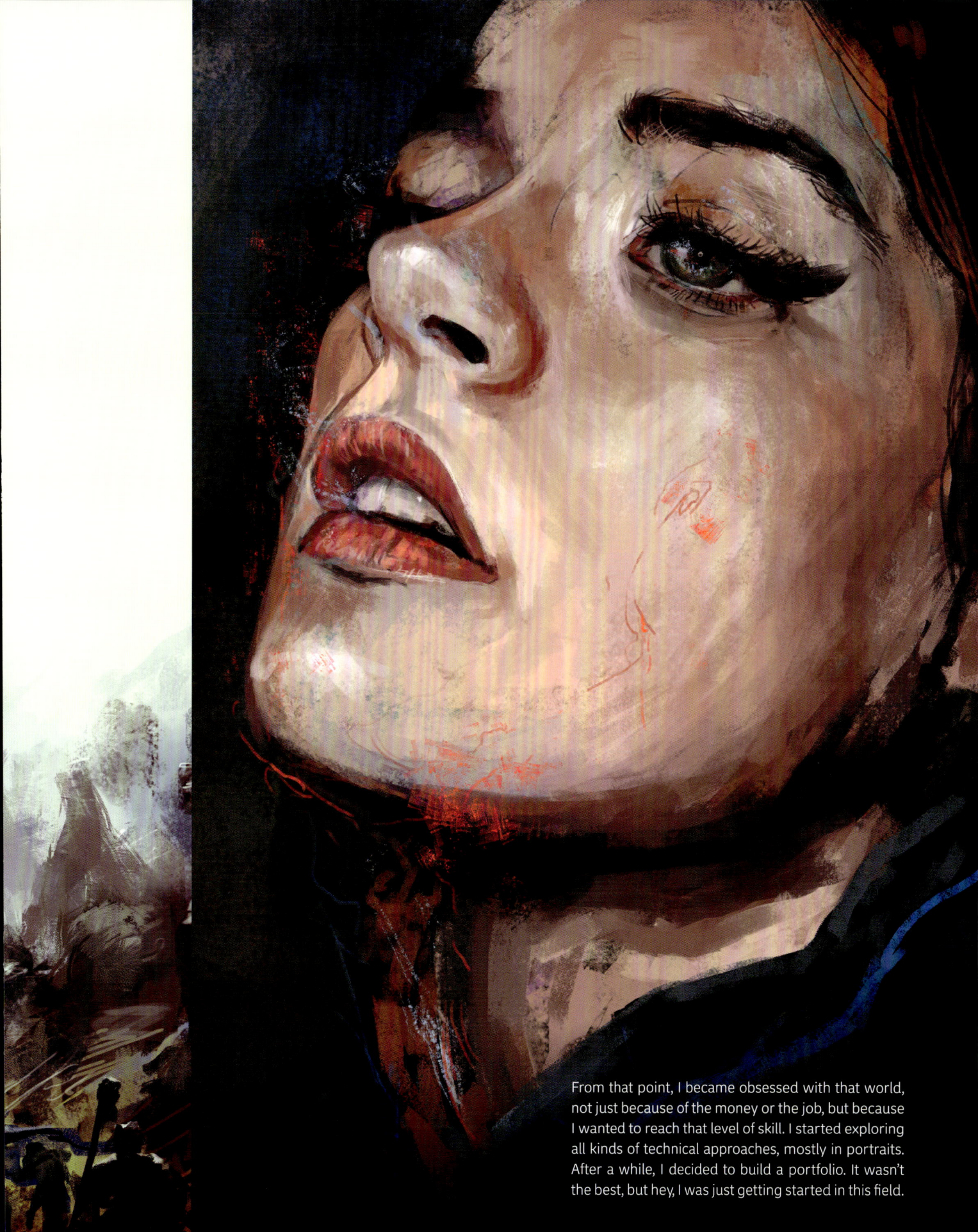

From that point, I became obsessed with that world, not just because of the money or the job, but because I wanted to reach that level of skill. I started exploring all kinds of technical approaches, mostly in portraits. After a while, I decided to build a portfolio. It wasn't the best, but hey, I was just getting started in this field.

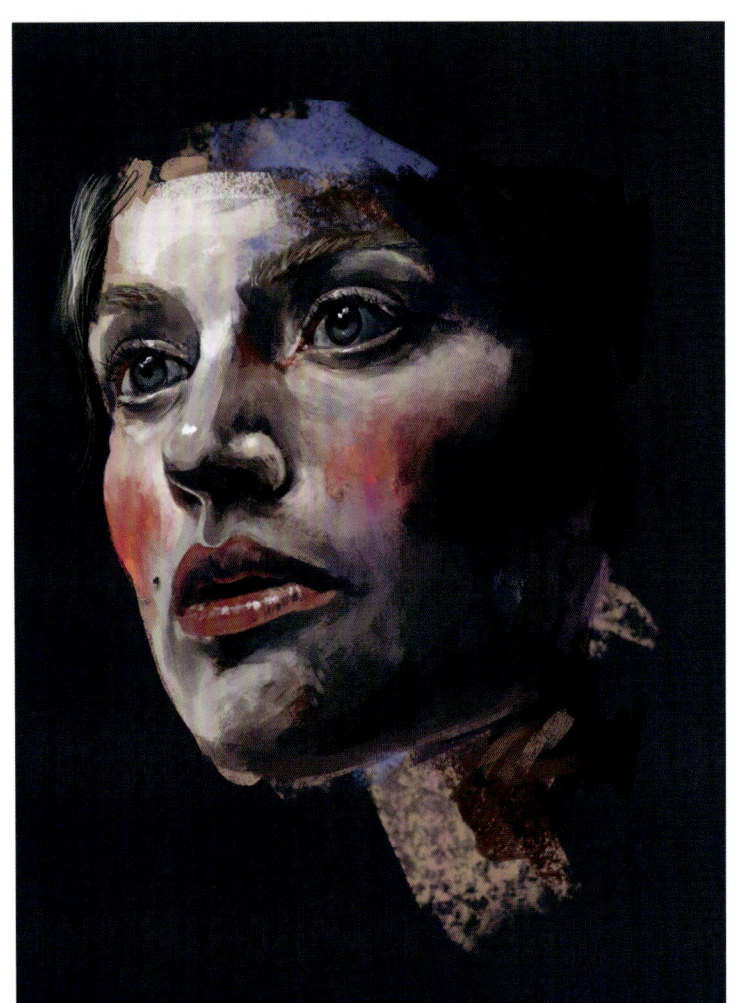

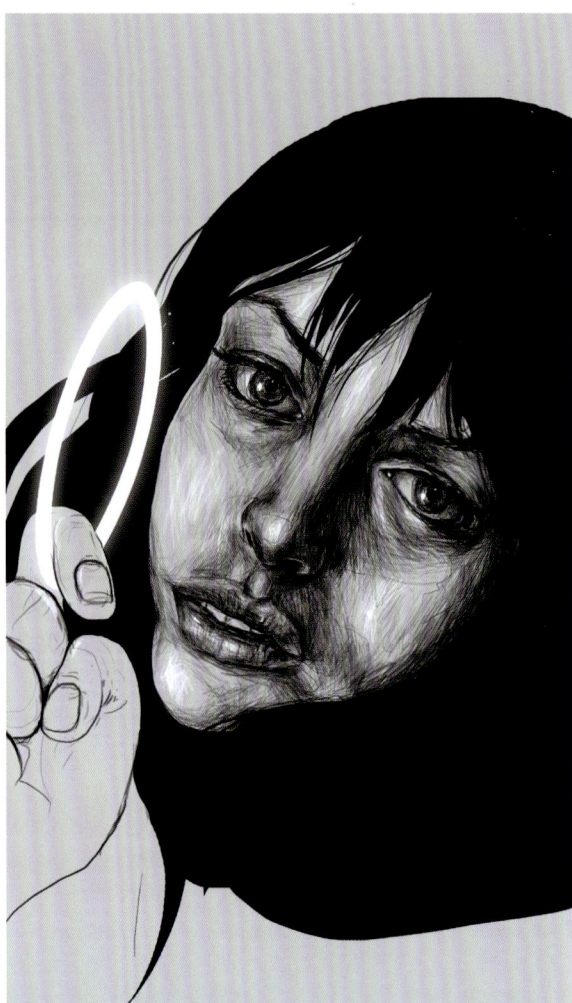

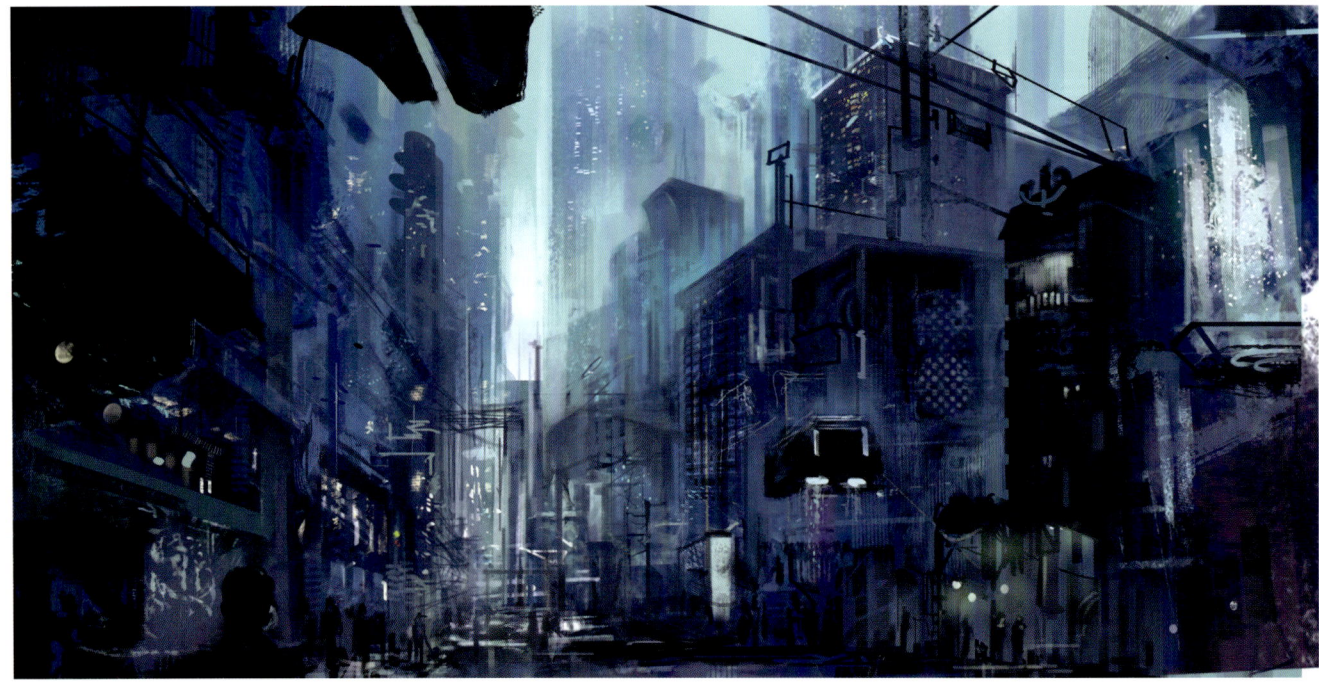

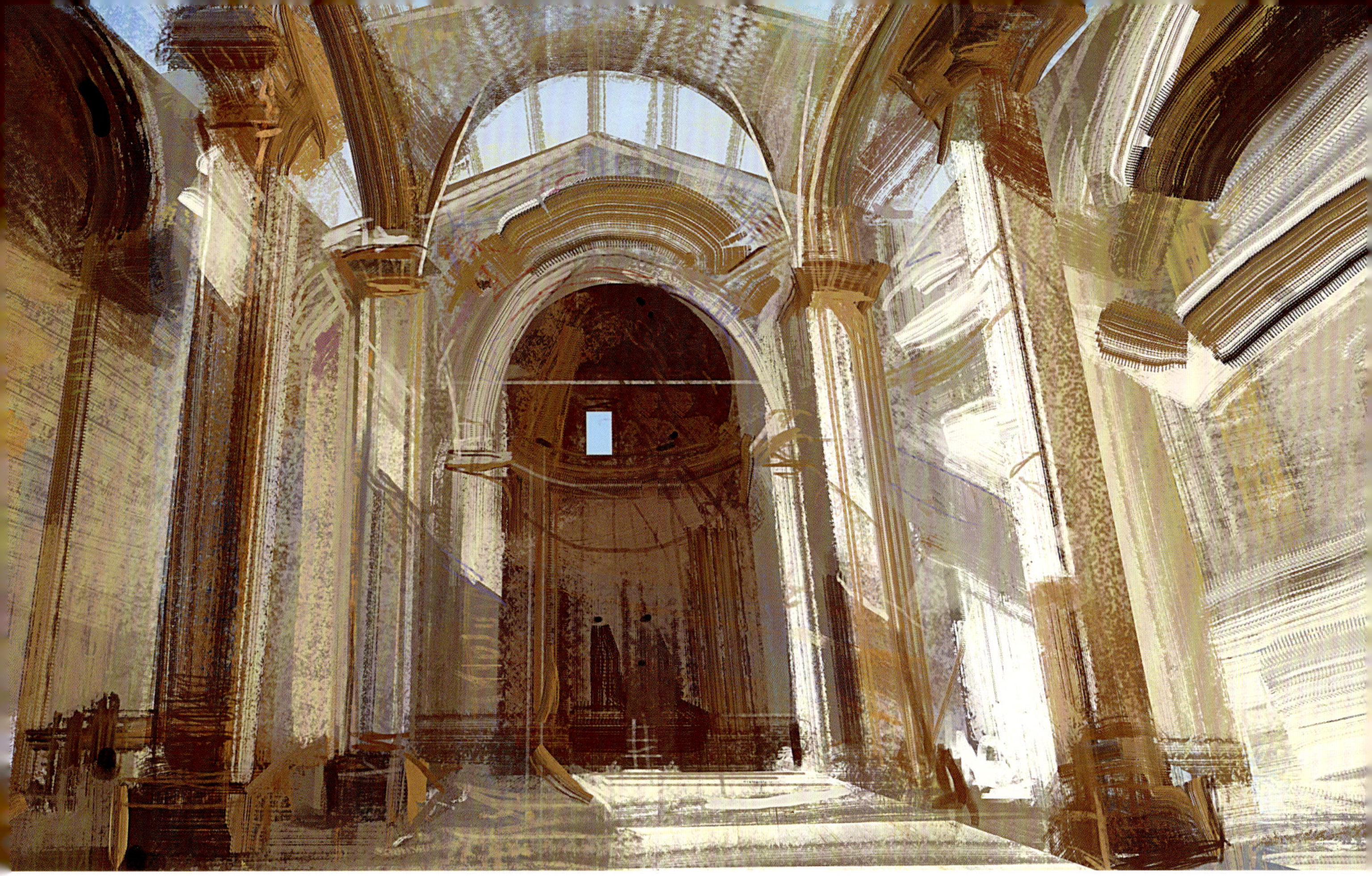
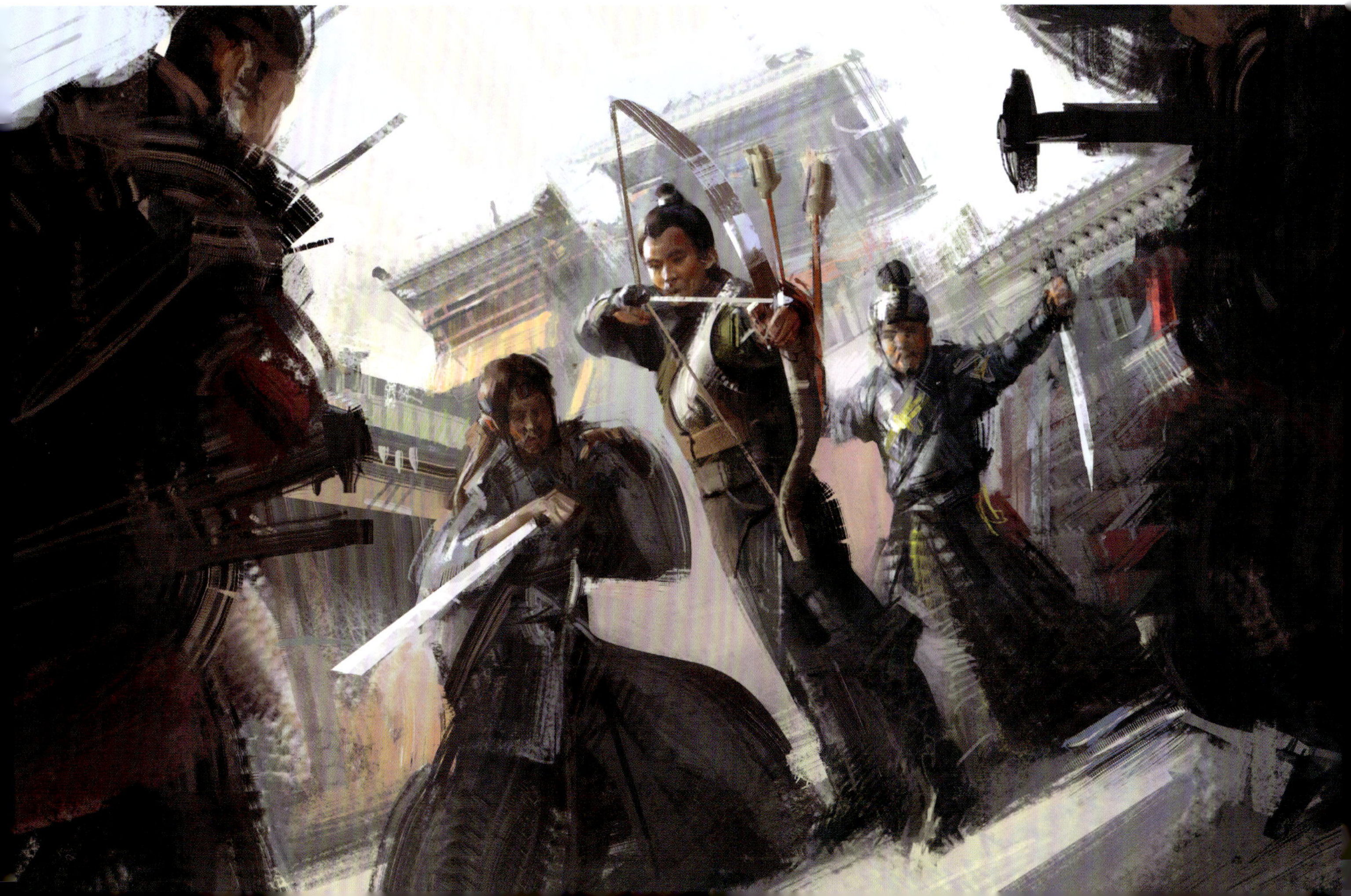

One study every day

While taking on some gigs as a graphic designer, I noticed that, despite applying to many jobs as a digital illustrator and concept artist, I wasn't getting much demand. Of course, my education and knowledge of the subject were very limited. Also, my focus on portraits alone wasn't enough to develop serious skills. So, I decided to paint a series of different topics every day for a long period, mostly using references I found on Pinterest related to subjects I was interested in. I used social media to share my daily sketch journey and slowly built a following.

I wasn't particularly focused on learning any specific thing, since I had no clear guidance. But sharing my work online and seeing the reaction was exciting. Back then, many digital artists were doing the same, and sometimes, they even noticed you. What can I say? I was young and it felt good to have someone you admired approve of your work with a little thumbs-up.

The interesting thing about these experiments was that by sharing, I started to understand what triggered more reactions. I began to notice that what made my sketches stand out wasn't just technical execution but the energy and personality I put into them.

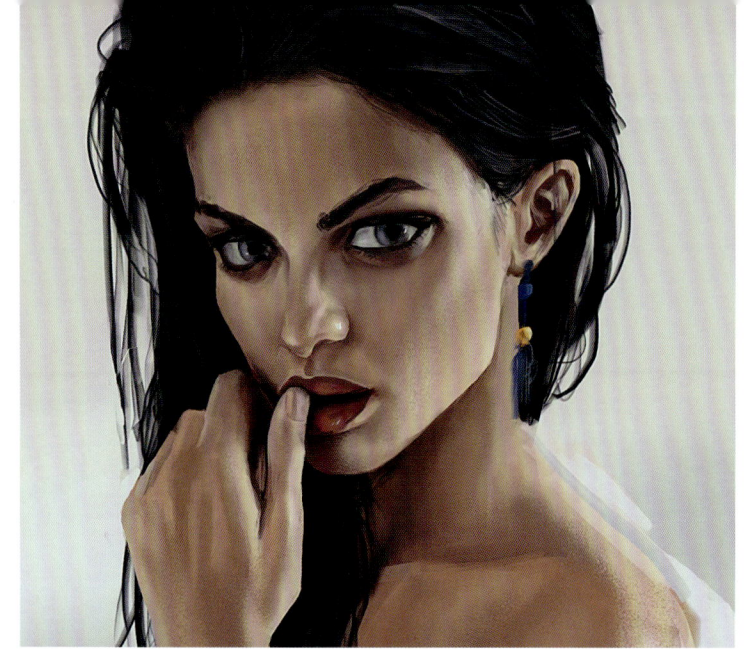

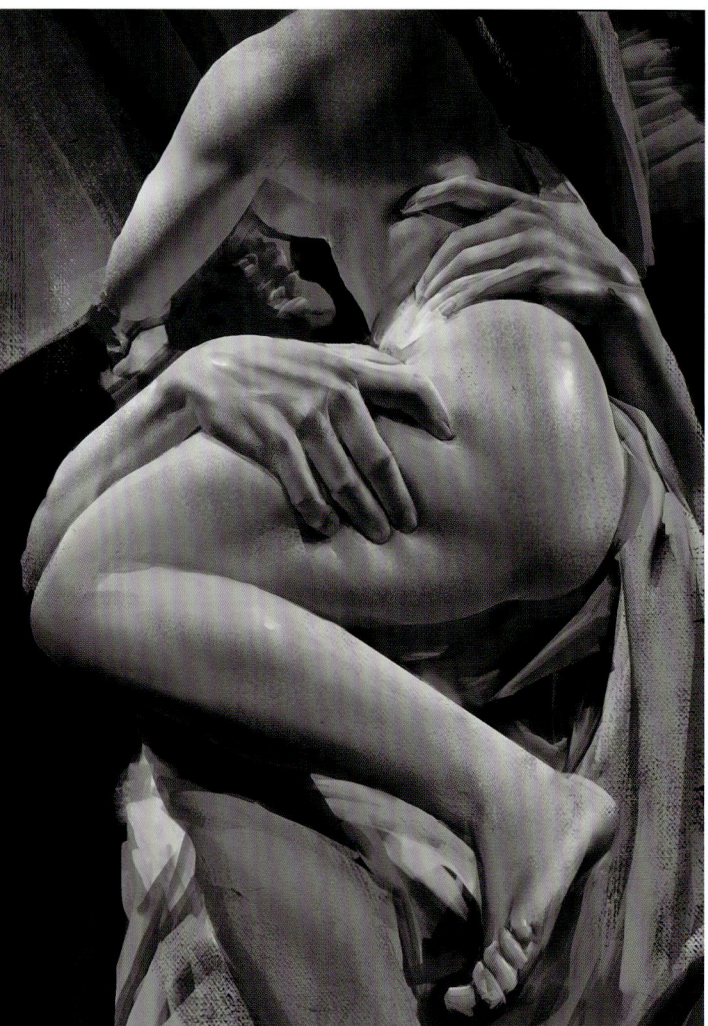

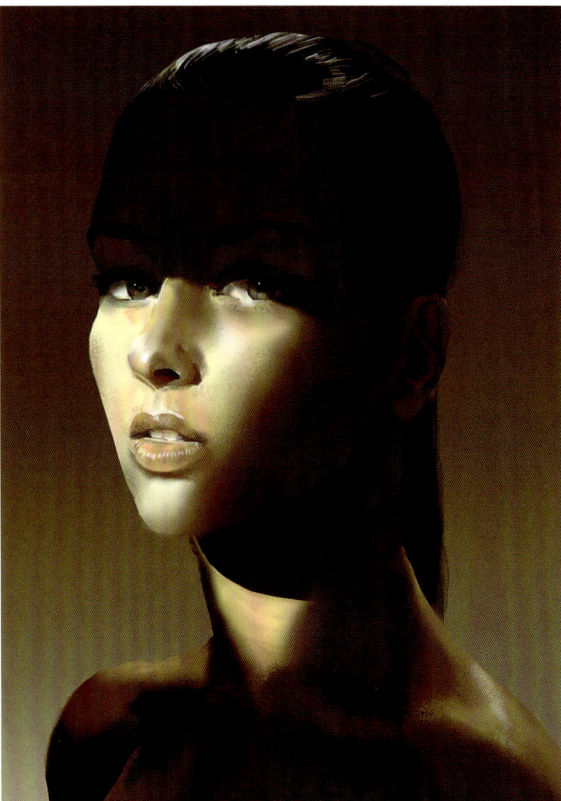

Each line and brush stroke became a tool to make the characters and scenes feel alive. I aimed to draw pretty faces with neutral expressions, but it was the strange ones, the highly expressive emotions, that really connected with people.

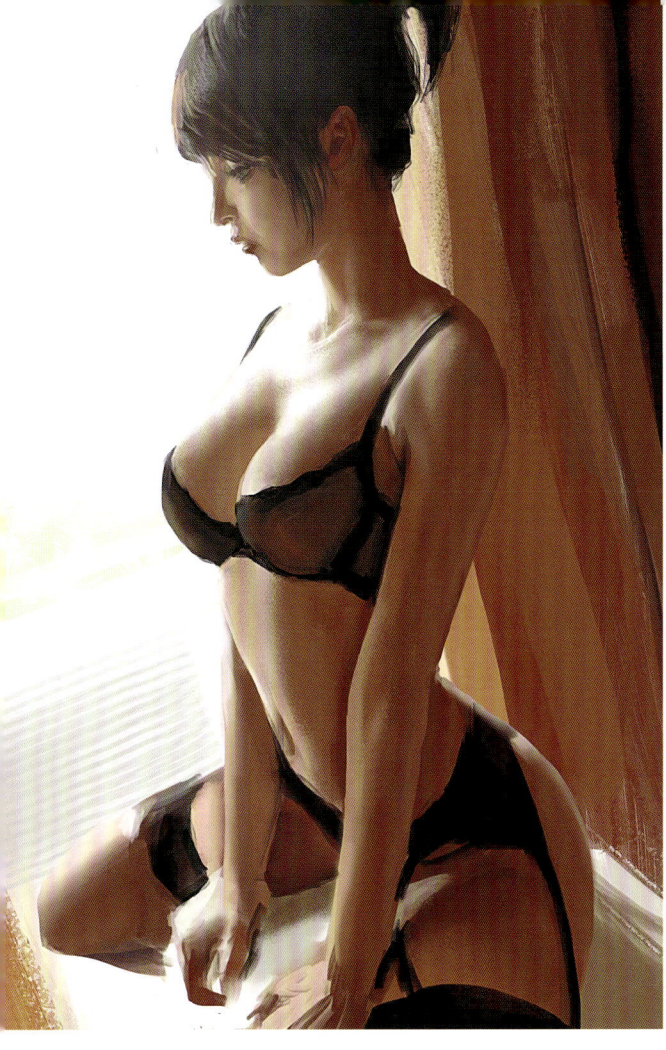

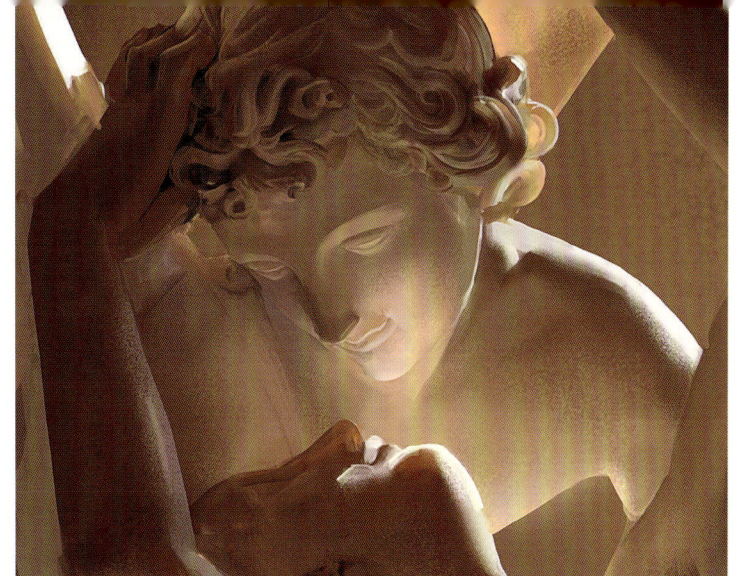

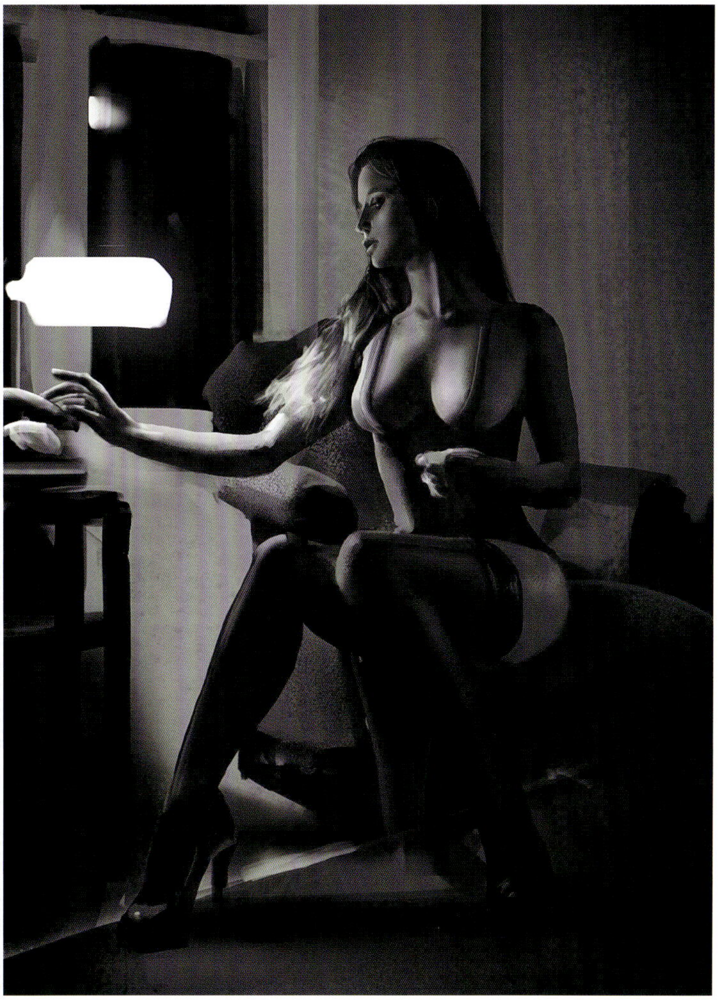

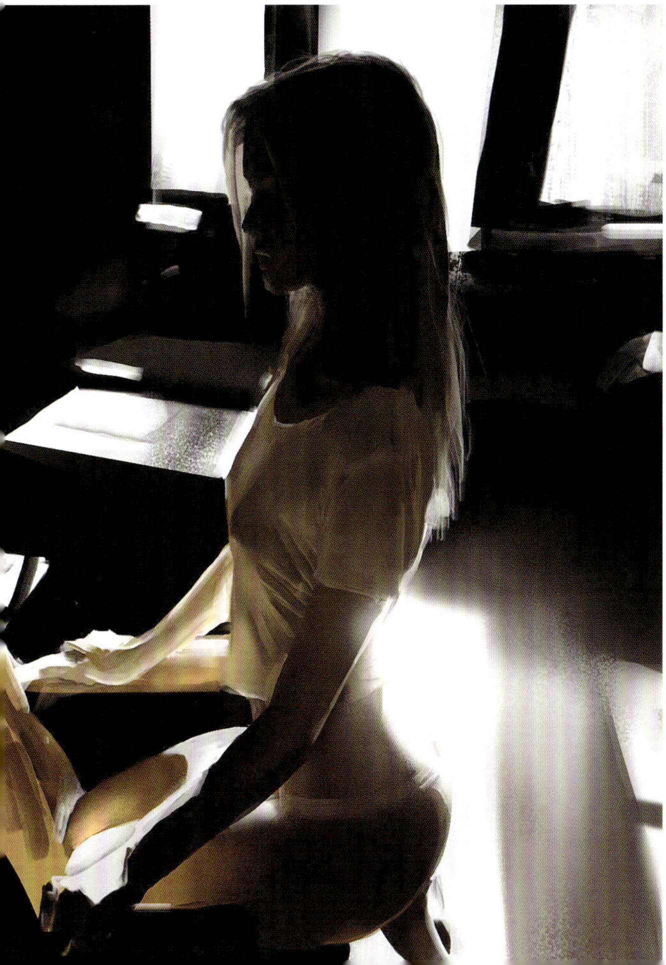

Of course, anything with a sexual theme proved popular, but it wasn't always about that. I also noticed how, in terms of values (light and shadow), high-contrast pictures tended to attract more attention.

This phase of my career was very revealing in terms of understanding what kind of artistic choices actually made an impact when sharing my work.

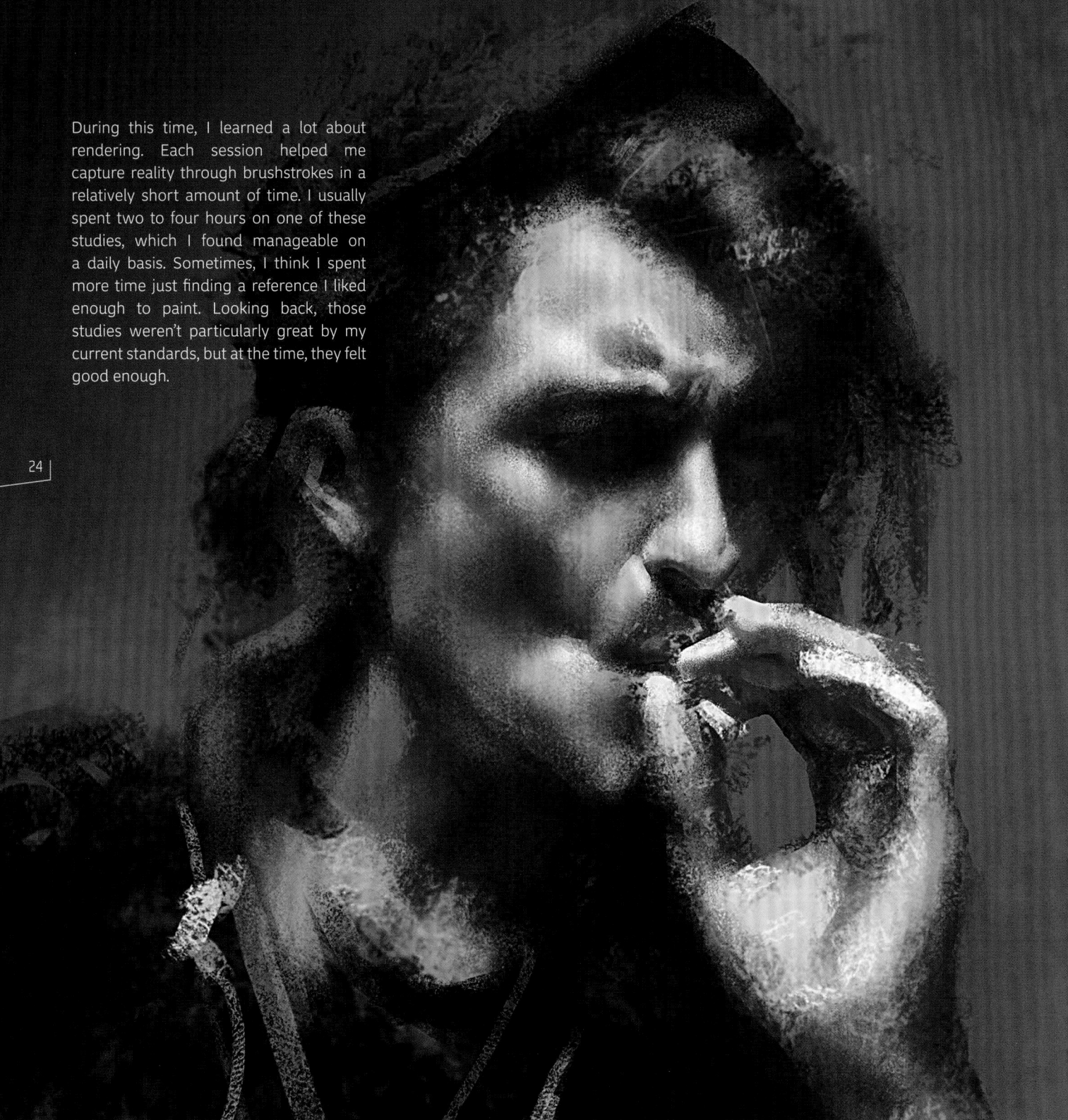

During this time, I learned a lot about rendering. Each session helped me capture reality through brushstrokes in a relatively short amount of time. I usually spent two to four hours on one of these studies, which I found manageable on a daily basis. Sometimes, I think I spent more time just finding a reference I liked enough to paint. Looking back, those studies weren't particularly great by my current standards, but at the time, they felt good enough.

How do you convince yourself that you're 'good enough'? I think a big part of it is focusing on one specific thing in your studies – like drawing a good pair of eyes or getting a solid render in one spot of the composition. Keeping things simple makes the task achievable and helps set your expectations straight, giving you small, clear goals that allow you to feel accomplished, at least to some degree.

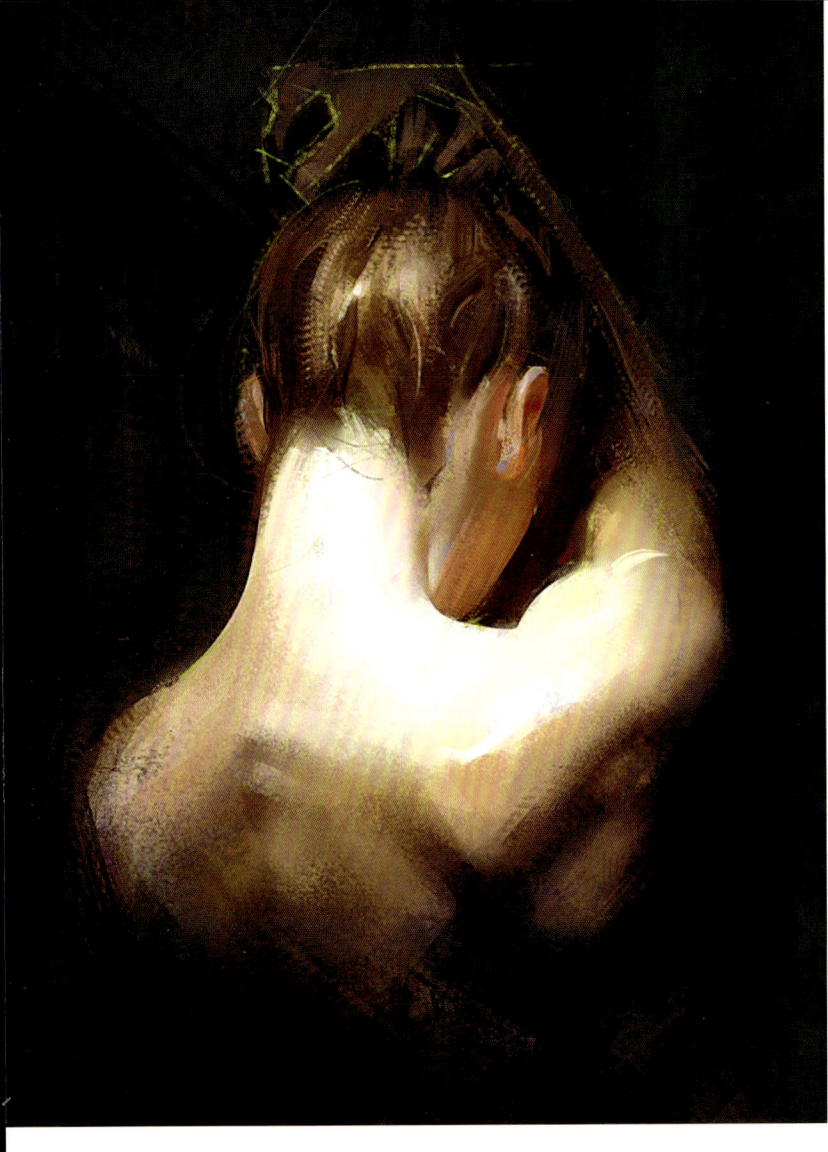

On an entrepreneurial level, my online presence started bringing in some commissions. Eventually, my daily shares on social media sparked interest from clients, particularly for illustration gigs. I wasn't reinventing the wheel conceptually, since my portfolio mostly consisted of painting studies. But as I gained traction, I figured it would be smart to start a Patreon and share my process.

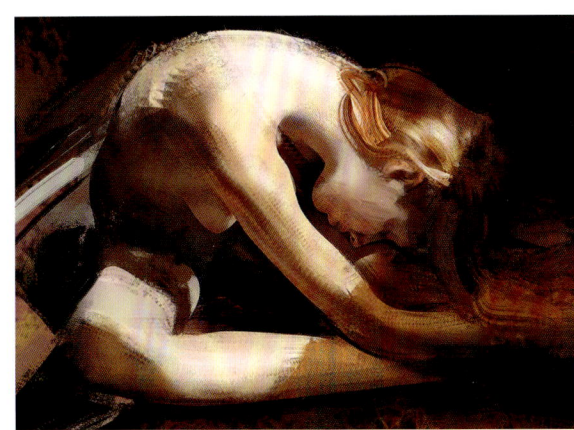

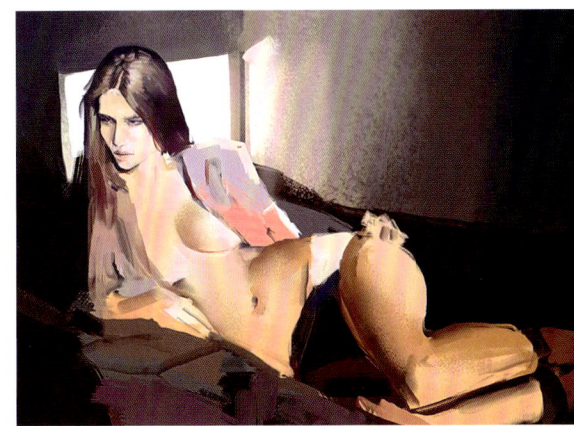

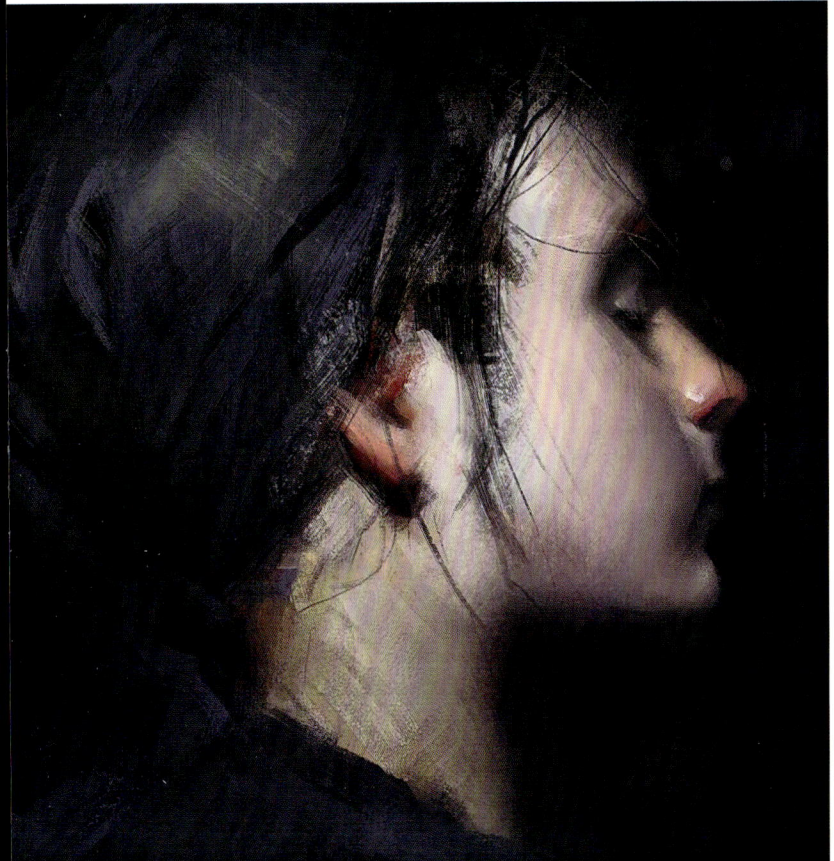

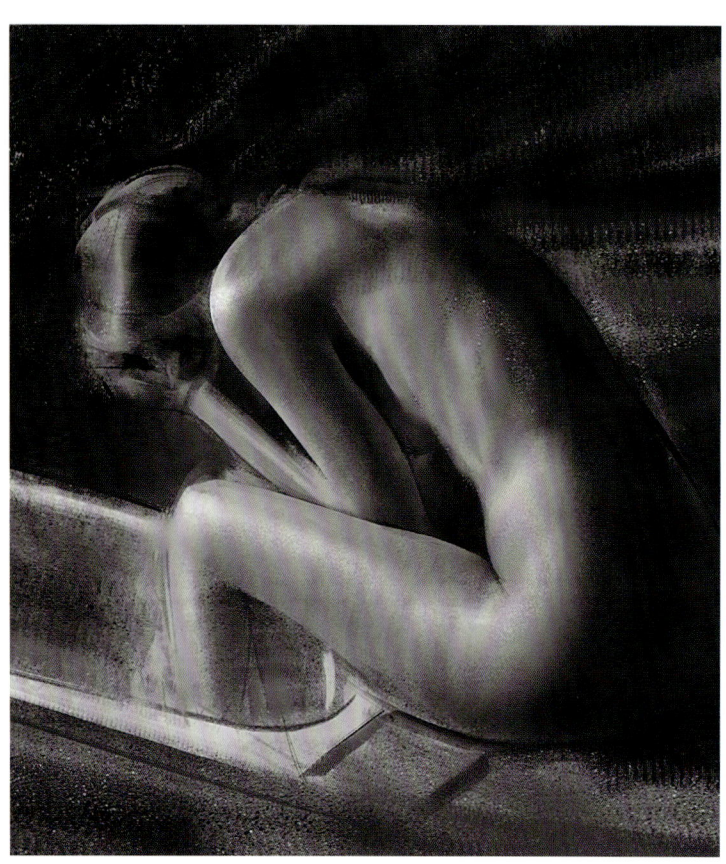

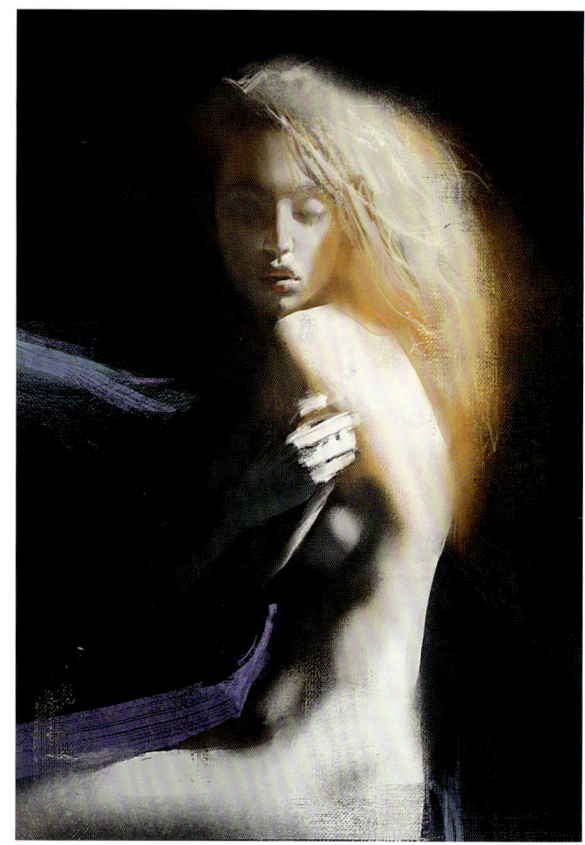

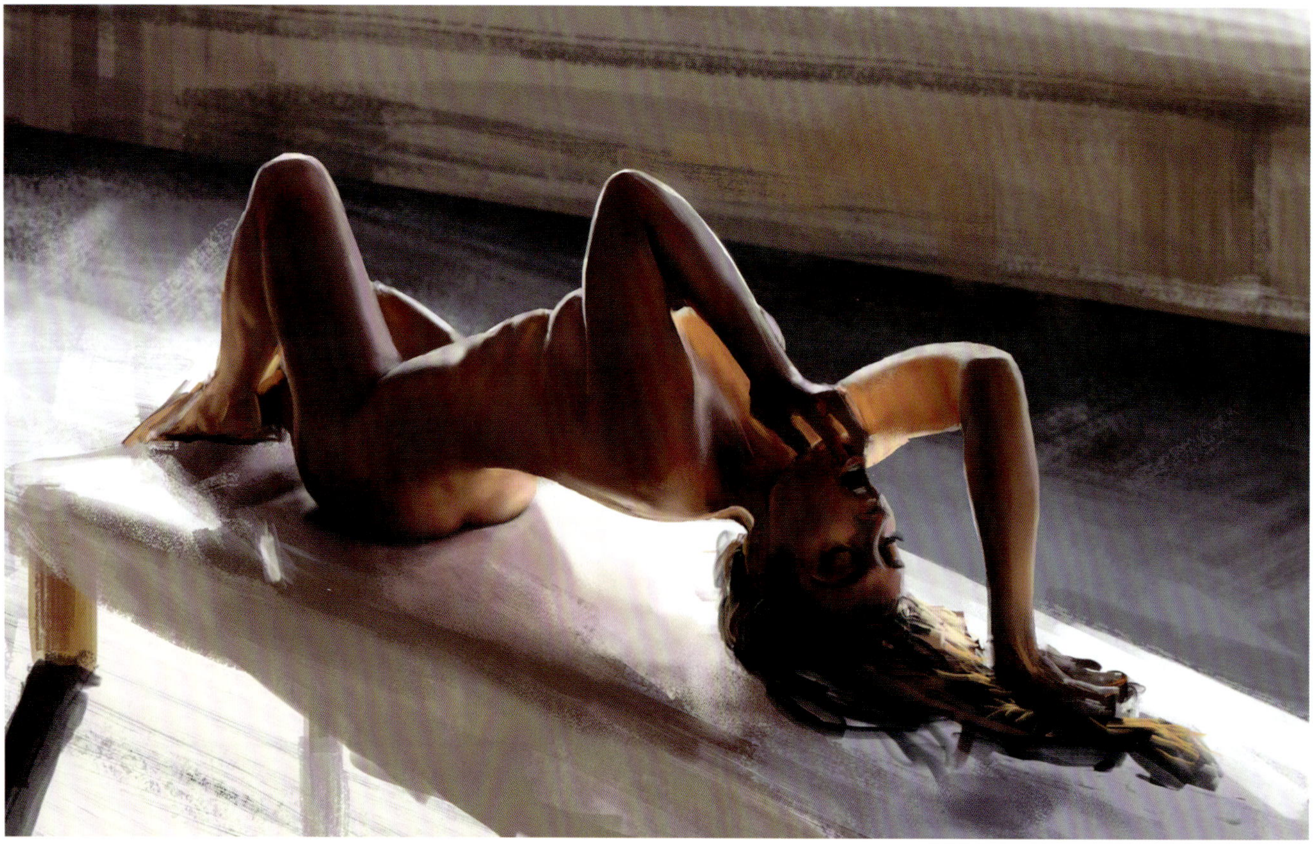

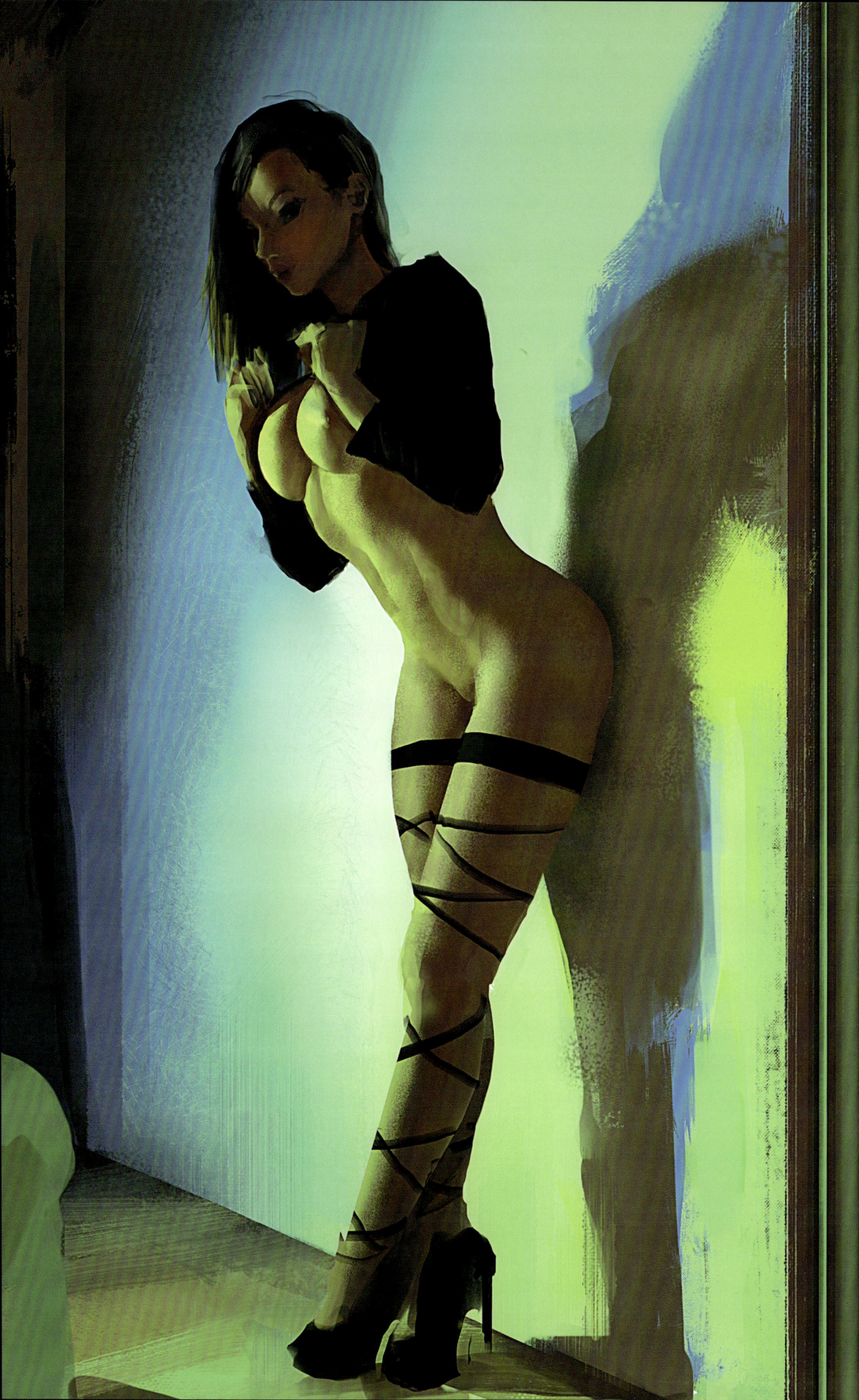

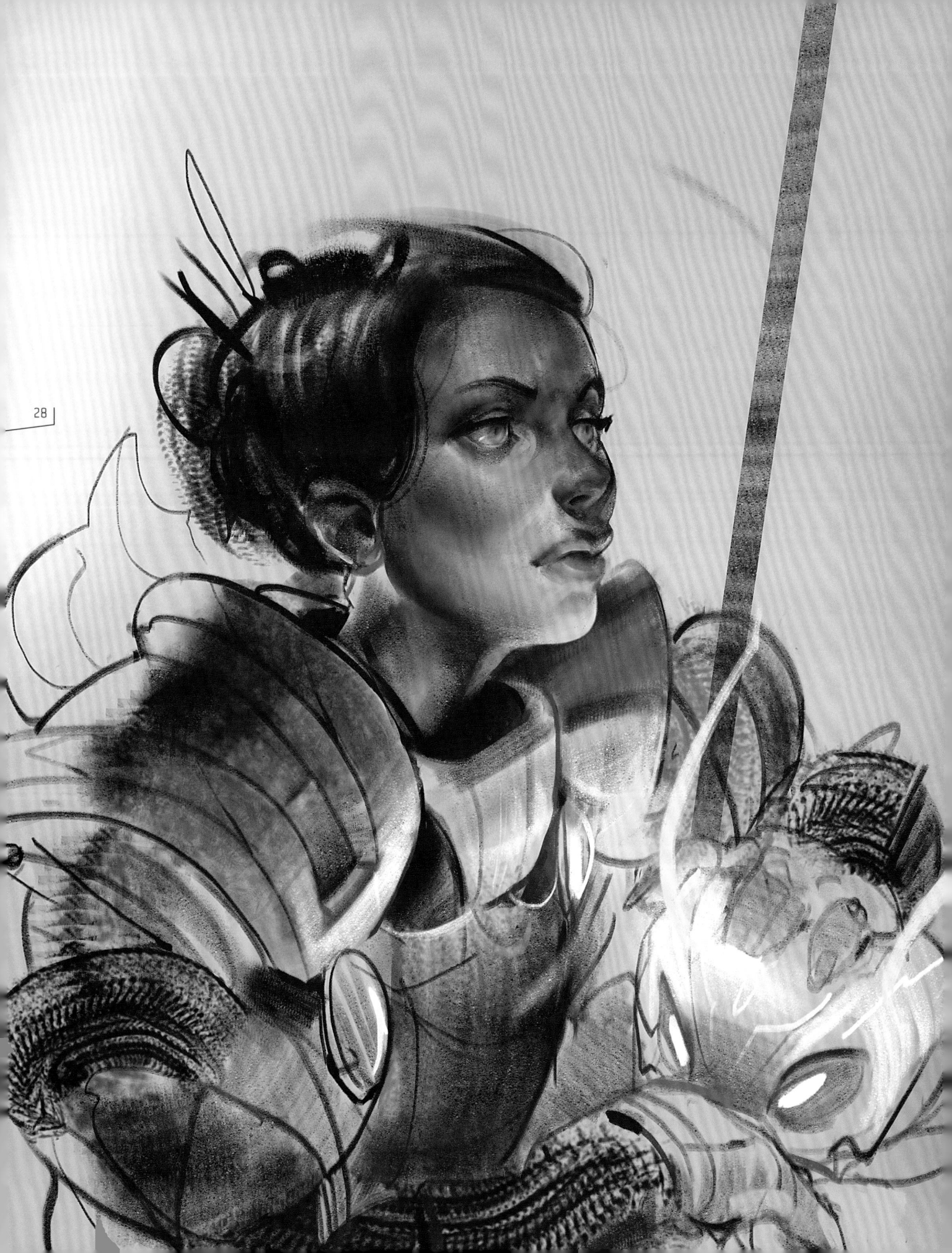

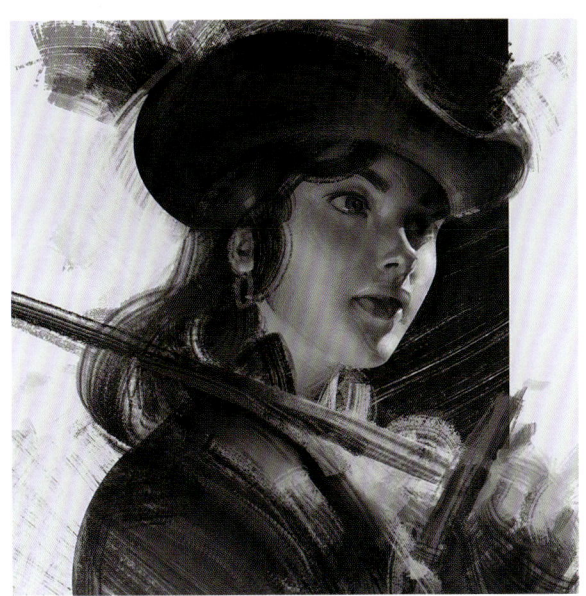

I must say, I never stopped working on my portfolio. Even though I was doing a lot of studies, on the days between them, I was always trying to apply new techniques to personal ideas.

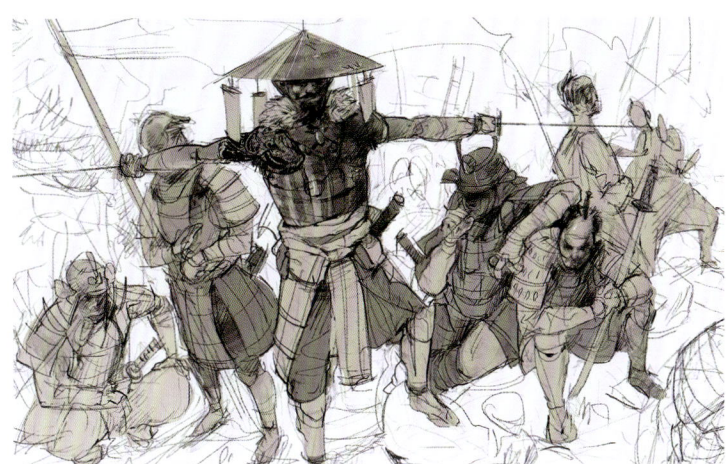

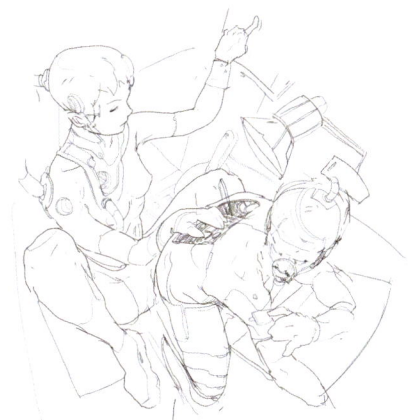

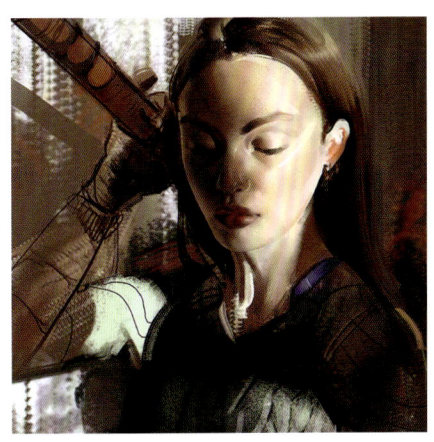

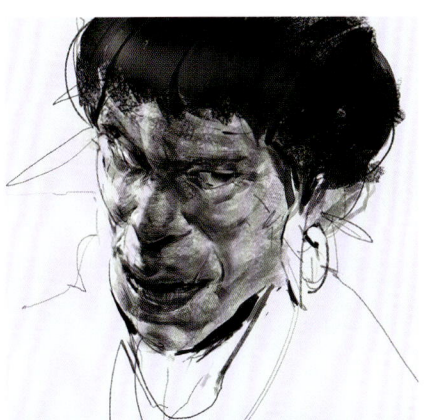

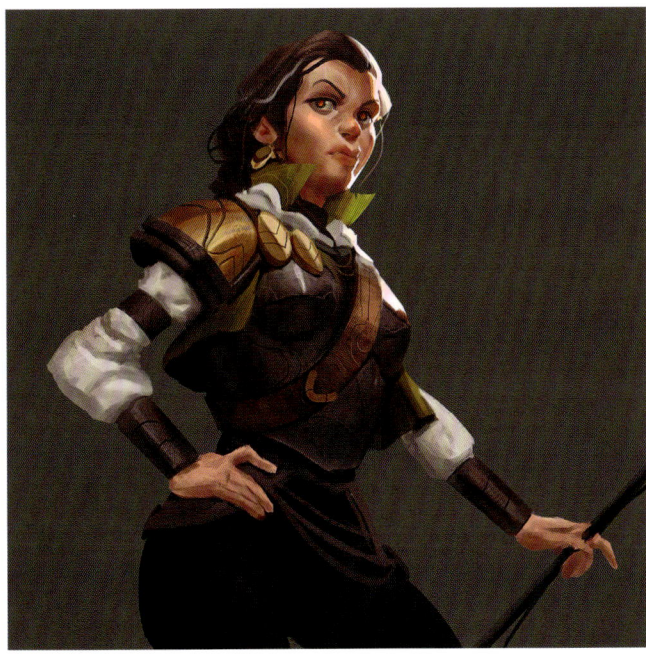

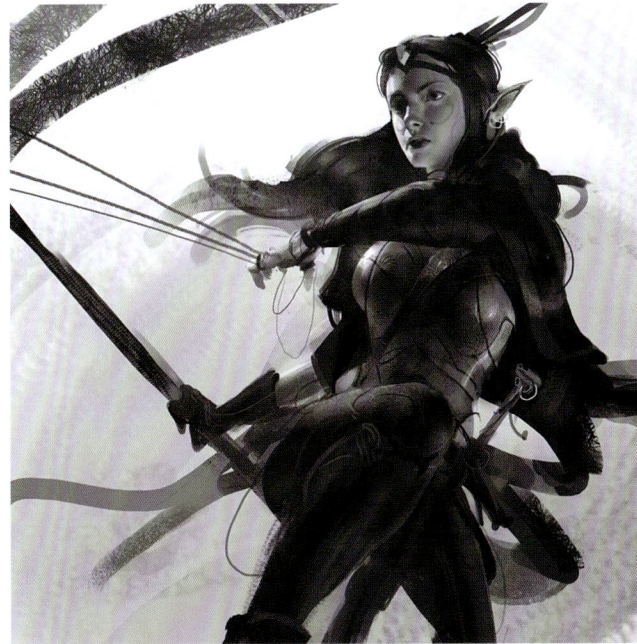

Lines

Although I was improving quite a lot compared to my early years, I had developed a strong dependency on references. I felt crippled when trying to create concepts from my imagination, so I decided to tackle what I thought was the very first step to creating something great (and still think to this day): line drawing. I can't believe it took me this long to focus on one of the most fundamental aspects of execution.

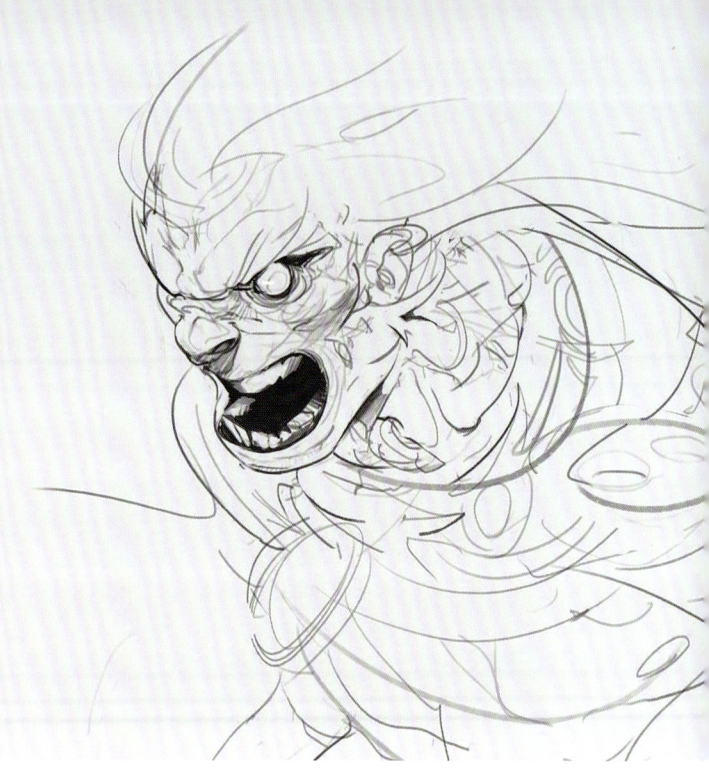

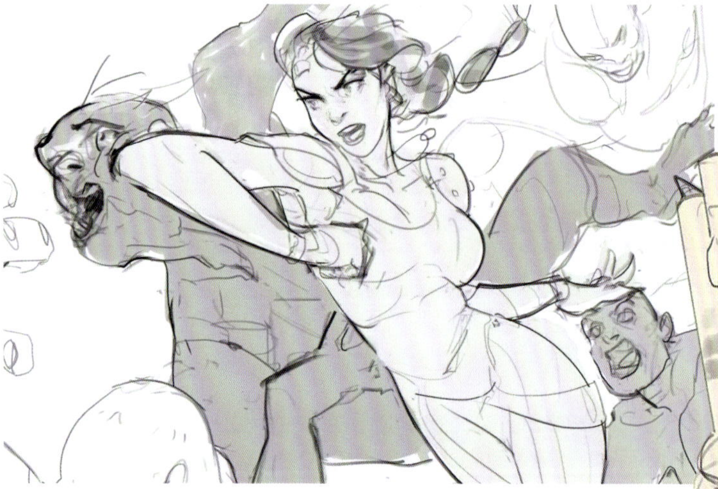

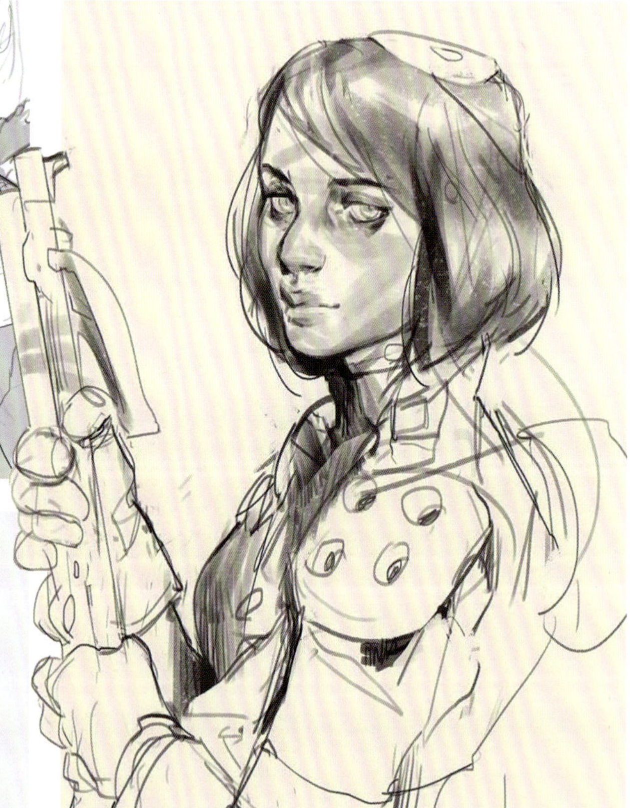

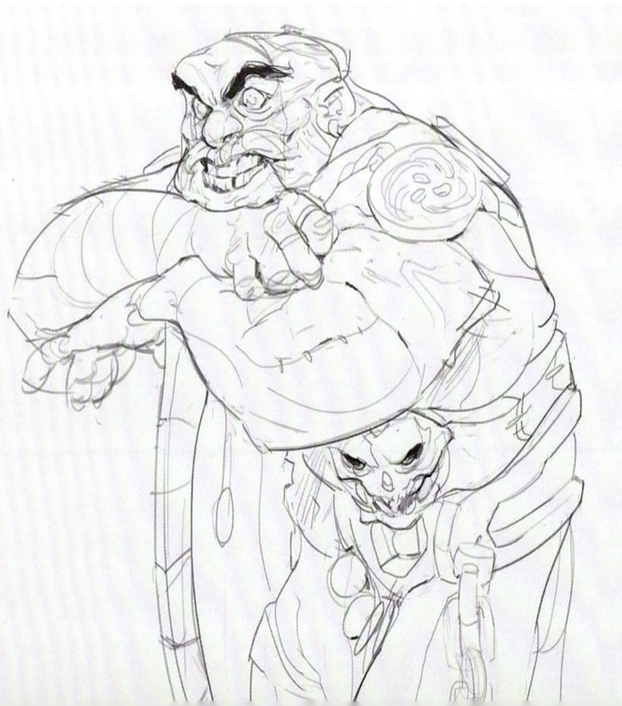

I had spent so much time trying to build images through nice textures, volume, and colours that I truly struggled to create something worthy using only lines – at least in my eyes. The art of saying a lot with a little and shaping forms through drawing was something I had neglected for too long.

After that, I slowly started integrating things I had learned during my painting-only routine. I noticed that some of my drawings and executions did not have the same traction. Surprisingly, very expressive, almost cartoonish characters got the most reactions, especially fan art. I was still using references from time to time, but attempted to create more based on ideas from my imagination.

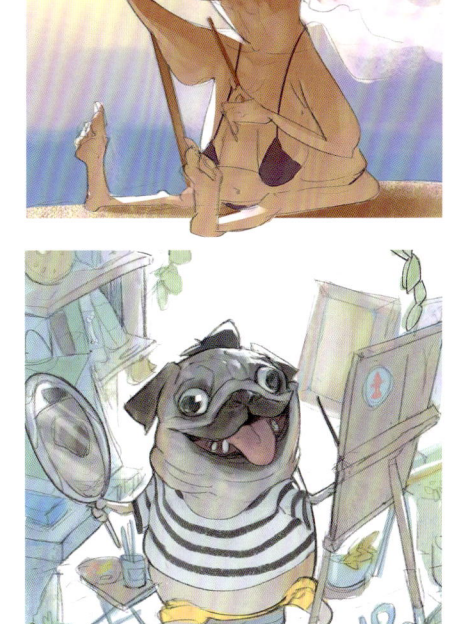

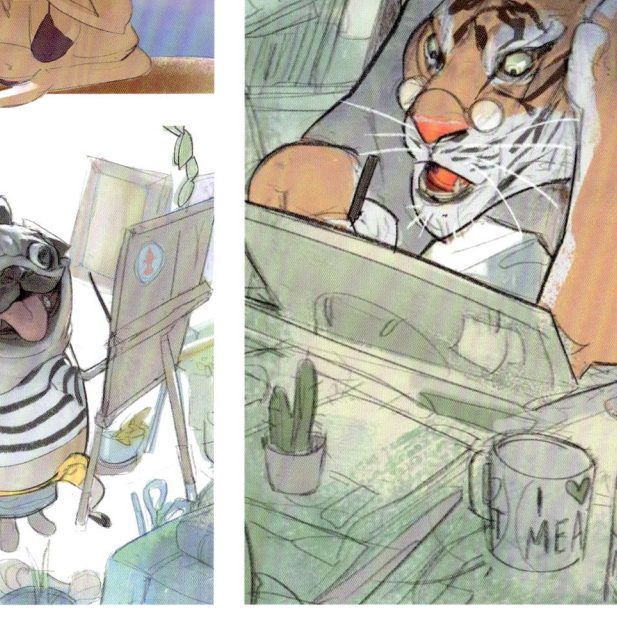

I realized many of my assumptions about art were wrong. It wasn't about the amount of detail, but about making the right choices – a careful selection of aesthetic decisions. Sometimes, a few well-placed lines with simple colours and values could generate more interest than overly complex pieces.

During this phase, I created one piece that still defines my art style to this day: fan art of a White Walker from *Game of Thrones*. It was a simple portrait, where I aimed to nail a thirty-minute sketch using just the necessary information. When I posted it, the reception was incredible. That made me decide to keep using this same technique for the next few days, and I kept getting a similar amount of traction.

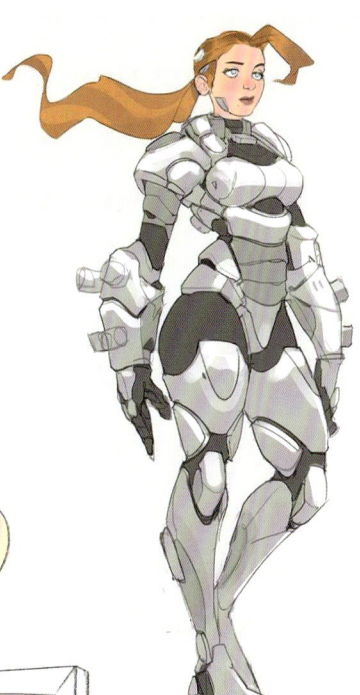

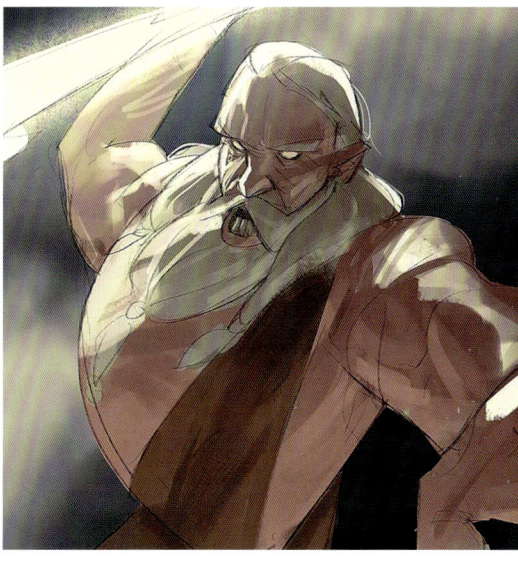

It's important to mention that by then, my online presence was growing. When I combined that with this particular technique, I caught the attention of recruiters and artists from Riot Games, landing a job at one of the best game-development companies. I'd love to credit one specific fan-art piece from back in those days, but honestly , I think it was the years of sharing my journey on social media that laid the foundation for them to reach out.

From lines up to now

FAN ART, CINEMATIC KEY FRAMES & ILLUSTRATION

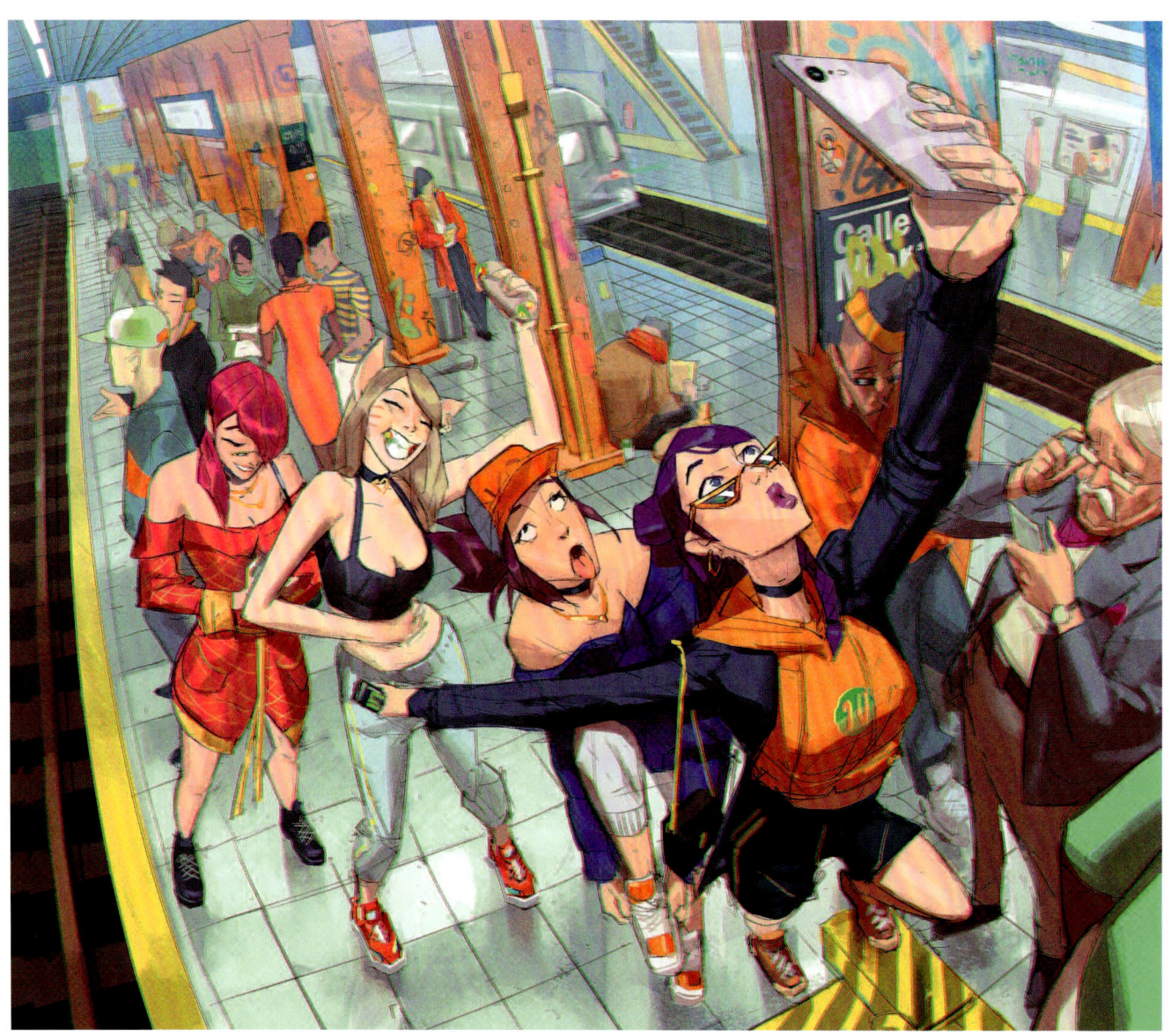

At the beginning of 2017, I was still very interested in making fan art, but I started thinking of ways to show popular characters in unusual situations. For example, if I drew a character from a big action movie, I'd show them doing something casual – like eating or doing laundry – instead of fighting or looking dramatic. I felt this would make them more relatable and different from what I often saw other artists doing.

If it was an actor from a well-known movie, I found it fun to imagine them from a different perspective – like how they would look in a frame of an animated film instead of live action. Since my style back then was heavily influenced by 2D animation, I thought this was a good way to get noticed while practising my technique.

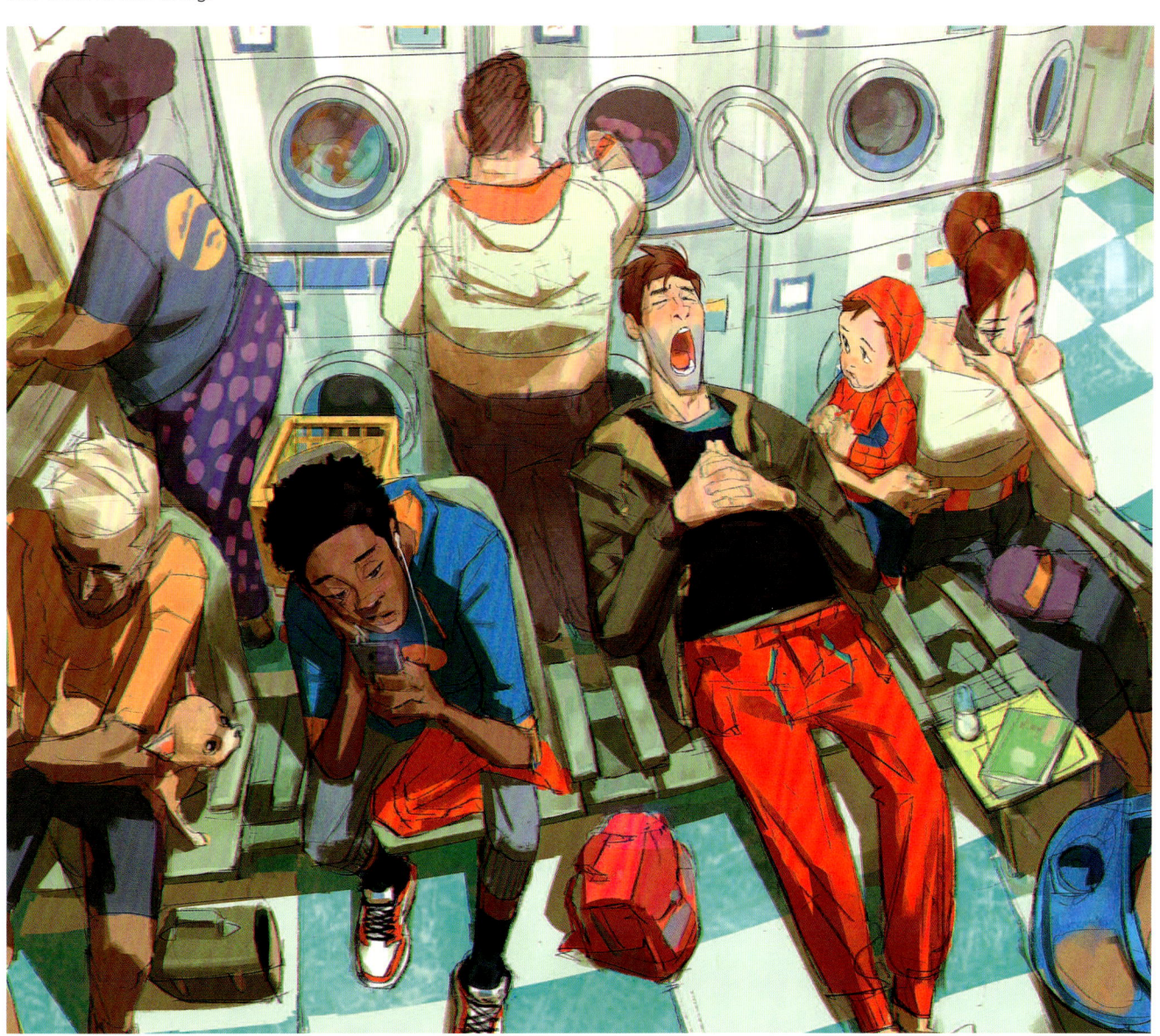

Maybe that's the 'life' people talk about when describing my work – just characters doing everyday things, like any of us.

ORIGINAL CINEMATIC KEY FRAMES & ILLUSTRATION

While doing these fan-art experiments, I was also trying to create original characters in between. I focused on dynamic curved lines for gestures and facial expressions to bring movement to my work. But my designs weren't very deep – they lacked strong shape, colour, and costume design, among other key fundamentals in character design – anything that made them feel like they existed. What can I say? They looked nice to me, but they didn't mean much.

Still, I created things like animals dealing with stressful situations, mythological creatures, and themes that were popular in concept art at the time – pirates, samurais, and so on. But most of my popularity came when I made a series of fan art based on *Game of Thrones*, which everyone was talking about at the time. A lot of those pieces ended up looking like they could be from an animated show.

Fan art is a good way to get noticed on social media because people already know the characters. Since there's a story behind them, it's easy for the art to spread. But this can backfire later when you want attention for your personal work. If people follow you for fan art, they might not care as much about your original ideas. That doesn't mean you're not good at what you do, but the reason people engage with your work isn't just about skill – it's also about the story behind the characters they already love.

I'd say it's best to do a mix of fan art and personal work, then slowly shift towards your own ideas if you want recognition for your original characters.

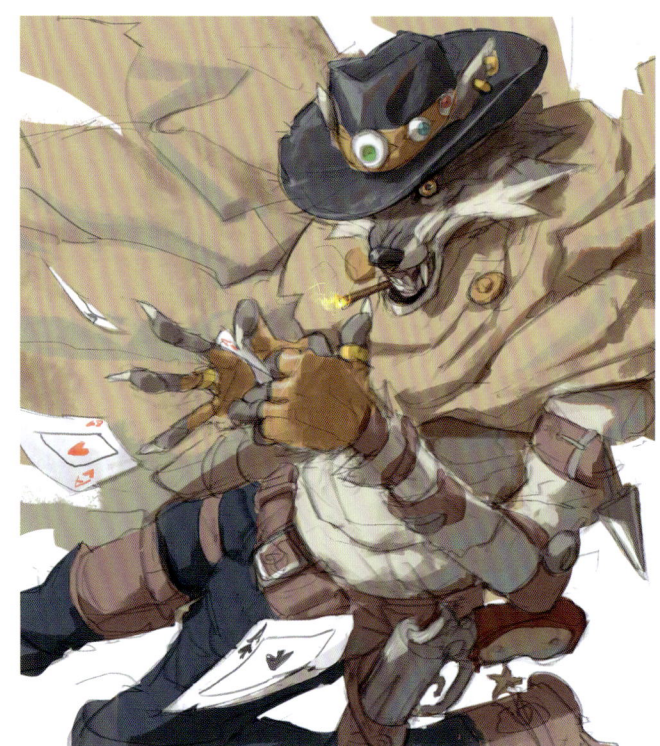

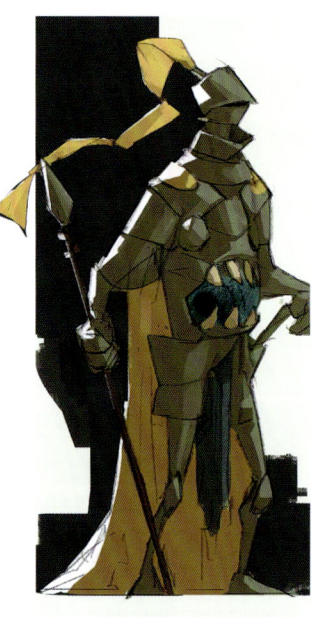

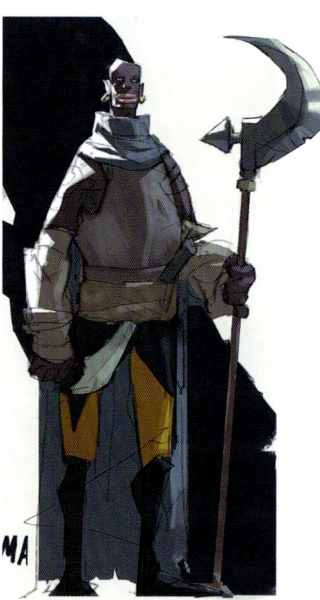

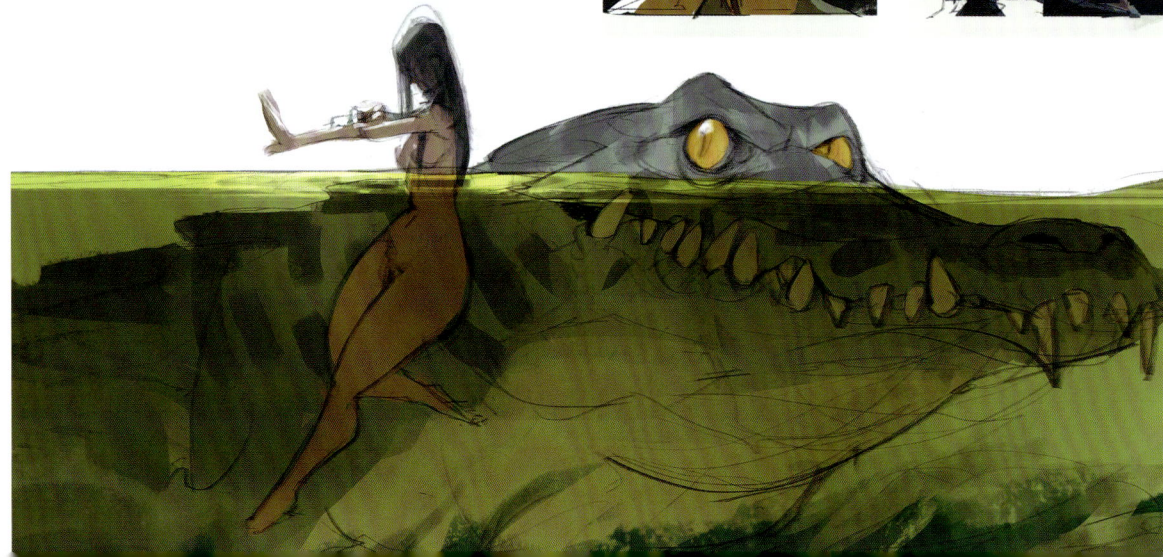

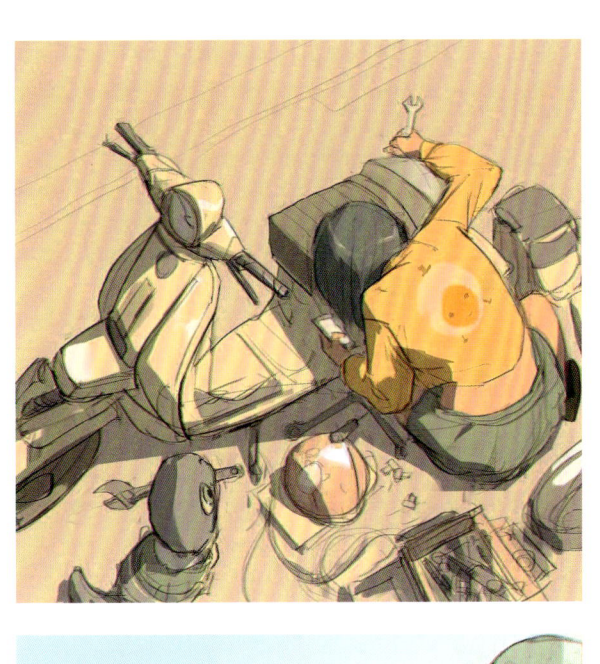
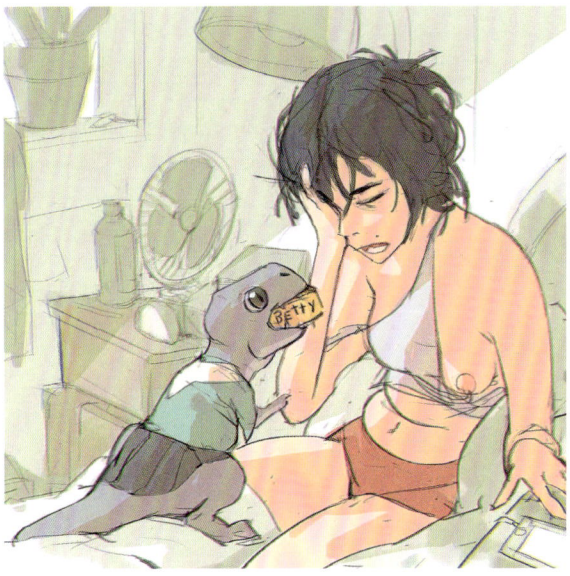

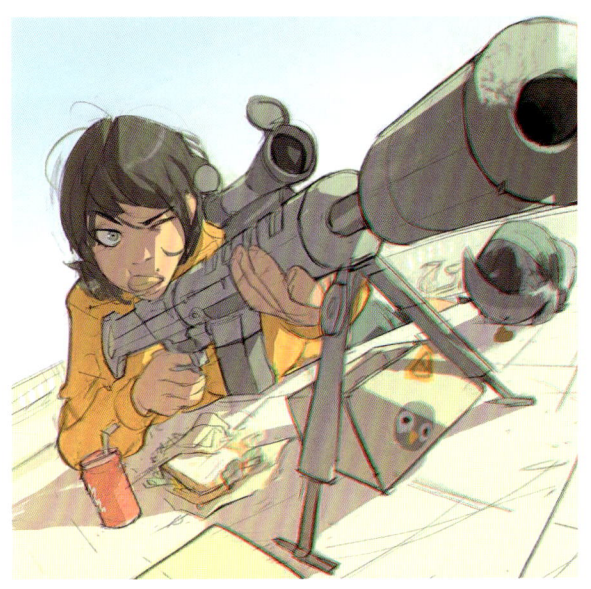
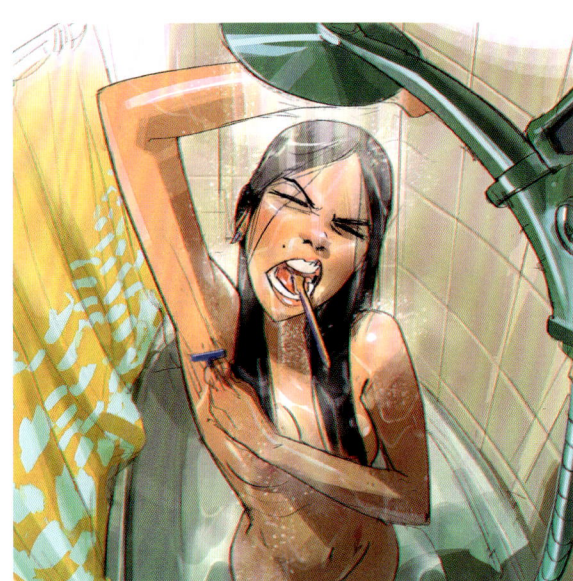
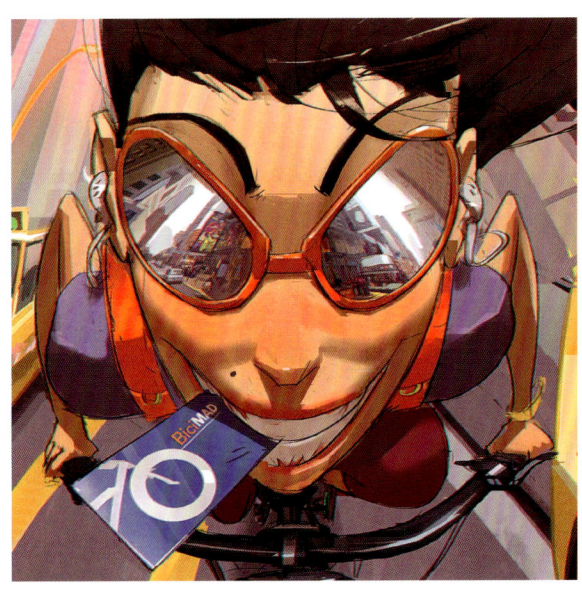
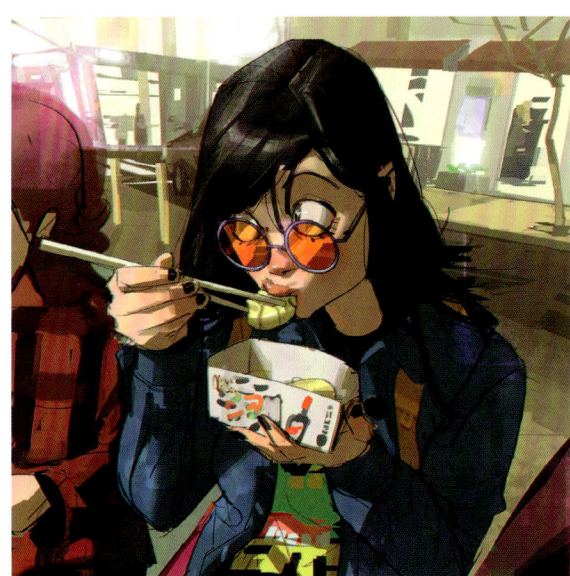

UNDERSTANDING ANIMATION

As I delved deeper into this 'animation frame' perspective, it struck me that I didn't know the creators behind the influential works from my childhood and recent years – many of them Japanese artists and directors. So, I started researching their processes, and also tried animating myself. I had a couple of animator friends who gave me tips while I worked on getting a few frames together, some a few minutes long, others just quick GIFs of characters doing simple things like eating.

My approach to this challenge was to think of a single frame, like an illustration I found interesting, and then create frames that came before and after. I didn't discover hot water here, as this is what storyboard artists do, but as with anything new, I mostly approached it through intuition.

I already knew animation was a powerful way to tell stories because I had grown up watching it, but I didn't fully understand that until I started making my own. A single drawing can say a lot, but even the simplest sequence of frames can create a stronger reaction. That's when I realized – the key was storytelling.

Over time, I understood that stories made concepts and characters feel real. And to me, animation felt like the most complete way to bring them to life. But who knows? Maybe I just wasn't good enough at other mediums. Maybe my judgement was shaped by social-media trends. I guess that's for others to decide.

This obsession with animation, stories, and characters eventually made me want to build my own world – somewhere my characters could exist and tell their stories. It's something I've been working on for years now, and hopefully, one day, I'll be able to make it a reality.

36

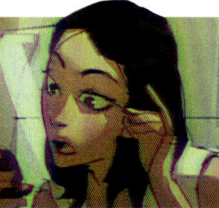 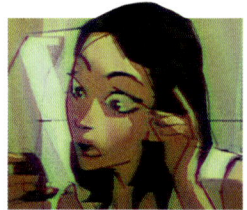 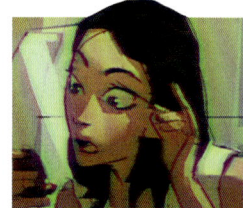 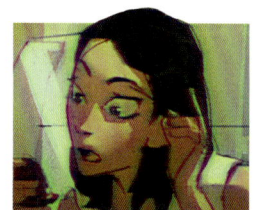 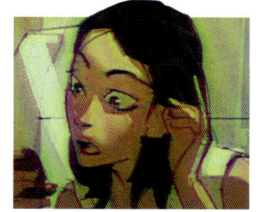 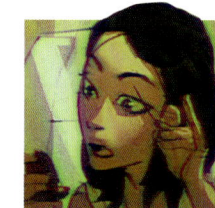

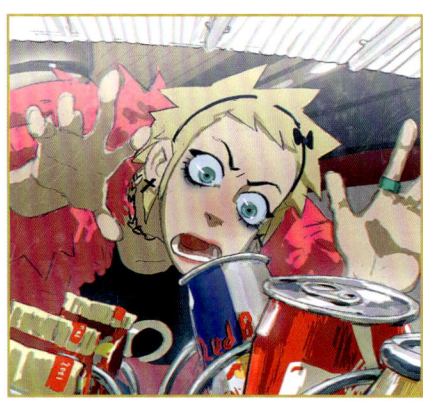 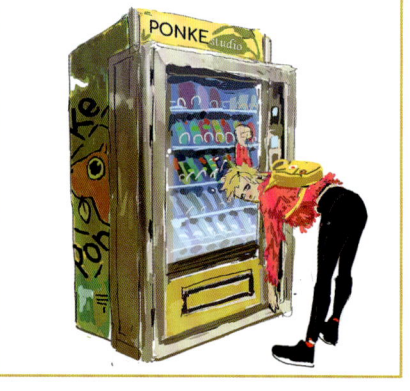 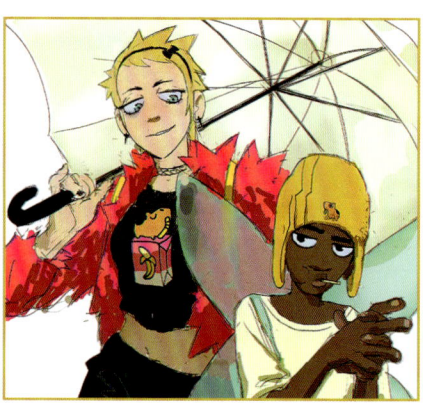

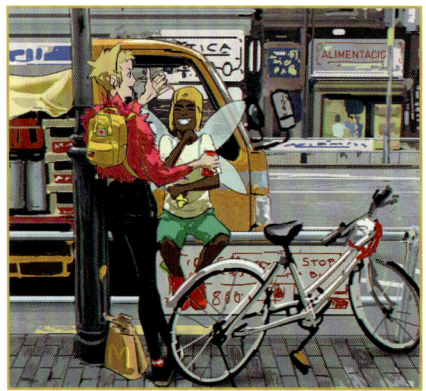 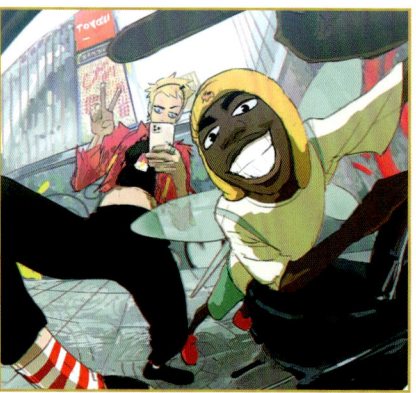

'I SLOWLY UNDERSTOOD THAT STORIES MADE CONCEPTS AND CHARACTERS FEEL REAL'

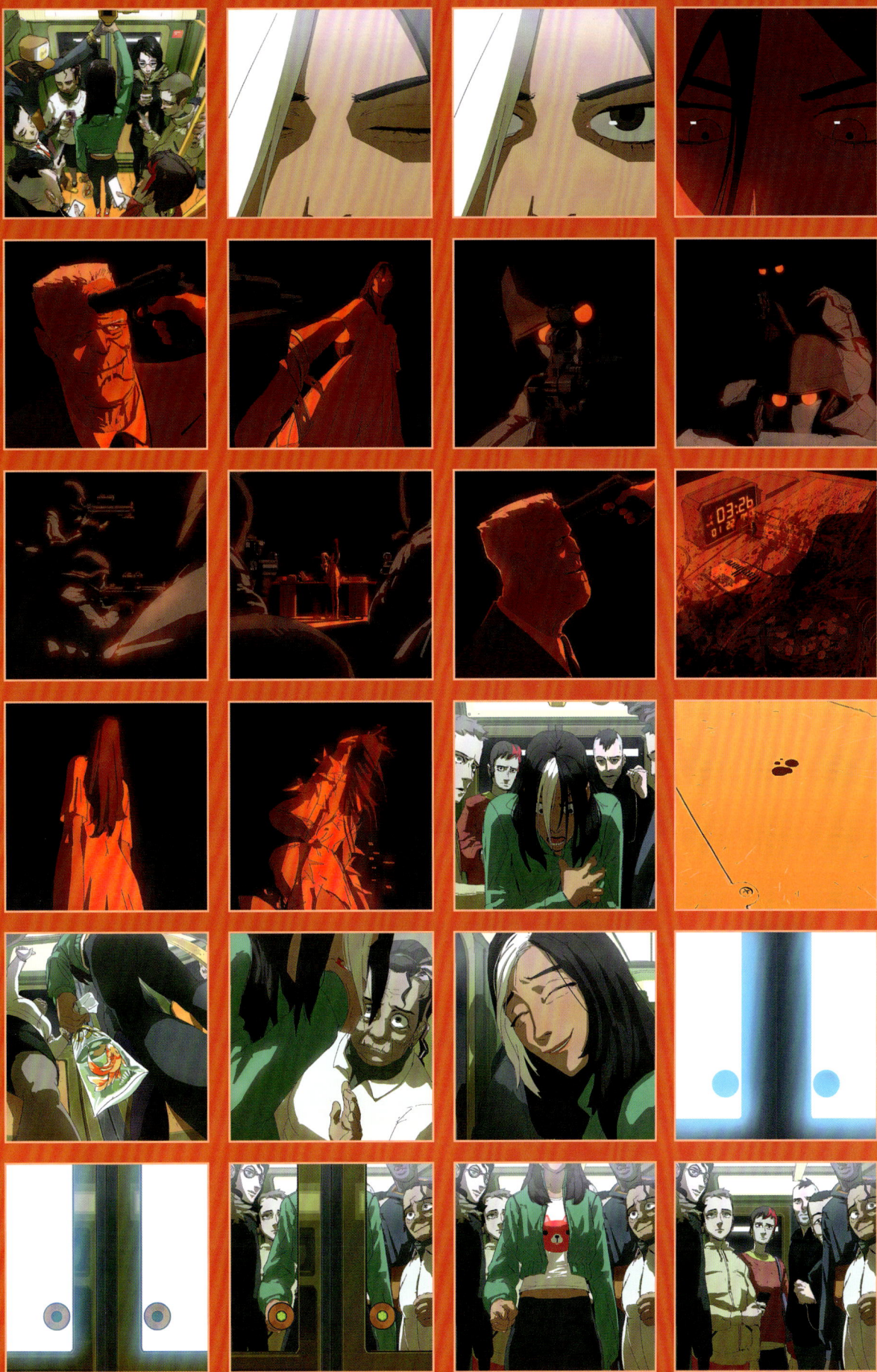

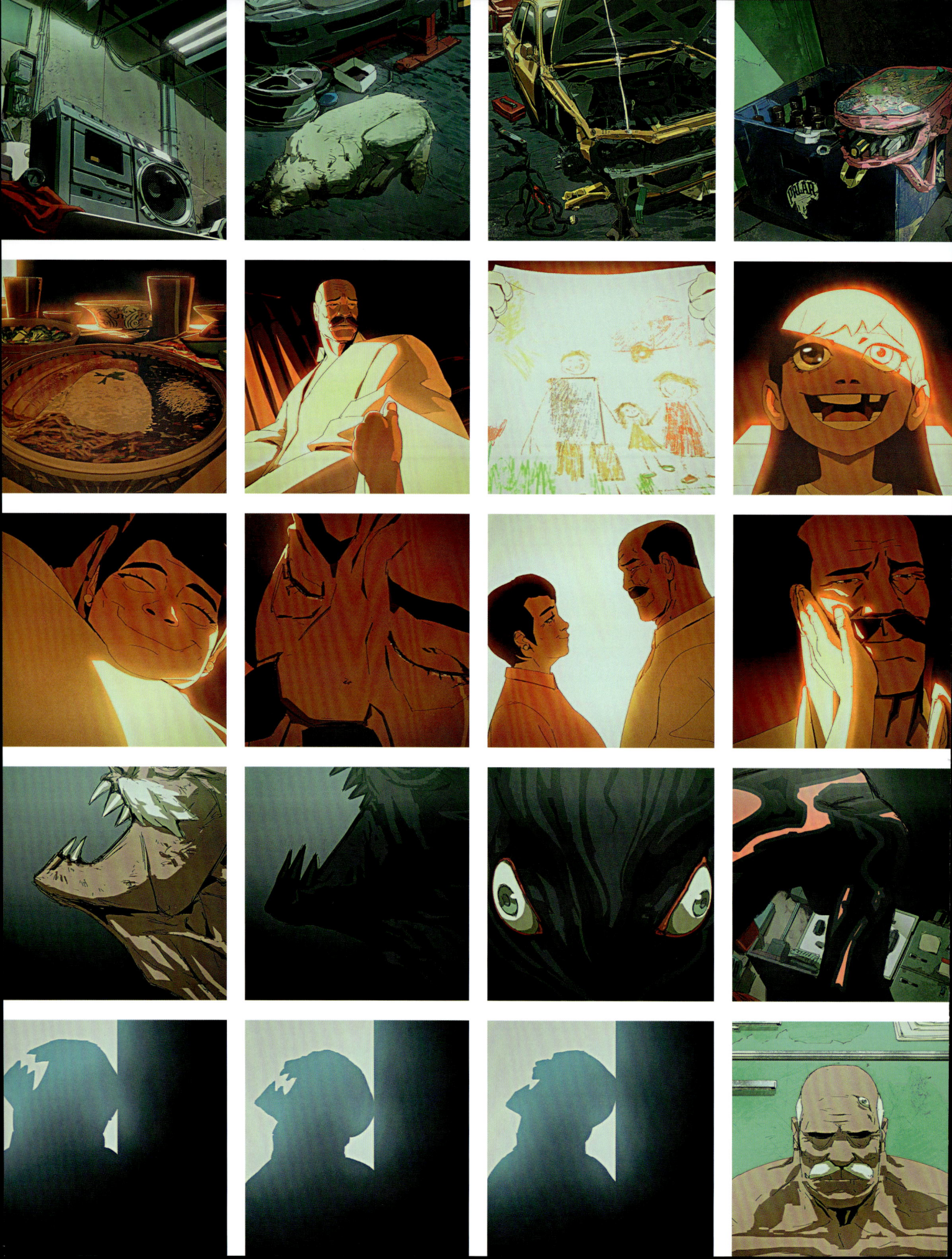

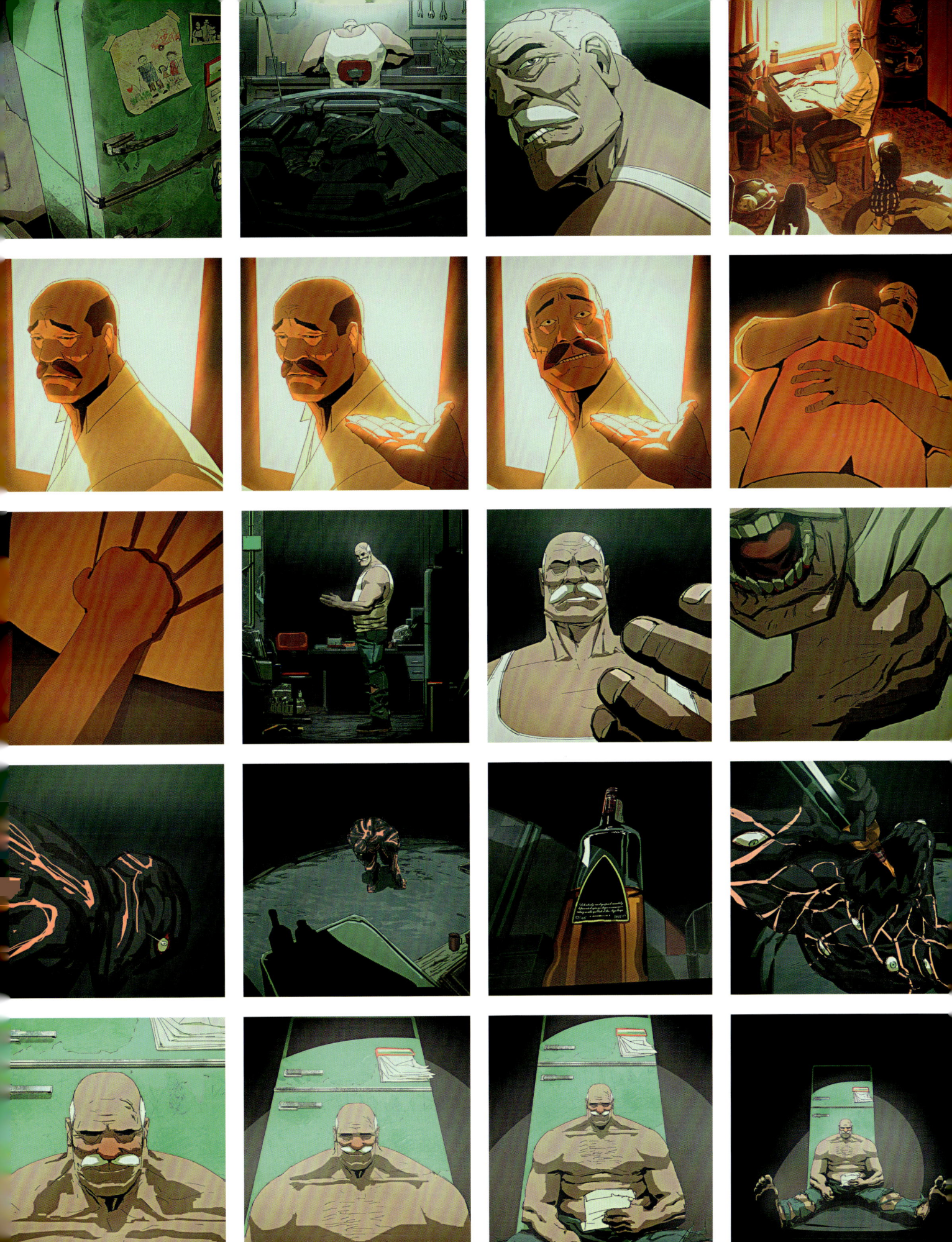

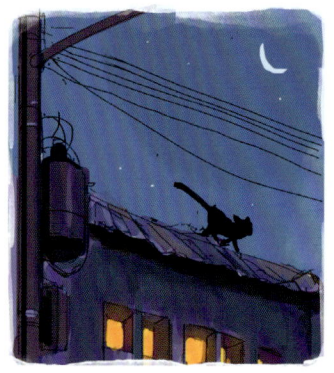

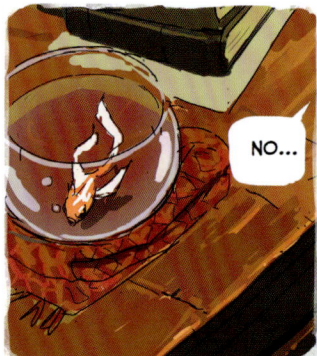

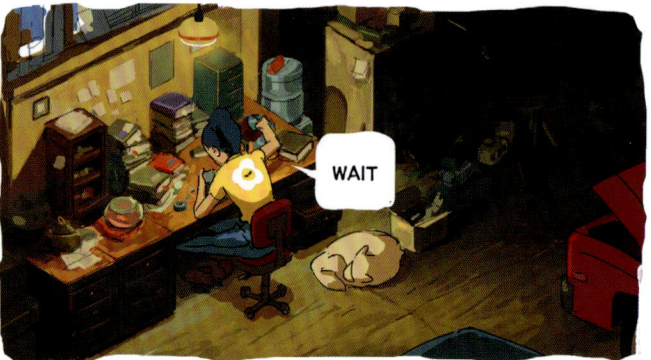

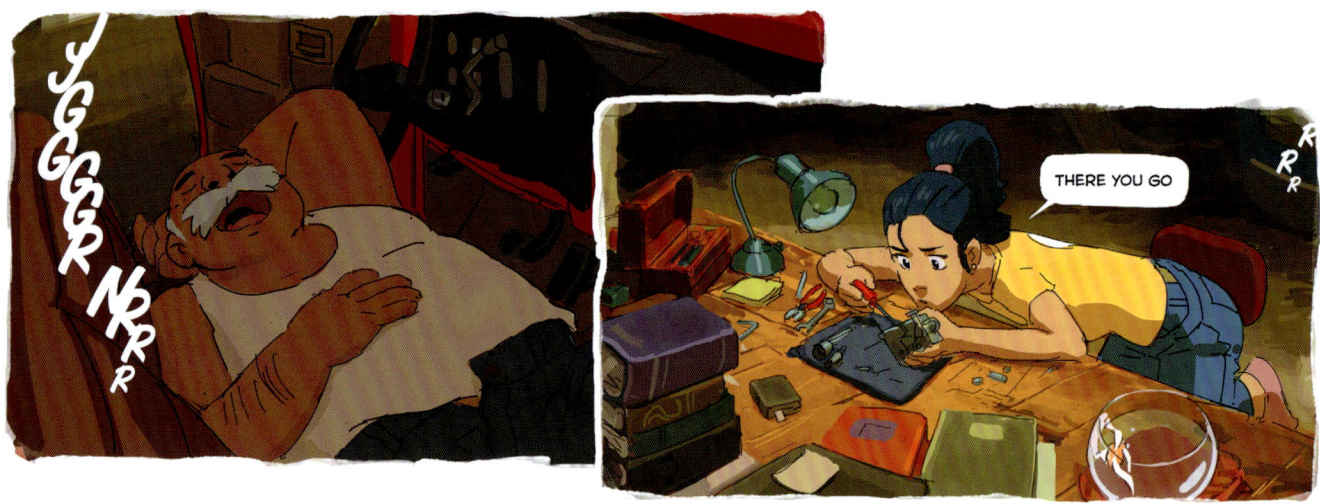

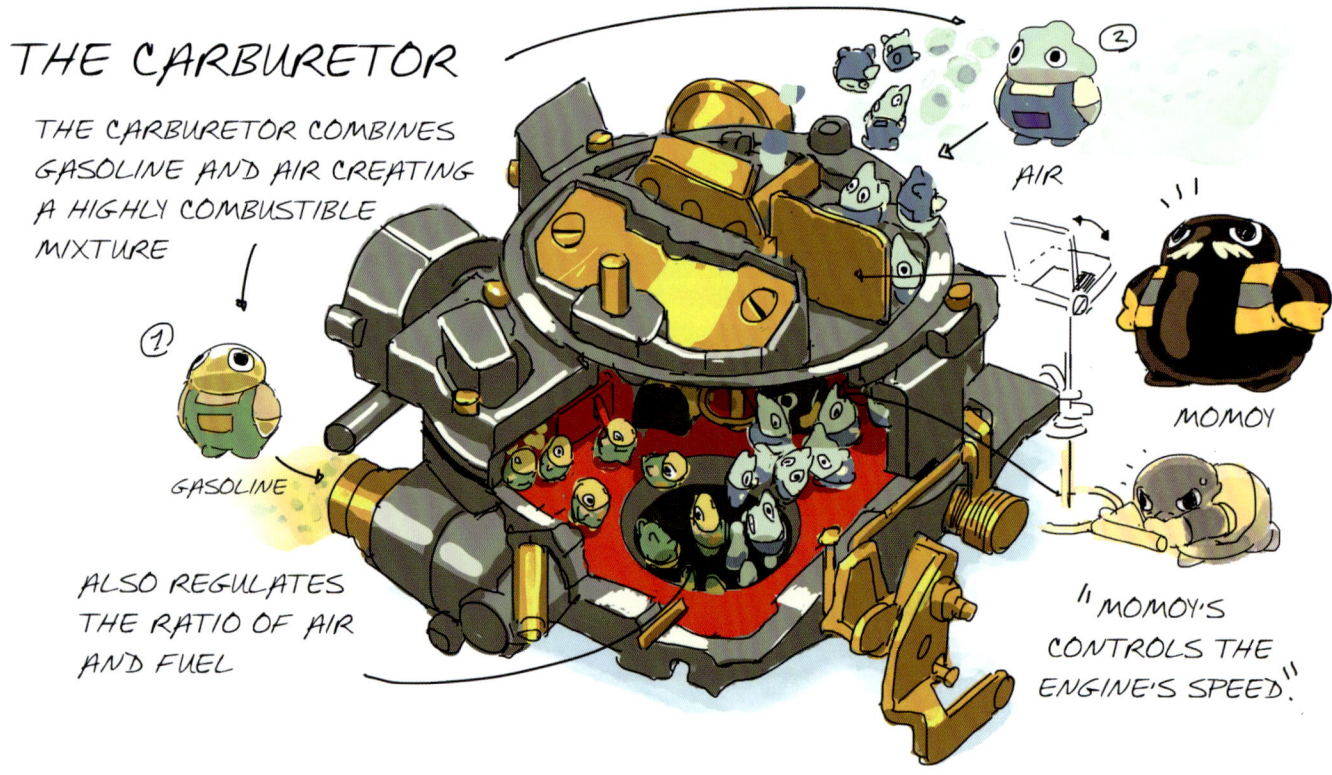

THE CARBURETOR

THE CARBURETOR COMBINES GASOLINE AND AIR CREATING A HIGHLY COMBUSTIBLE MIXTURE

① GASOLINE

② AIR

MOMOY

ALSO REGULATES THE RATIO OF AIR AND FUEL

"MOMOY'S CONTROLS THE ENGINE'S SPEED"

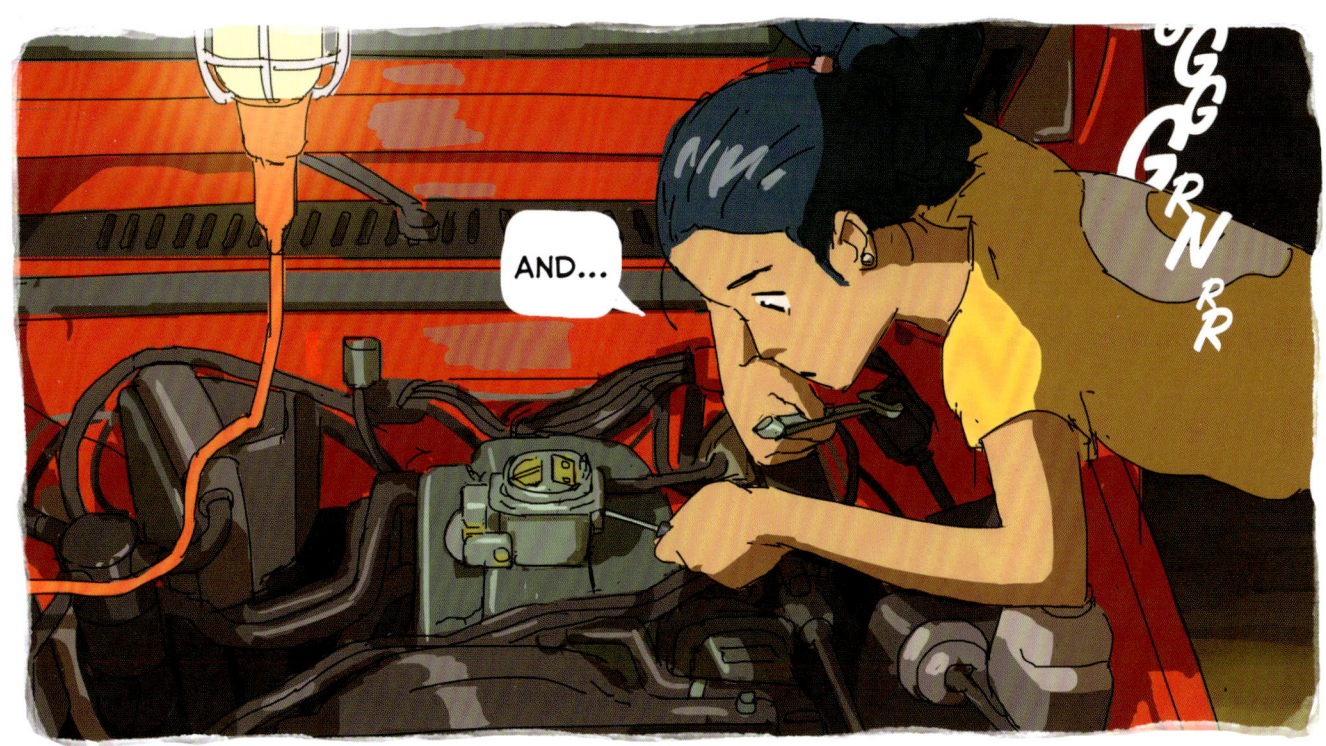

41

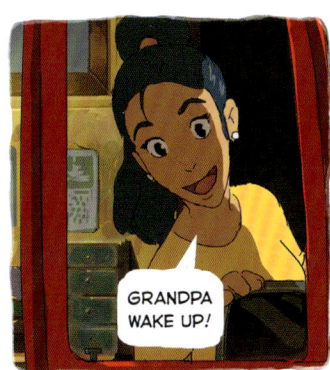

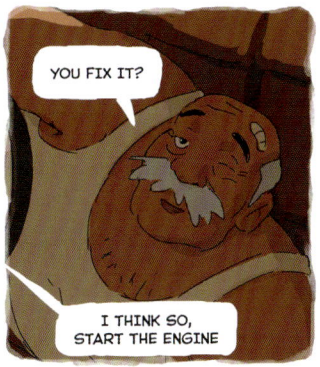

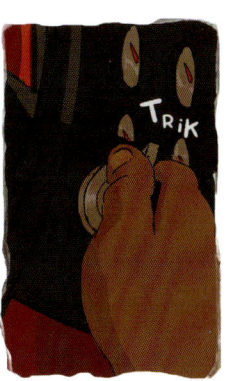

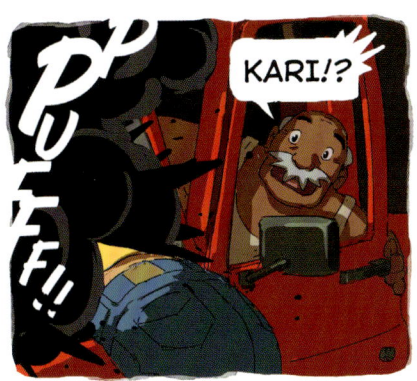

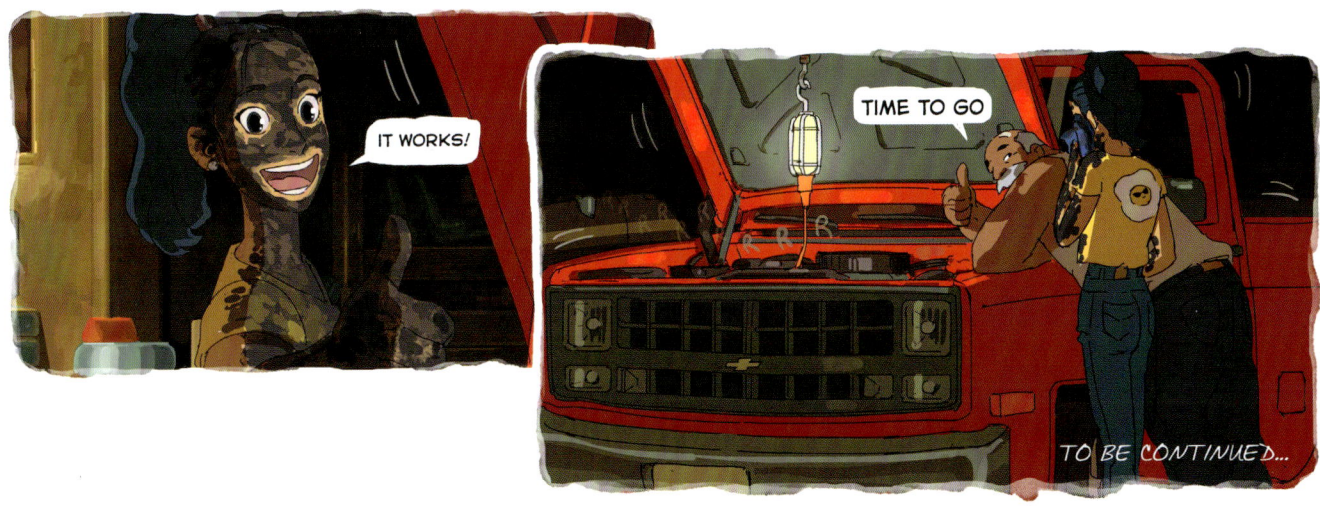

TO BE CONTINUED...

CHARACTER DESIGN OUT OF EVERYTHING

In recent years, I focused on building my projects and stepped away from social media. But one artist really inspired me to come back – a Korean artist called Rinotuna, who creates characters based on everyday objects, animals, and random themes he finds interesting.

Beyond his great techniques and concepts, his art just makes me feel good. I can't explain it, and I think that's fine. Art does not need to be described in detail for you to understand it; it must be experienced first. Then maybe you can try to define and discuss it – but first, it must evoke something within you.

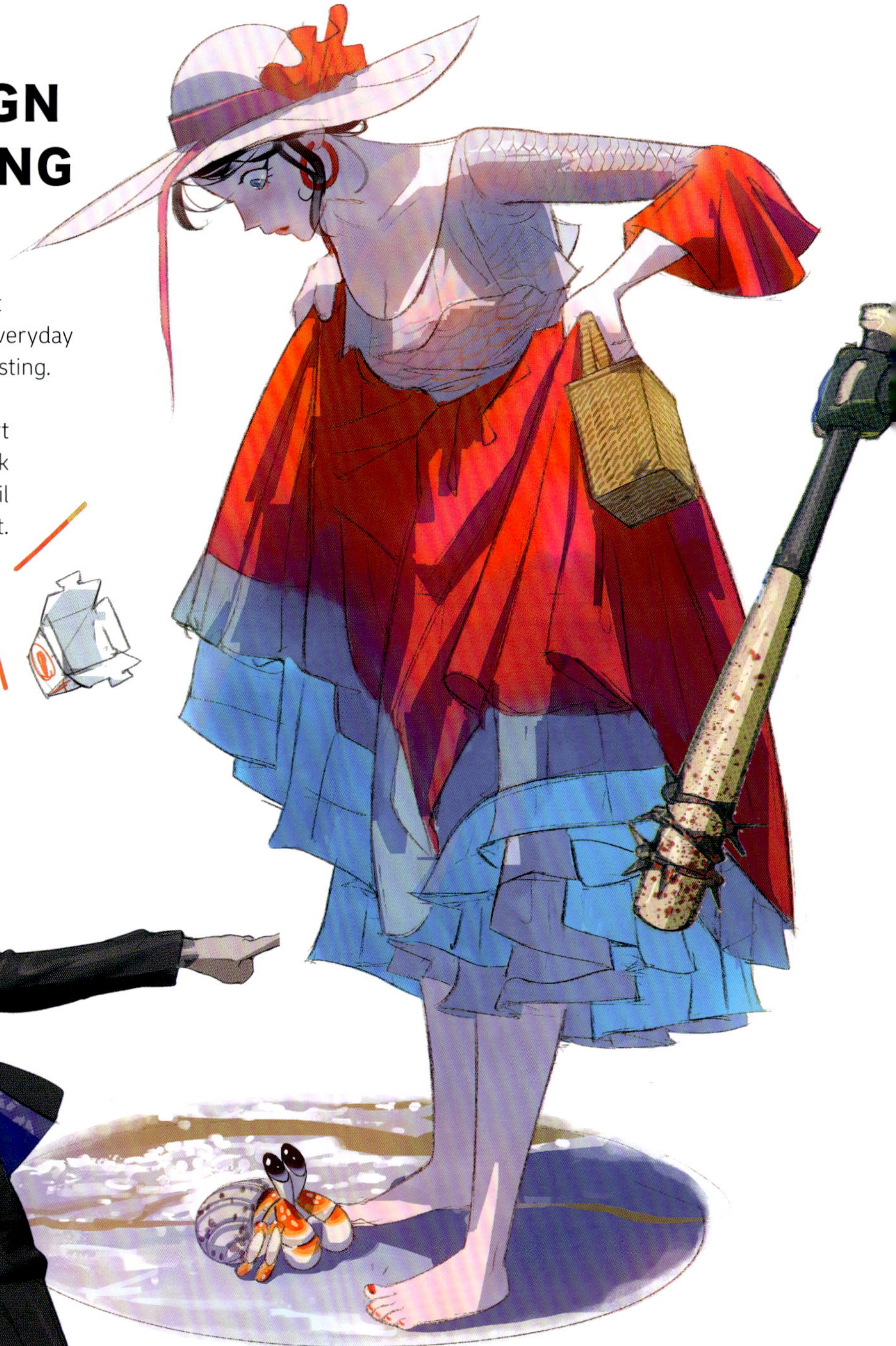

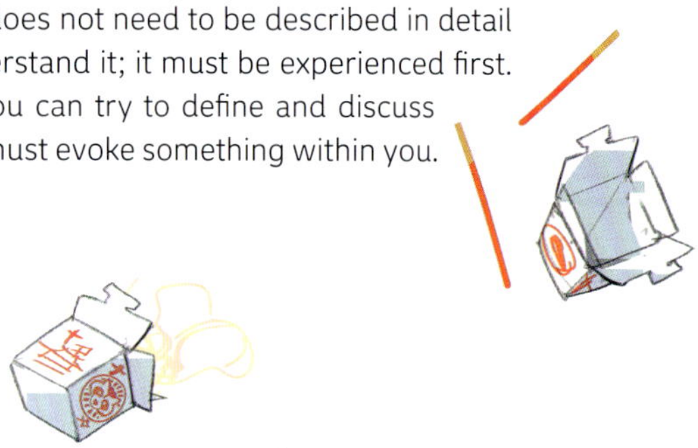

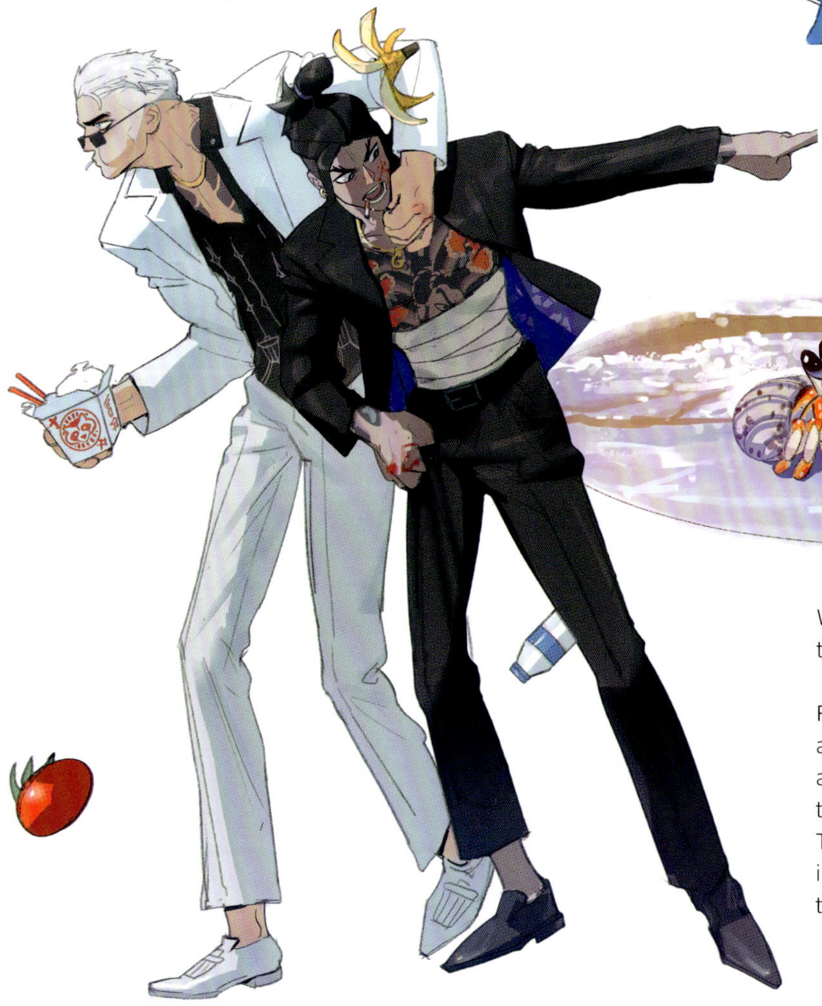

Whatever his work did, it was so inspiring that I wanted to try it myself, and I did.

For quite a while, I took random references, as well as inspiration, from Rinotuna's art, and tried to think of ways in which they could be portrayed as characters. This approach to concept development in character design taught me a lot – things I had never felt I could reach before.

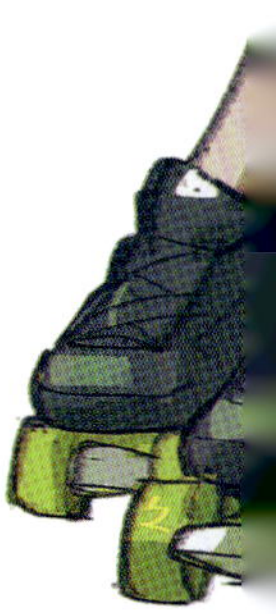

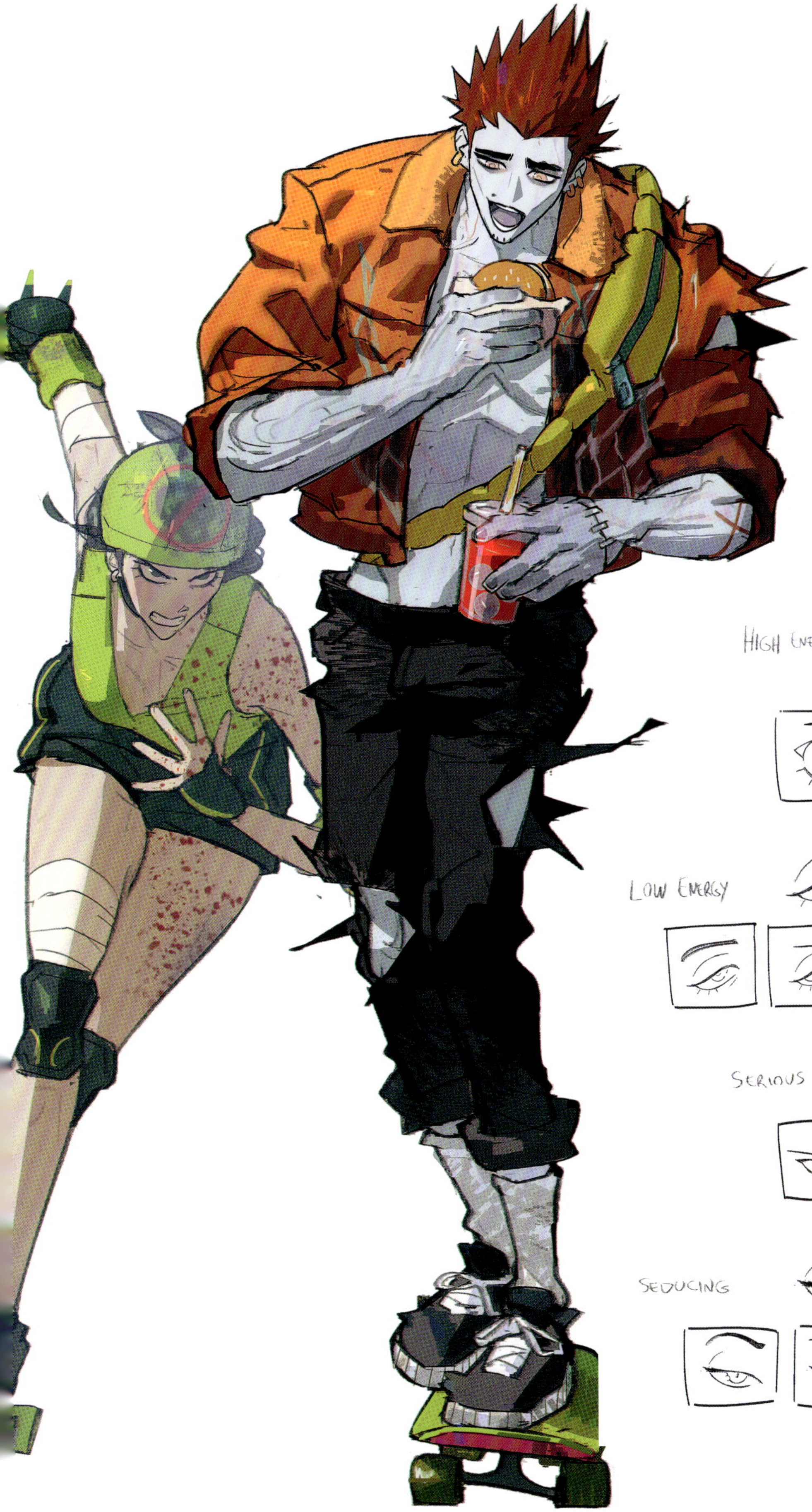

Combined with my previous experience, it became the missing piece that helped me shape characters that feel like they have a life beyond the illustrations themselves.

Much of what I share in this book comes from these phases of my journey, as well as the techniques from my previous years. I hope you enjoy them.

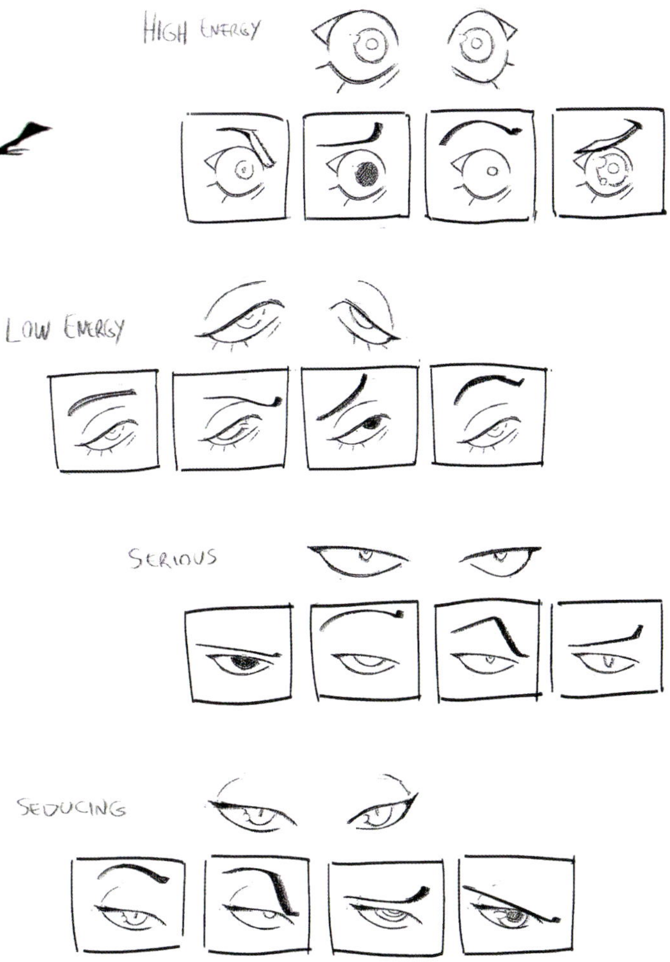

HIGH ENERGY

LOW ENERGY

SERIOUS

SEDUCING

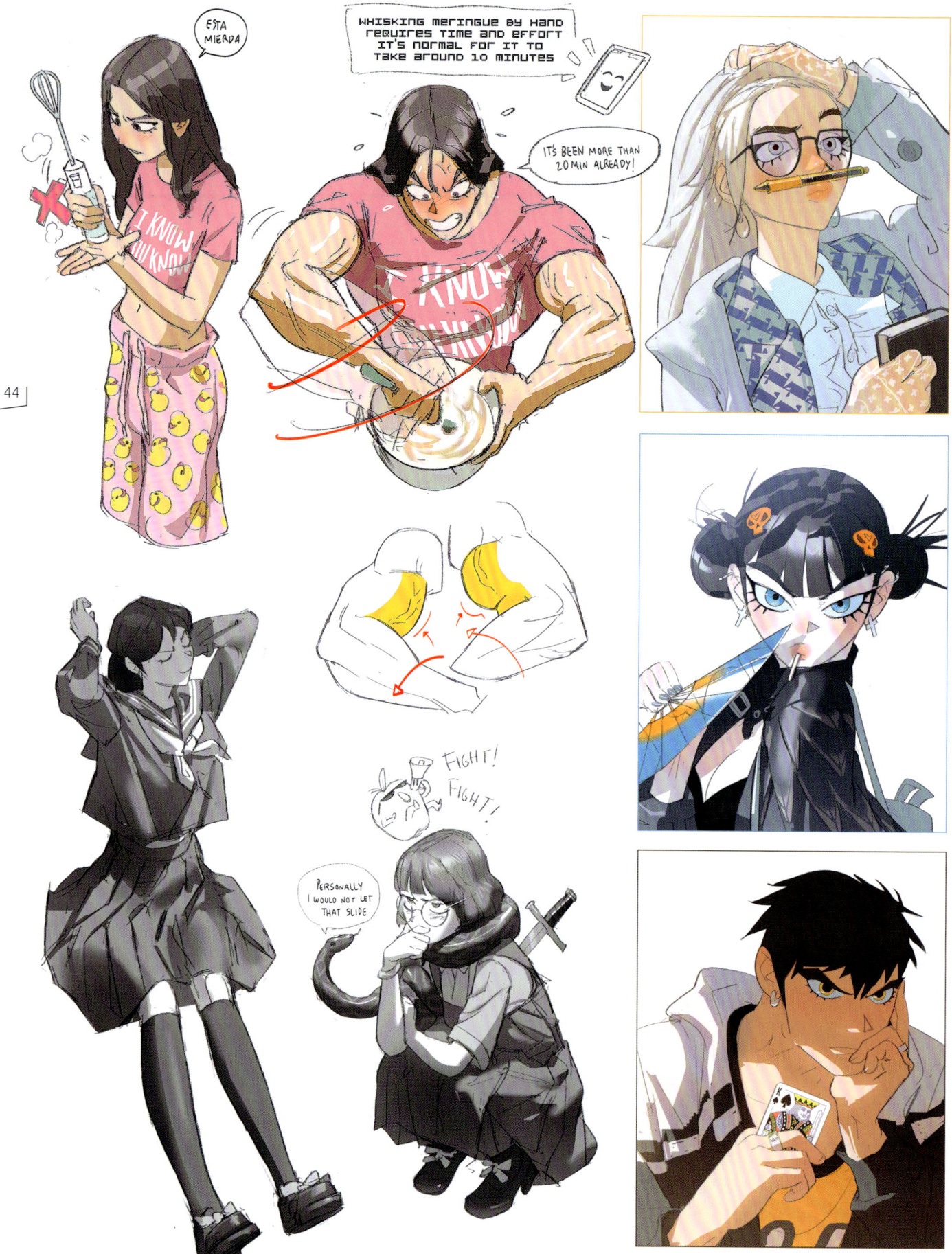

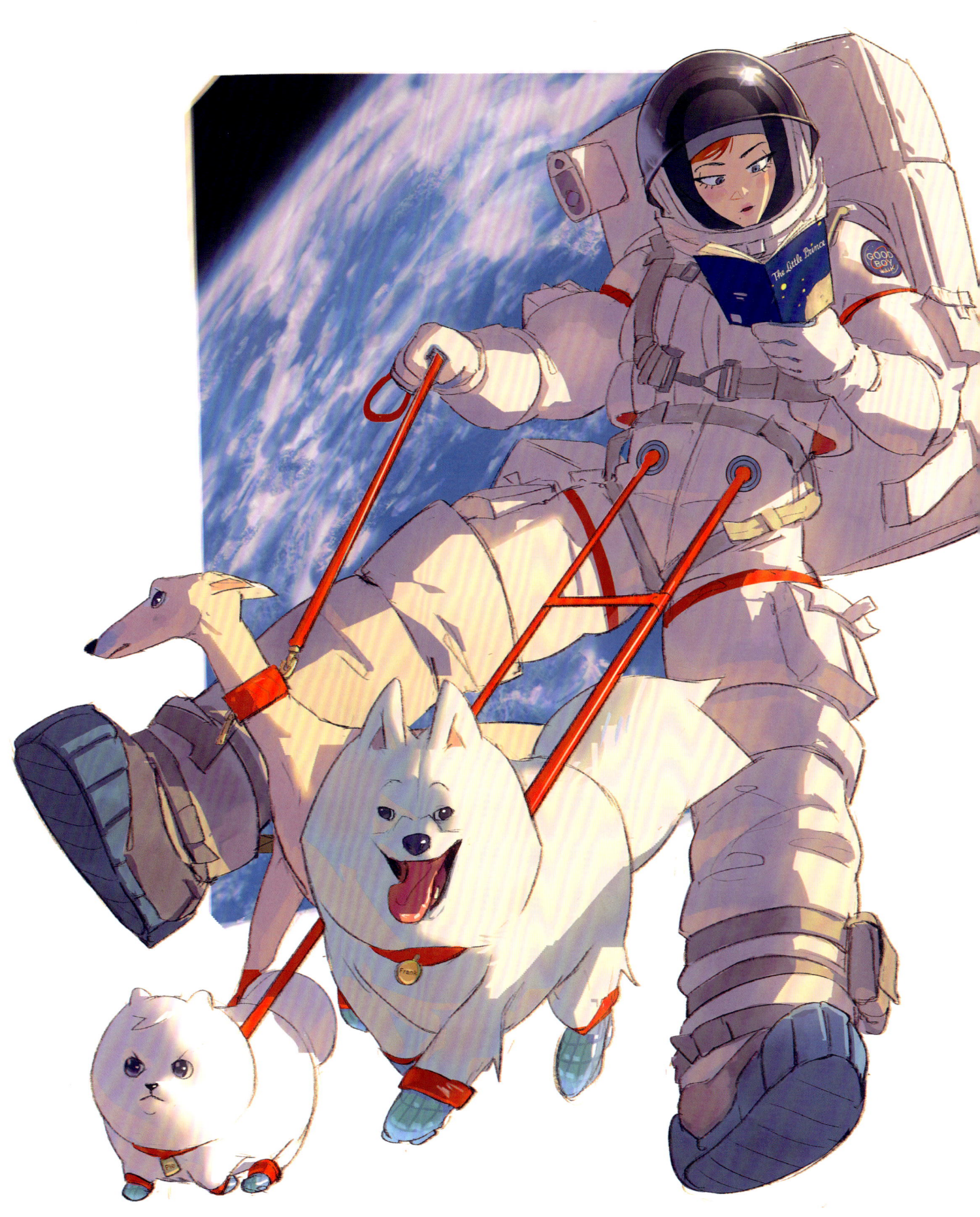

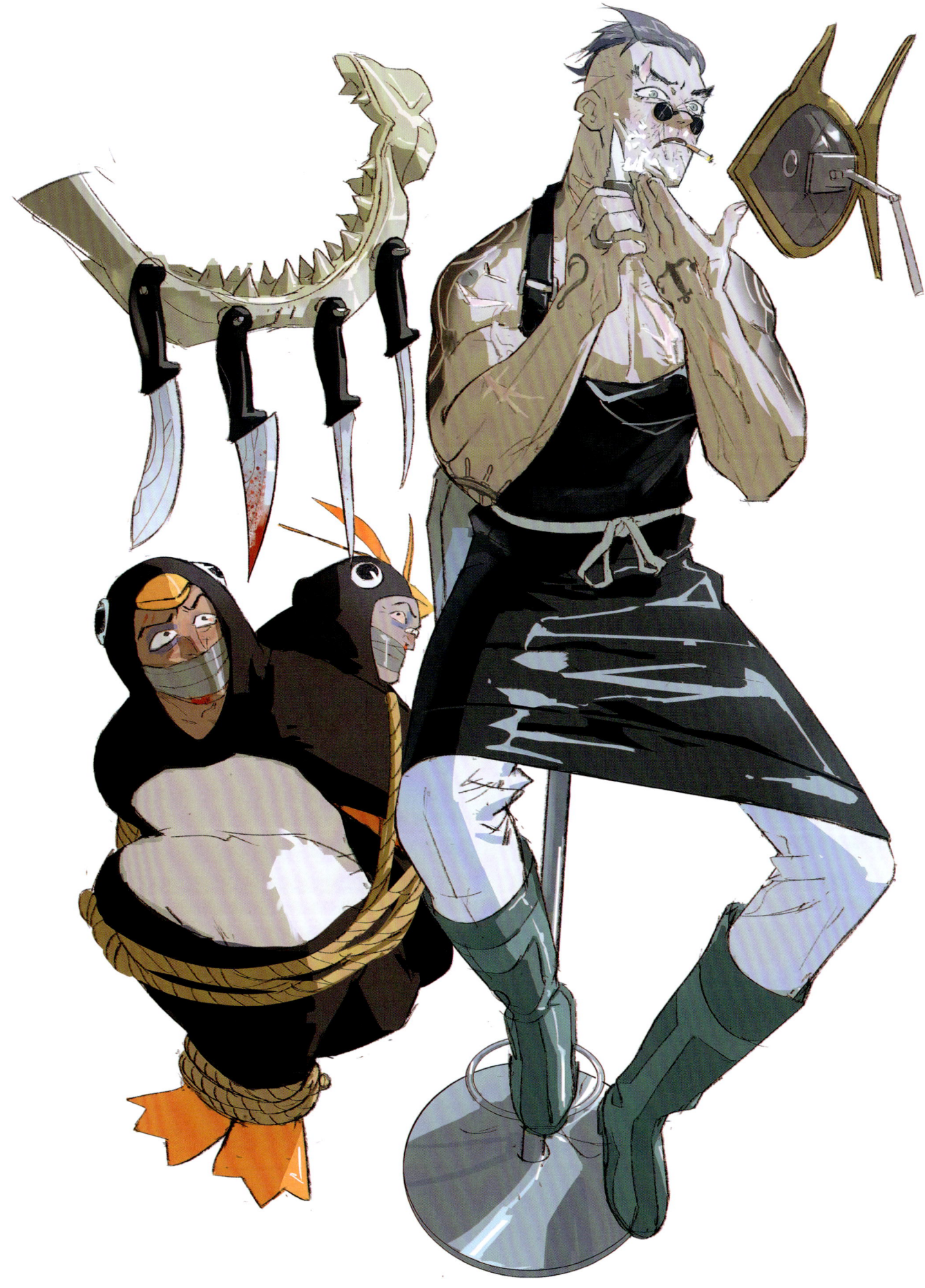

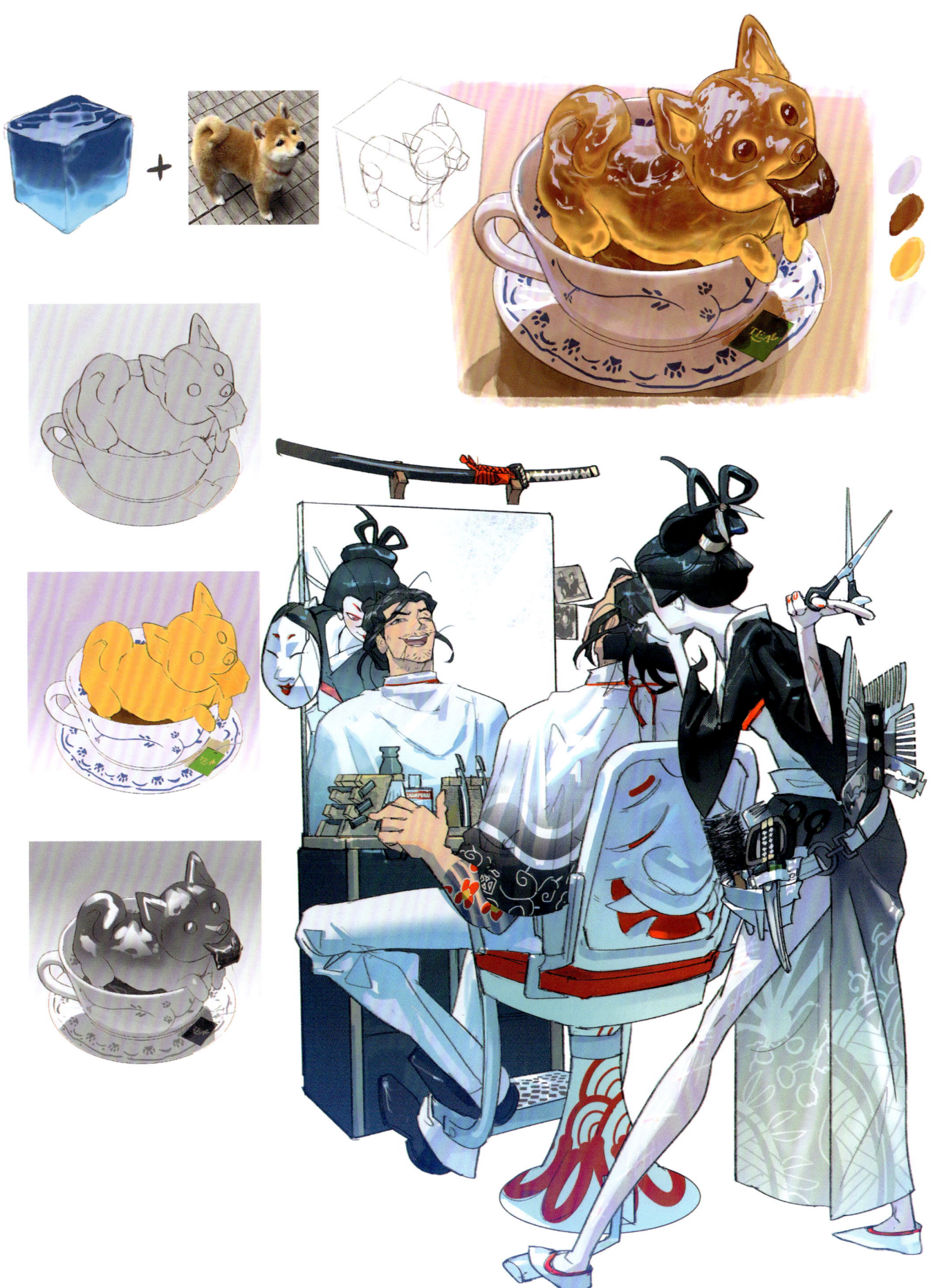

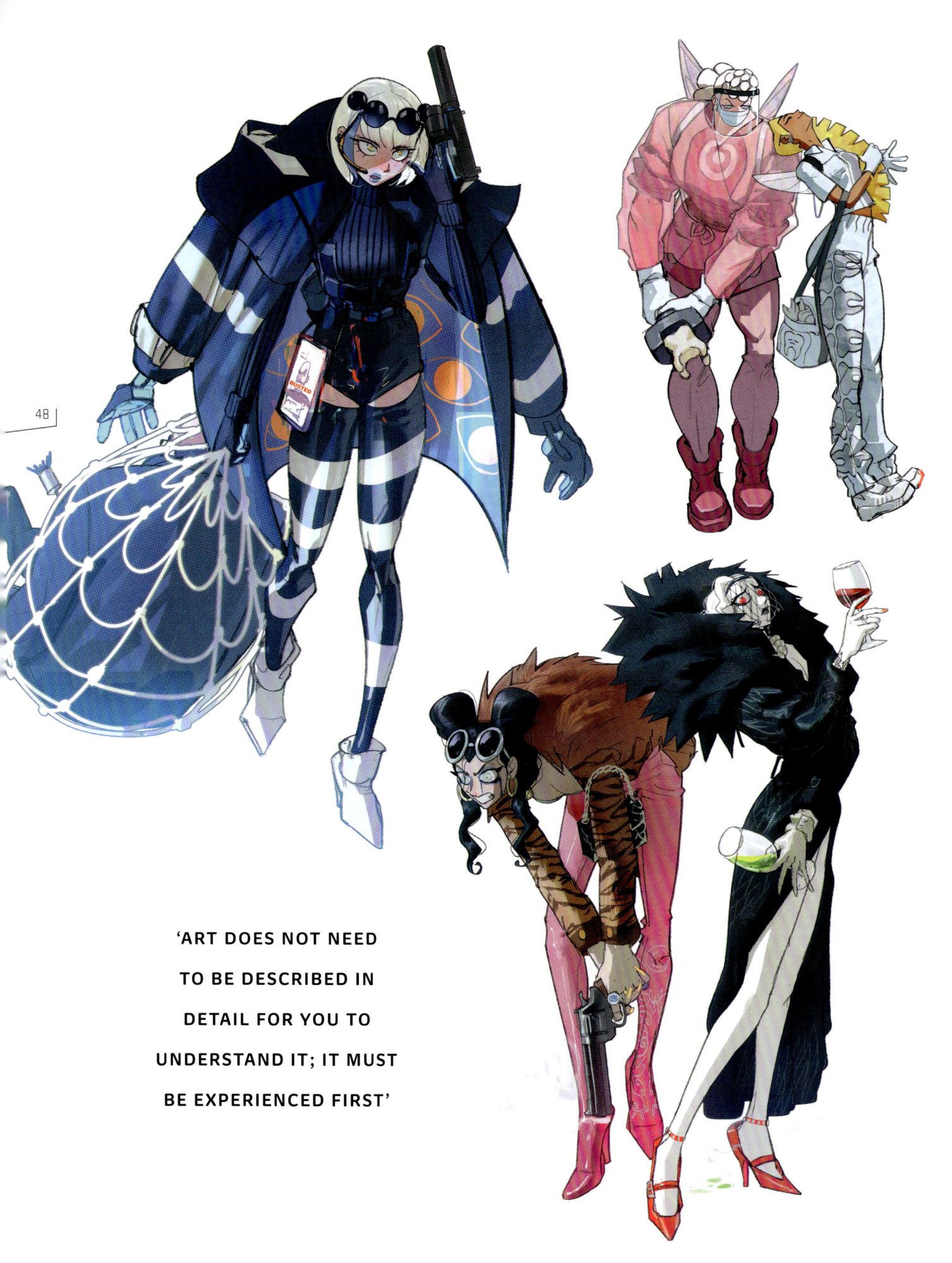

48

'ART DOES NOT NEED
TO BE DESCRIBED IN
DETAIL FOR YOU TO
UNDERSTAND IT; IT MUST
BE EXPERIENCED FIRST'

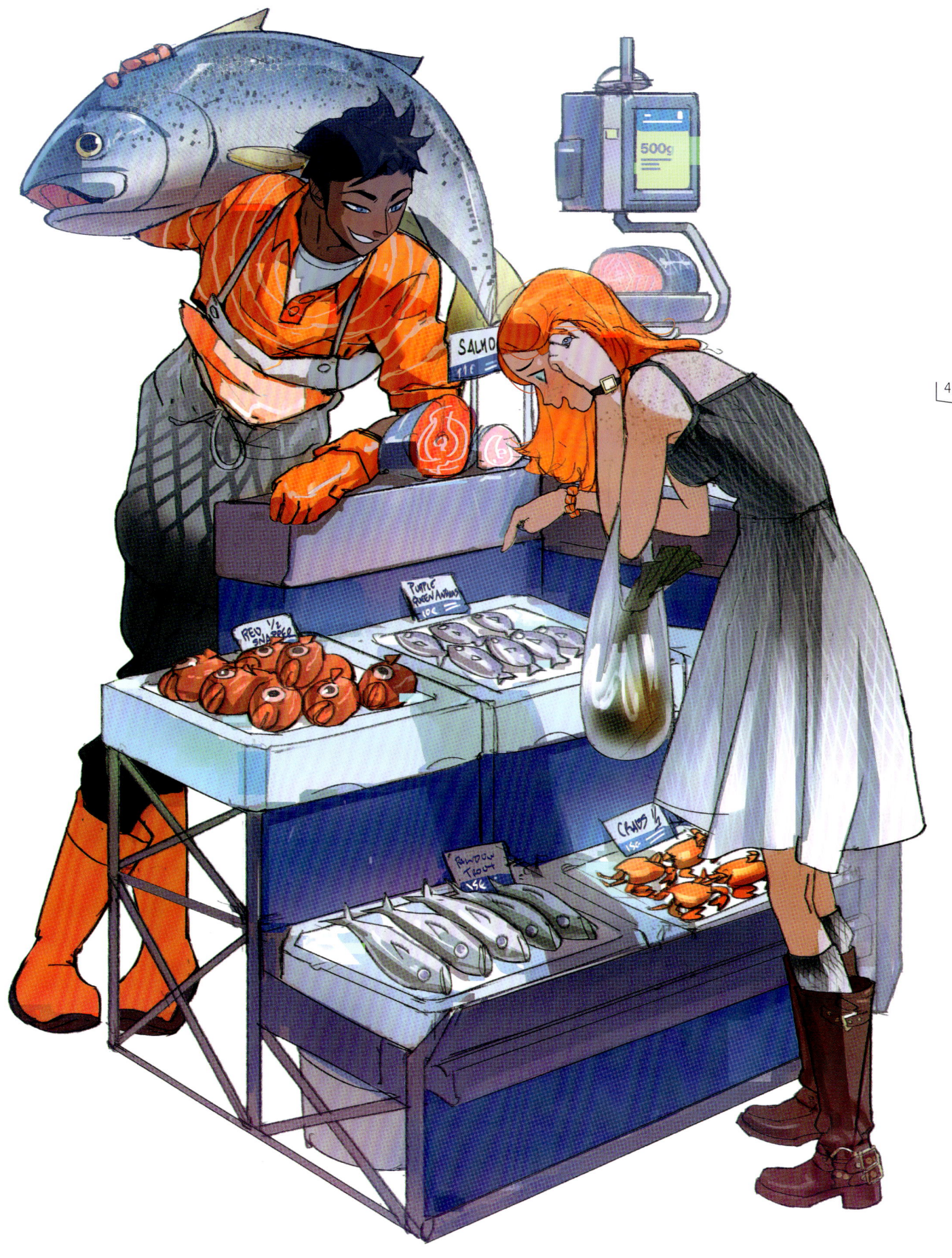

500g

SALMO

PURPLE
QUEEN ANTHIAS
10¢

RED 1/2
SNAPPER

CRABS 1/
15¢

RAINBOW
TROUT
15¢

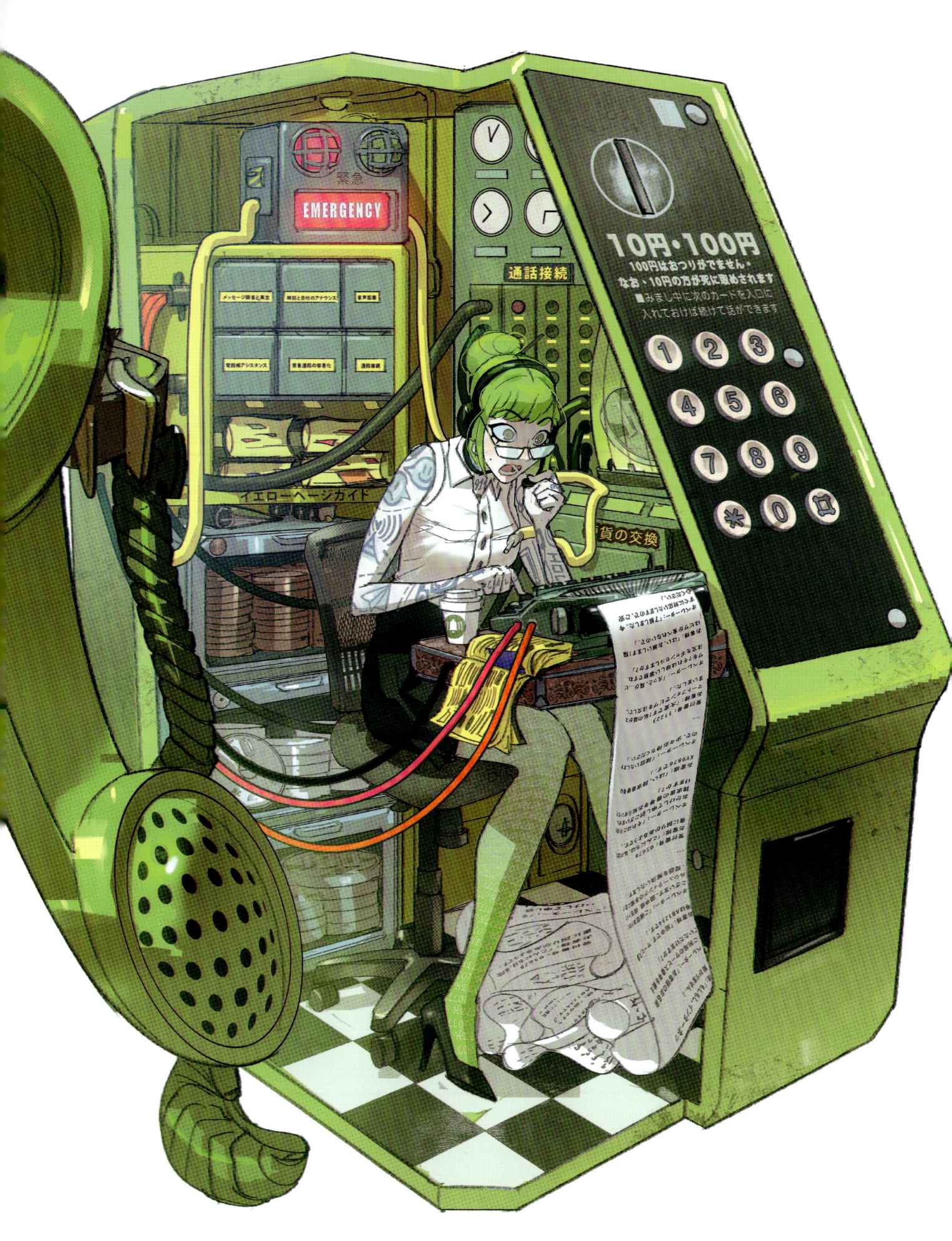

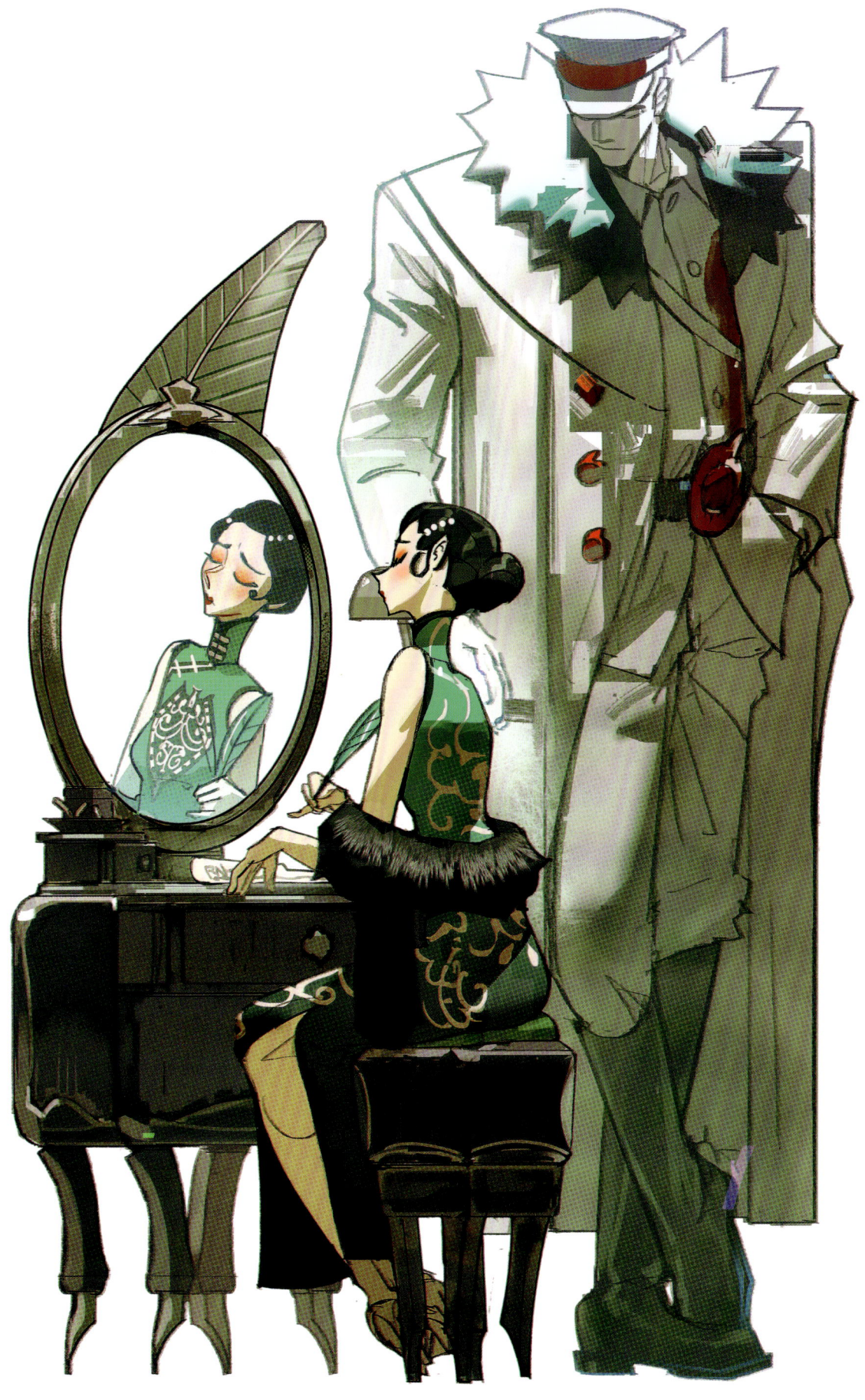

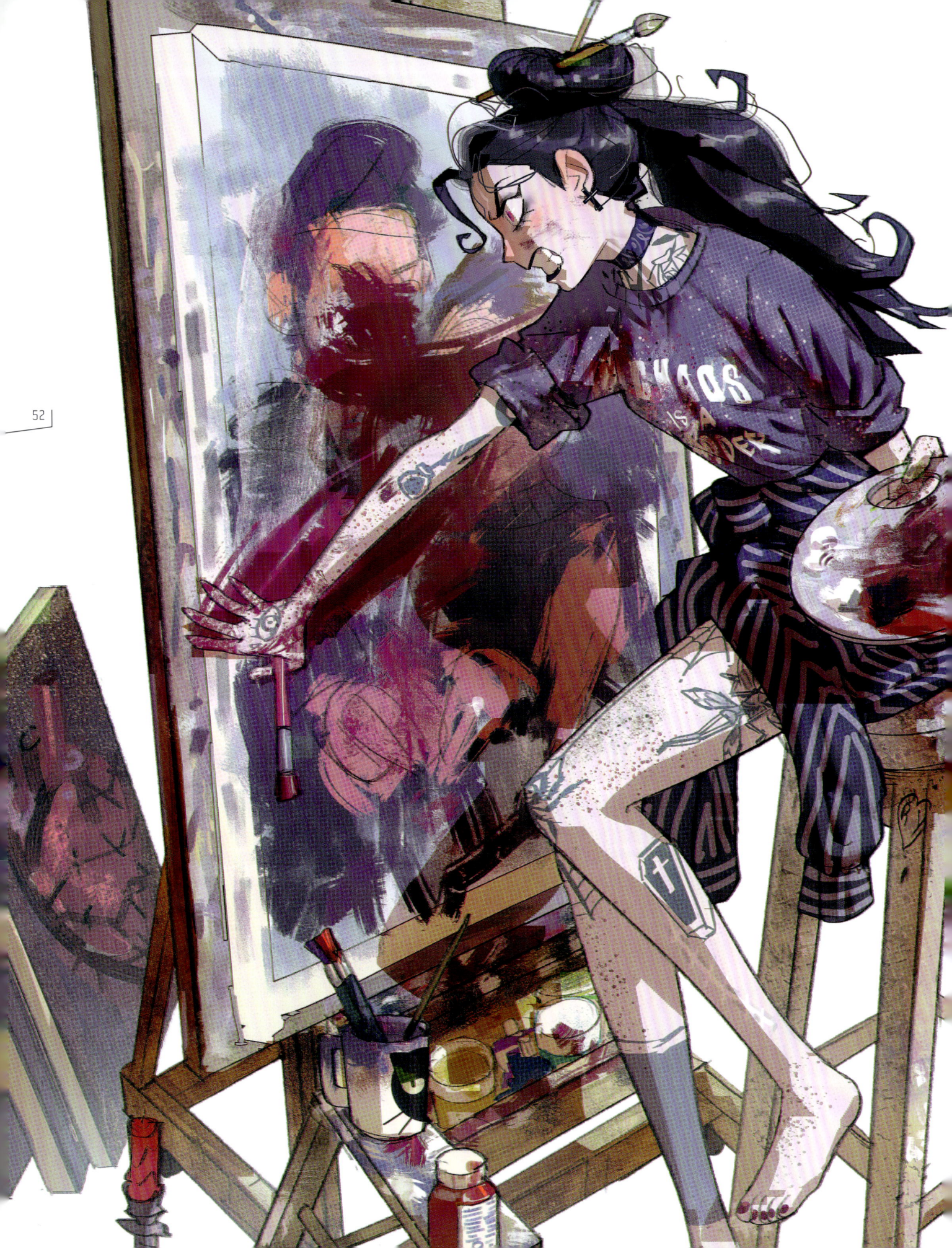

MY CREATIVE PROCESS

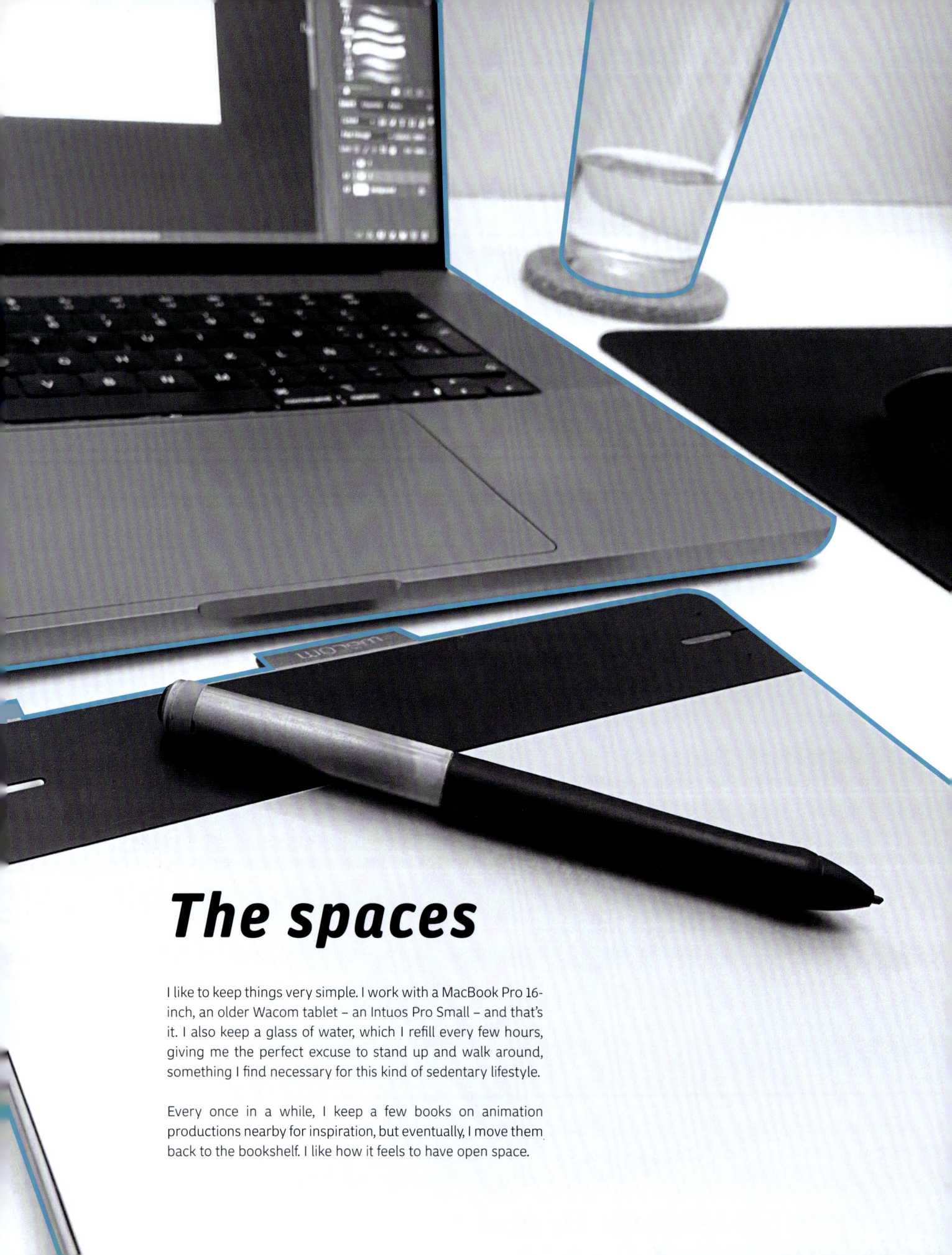

The spaces

I like to keep things very simple. I work with a MacBook Pro 16-inch, an older Wacom tablet – an Intuos Pro Small – and that's it. I also keep a glass of water, which I refill every few hours, giving me the perfect excuse to stand up and walk around, something I find necessary for this kind of sedentary lifestyle.

Every once in a while, I keep a few books on animation productions nearby for inspiration, but eventually, I move them back to the bookshelf. I like how it feels to have open space.

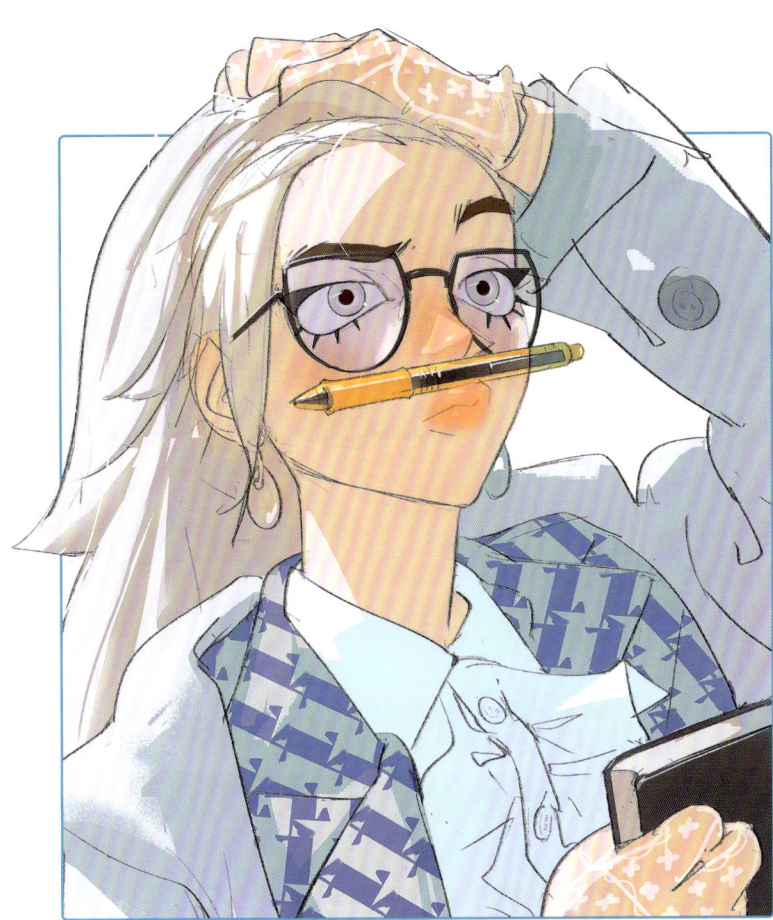

I USE PHOTOSHOP FOR ALL MY WORK. LIKE MY DESKTOP, MY WORKSPACE IS SIMPLE, WITH A FOCUS ON EFFICIENCY

My canvas size is 6000x7505 at 300 pixels/inch for cleaner line art.

My most-used tools include the Magic Wand tool, Paint Bucket tool, Brush tools, Eraser tool, and Zoom tool.

I rely on a set of eight brushes, each with specific functions, and use various layer-blending modes like Multiply, Color Burn, Overlay, Screen, and Color Dodge for different effects.

For a cinematic touch, I use filters like Selective Color, Smart Sharpen, and Pixelate/Color Halftone.

Finally, I export my work in PNG format, resizing the longest side to 1920 pixels for digital sharing.

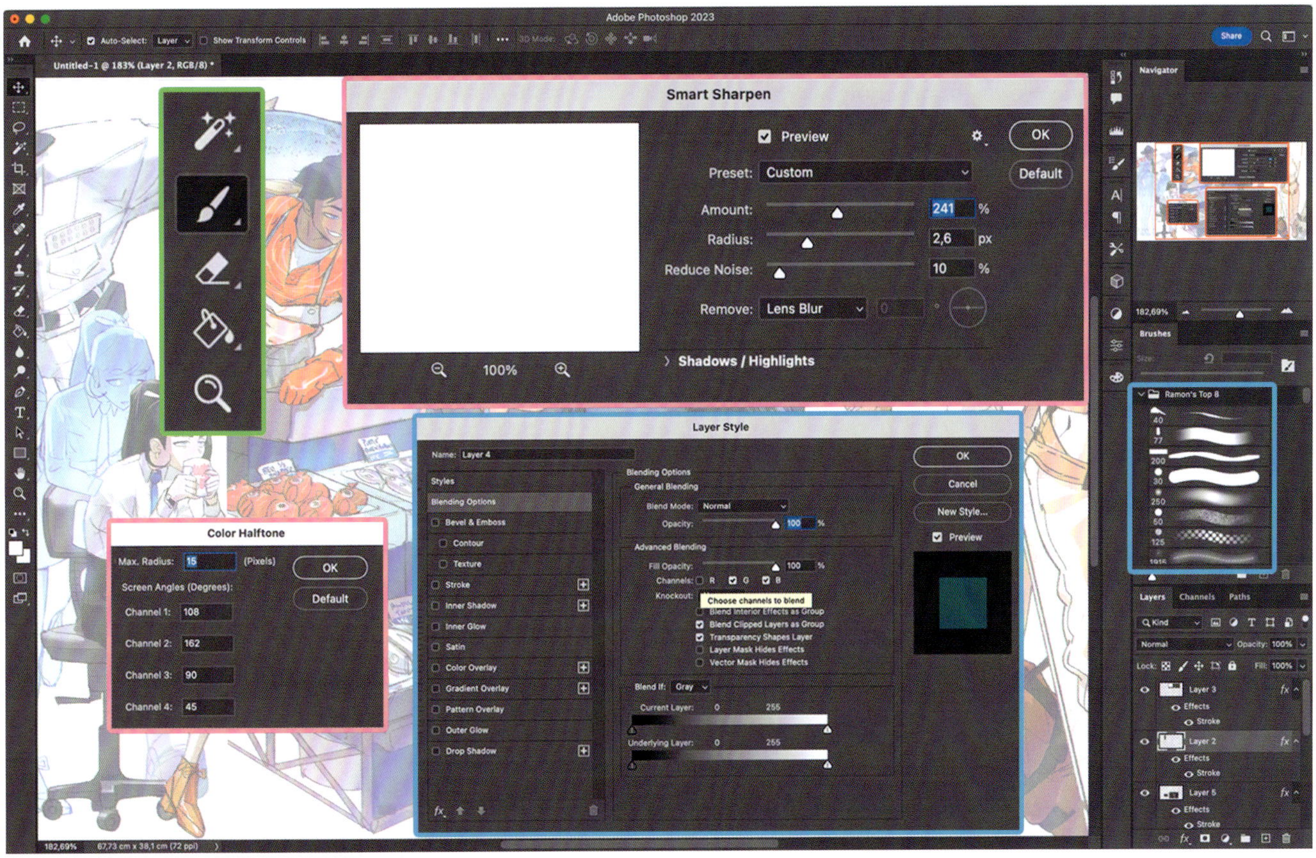

Smart Sharpen

Preview

Preset: Custom

Amount: 241 %
Radius: 2,6 px
Reduce Noise: 10 %

Remove: Lens Blur

> Shadows / Highlights

Color Halftone

Max. Radius: 15 (Pixels)

Screen Angles (Degrees):
Channel 1: 108
Channel 2: 162
Channel 3: 90
Channel 4: 45

Layer Style

Name: Layer 4

Styles
Blending Options
  Bevel & Emboss
  Contour
  Texture
  Stroke
  Inner Shadow
  Inner Glow
  Satin
  Color Overlay
  Gradient Overlay
  Pattern Overlay
  Outer Glow
  Drop Shadow

Blending Options
General Blending
Blend Mode: Normal
Opacity: 100 %

Advanced Blending
Fill Opacity: 100 %
Channels: R G B
Knockout: Choose channels to blend
  Blend Interior Effects as Group
  Blend Clipped Layers as Group
  Transparency Shapes Layer
  Layer Mask Hides Effects
  Vector Mask Hides Effects

Blend If: Gray
Current Layer: 0 255
Underlying Layer: 0 255

The process

My process for original concepts is pretty straightforward. I spend a fair amount of time thinking about what I want to create. Once I feel I have something visually interesting to produce, I move on to the execution phase, which starts with shapes (only line art), then colour, and finally values (light and shadows). This process may vary, but it generally follows the same structure. In simple terms:

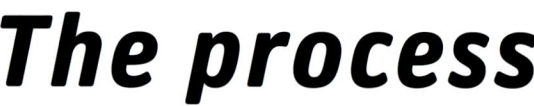

CONCEPT: idea, inspiration, reference
SHAPE: anatomy, gesture, costume, composition, perspective
COLOUR: colour theory, composition, balance
VALUE: lighting, shadow, volume, textures

It wasn't always this way, and I'm sure it might change in the future. In my opinion, being an artist requires you to change your approach to art every once in a while to make the process less predictable, and more fun and engaging. Art is not always about the end result, but the process itself. The process I described is simply one of the most efficient I've found in my career.

LET'S JUMP INTO EACH POINT.

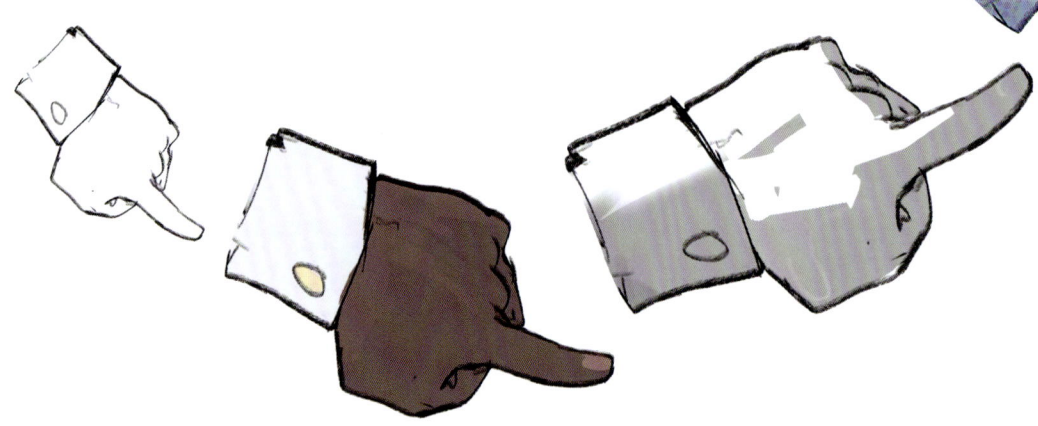

CONCEPT

In this step, I try to combine simple and relatable ideas that inspire my characters. The combination consists of casual objects, animals, and everyday situations. On top of that, I add extra details in terms of costume design, and sometimes I like to mix a bizarre situation with something funny to create novelty through unconventional twists. For instance, here's the concept exploration behind one of my illustrations, *Wake Up*:

REFERENCE: Coffee maker

COLOUR: White, grey, and a little black

ACTION: Someone recently awake;
a military figure putting versions
of the character together

COSTUME: Military uniform, office outfit

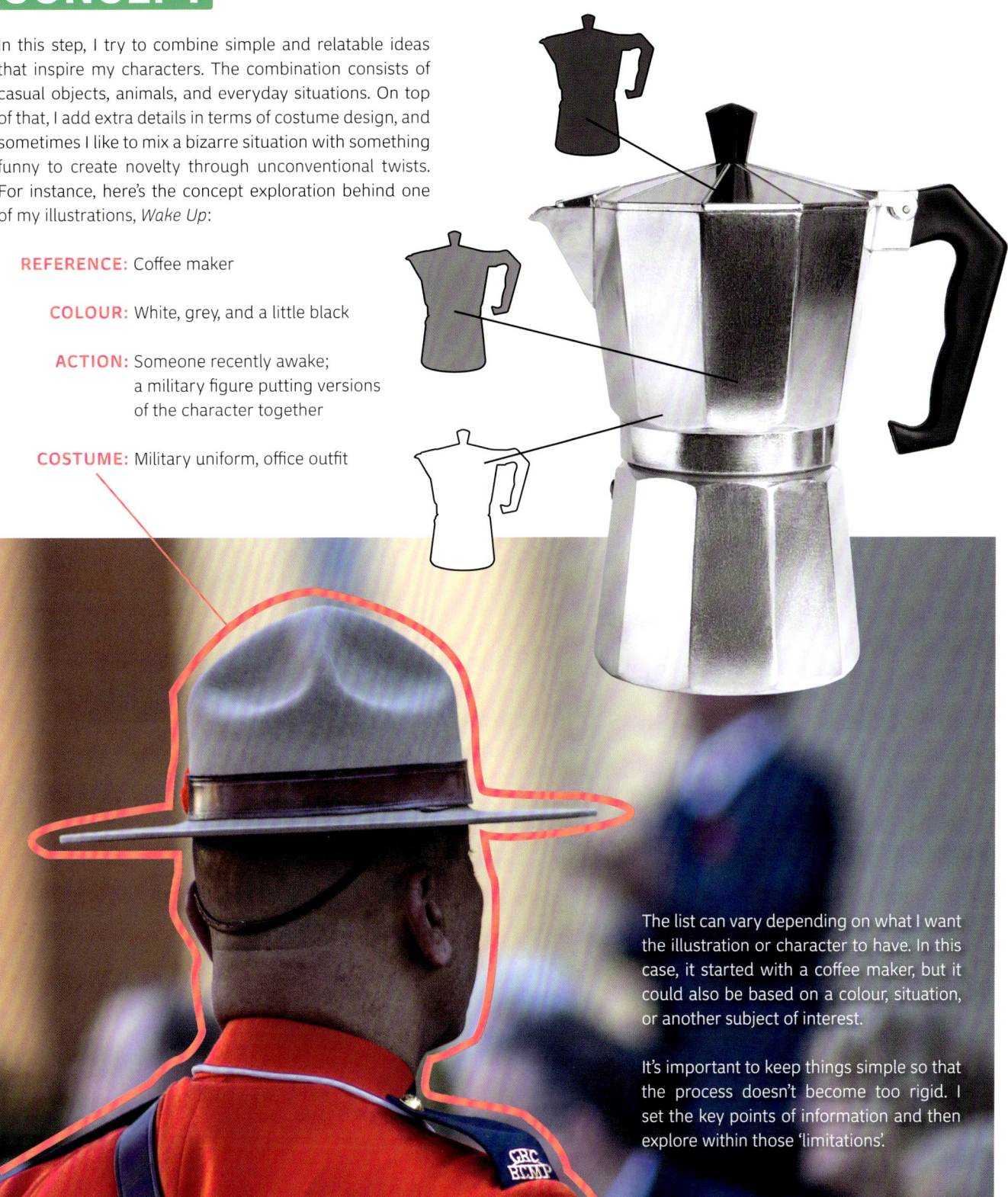

The list can vary depending on what I want the illustration or character to have. In this case, it started with a coffee maker, but it could also be based on a colour, situation, or another subject of interest.

It's important to keep things simple so that the process doesn't become too rigid. I set the key points of information and then explore within those 'limitations'.

SHAPE

In this context, shapes refer to everything I build using line-art drawings. In character design, this includes anatomical and costume silhouettes, while outside of characters, it applies to environments, objects, and more. This phase is influenced by other fundamentals like composition and perspective.

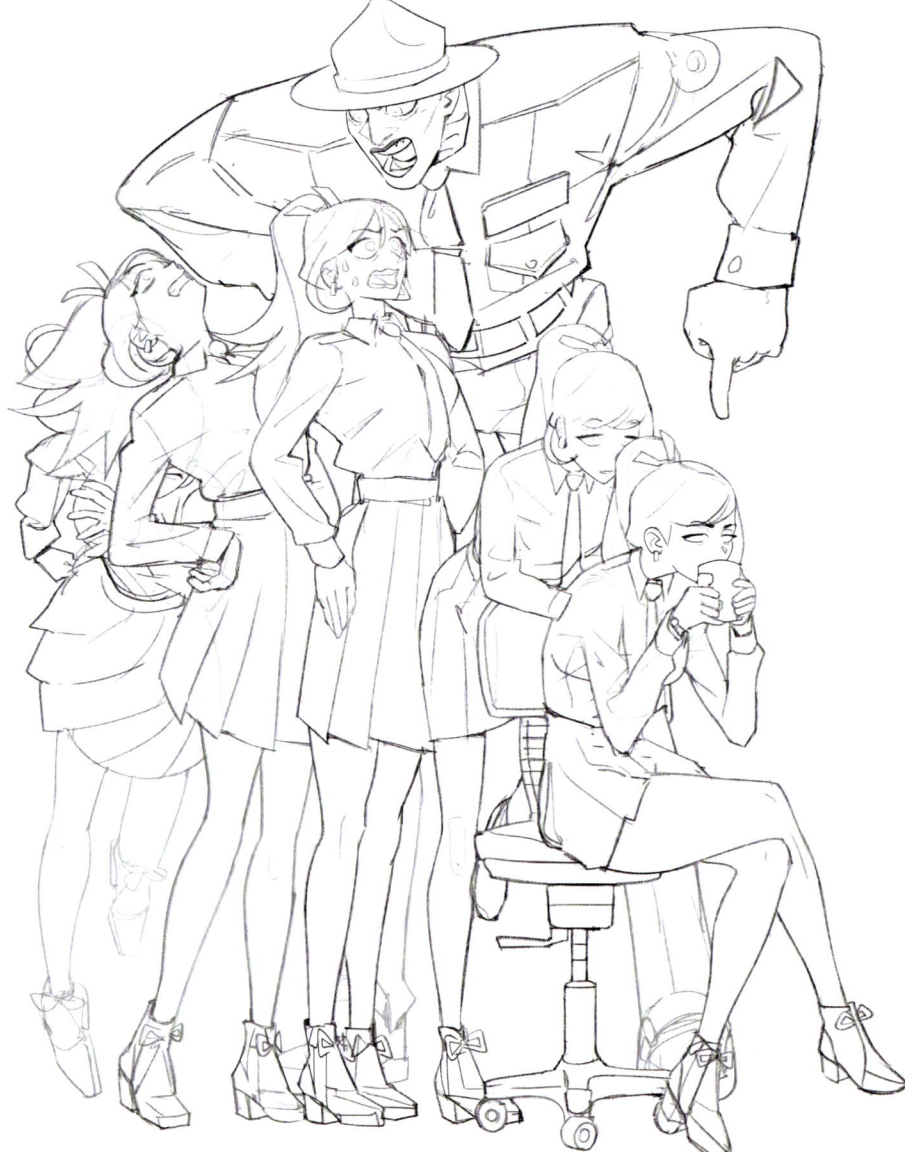

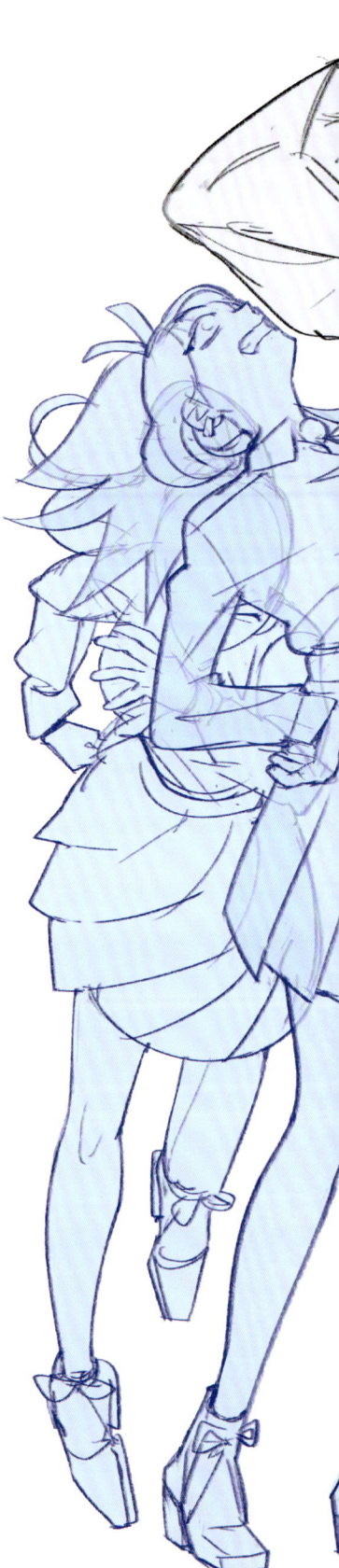

Most of the hard work happens during this stage, as the line art acts as a foundation for the next steps, such as colours and values. This is also where most of my stress and anxiety comes in, as I'm shaping the conceptual points mentioned earlier, and it's not always a straightforward process.

DRAWING IS HARD, BUT WHEN IT GOES WELL, I ENJOY IT MUCH MORE

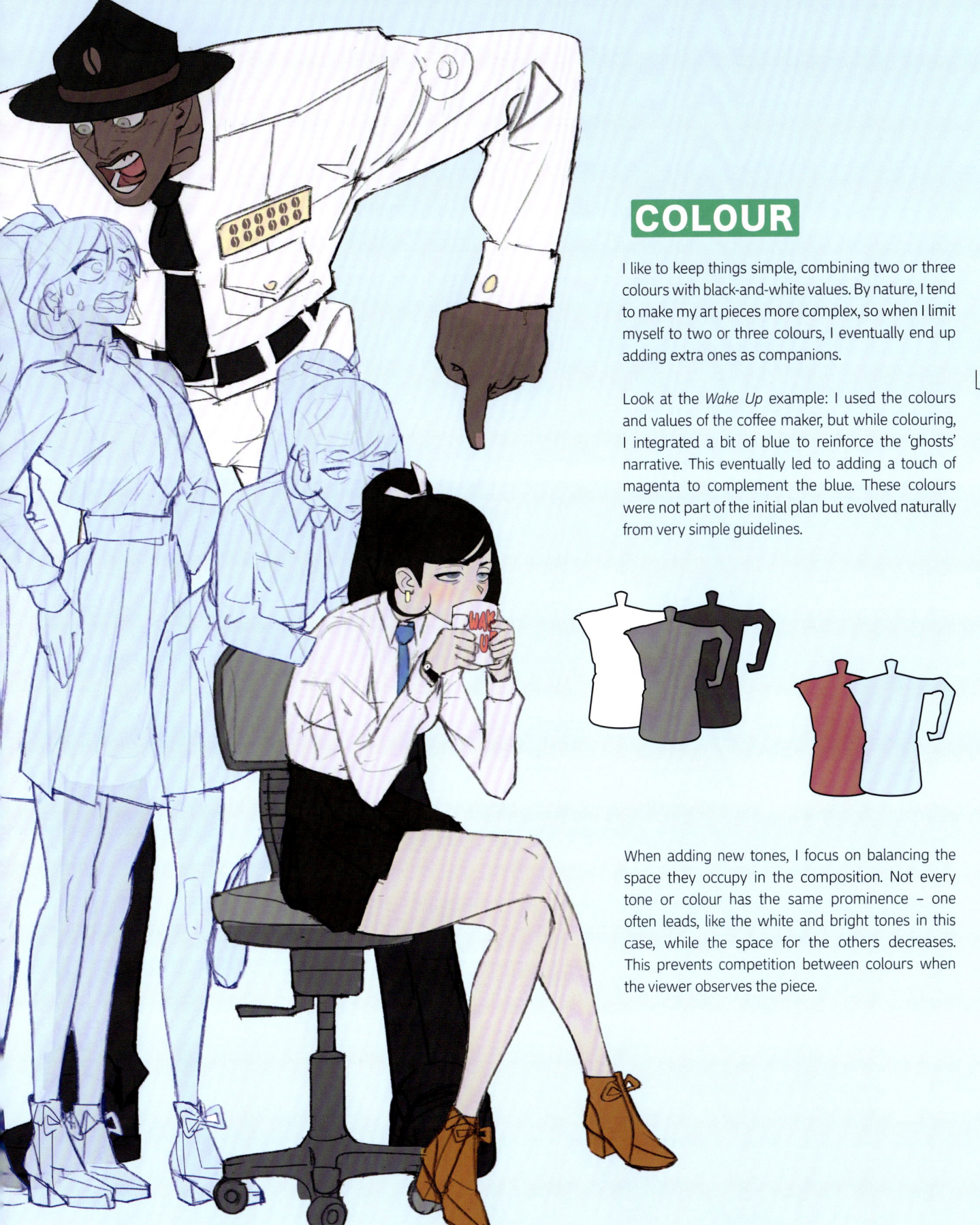

COLOUR

I like to keep things simple, combining two or three colours with black-and-white values. By nature, I tend to make my art pieces more complex, so when I limit myself to two or three colours, I eventually end up adding extra ones as companions.

Look at the *Wake Up* example: I used the colours and values of the coffee maker, but while colouring, I integrated a bit of blue to reinforce the 'ghosts' narrative. This eventually led to adding a touch of magenta to complement the blue. These colours were not part of the initial plan but evolved naturally from very simple guidelines.

When adding new tones, I focus on balancing the space they occupy in the composition. Not every tone or colour has the same prominence – one often leads, like the white and bright tones in this case, while the space for the others decreases. This prevents competition between colours when the viewer observes the piece.

VALUE

By values, I mean how light creates volume out of shapes. In this phase, I focus on forming three-dimensional structures through what we call rendering in painting or illustration. In other words, this is what makes things look realistic.

Light projected onto shapes allows the eyes to perceive the form of a face, cloth folds, object surfaces, and textures of all kinds, such as water, leather, and skin. When someone aims for a realistic look in a piece of art, it's mostly a matter of values. Shapes and colours play an important role, but in my opinion, a well-distributed range of values is the most crucial factor in achieving that goal.

In the next example, you'll see a values treatment applied within the character's silhouette, with the colour layers turned off.

After years of painting studies and practice, I've chosen to keep my process very simple. The values created by light on my characters are a combination of shadows, middle tones, and some highlights.

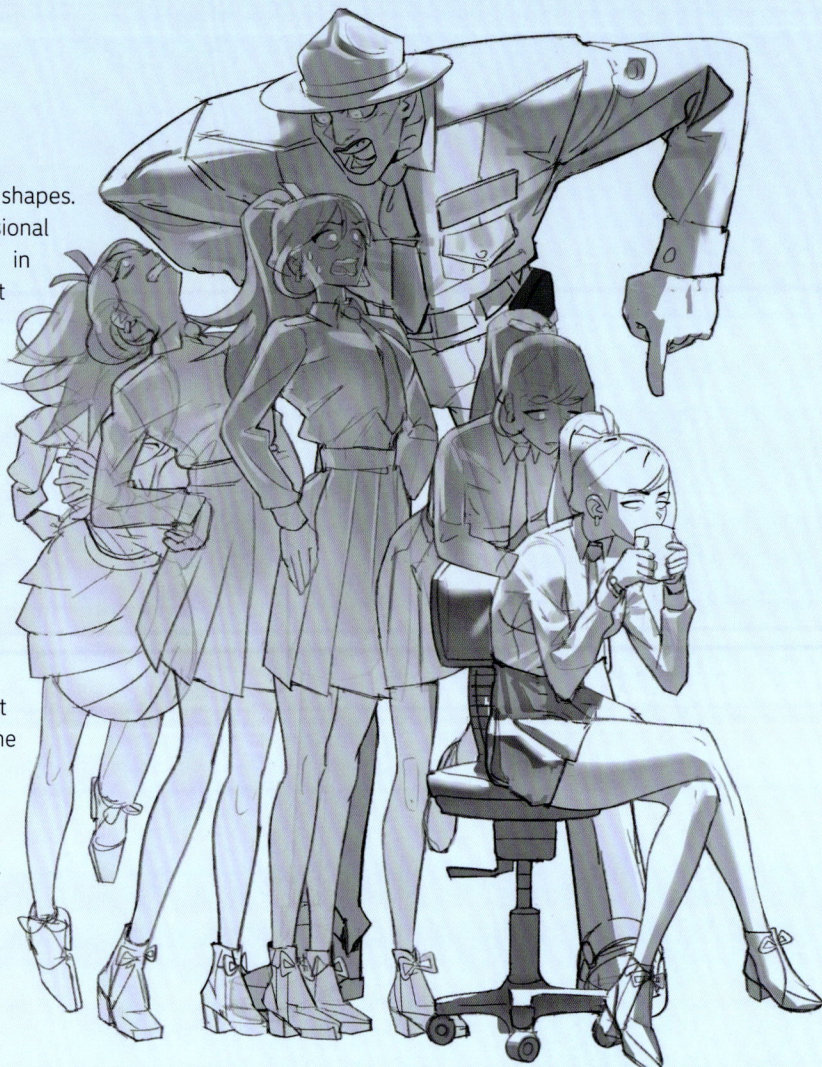

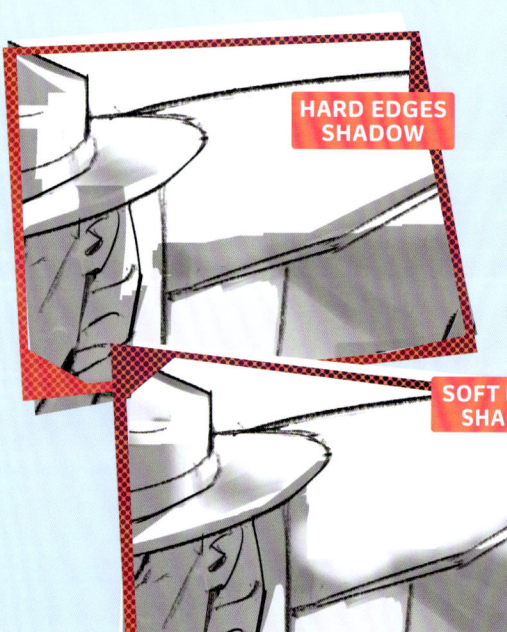

HARD EDGES SHADOW

SOFT EDGES SHADOW

Most of my shadows are created with a hard brush using the same exact tone. I focus more on the shape of the shadow than its colour, often using very desaturated and bright colours. I take great inspiration from animation, which relies on the cel-shading technique. Value shades are often hard-edged rather than softly blended, which adds to the distinctive style.

However, when I try to convey a more realistic approach, I add more layers of shading to the characters, or soften the silhouette of the shadow.

DETAILS

Last but not least, during this final phase, I mainly make adjustments using tools like Selective Color, Smart Sharpen, and Pixelate/Color Halftone. I like the distorted look that some old television series and movies had, bringing a nineties vibe to the canvas.

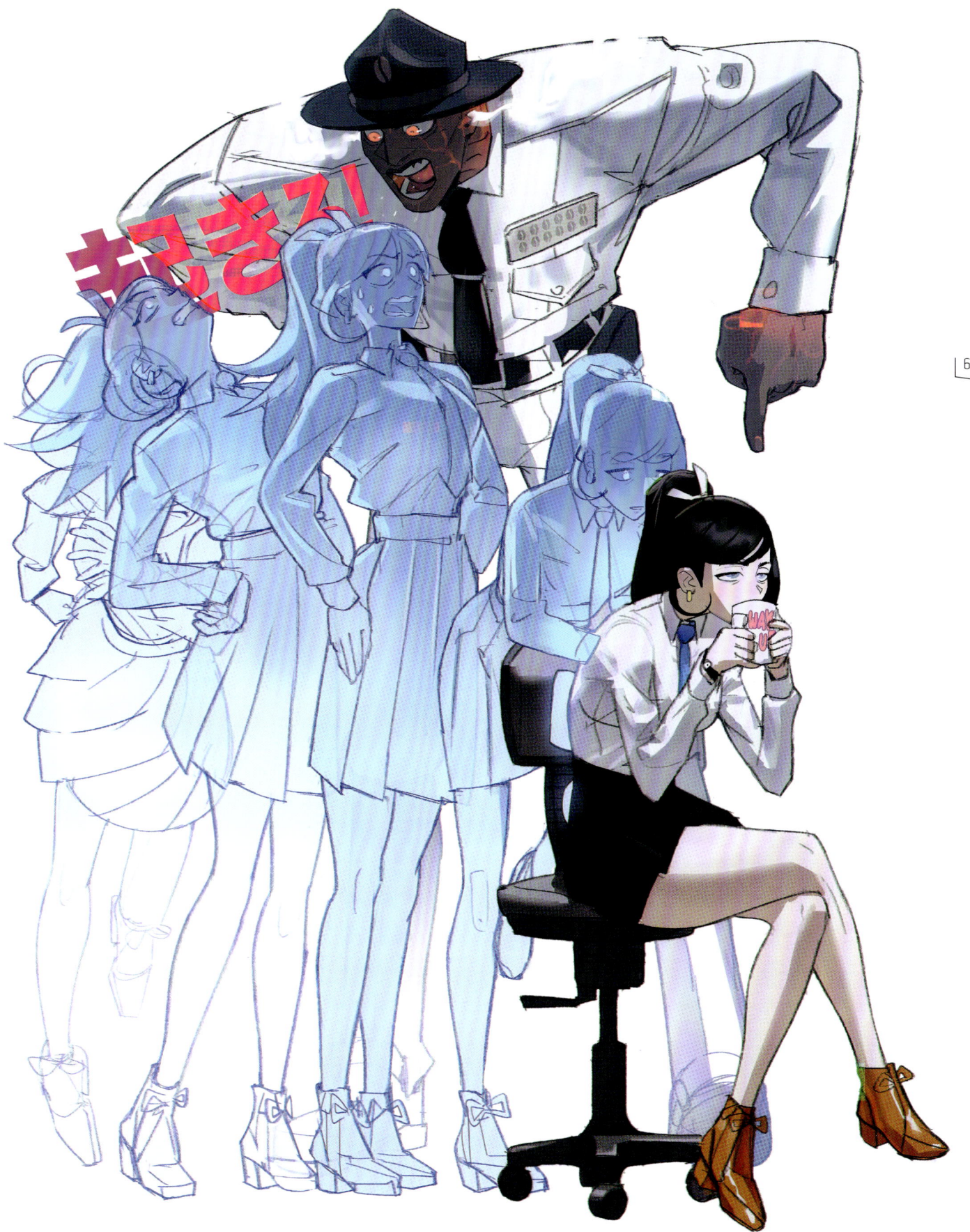

Influences

I've been influenced by several artists, especially those in Japanese animation such as Katsuhiro Otomo, Hayao Miyazaki, and others behind classic animation and anime series from the eighties and nineties.
I've never been into reading or buying books, but in recent years, I've become drawn to storyboard work from productions like *Akira*, *Spirited Away*, *Ghost in the Shell*, and *Furi Kuri*.

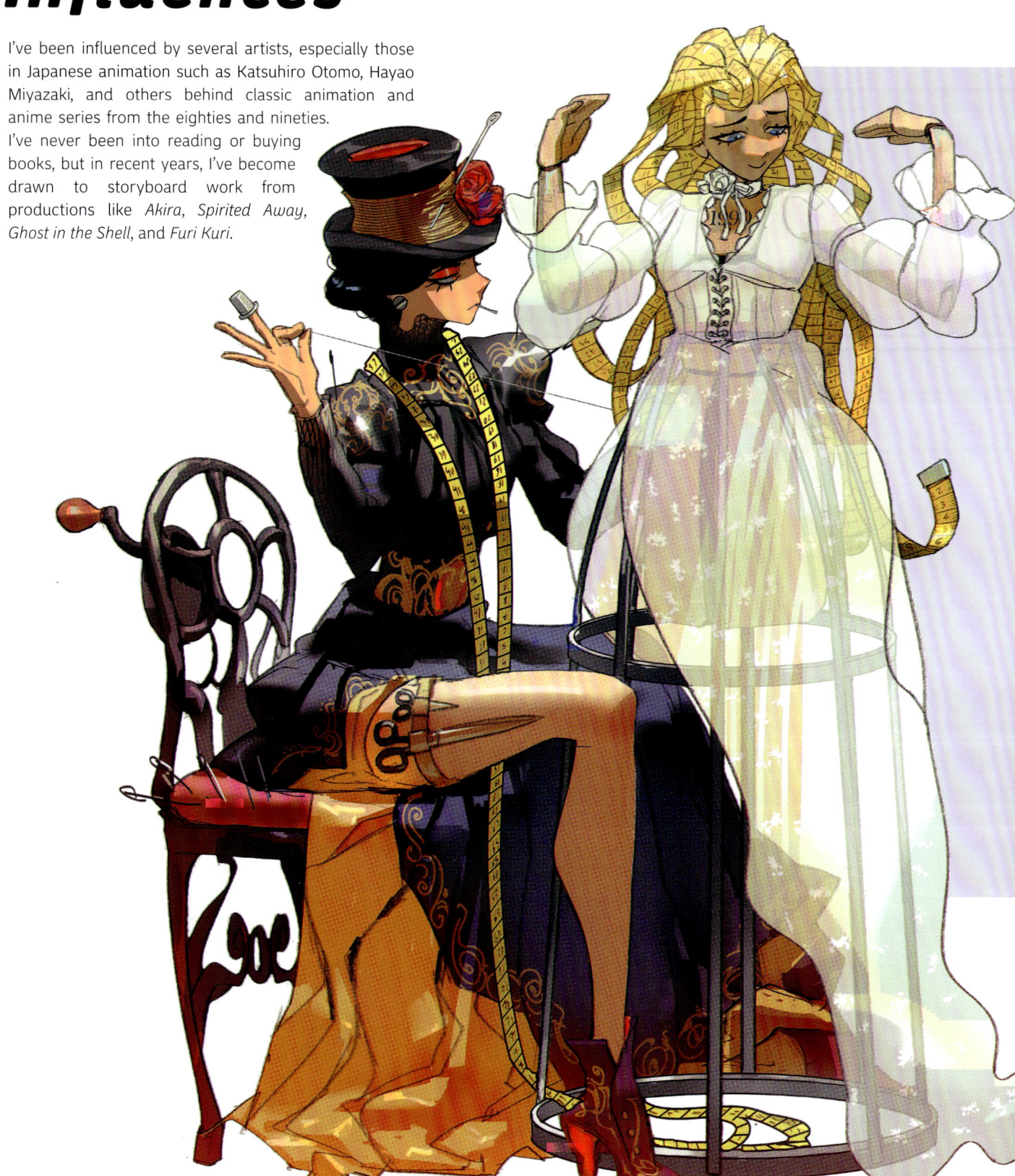

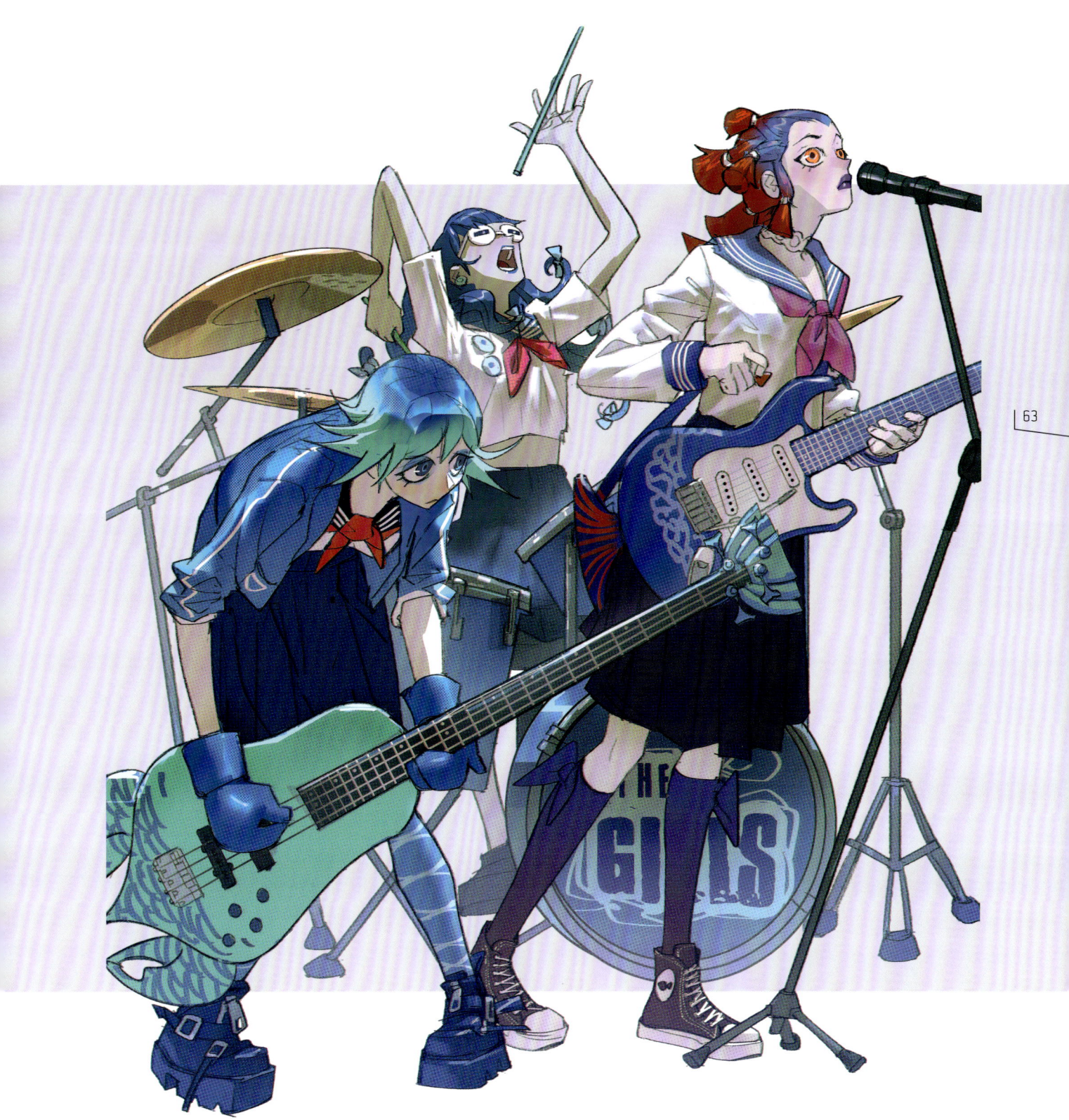

When I have some time or need a boost of inspiration, I revisit one of those books or cinematic classics. It brings such a fresh perspective, reminding me to be as creative, bizarre, and fun as I can be.

Struggles & creative block

Like every artist, I often deal with struggles that affect my creative process:

ANXIETY   **BURNOUT**

CREATIVE BLOCK

STRESS

These are things I'm sure you have experienced as well. I've developed a series of solutions that help me overcome some of these challenges, but those solutions eventually expire, leading to new strategies, and the cycle continues.

By that, I mean there is no absolute solution that will remove the suffering from creating art – or just living – but it's true that some unchanging habits have kept me afloat over the years.

These standard habits include proper sleep, rest, eating healthy food (or at least avoiding junk), exercising at least once per week (though I recommend more), and having casual social encounters with family or friends. It might sound silly – what does this have to do with art? Well, it turns out that when properly integrated into daily life, these habits help me stay calm (or at least less anxious) when I sit down for more than an hour to make art.

If you've already got a fair handle on these basics, we can move forward with my practical solutions to one of the biggest struggles many artists face: creative block.

1 ASK QUESTIONS!

Life is tough, and there will always be reasons to worry beyond art. We cannot avoid life, but we can be aware of the reason behind our creative block. Is it because of the art itself, or is there something else we need to address first? If it's not art-related, try to resolve it as best you can. Once that's done, move forward with some art-related questions, such as:

— **WHAT DOES IT MEAN TO BE CREATIVE?**

— **WHAT KIND OF FEELINGS DO YOU WANT TO EVOKE WITH YOUR PIECE?**

— **DEPENDING ON THE GOAL, HOW SHOULD A COMPOSITION OR CHARACTER BE VISUALLY STRUCTURED TO ACHIEVE IT?**

— **IS THE ANSWER IN THE SHAPES, COLOURS, OR VALUES?**

The more specific your questions, the better – you'll expose yourself to information that helps shape your concept and execution.

As I mentioned earlier in the book, a rigid and strict path is not ideal. But having at least a few clear points of focus will increase your chances of reaching your goal and bringing your ideas to life.

2 REFERENCES

Another thing I do to avoid creative block is visit my Pinterest boards. I've saved everything that has inspired me at some point in my life. It doesn't matter if it's silly, unrelated to my art, or even if it's another tool – the point is to build a place I can return to whenever I need inspiration.

HERE ARE THREE SIMPLE TIPS!

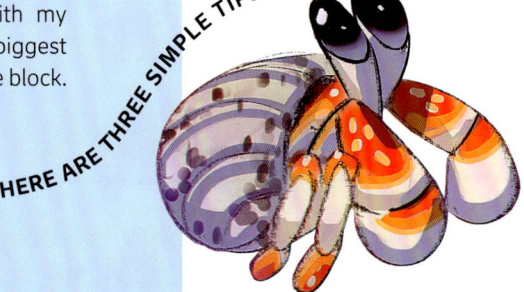

3 DO IT!

Last but not least, high expectations often build a wall that many of us struggle to break through. This happens because of the weight a piece of art might carry – maybe it's for someone special, maybe it's for an important client, or maybe we just want to do our best and don't know where to start.

I've noticed that the best way is simply to start. But you already knew this, didn't you? The trick is to break your task into small steps – small enough that it doesn't intimidate you. Taken to an extreme, this could mean drawing just one line per day. You might laugh at that, but hey, if you're completely paralyzed by the process, one line is better than nothing. I give you this example because your challenge isn't to finish the work – it's to start it. And if making the task easy enough helps you take that first step, then I'm sure you'll reach your goal.

TRY THIS:

DAY 1:
Draw the eyes – maybe for an hour or just thirty minutes – focusing on getting them right. What kind of motivation does your character have? What expression would capture that personality?

DAY 2:
How about drawing the nose, mouth, or even the ears? Something that matches the eyes you drew the day before. Look at yourself in the mirror and try to nail that combination.

DAY 3:
Now, how tough is it to draw the head? Struggling with same-face syndrome? Not great at perspective? No worries – take a picture of yourself and use it as a reference. If after an hour it's still not working, stop. Take a break, then come back with a fresh mind and ask yourself: why isn't it working? What are you missing? You can even overlay your reference image – not to trace, but to identify what's off and correct it.

Don't despair if you don't get it right at first – you're already making progress just by trying. Learning to draw works like that: you fail so many times that you get used to it. Eventually, you stop hesitating and keep going until it's right. Of course, some artists won't need three days to get to this point, but I'm making the case for someone who's scared to move forward. We've all been there.

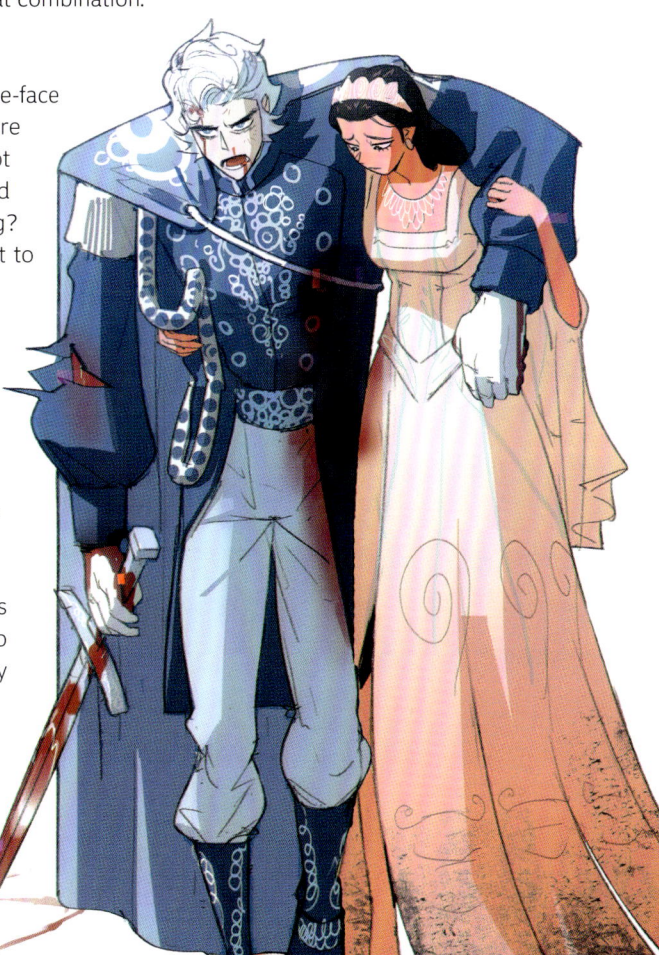

Even if your idea isn't perfect, creating art is about the process itself. Sometimes, the best ideas come during execution. So go ahead and take that first step, even if nothing turns out the way you'd like it to.

Having a relatively balanced life will help you deal with burnout, anxiety, and stress, but that alone won't necessarily pull you out of a creative block. You need to ask yourself the right questions, draw inspiration from your personal space, and most importantly – take that first step.

JUST START IT!

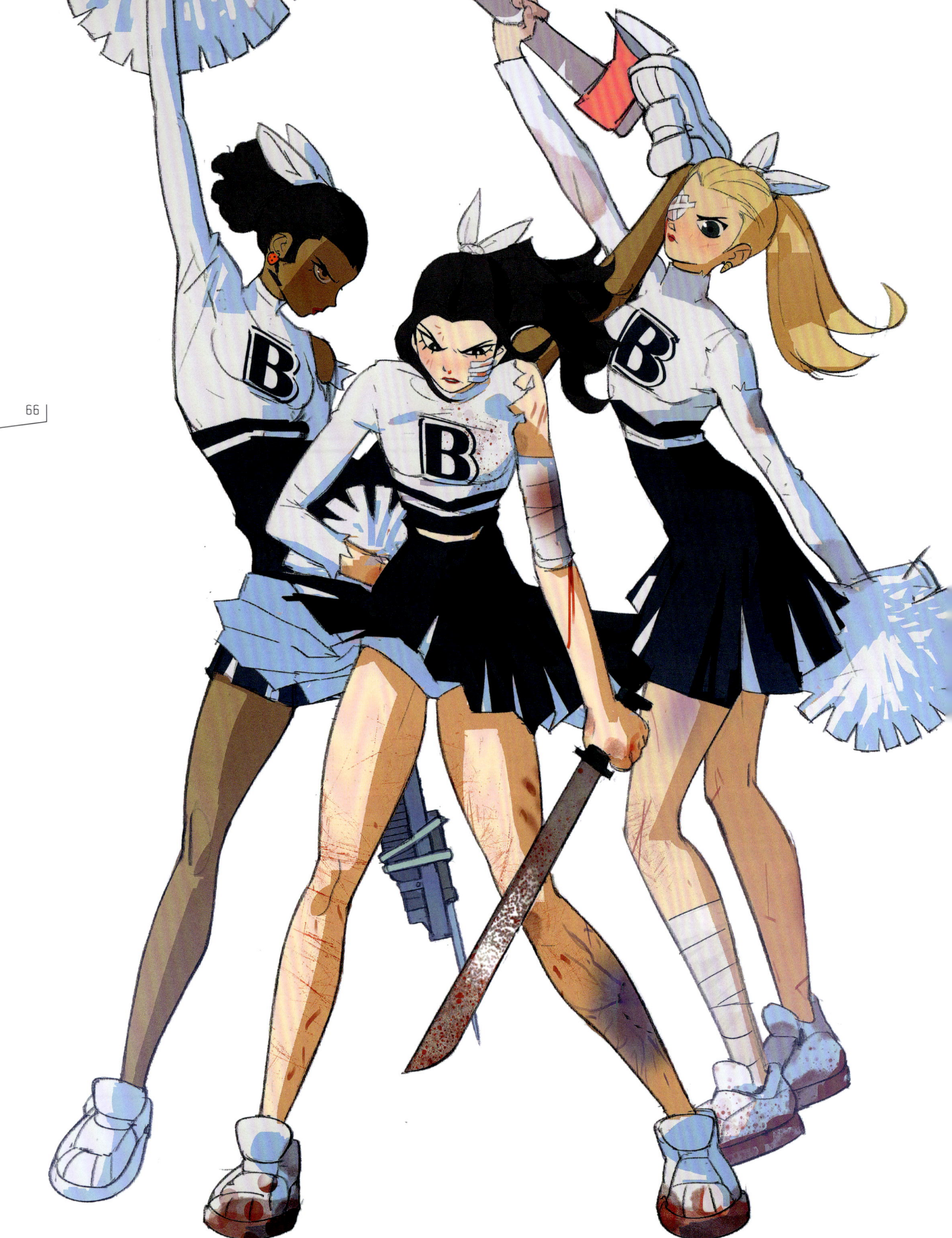

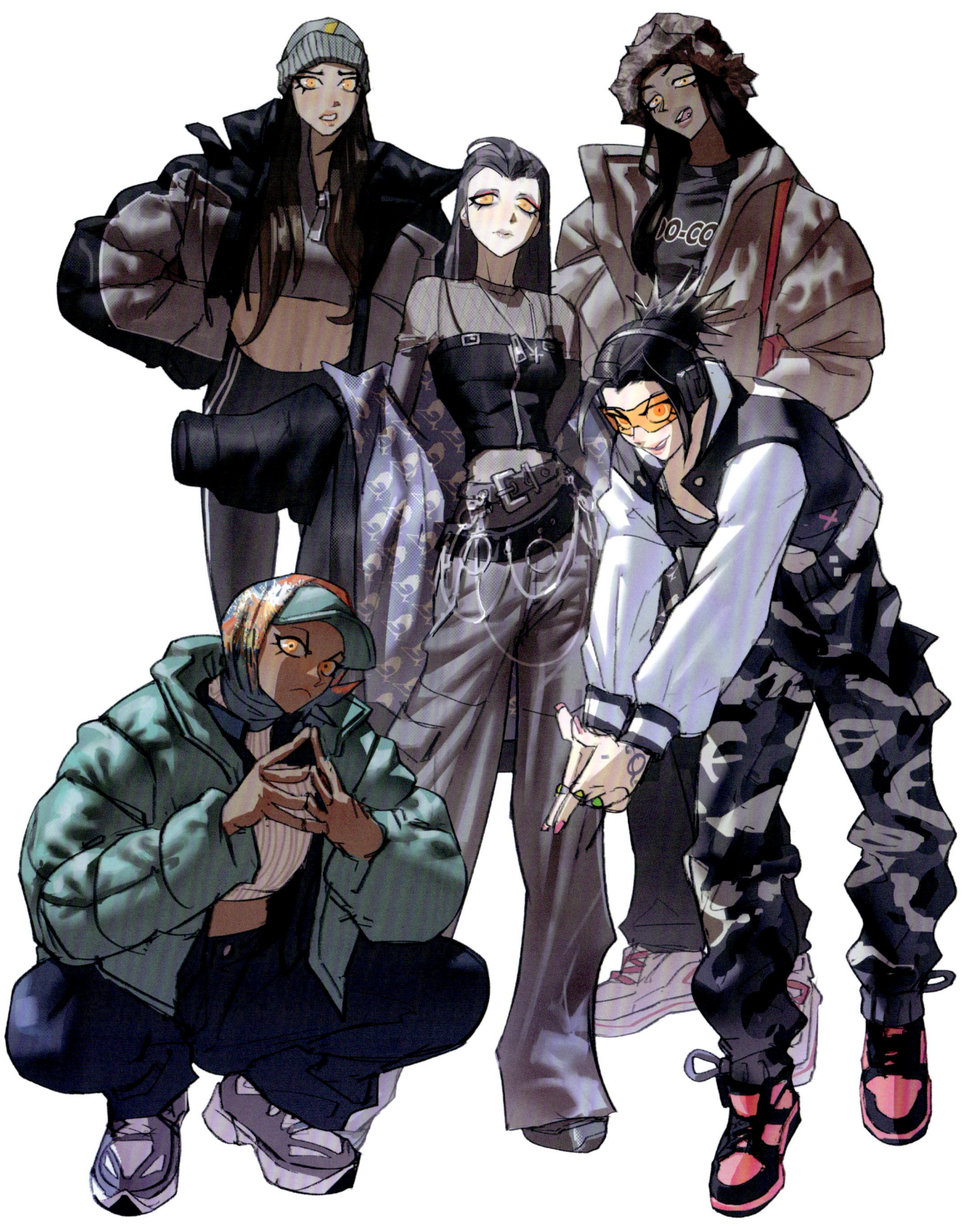

GALERÍA

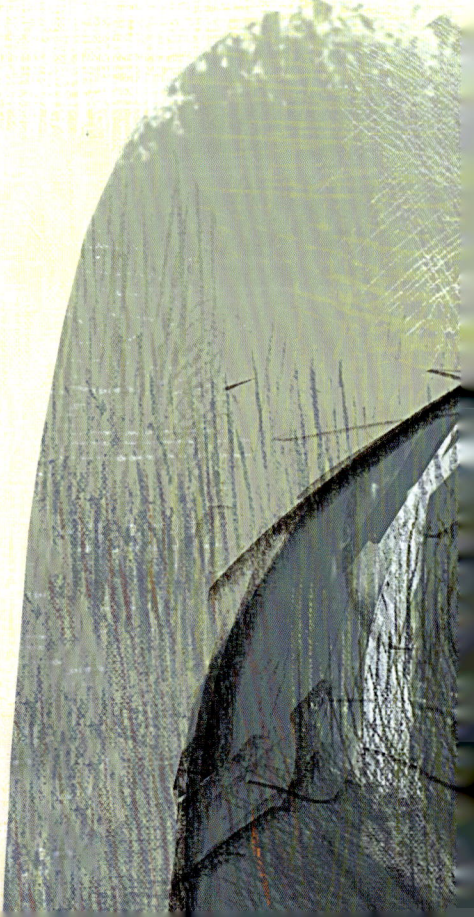

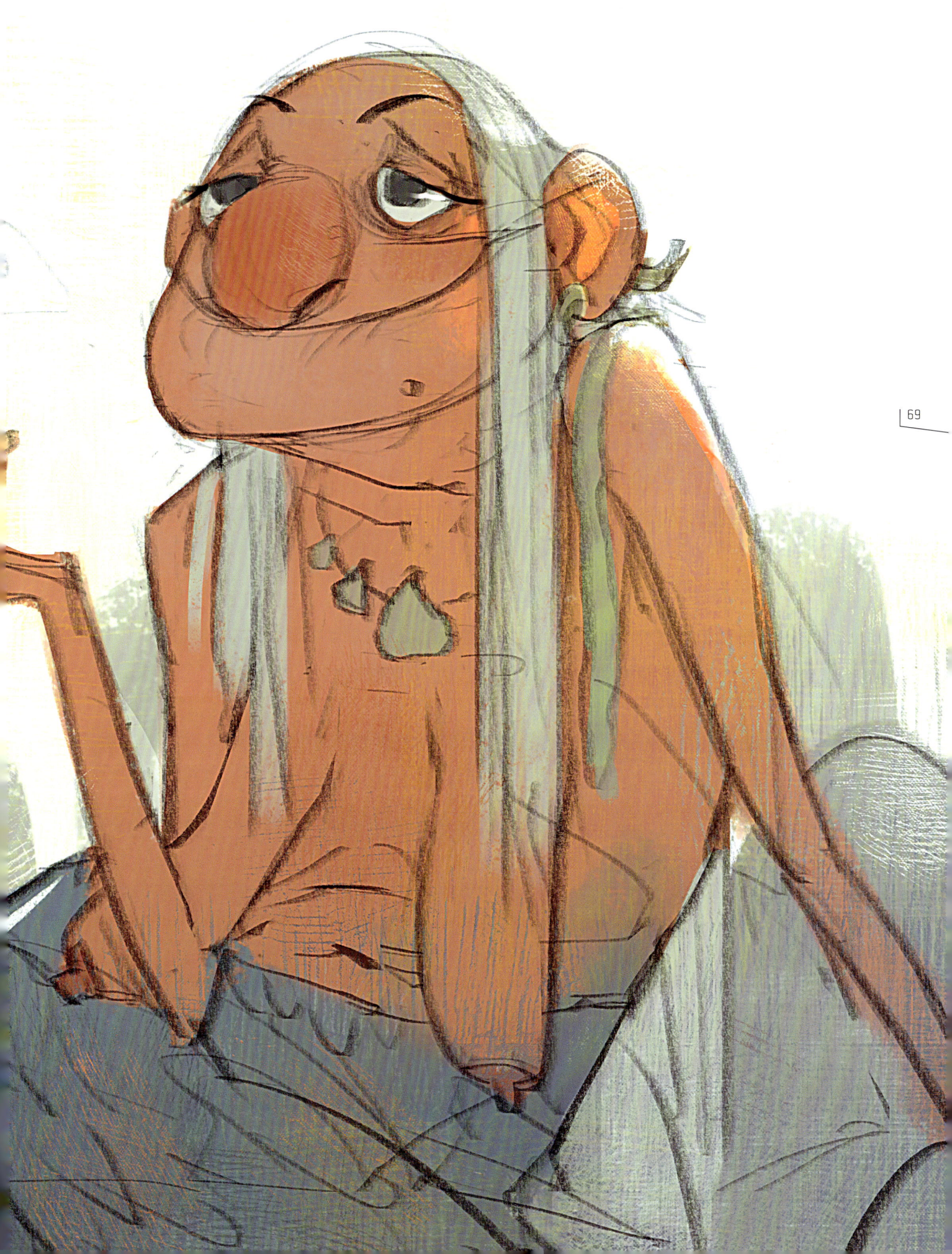

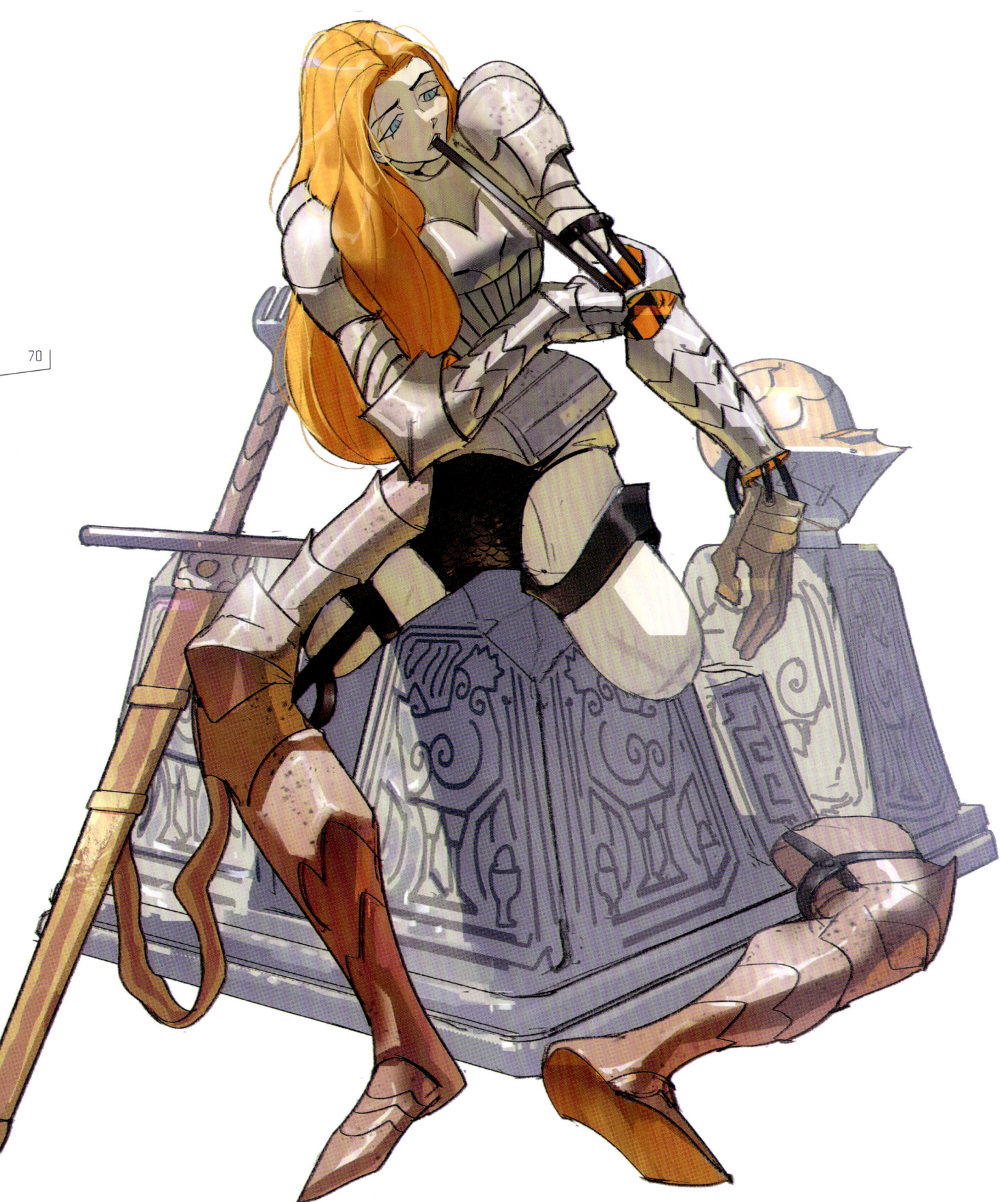

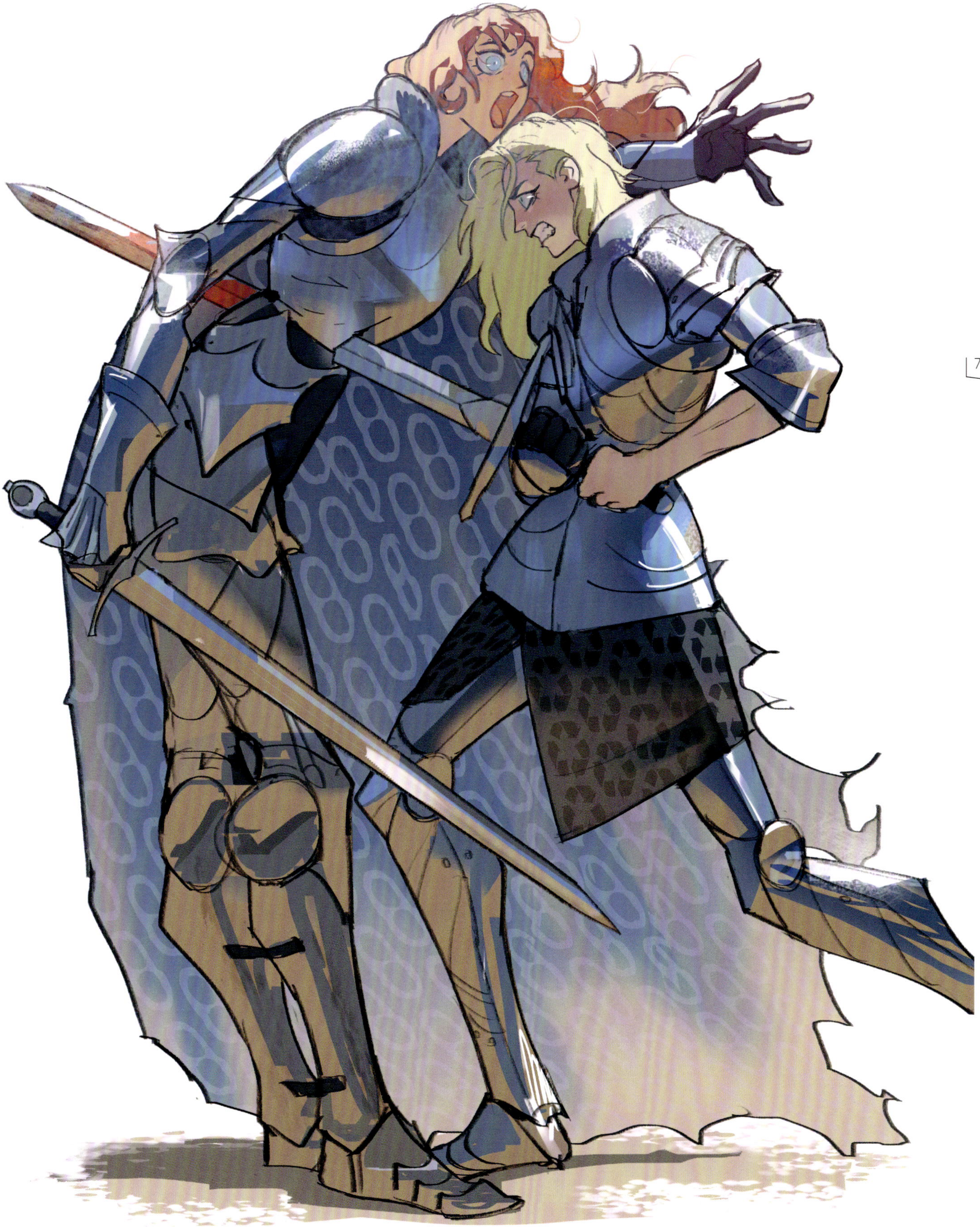

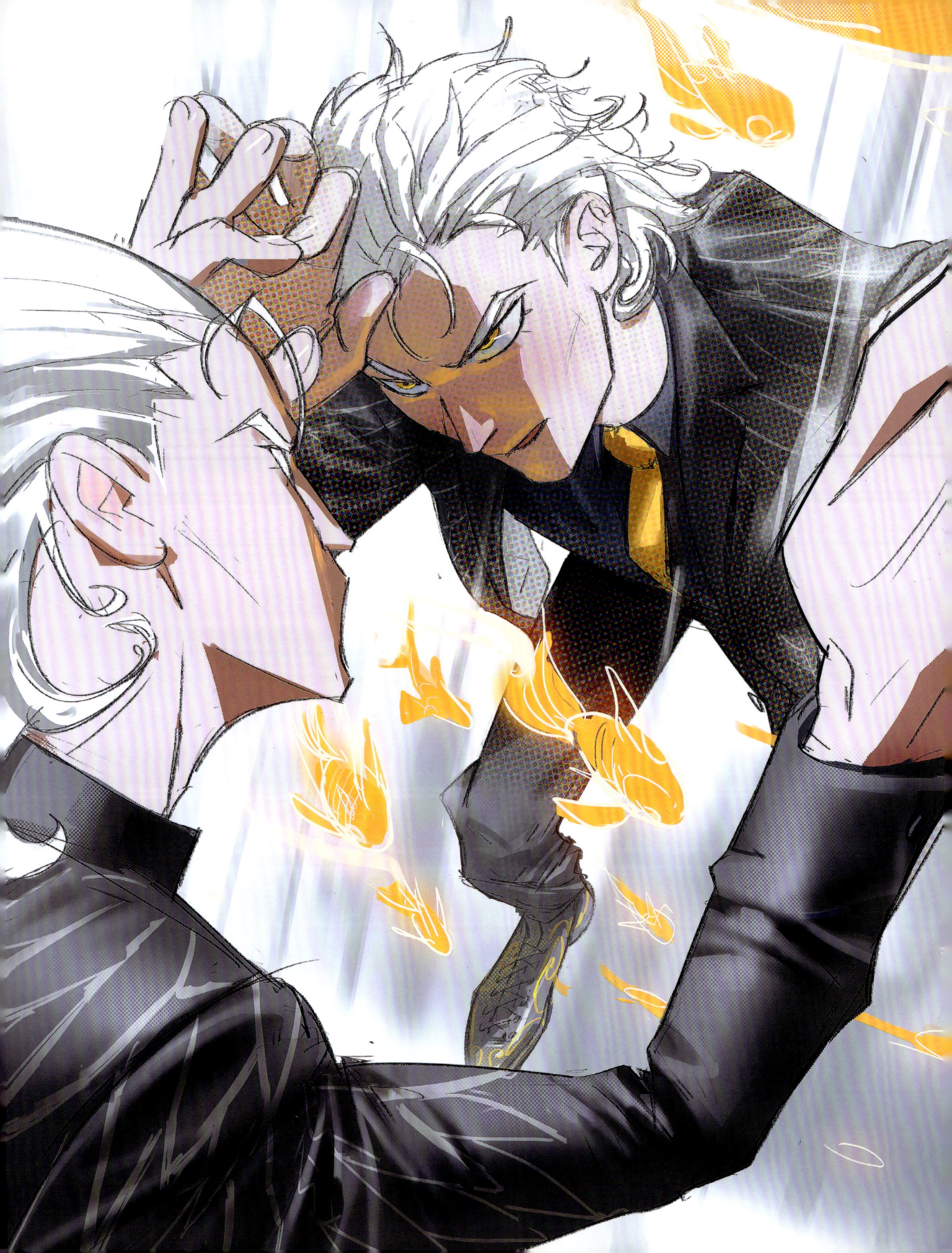

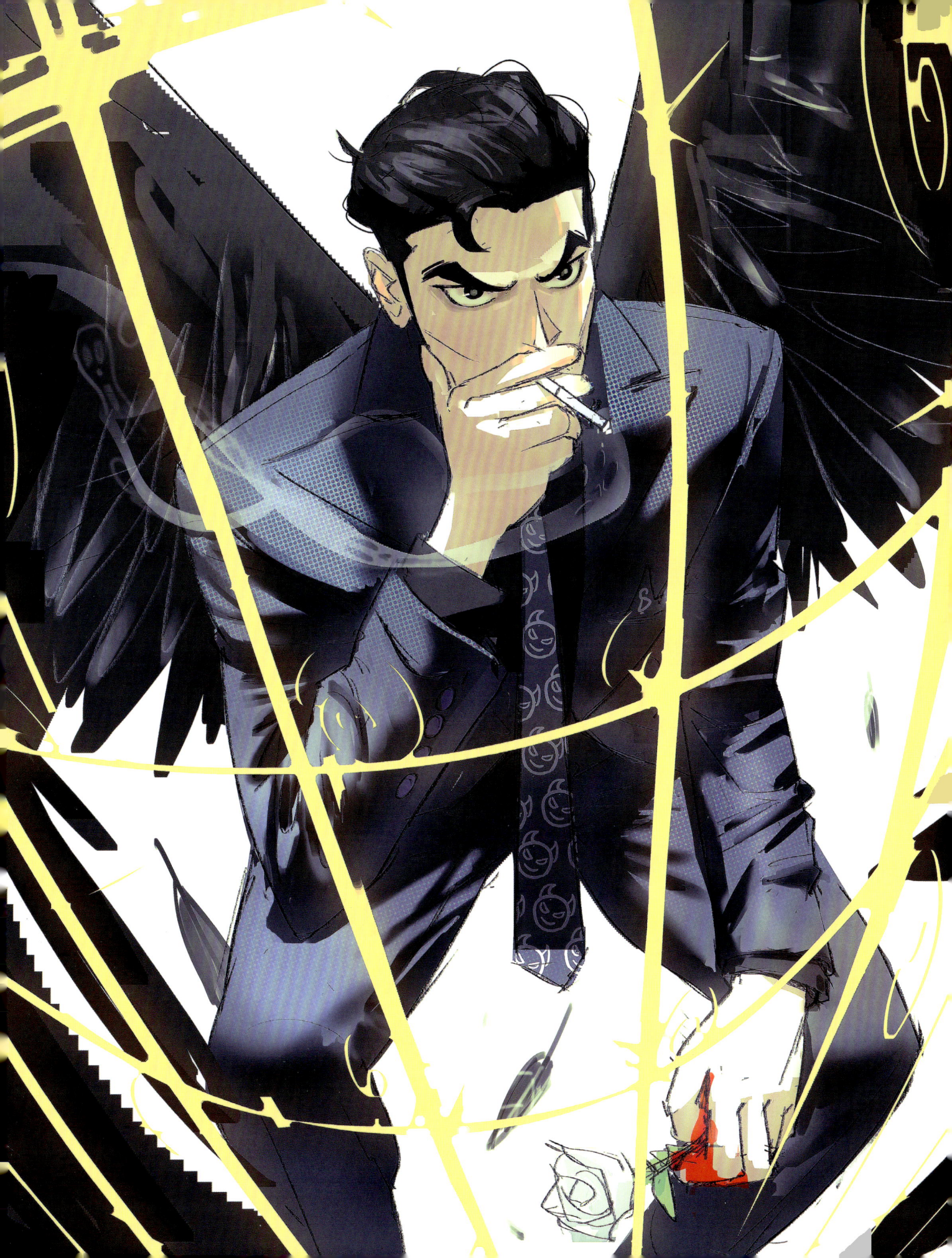

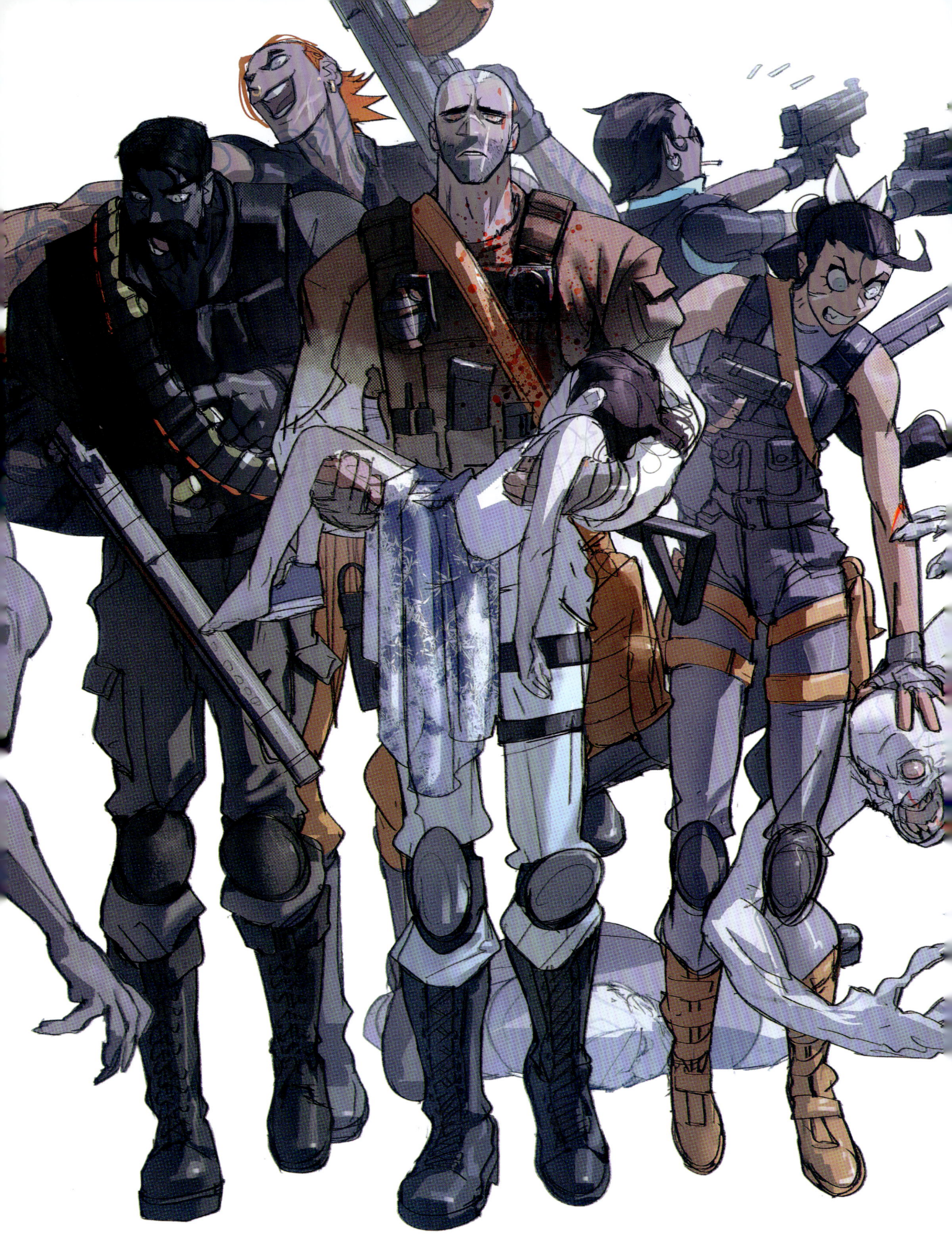

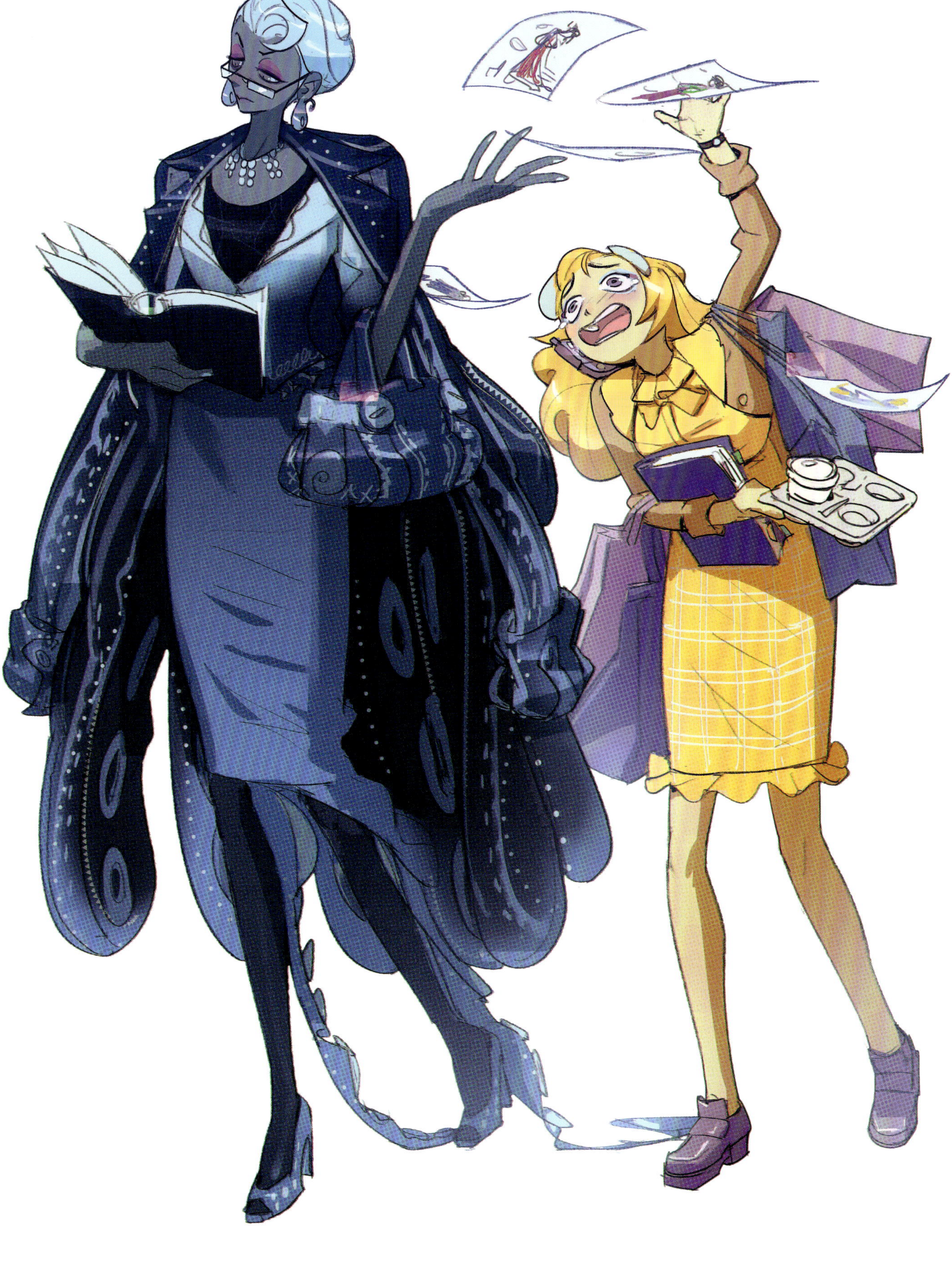

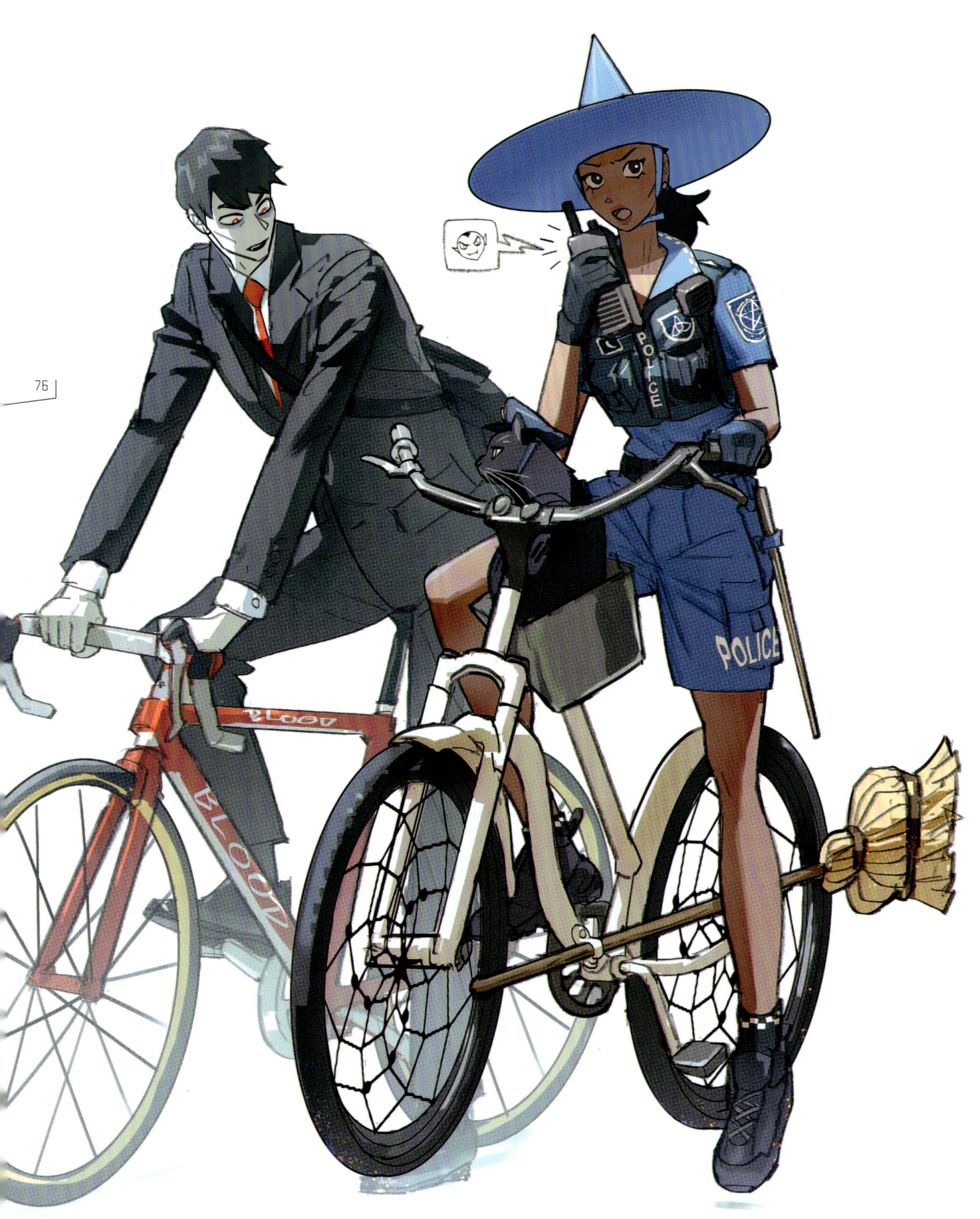

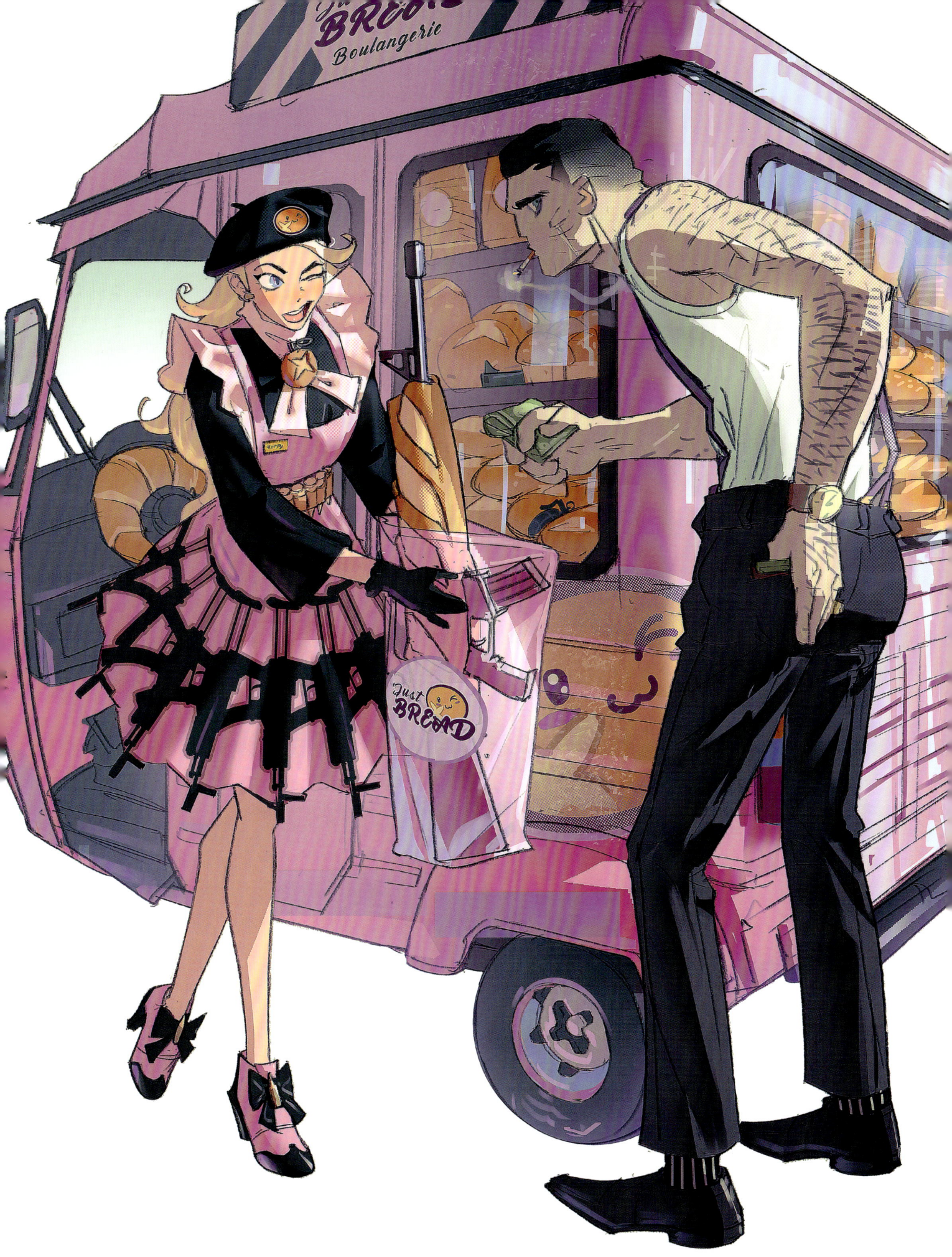

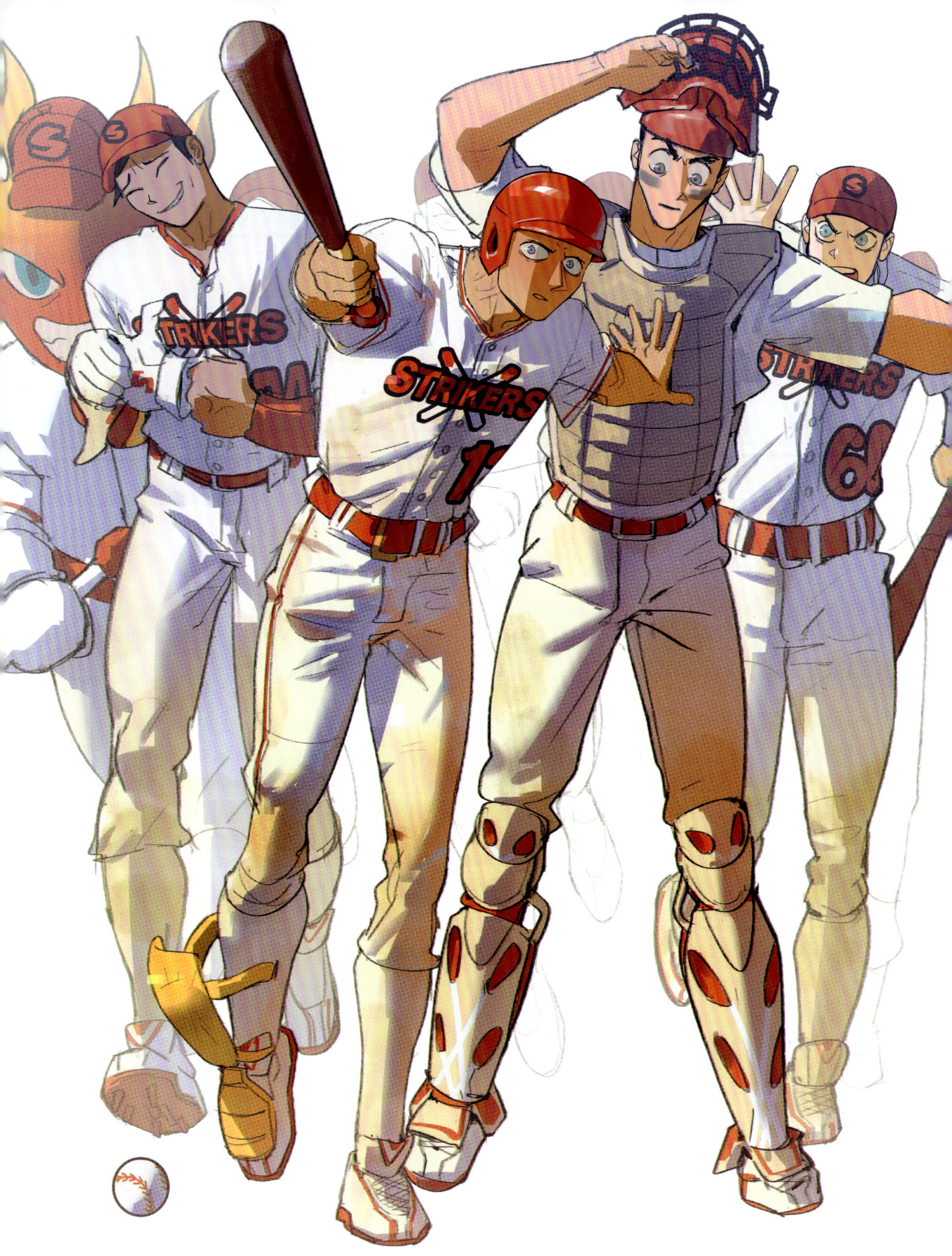

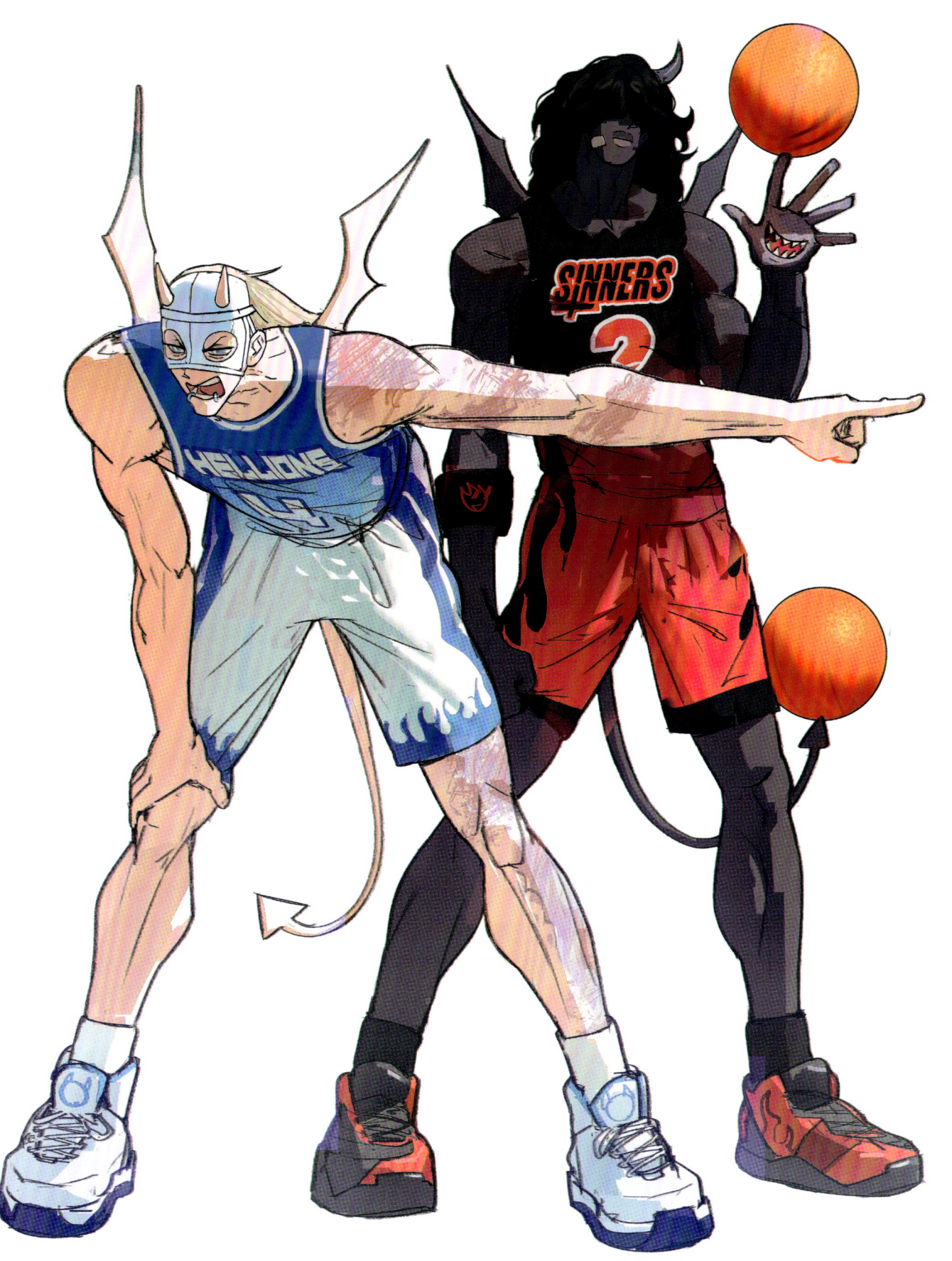

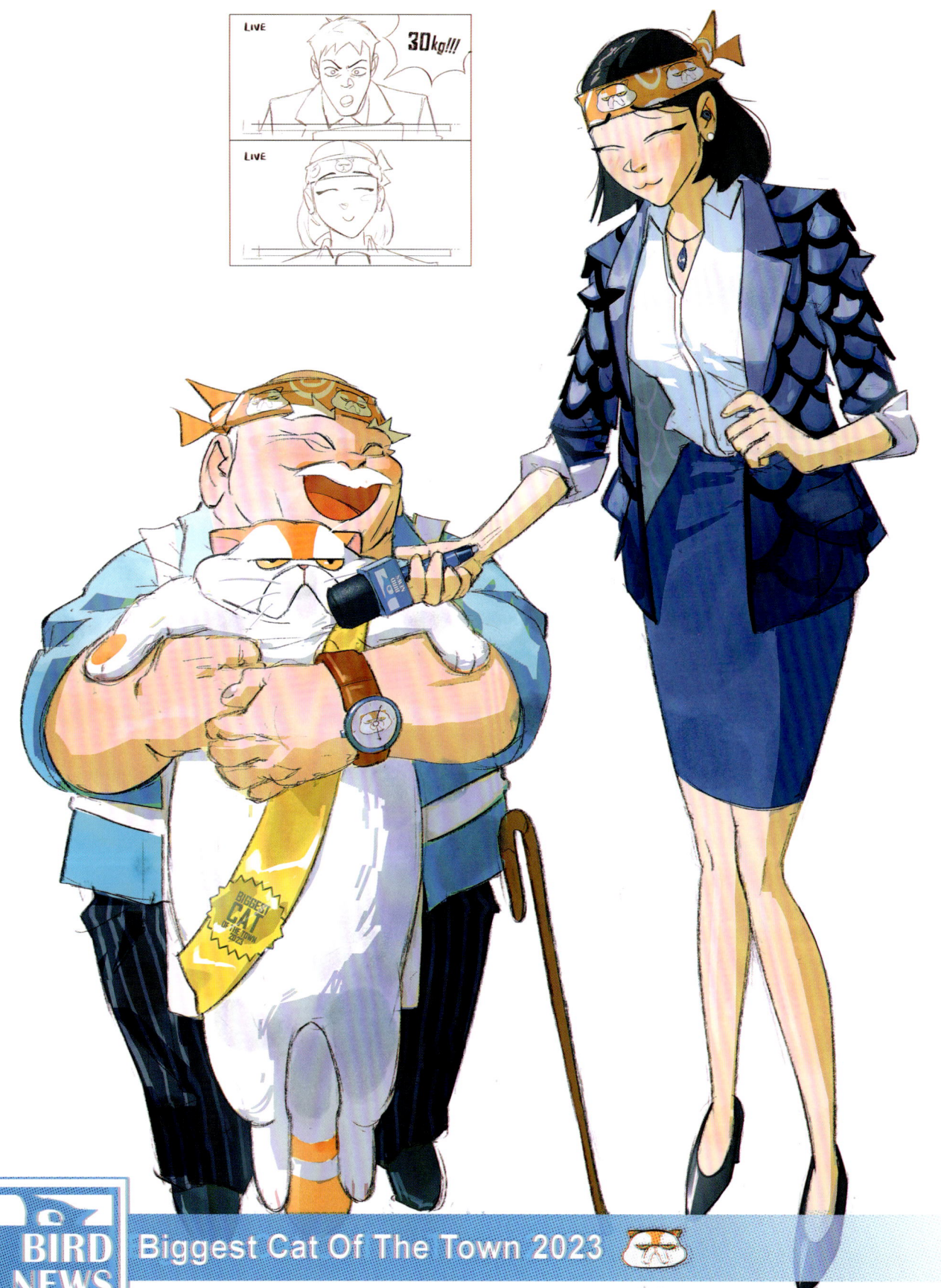

LIVE
30kg!!!
LIVE

BIGGEST CAT OF THE TOWN 2023

BIRD NEWS Biggest Cat Of The Town 2023

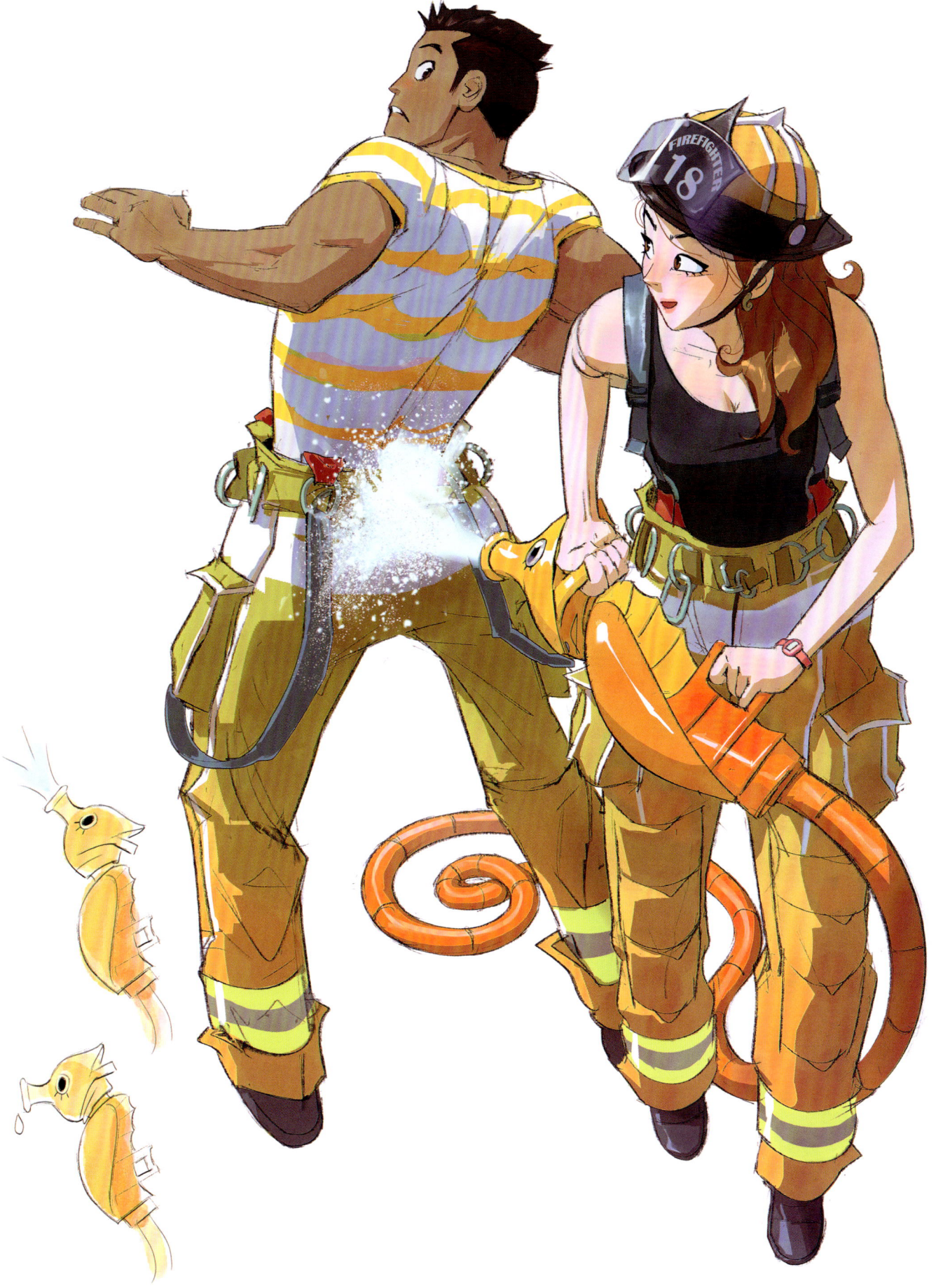

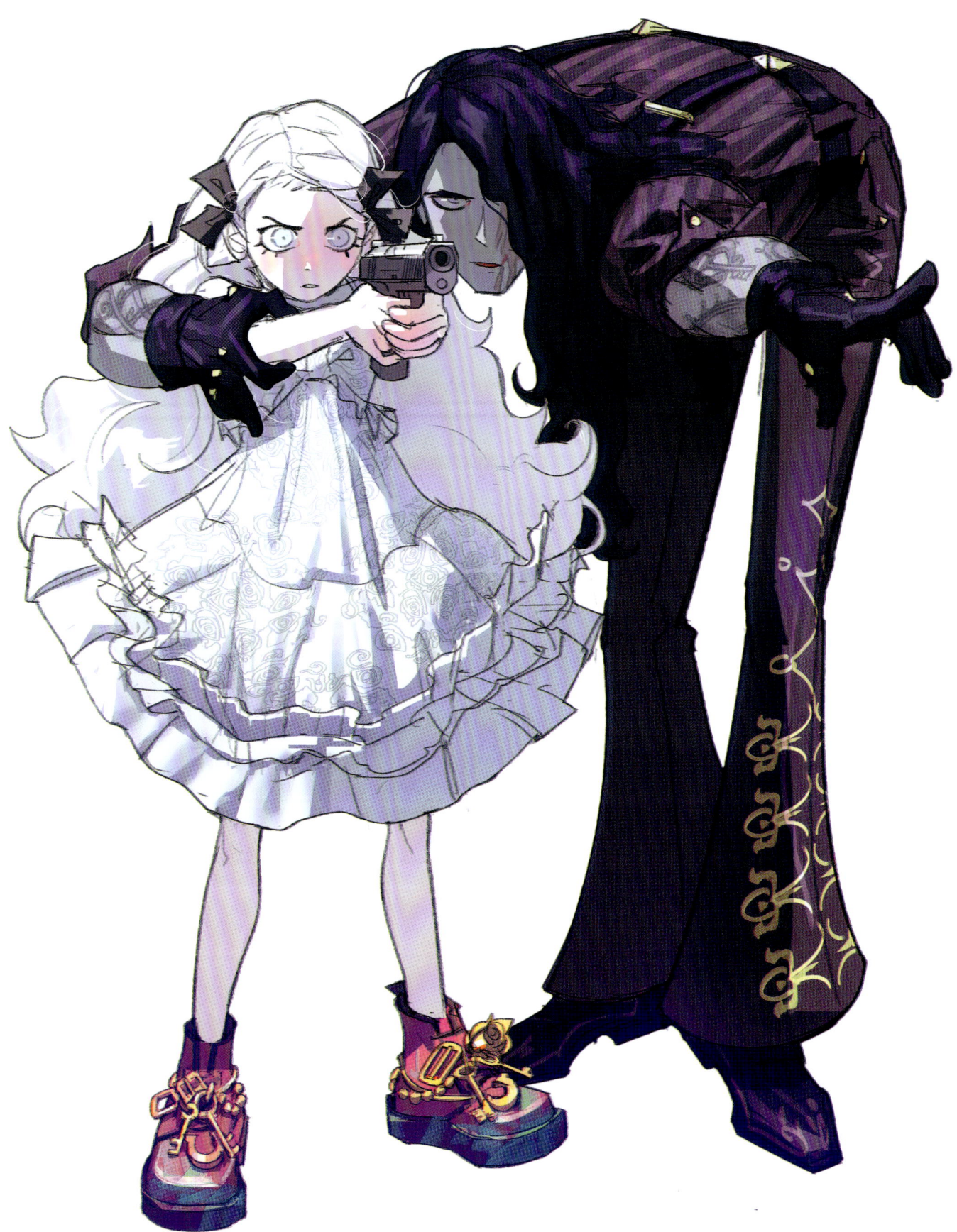

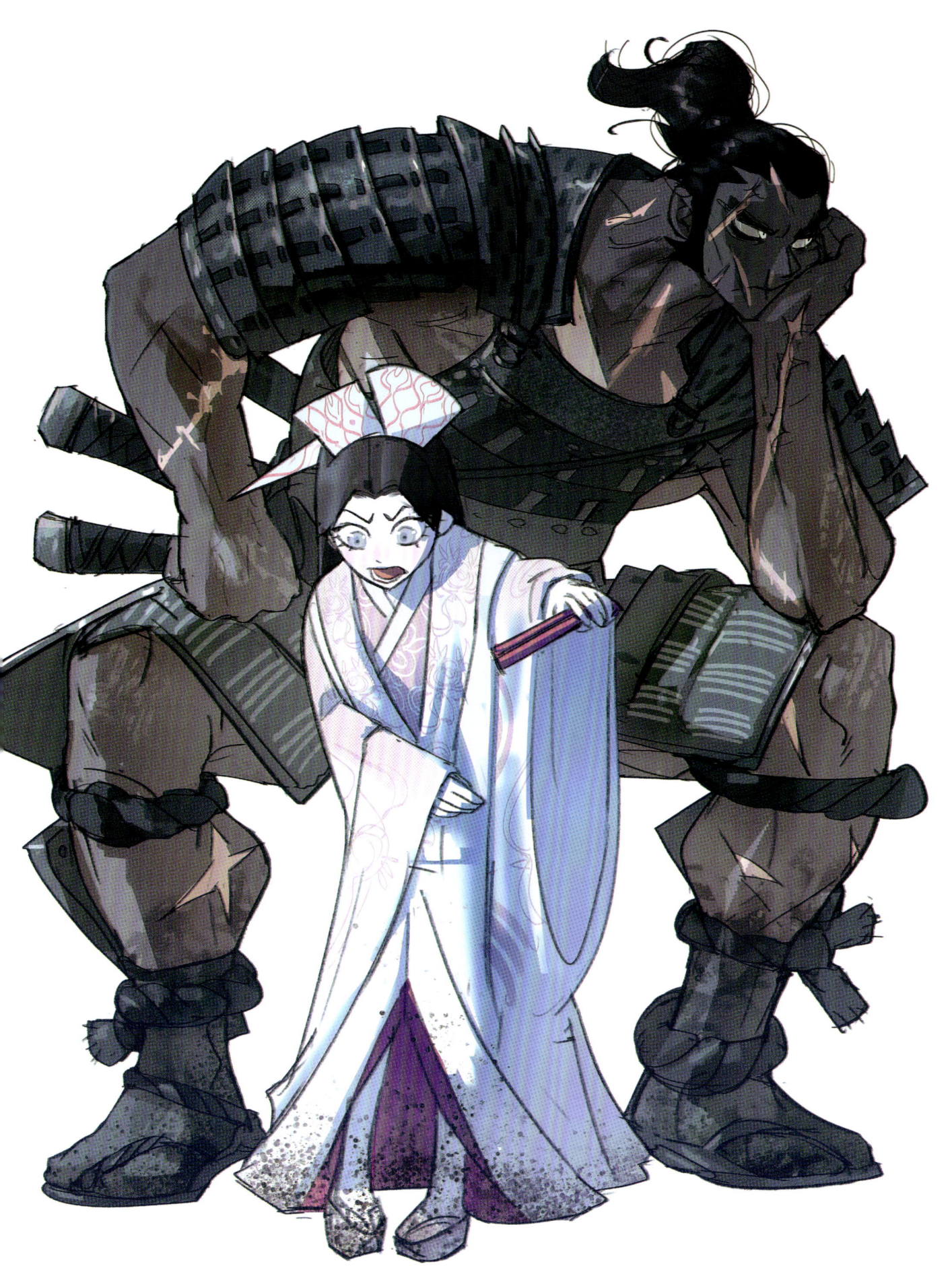

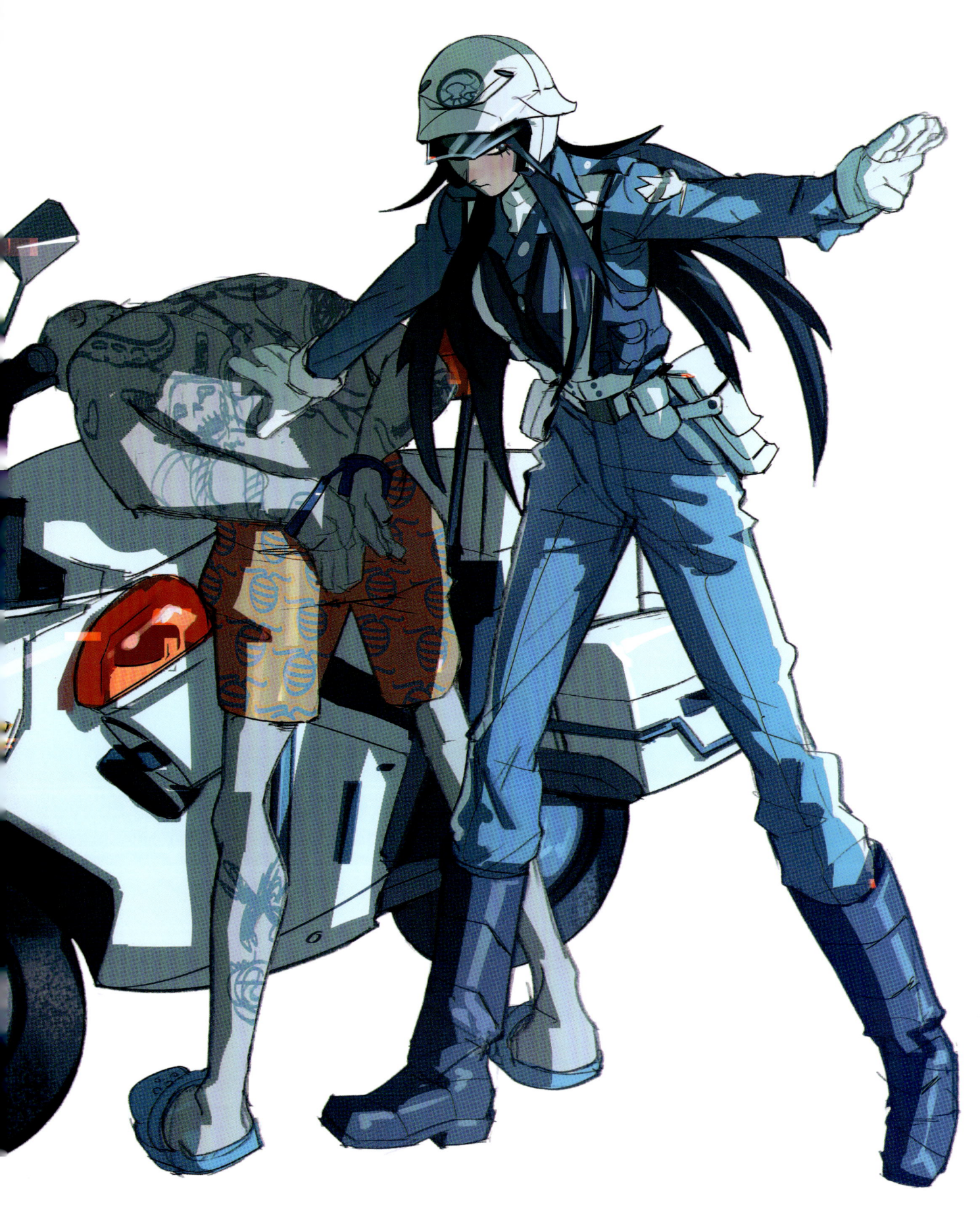

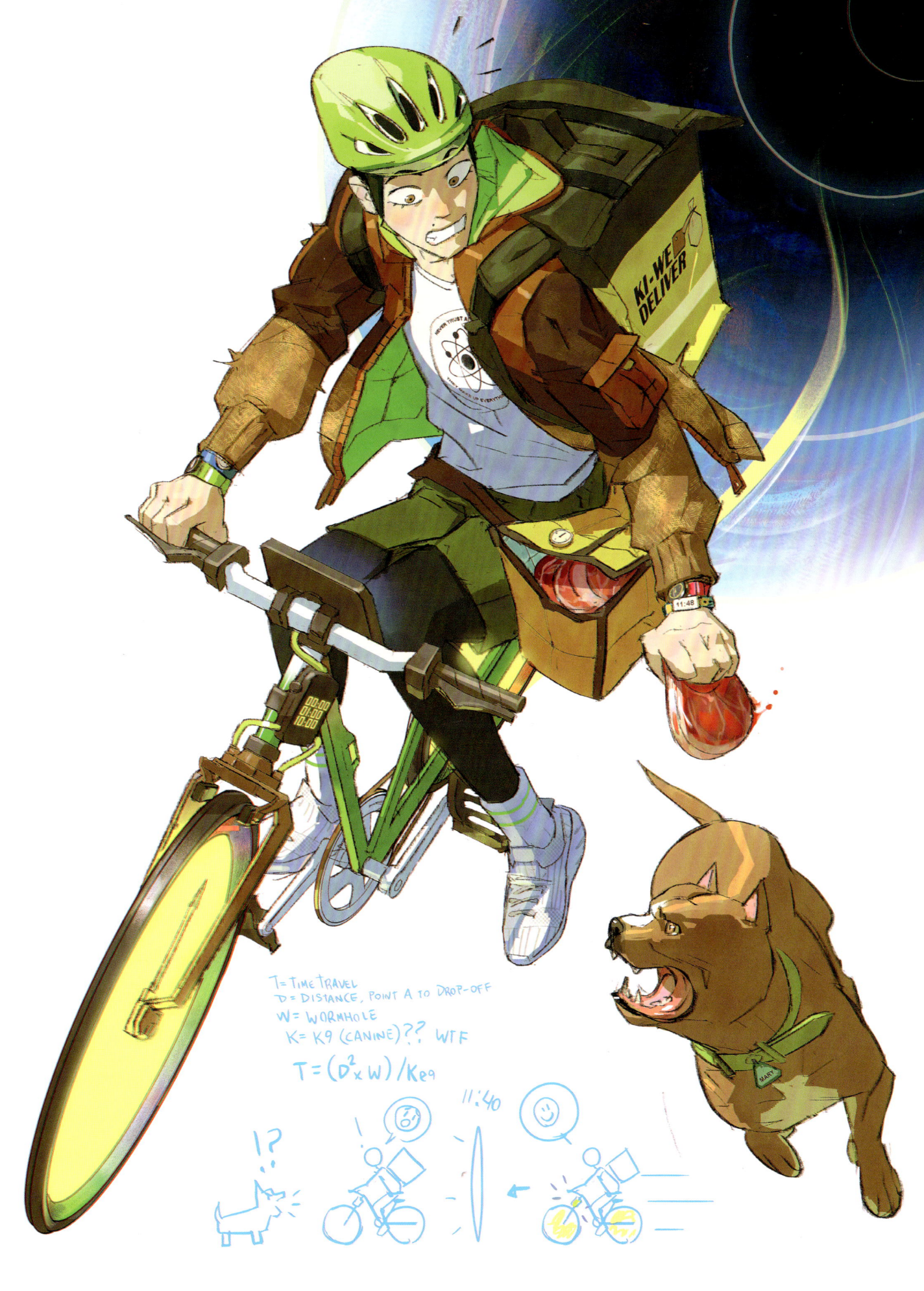

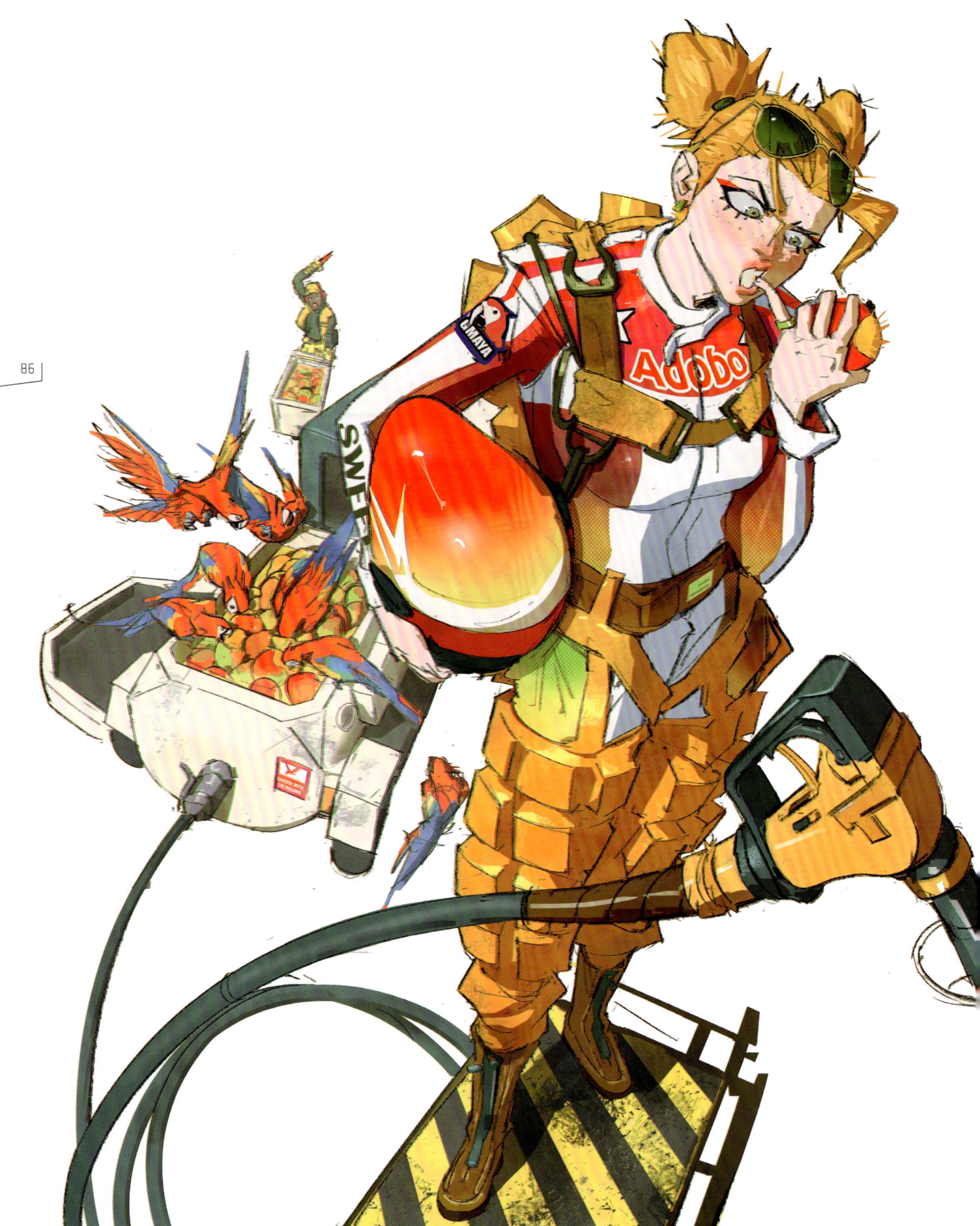

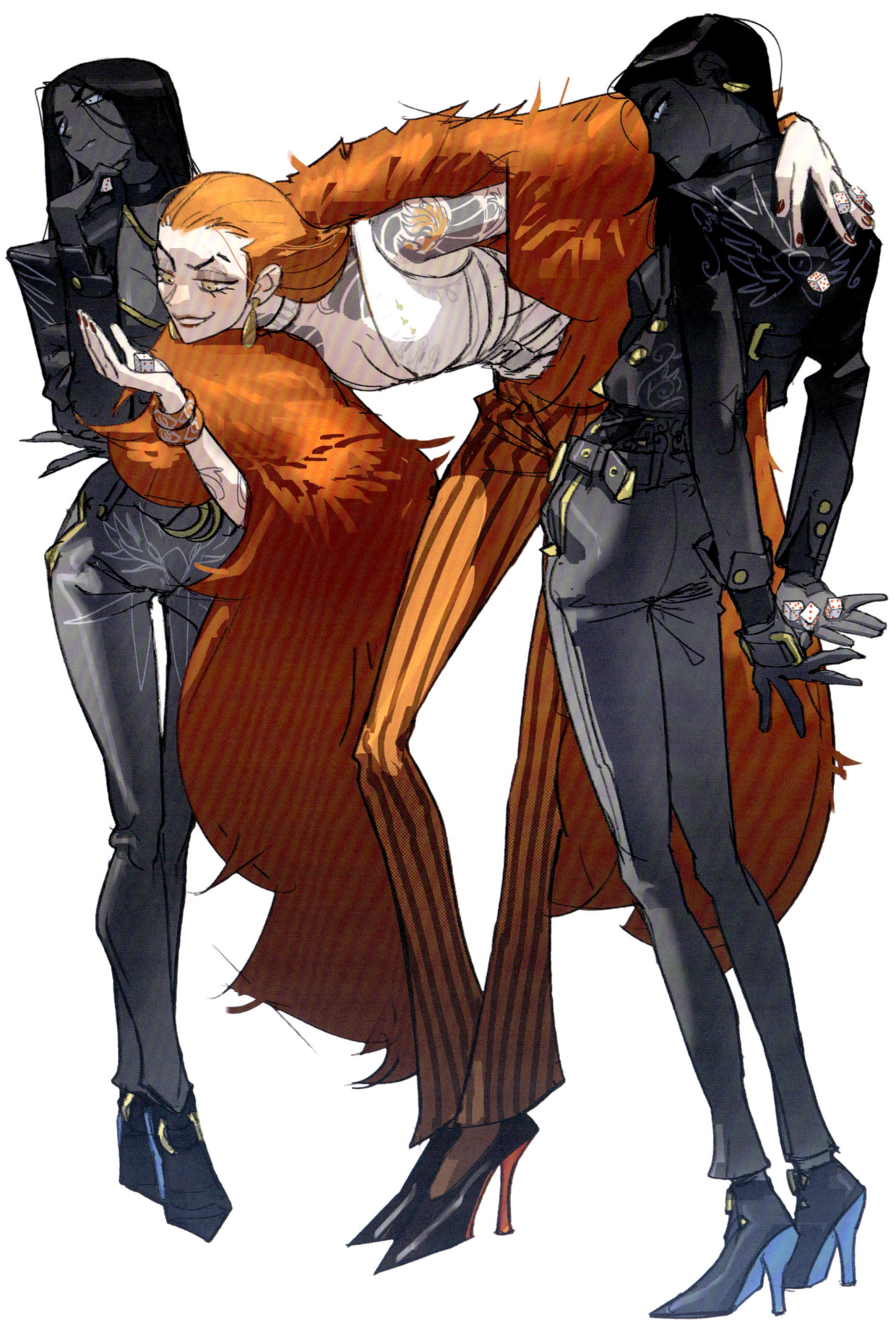

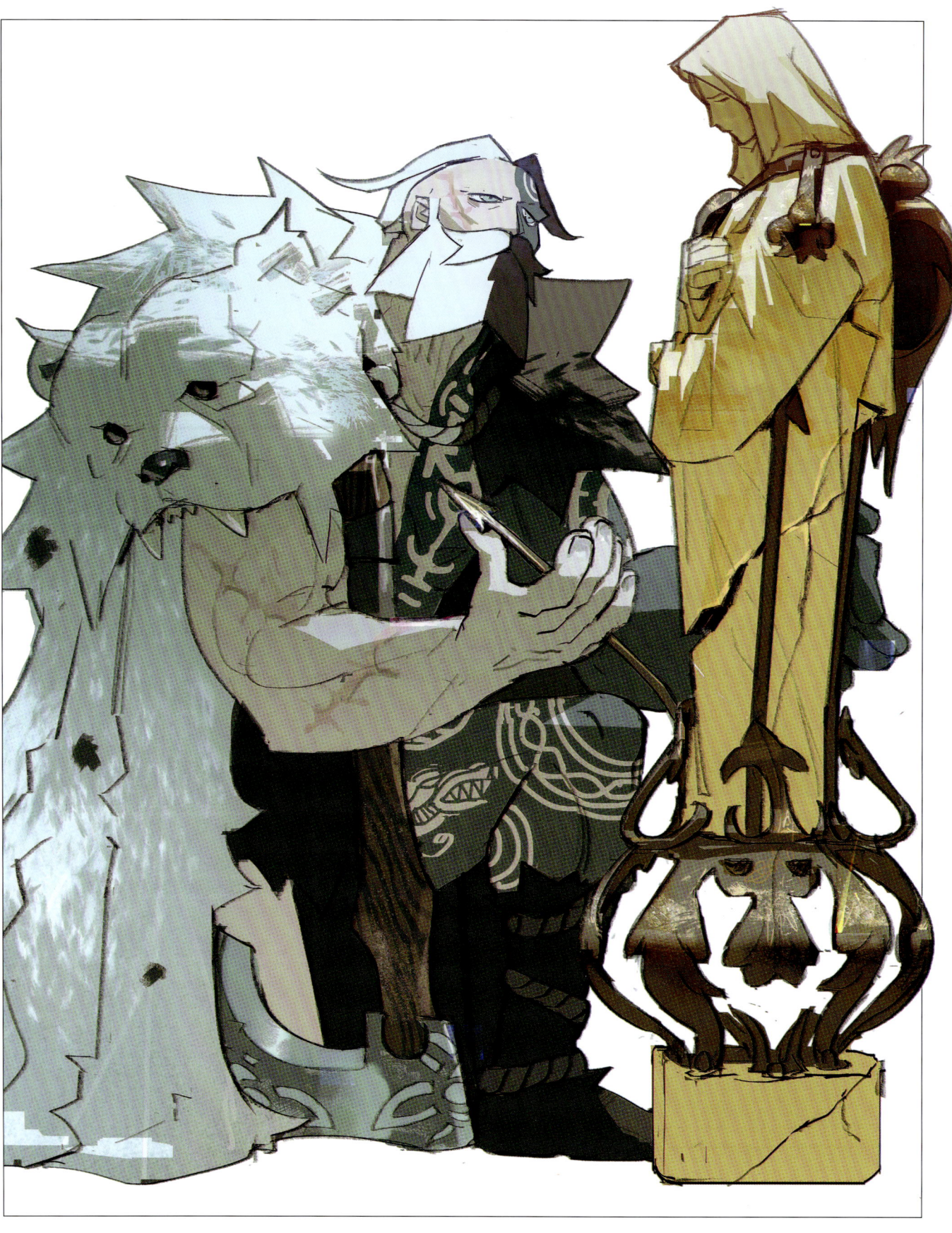

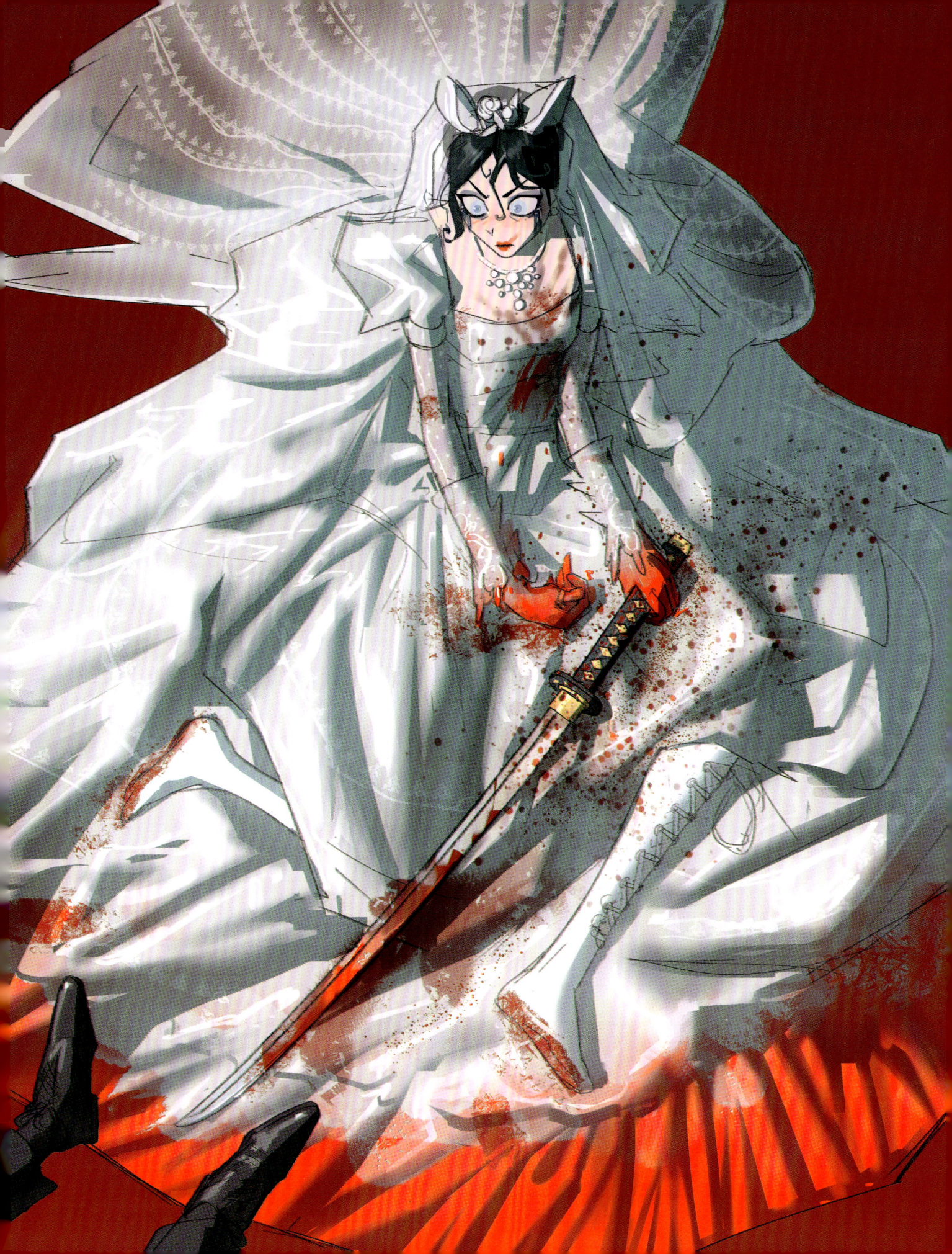

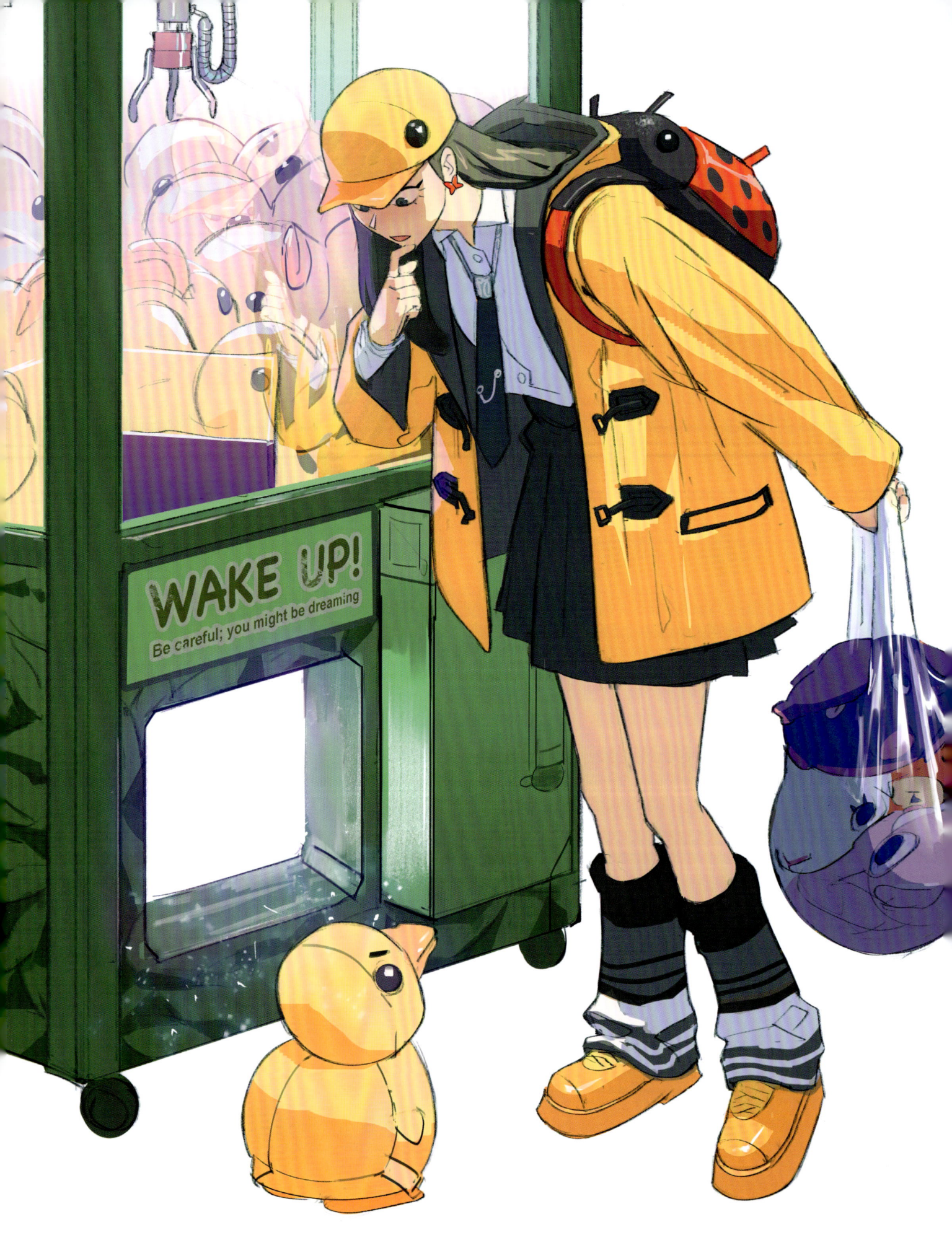

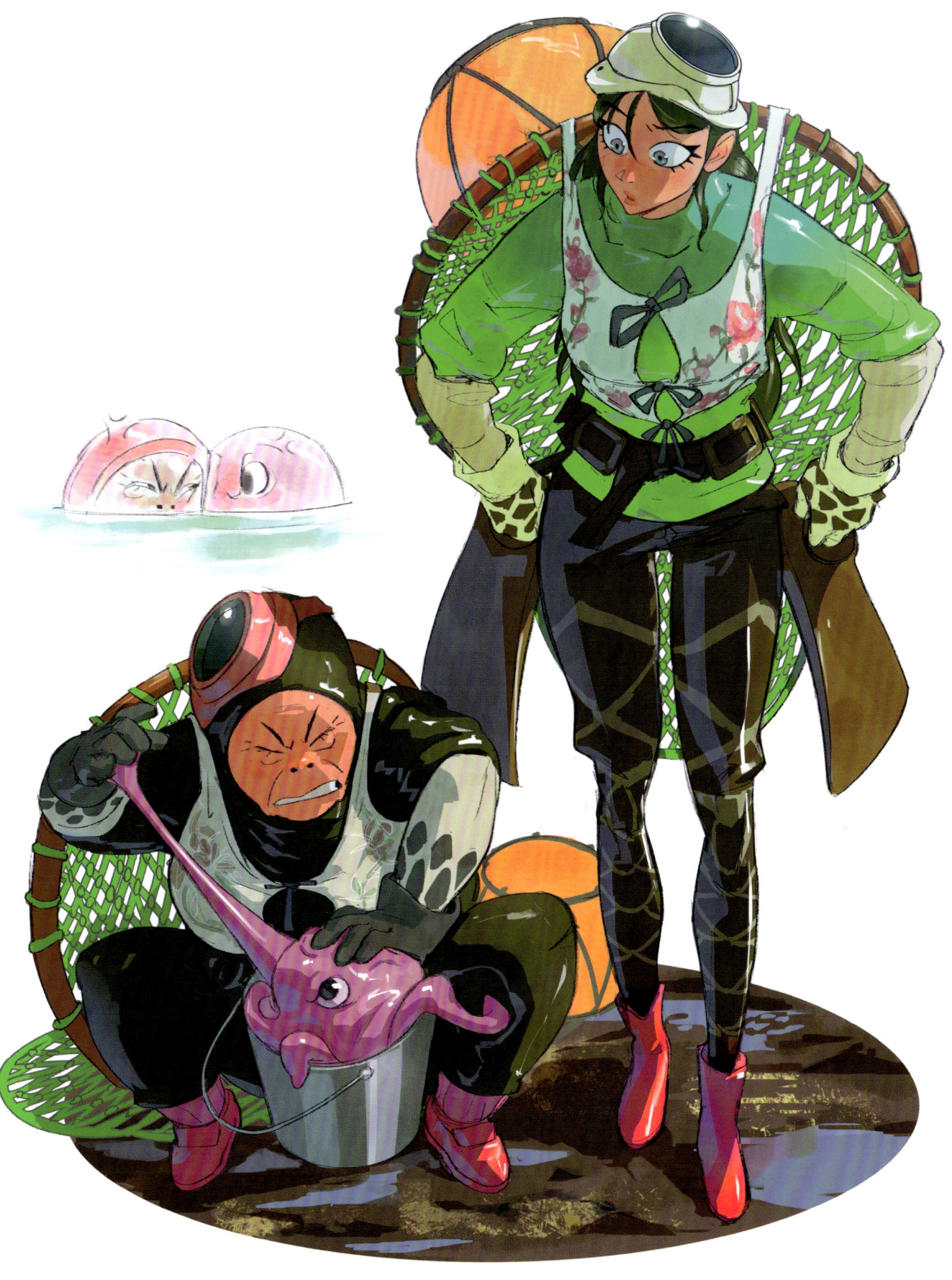

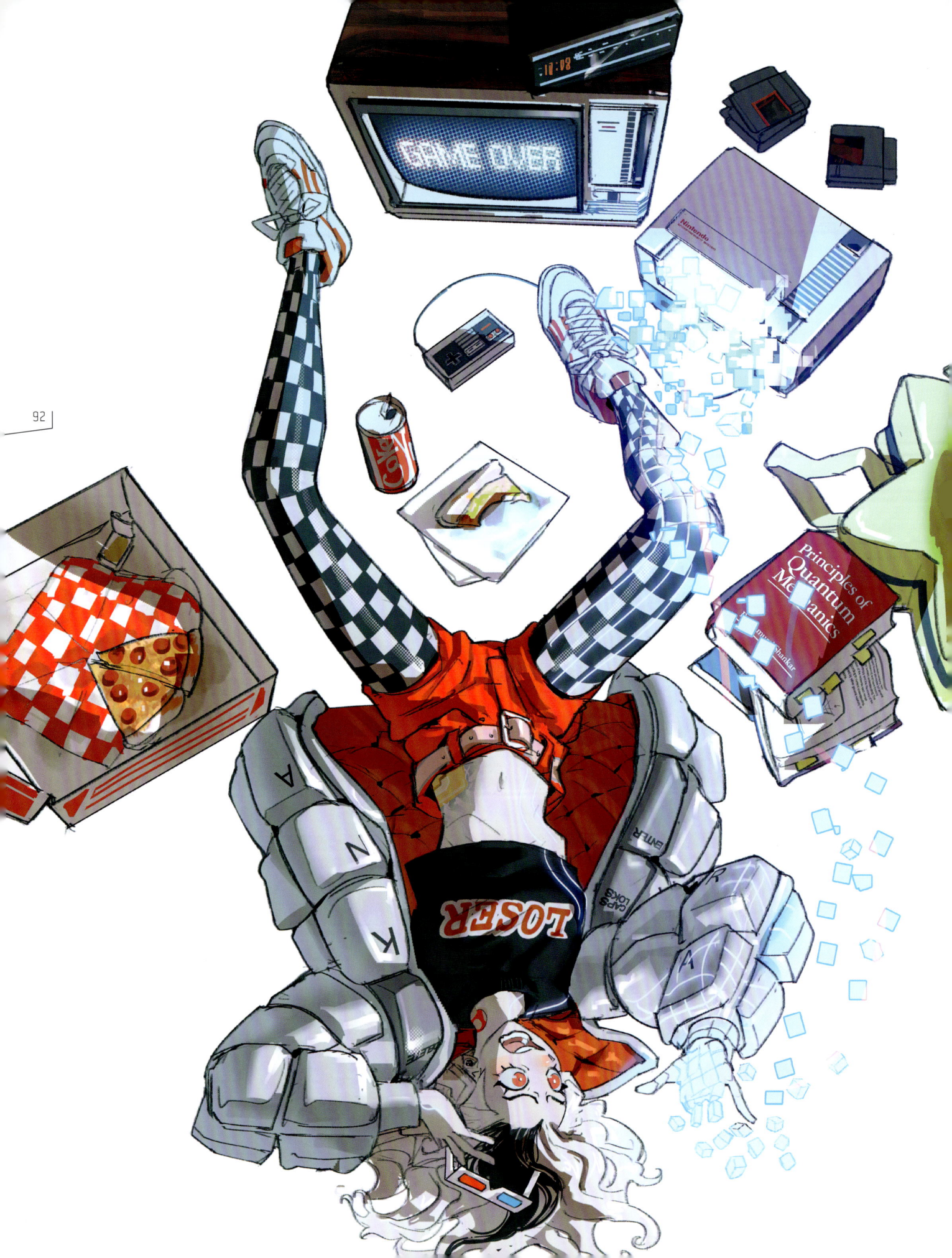

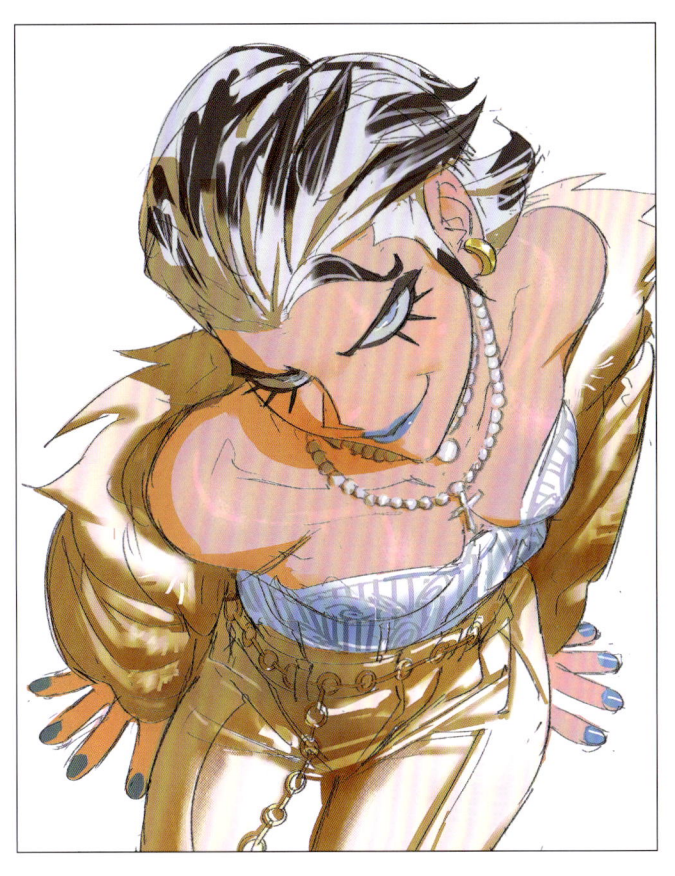

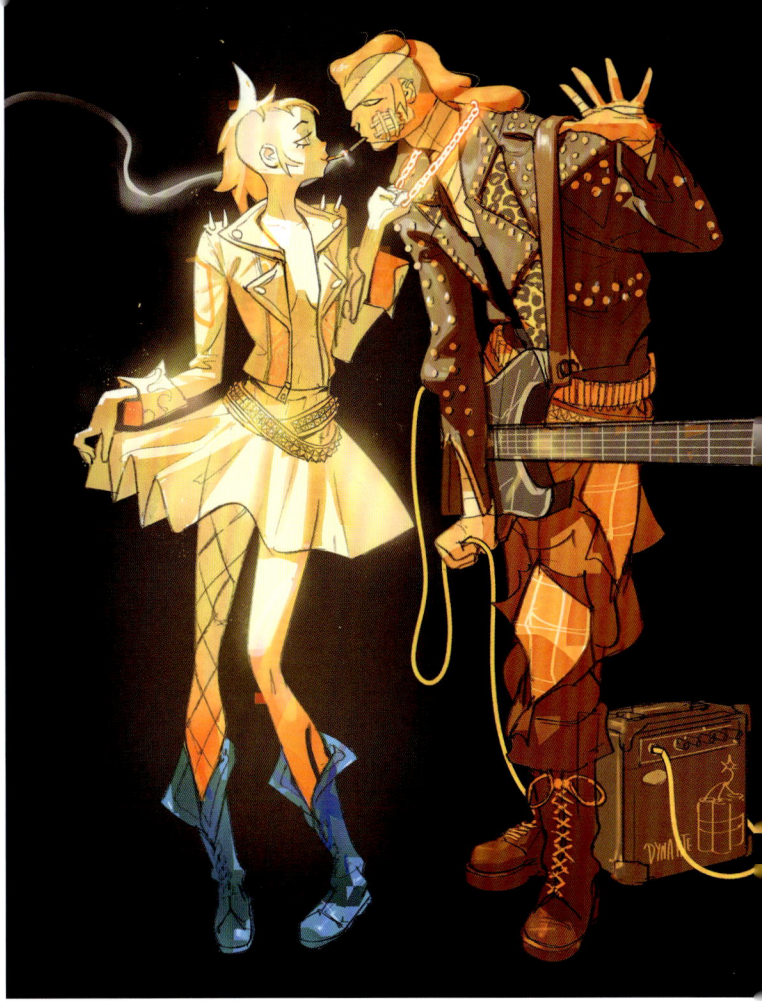

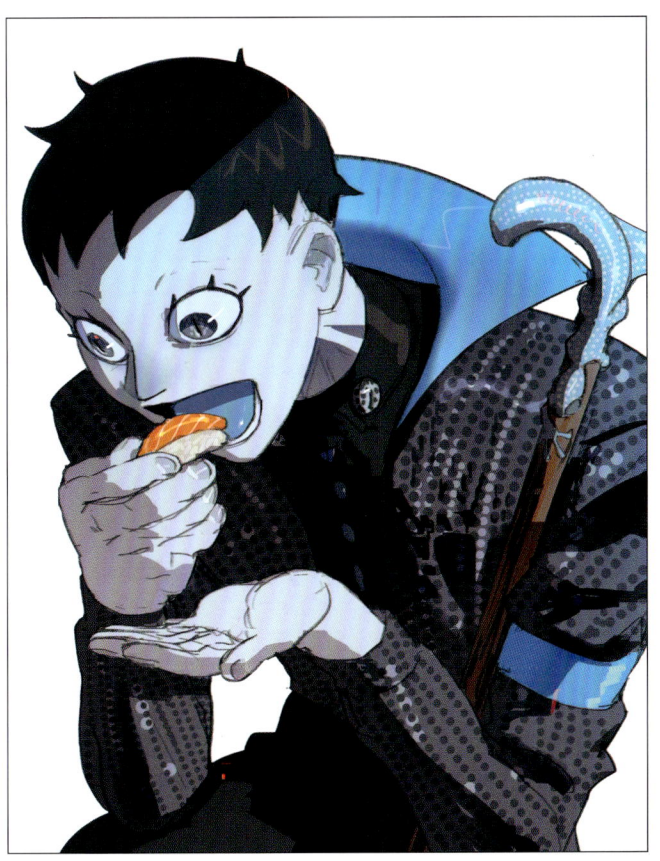

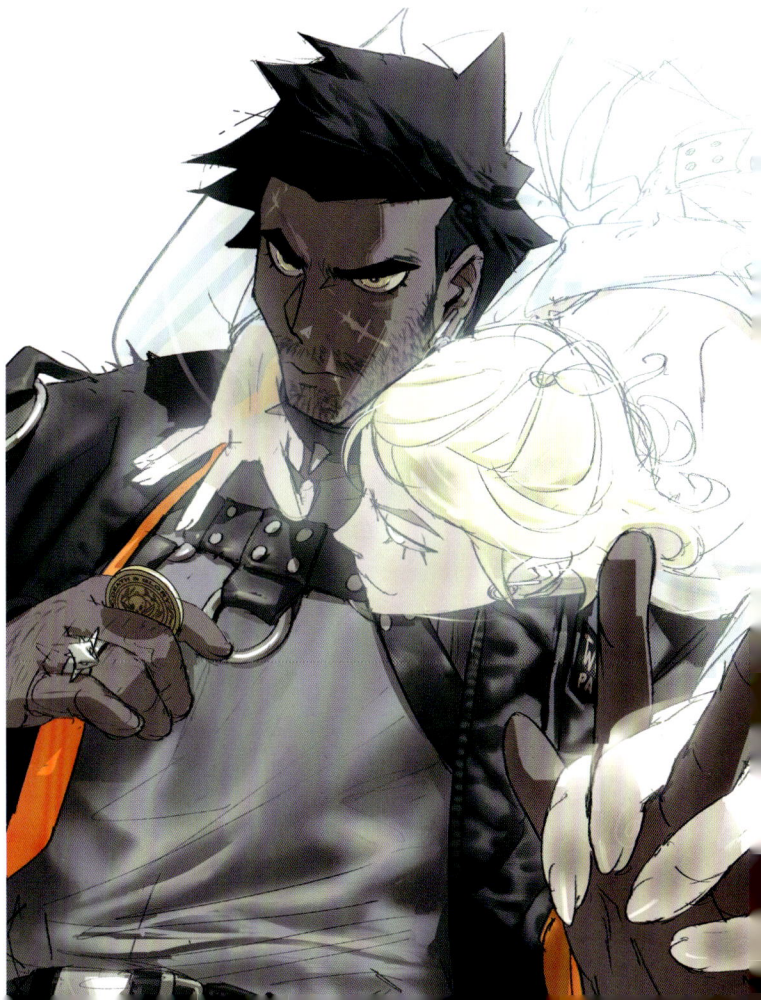

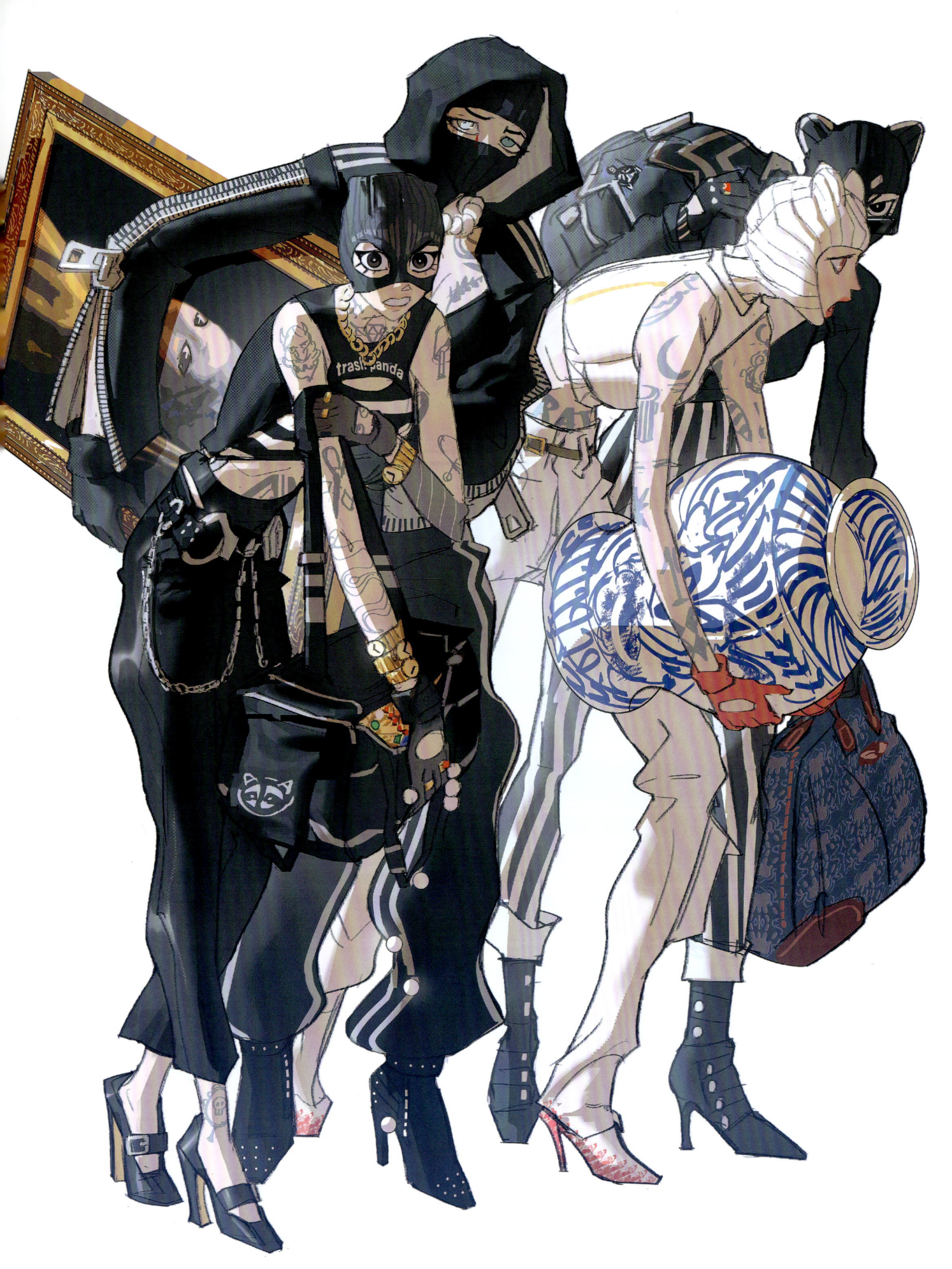

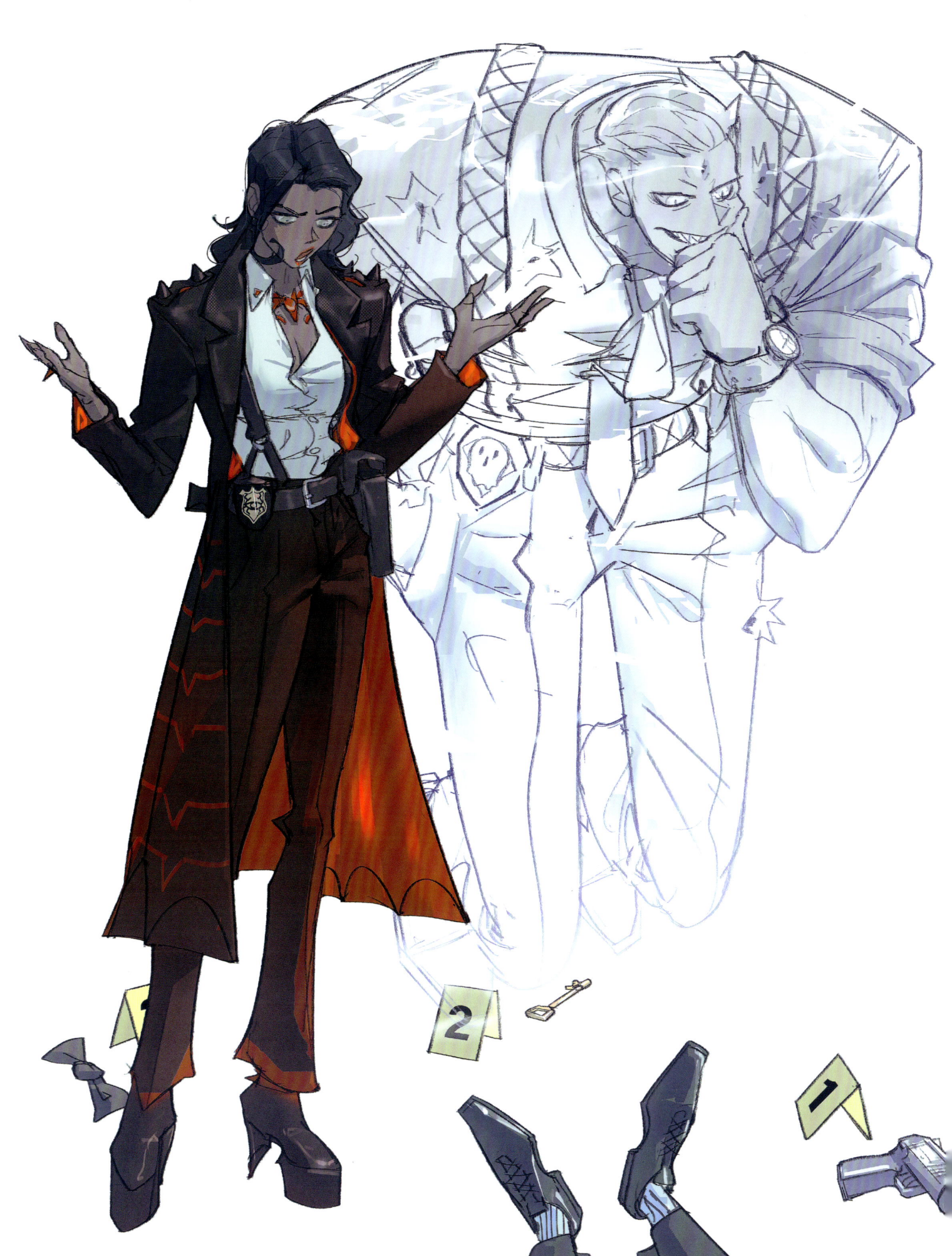

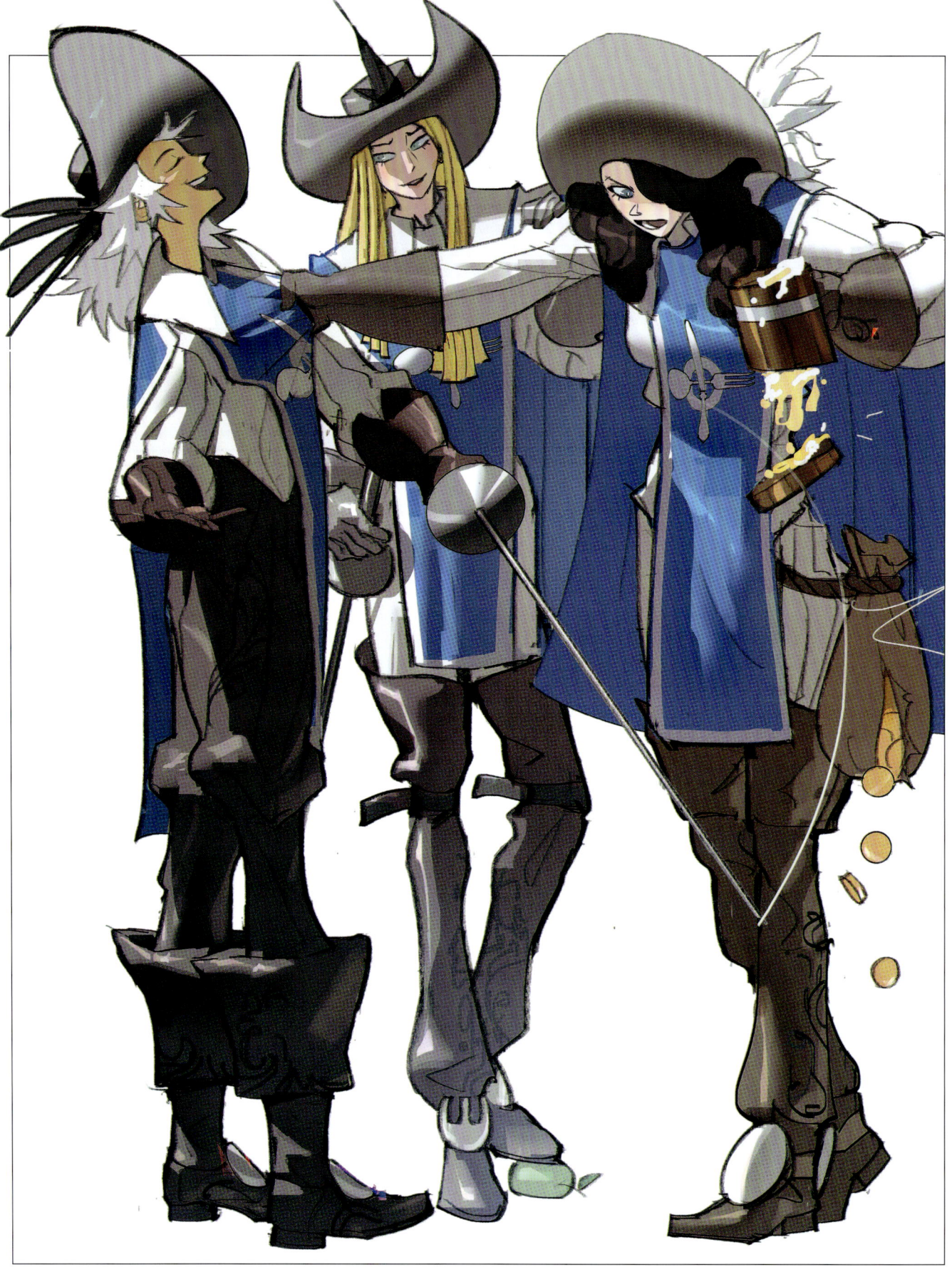

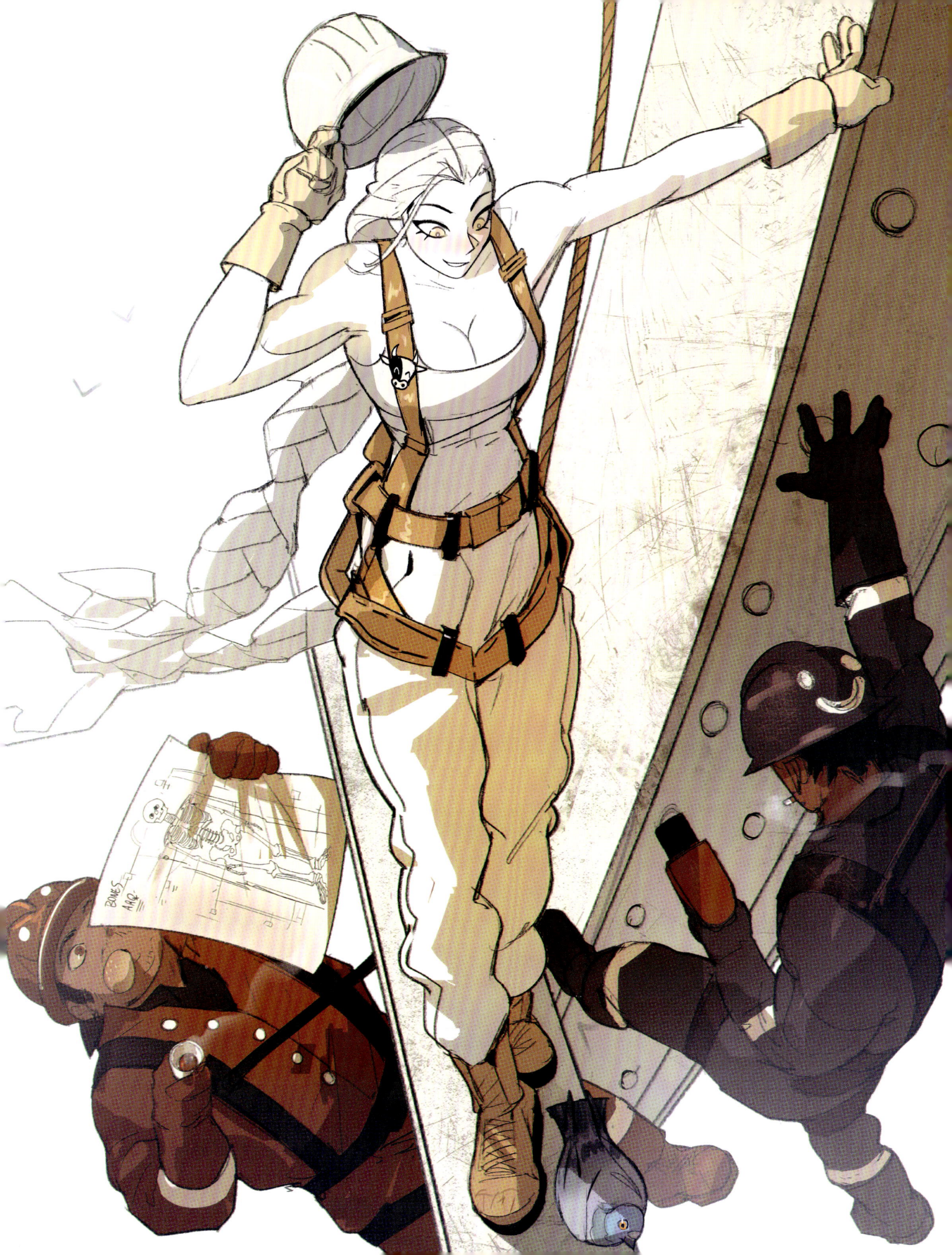

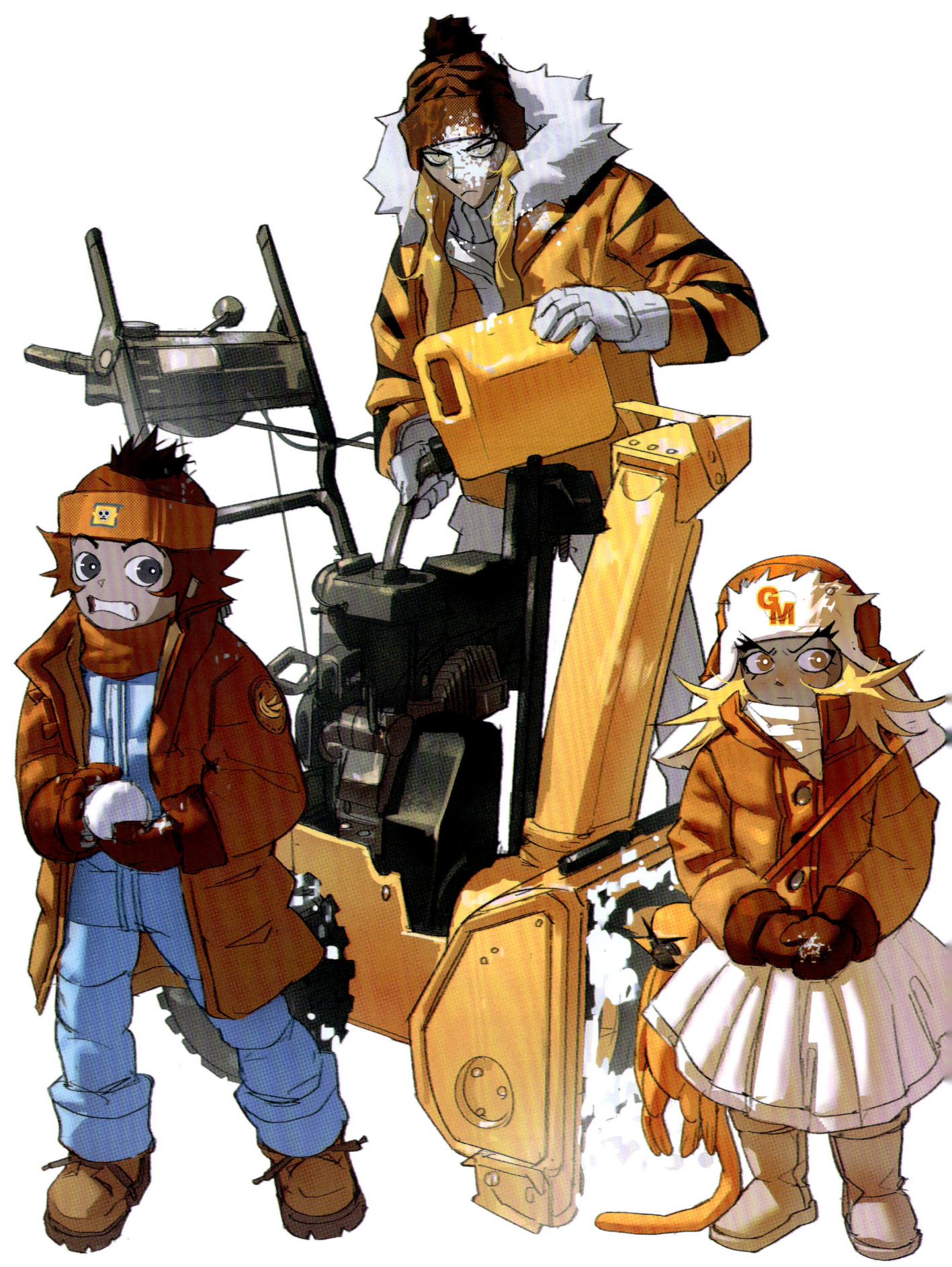

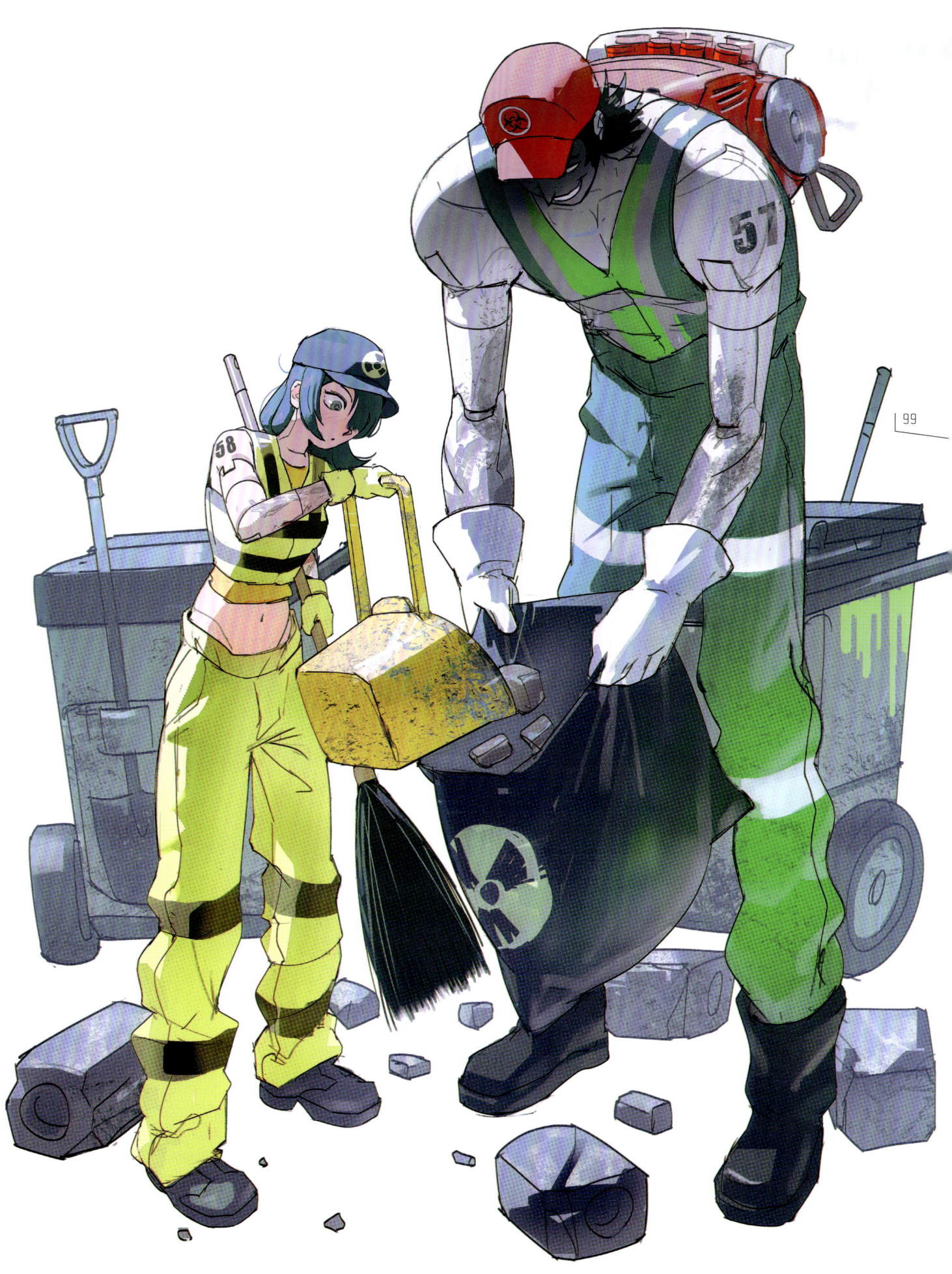

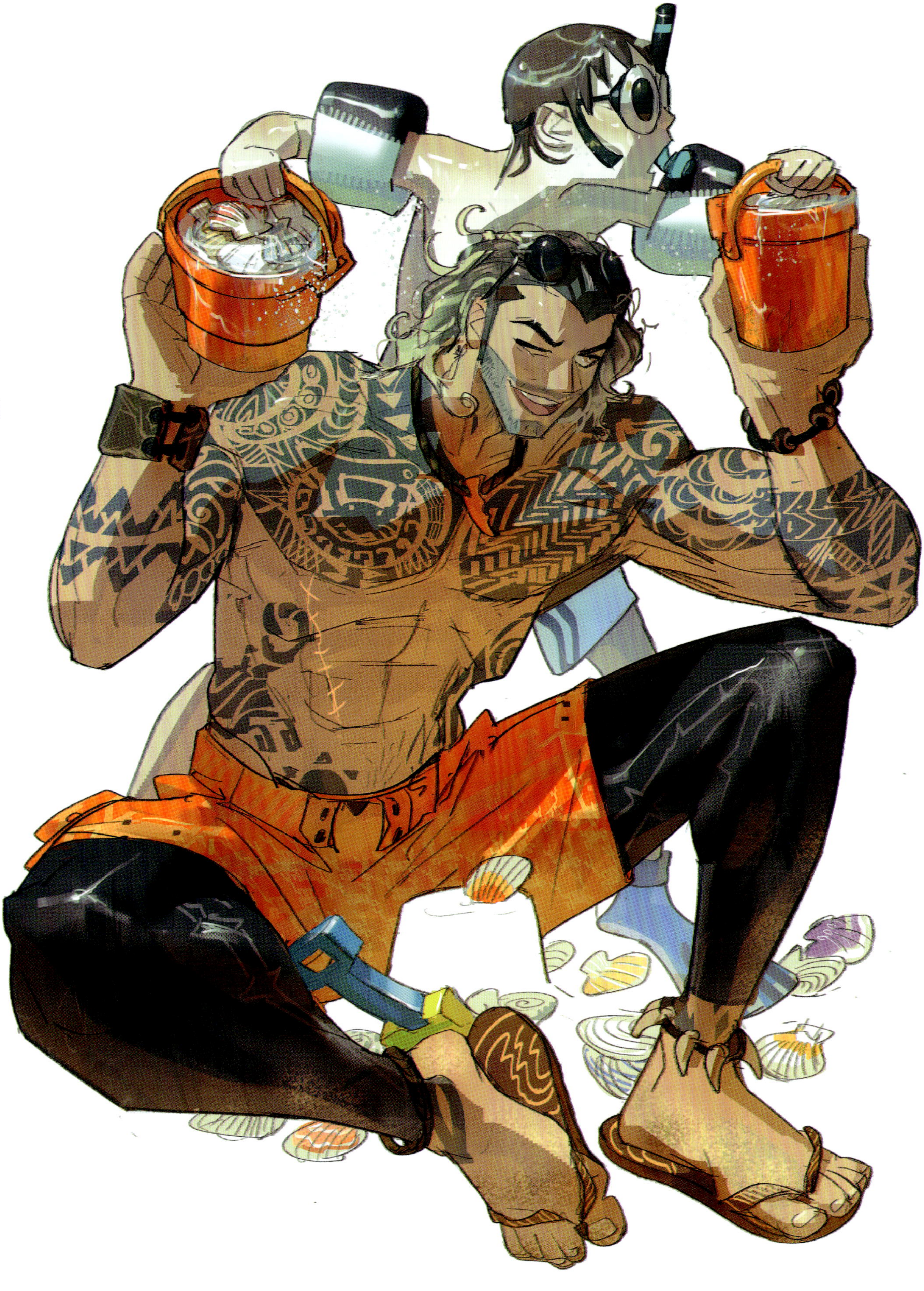

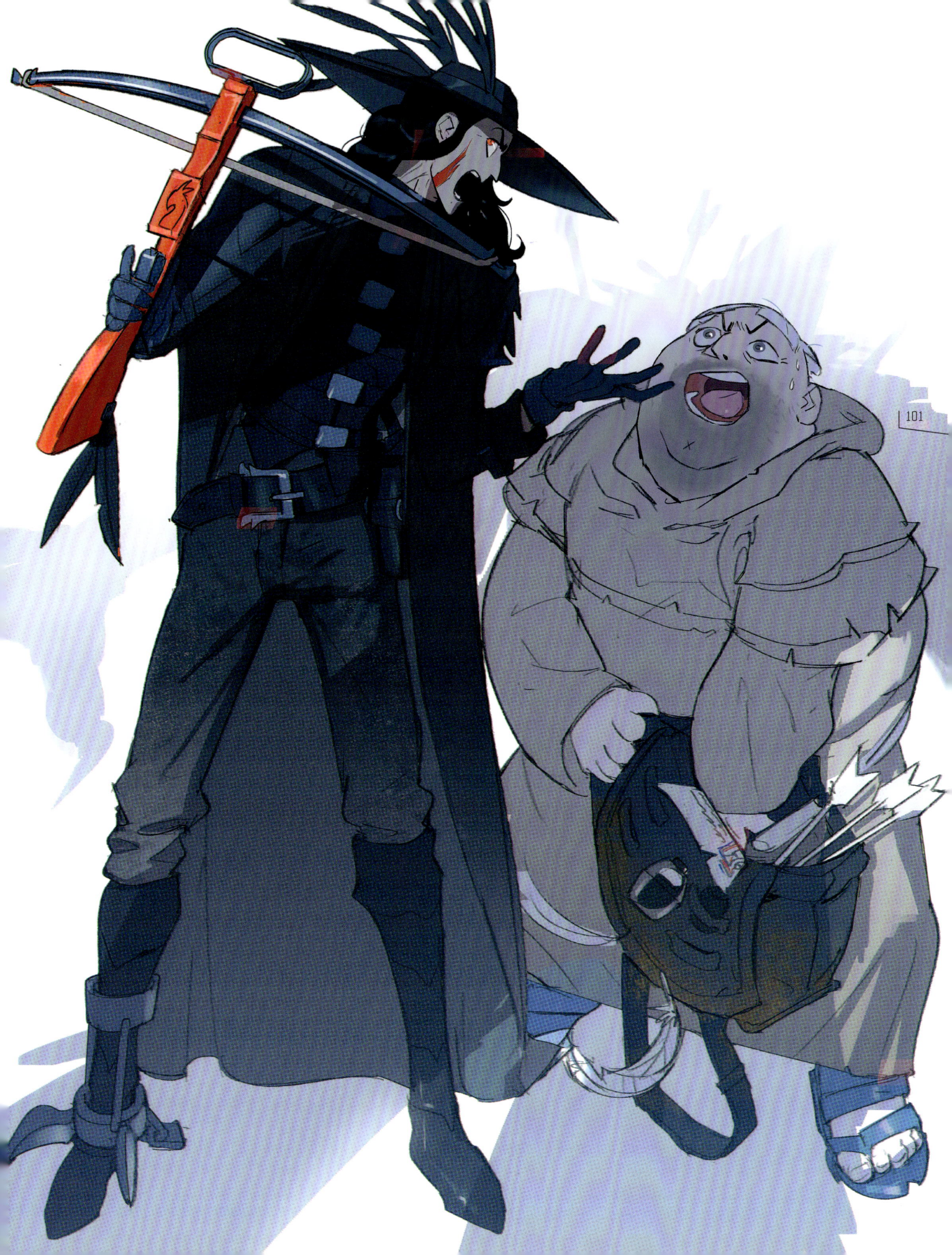

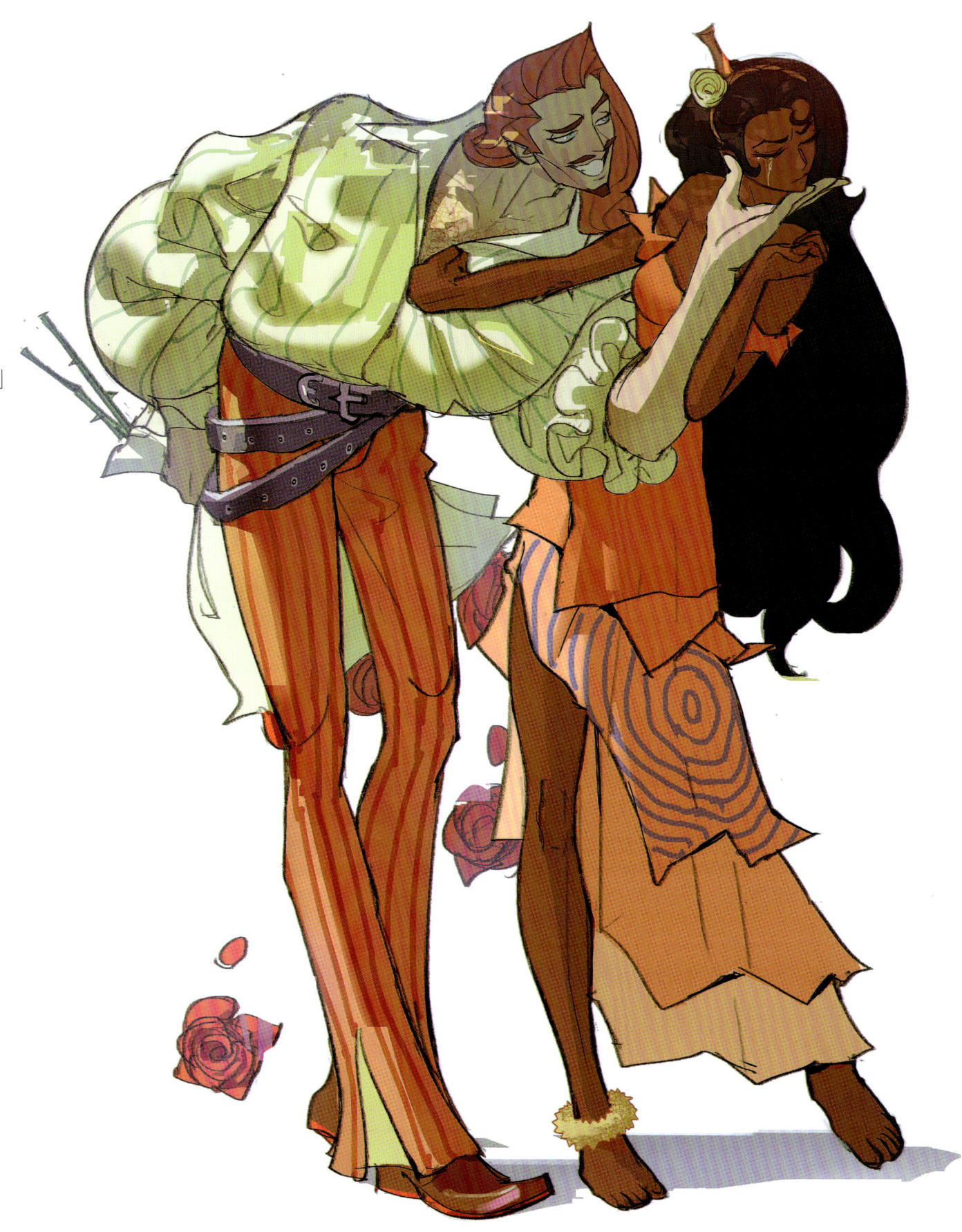

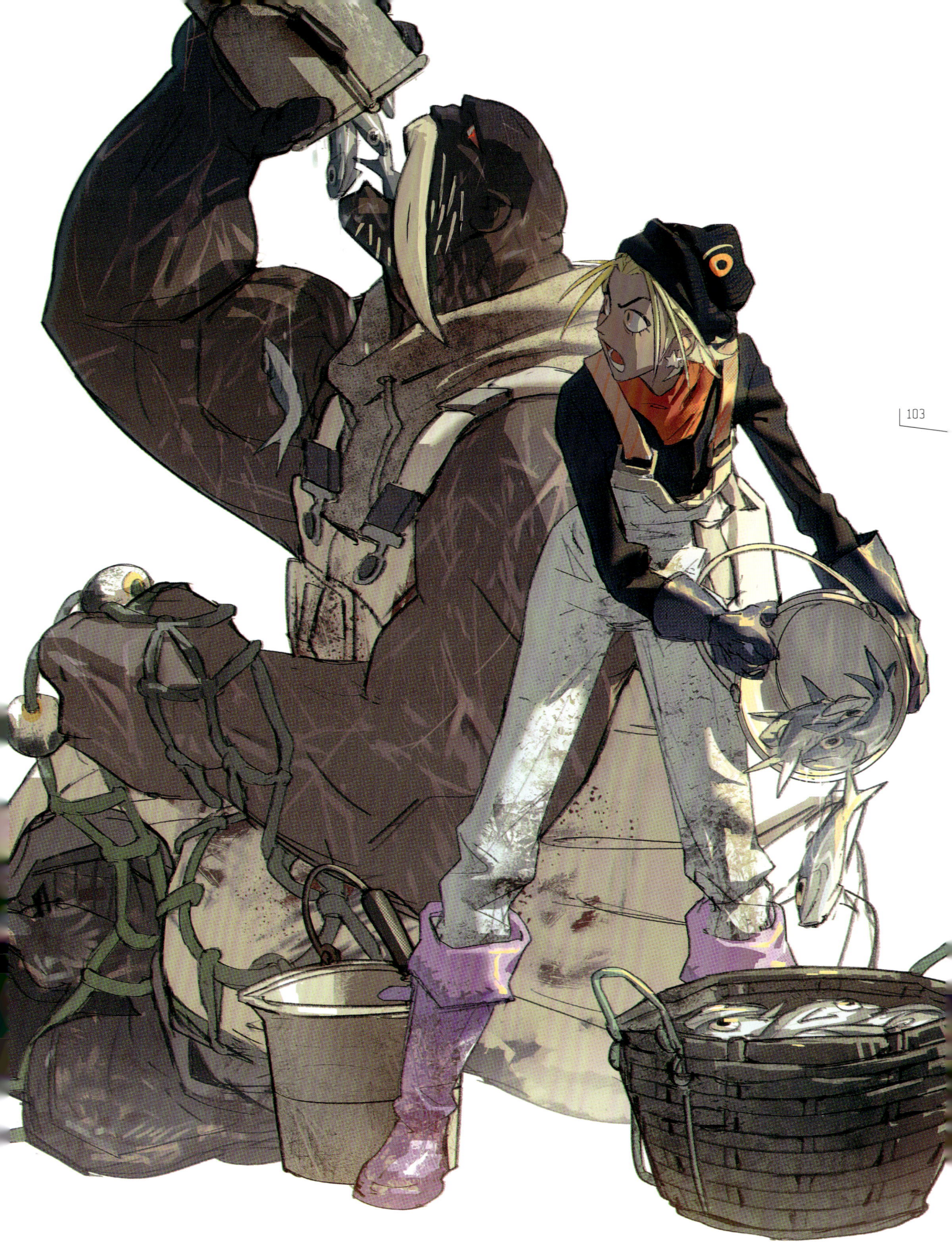

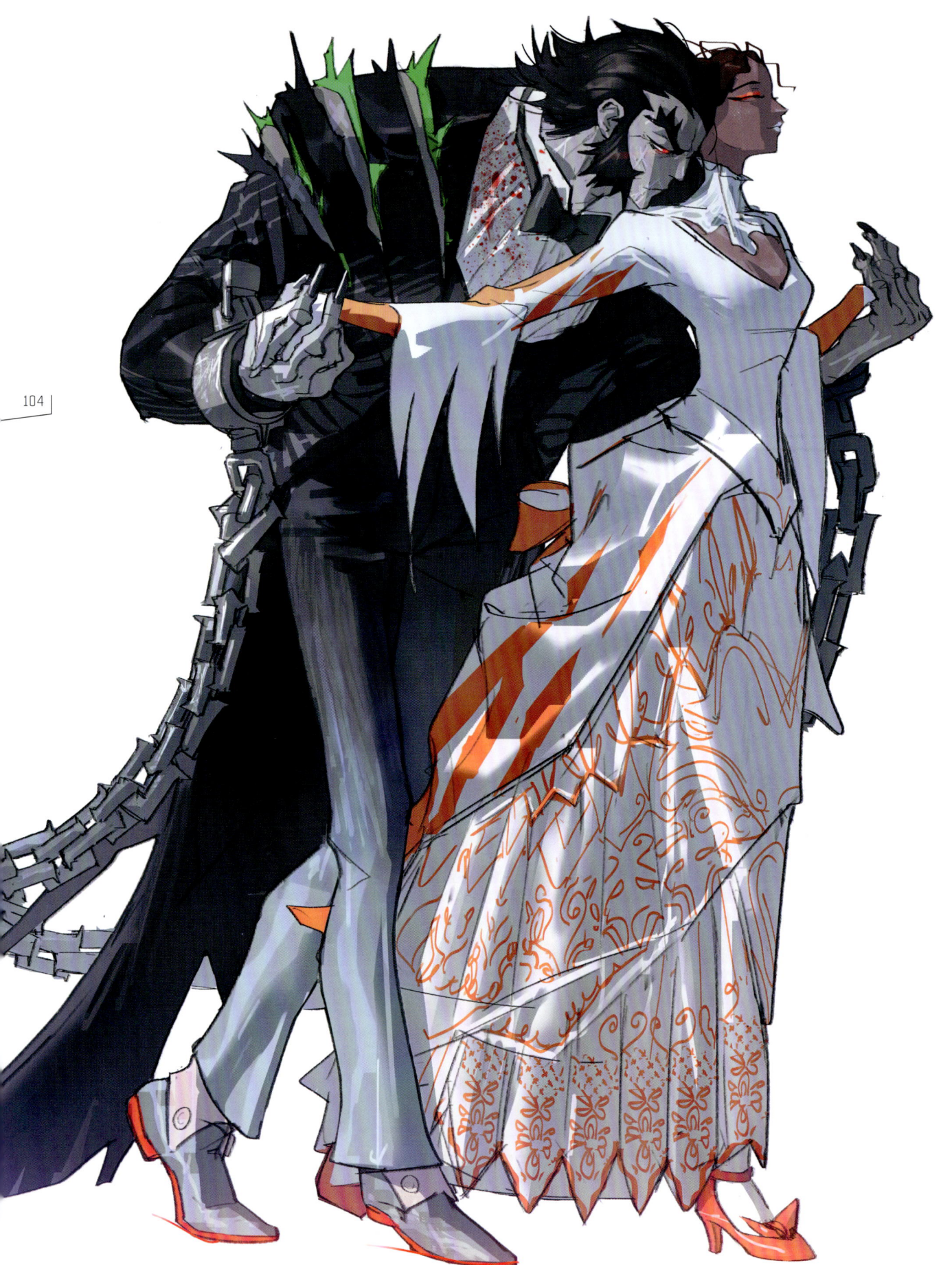

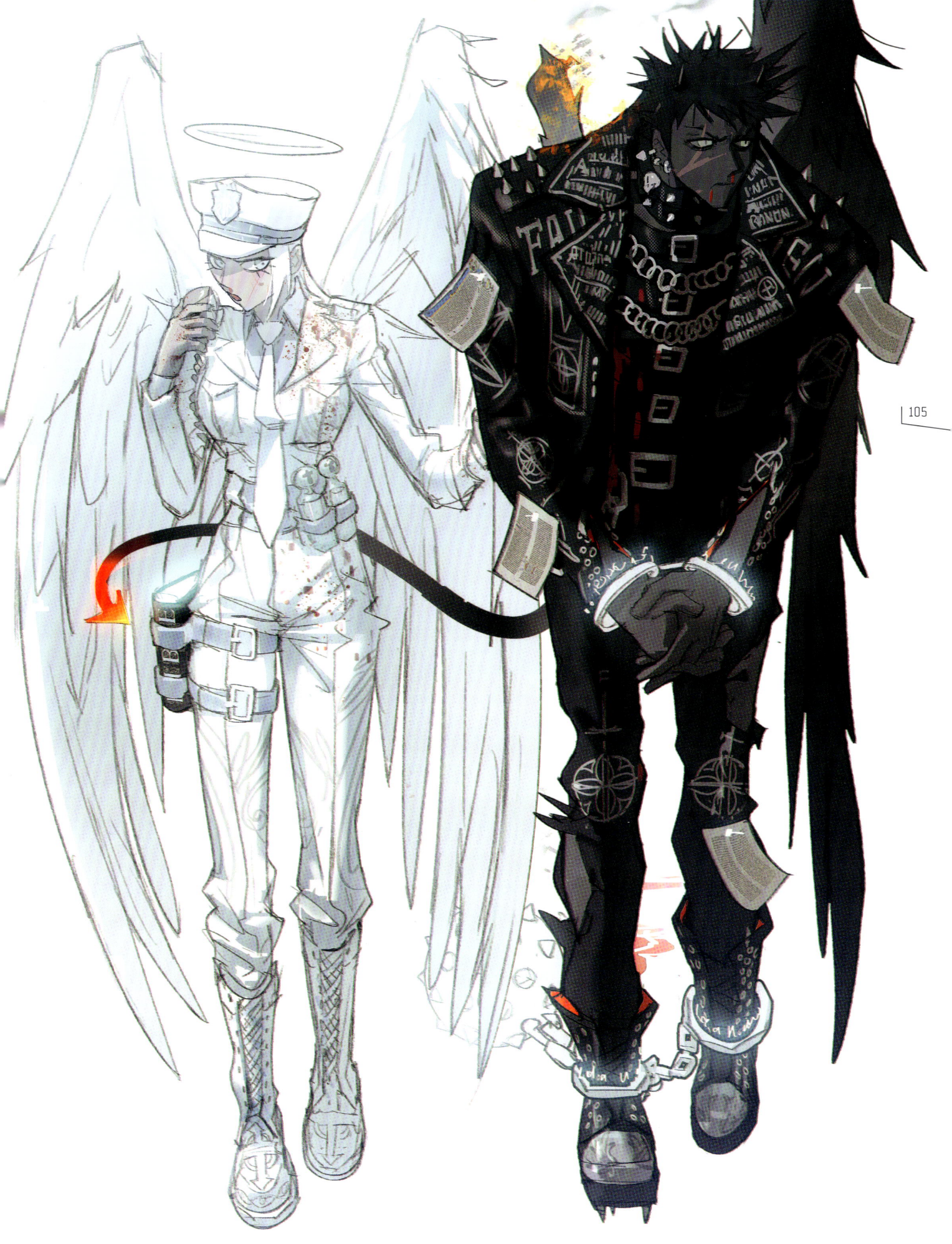

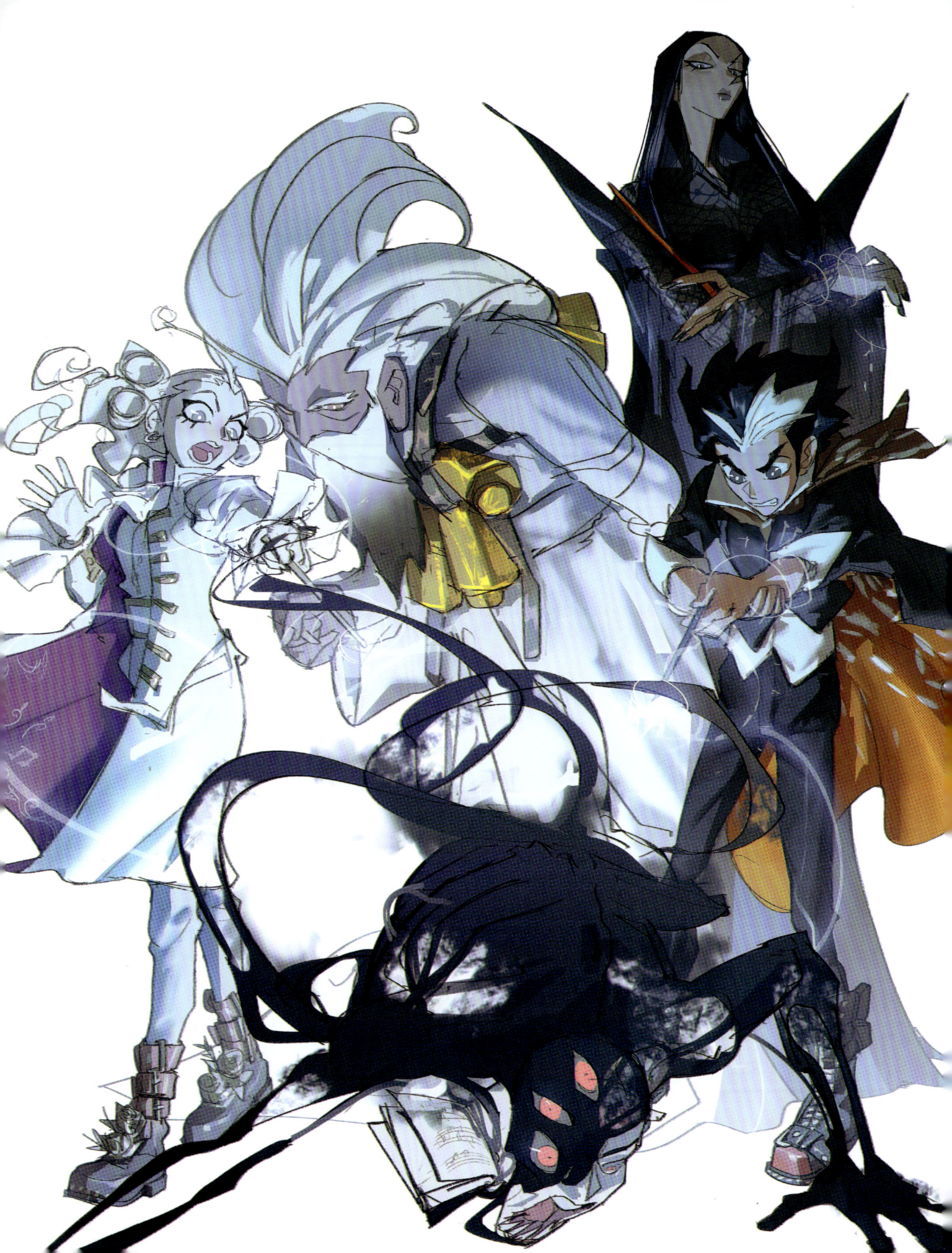

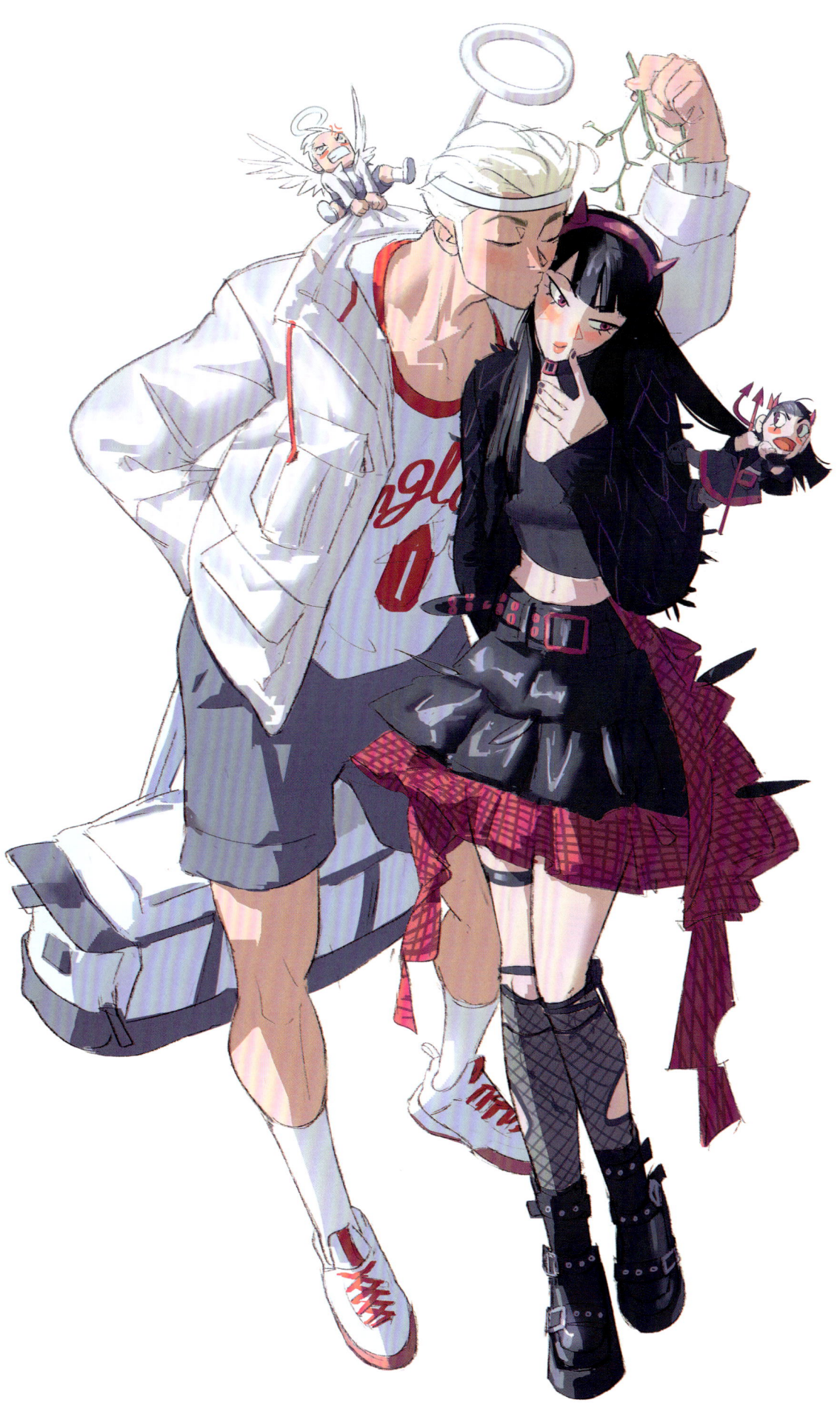

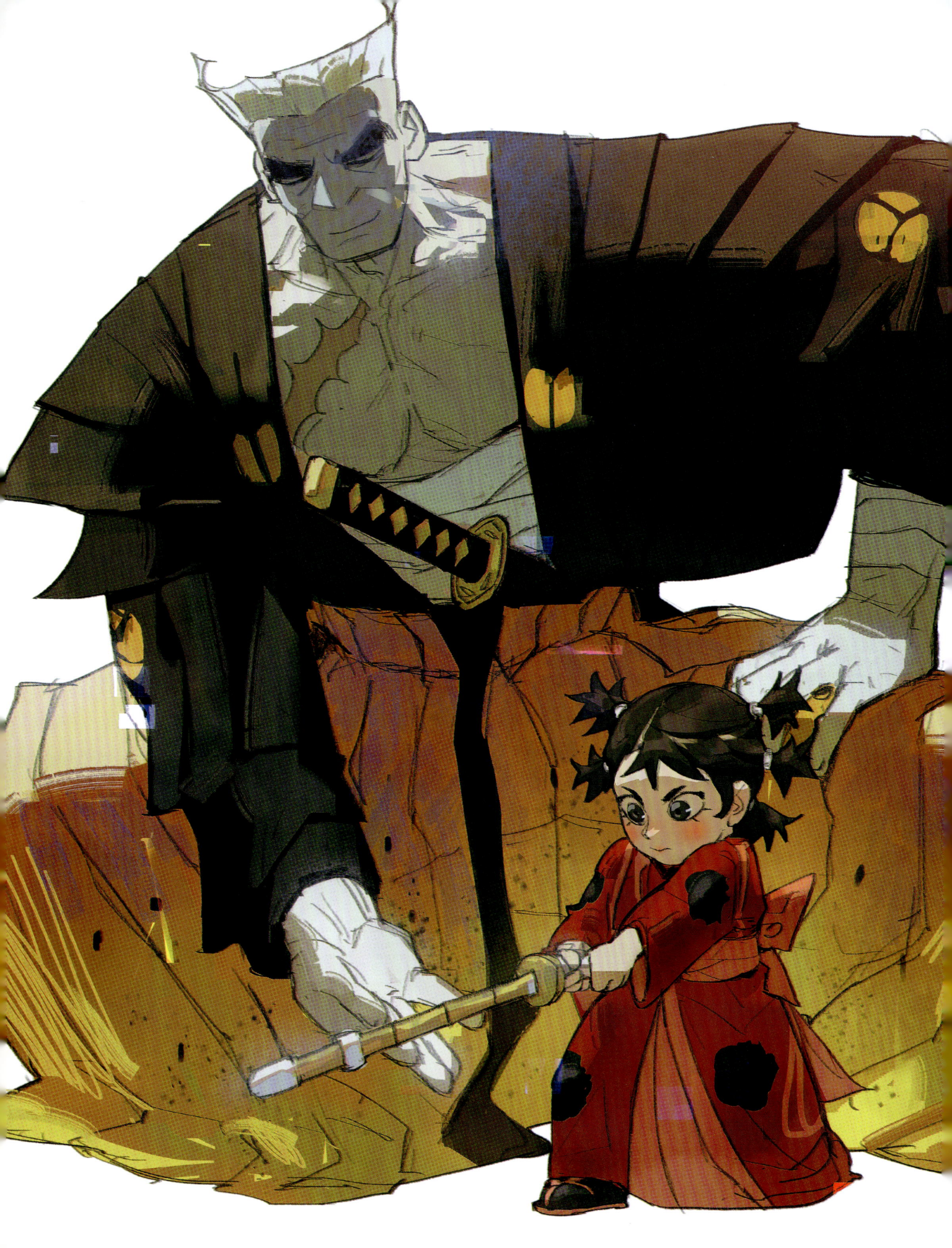

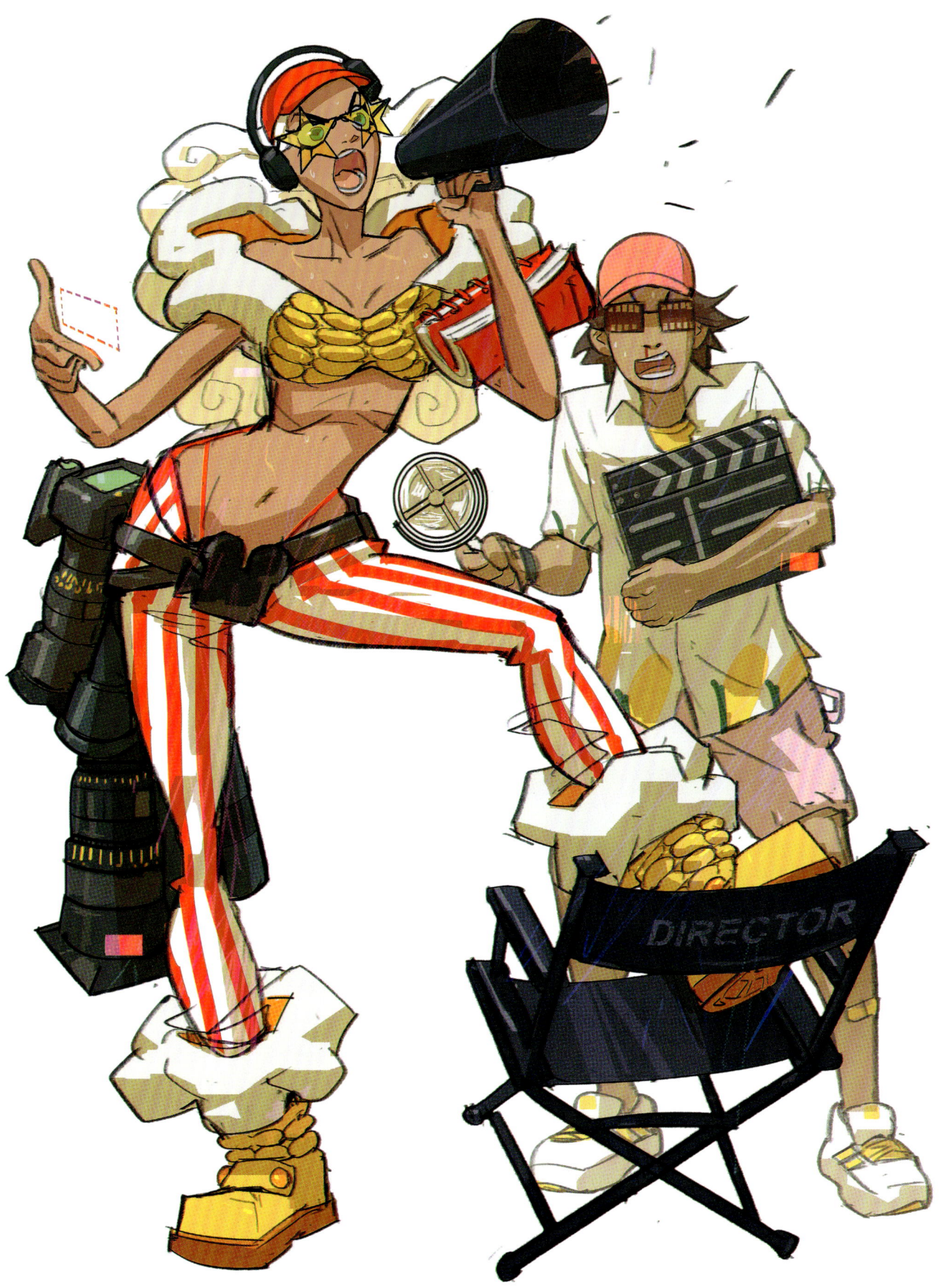

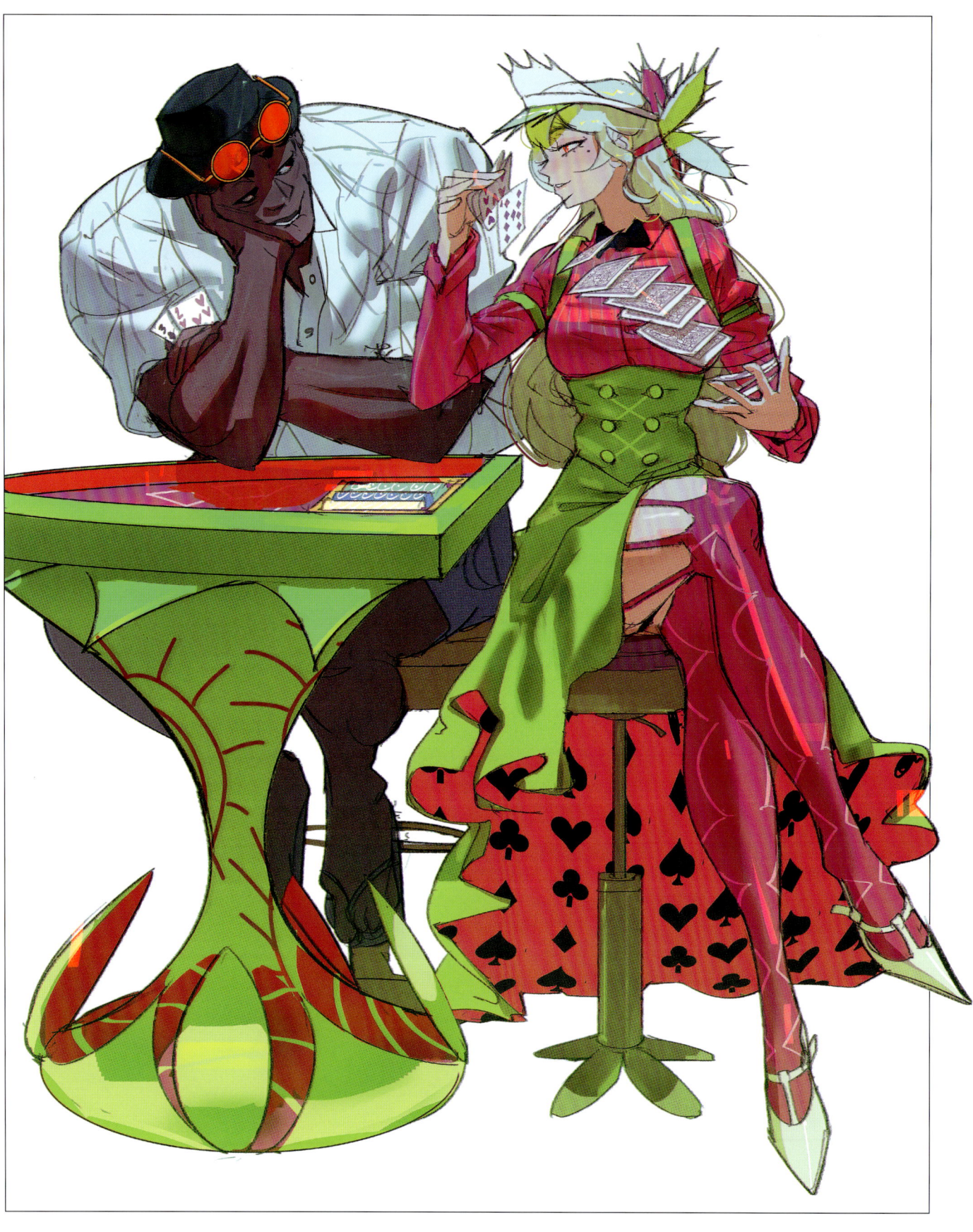

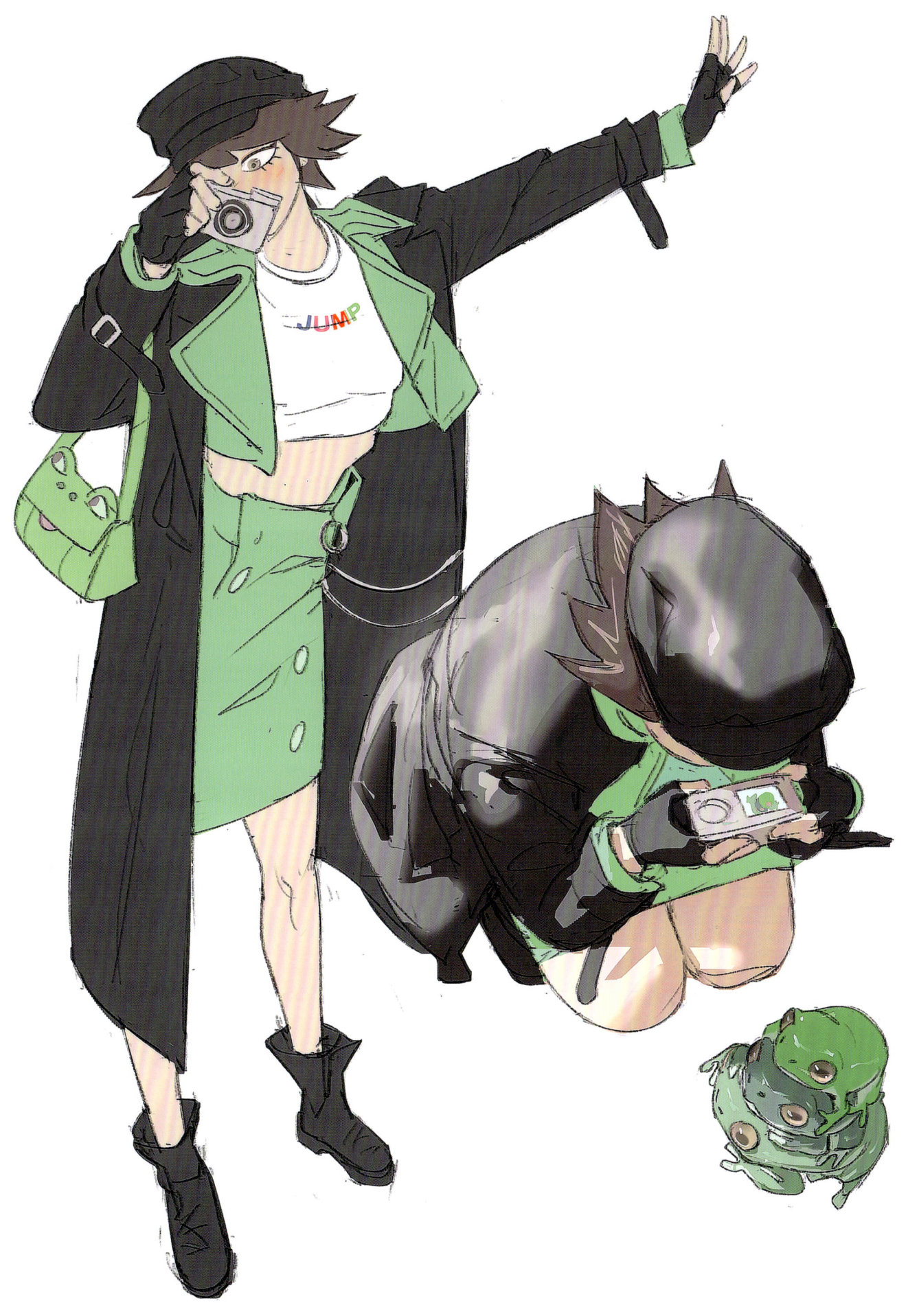

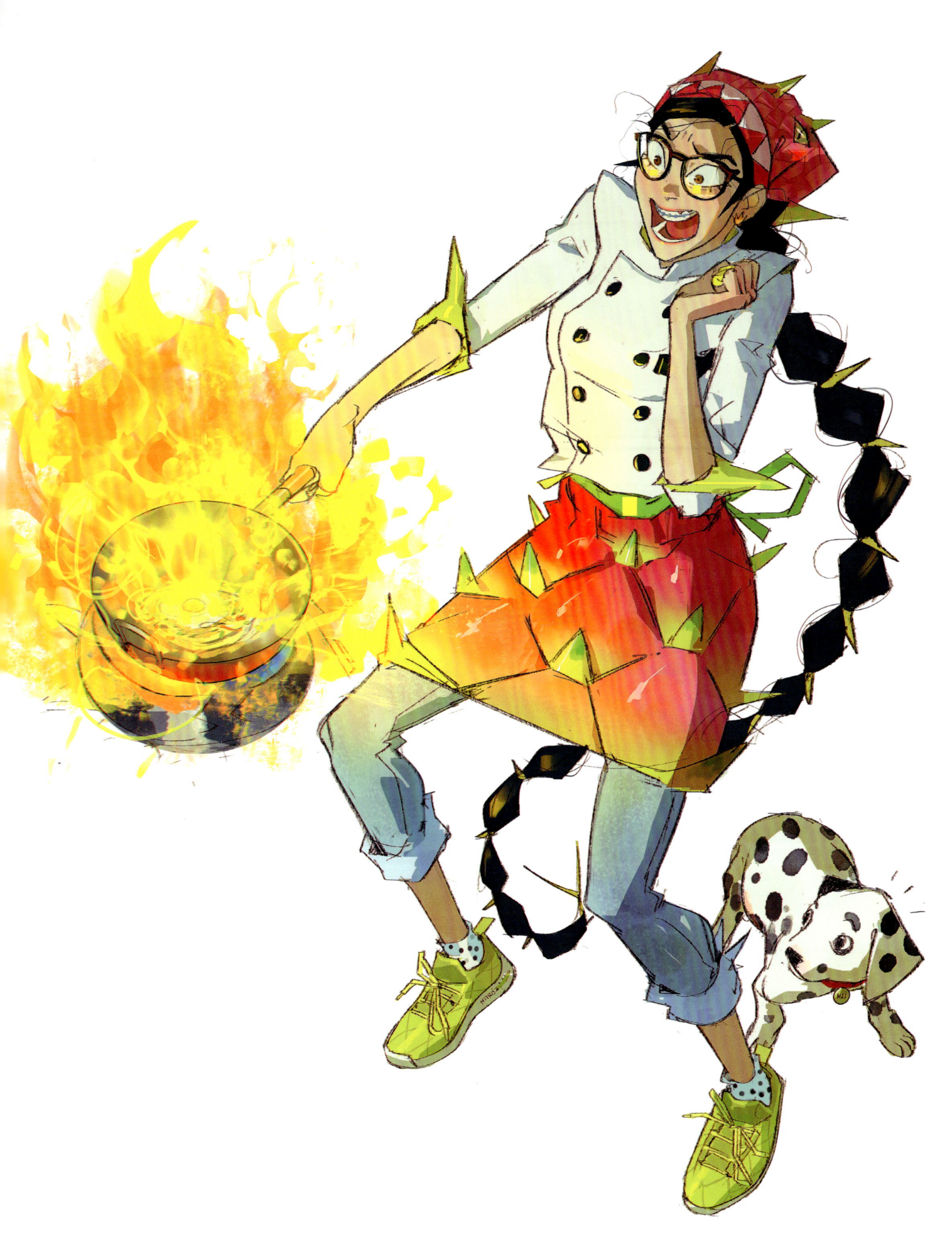

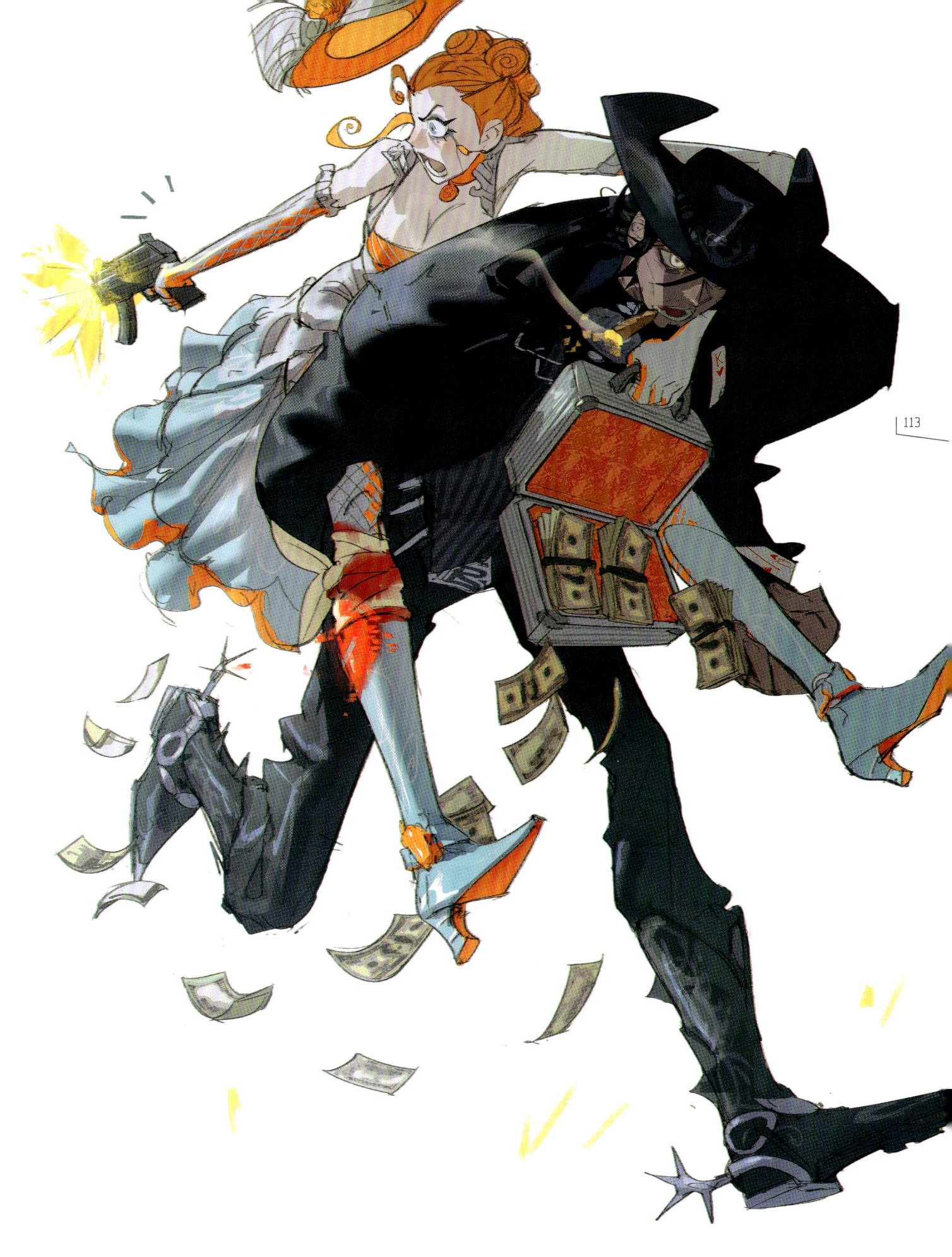

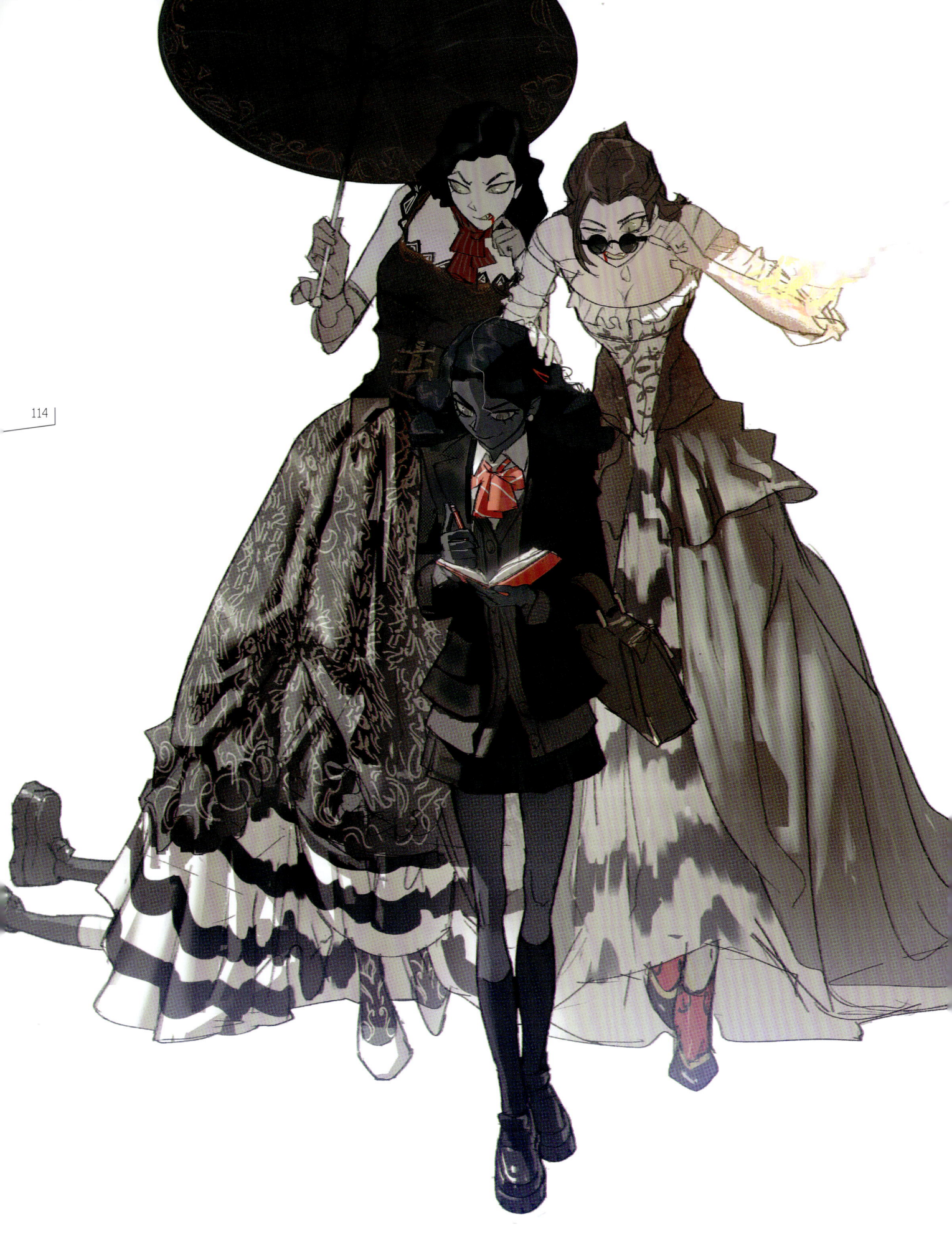

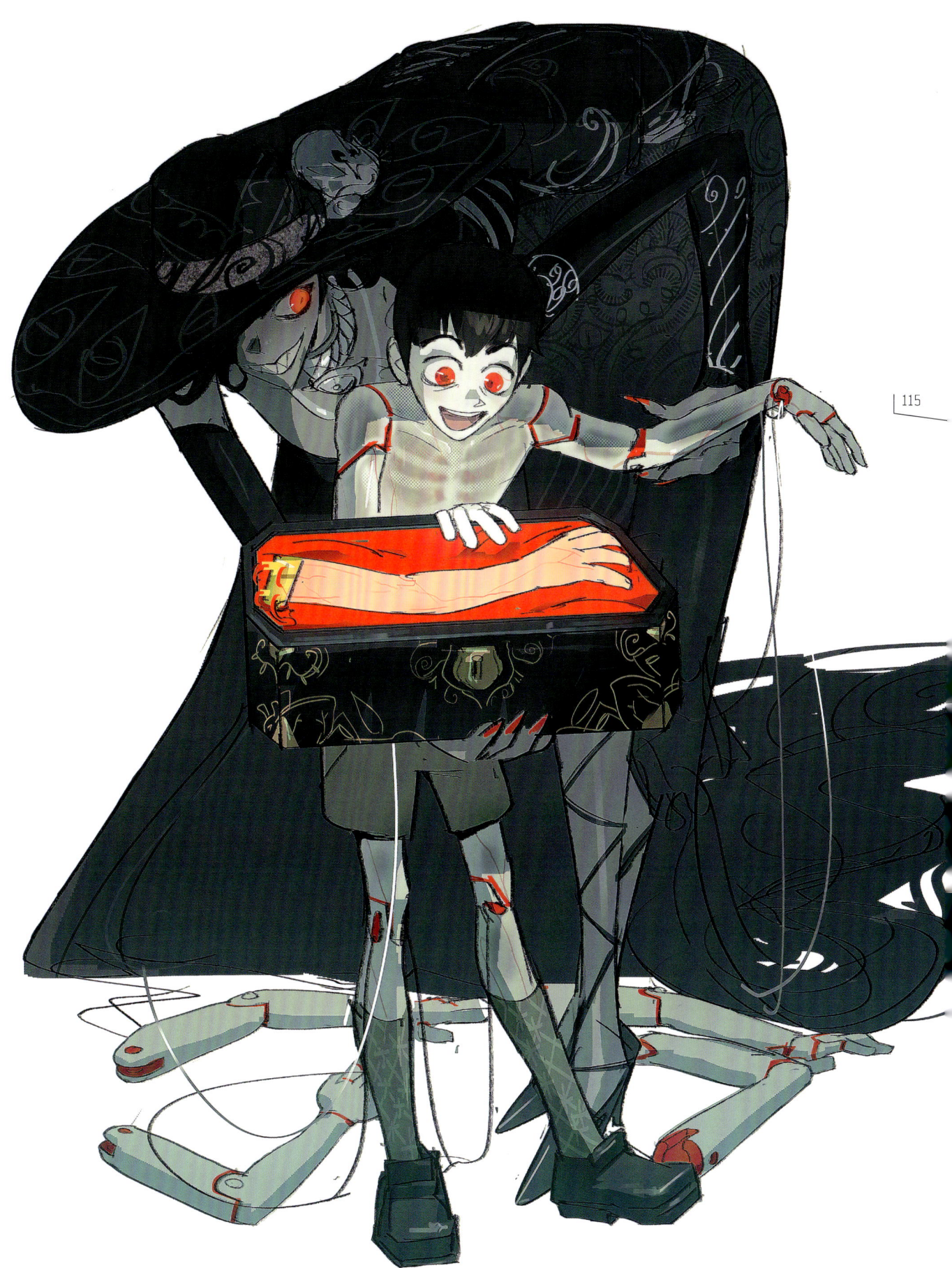

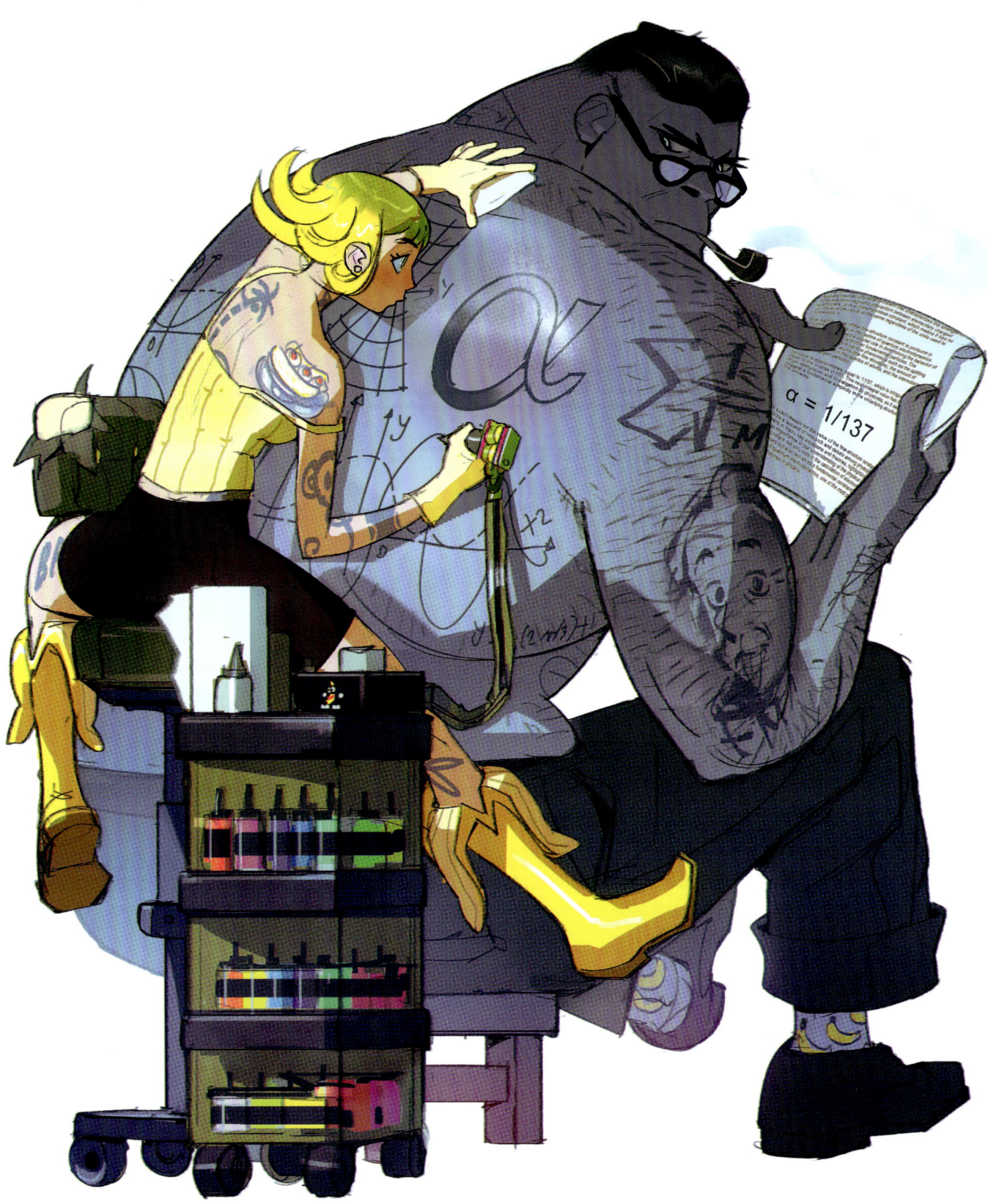

$\alpha = 1/137$

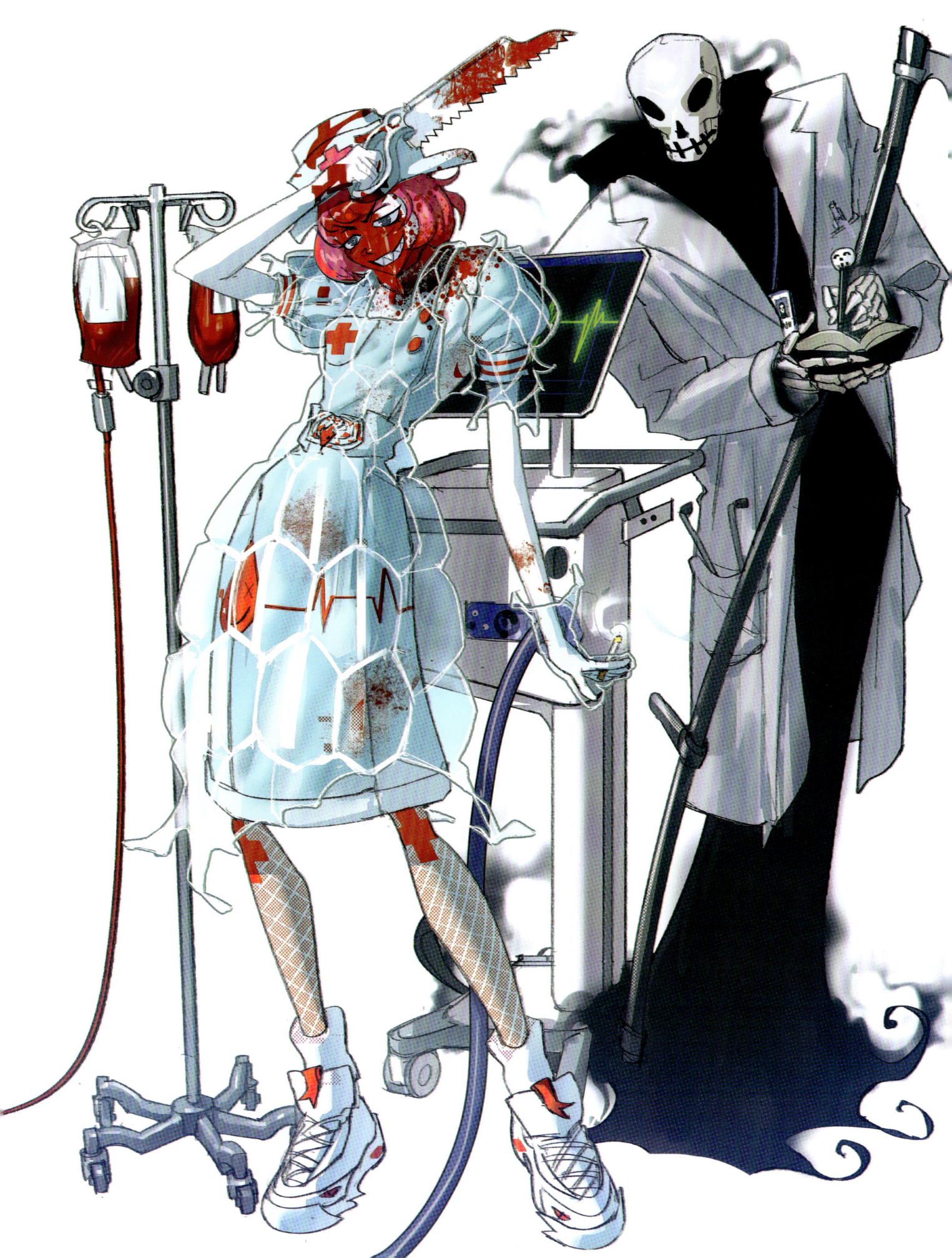

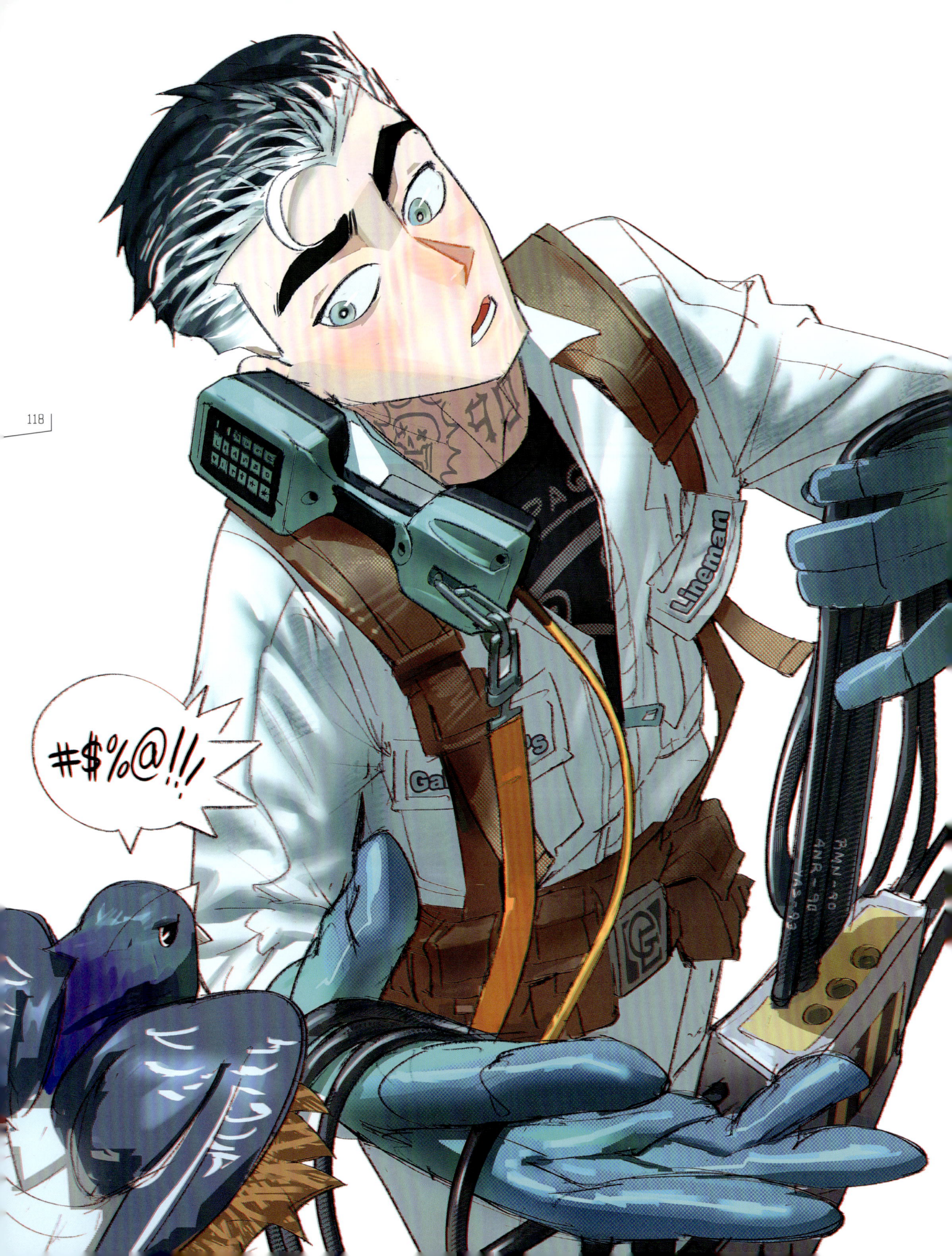

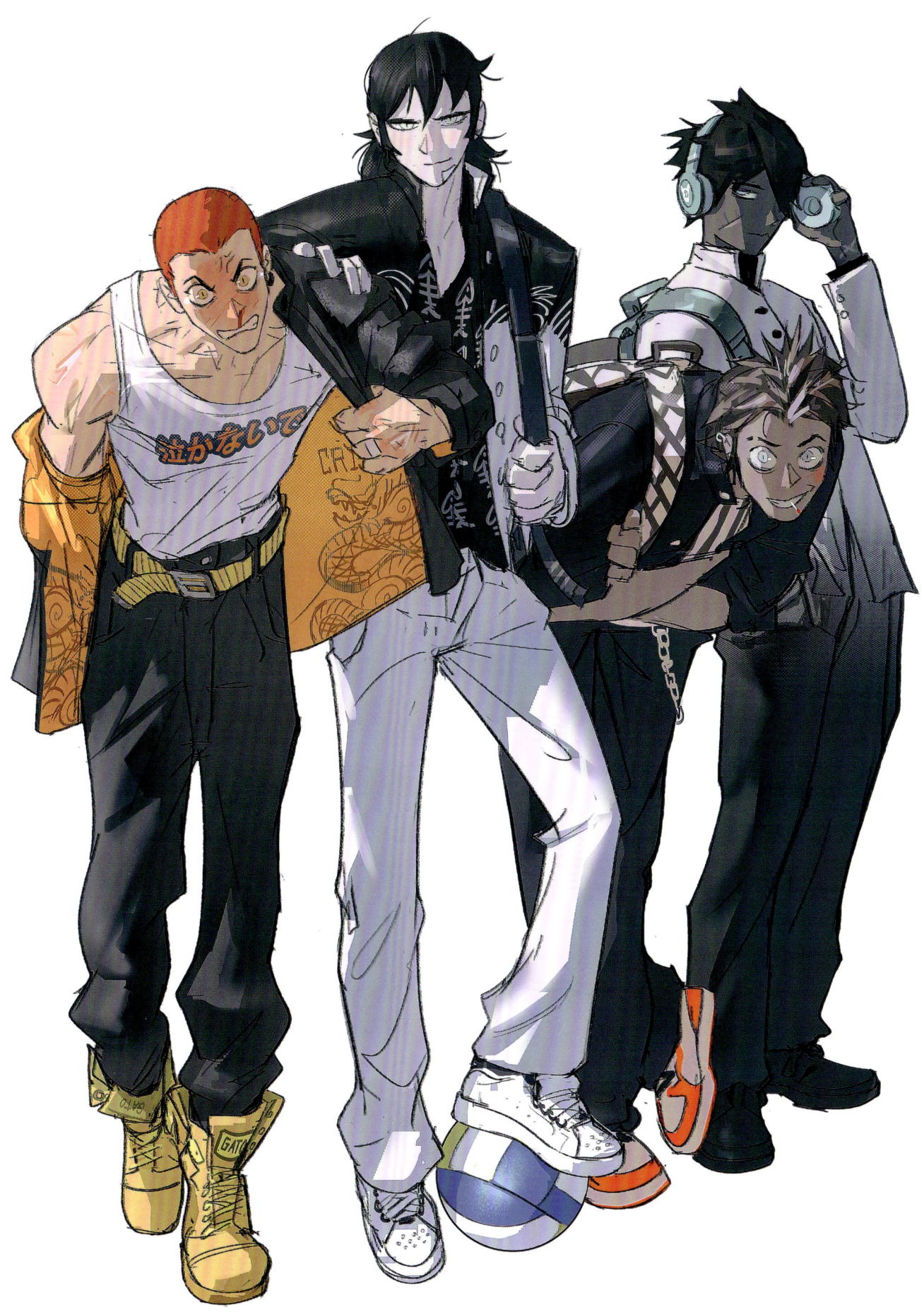

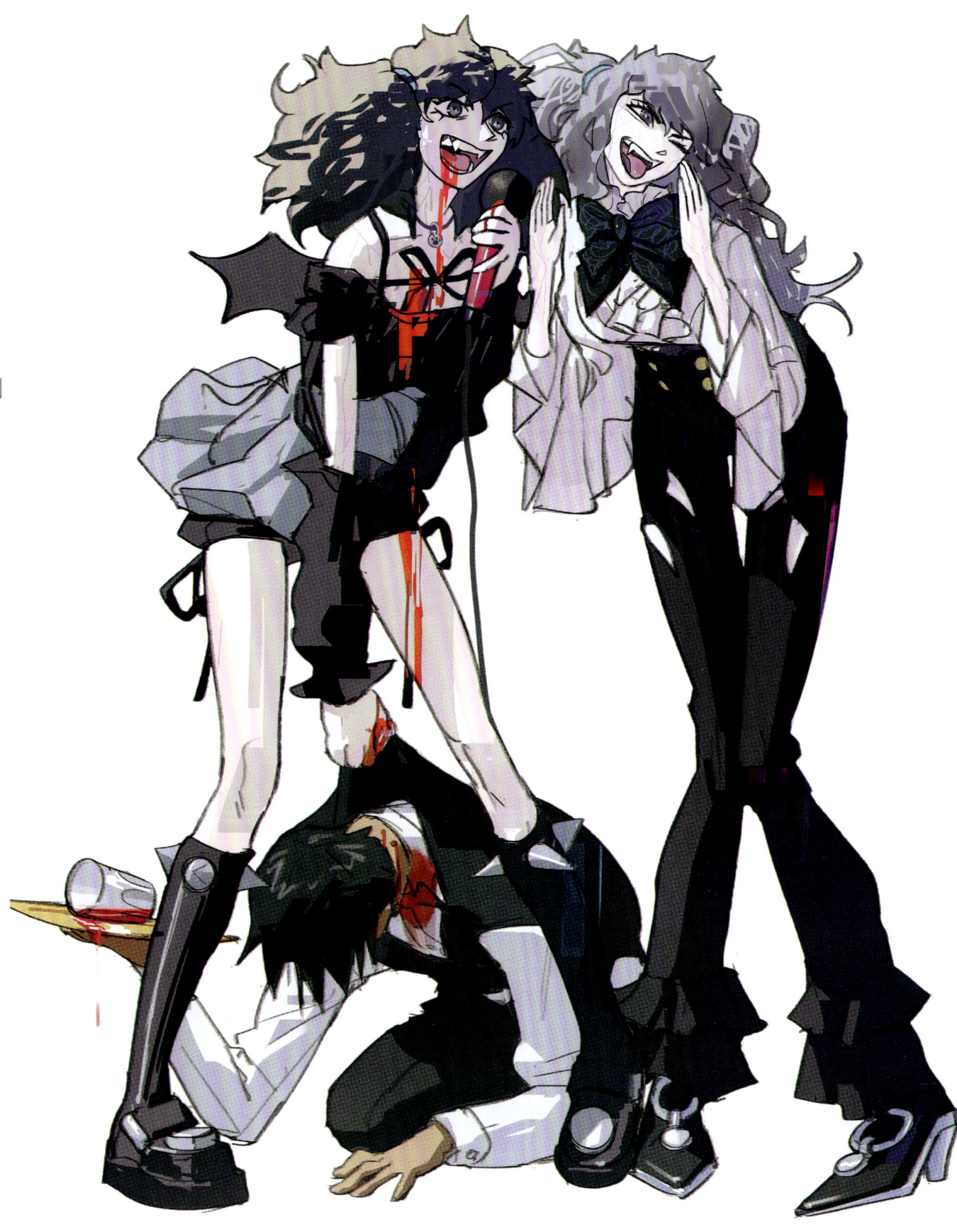

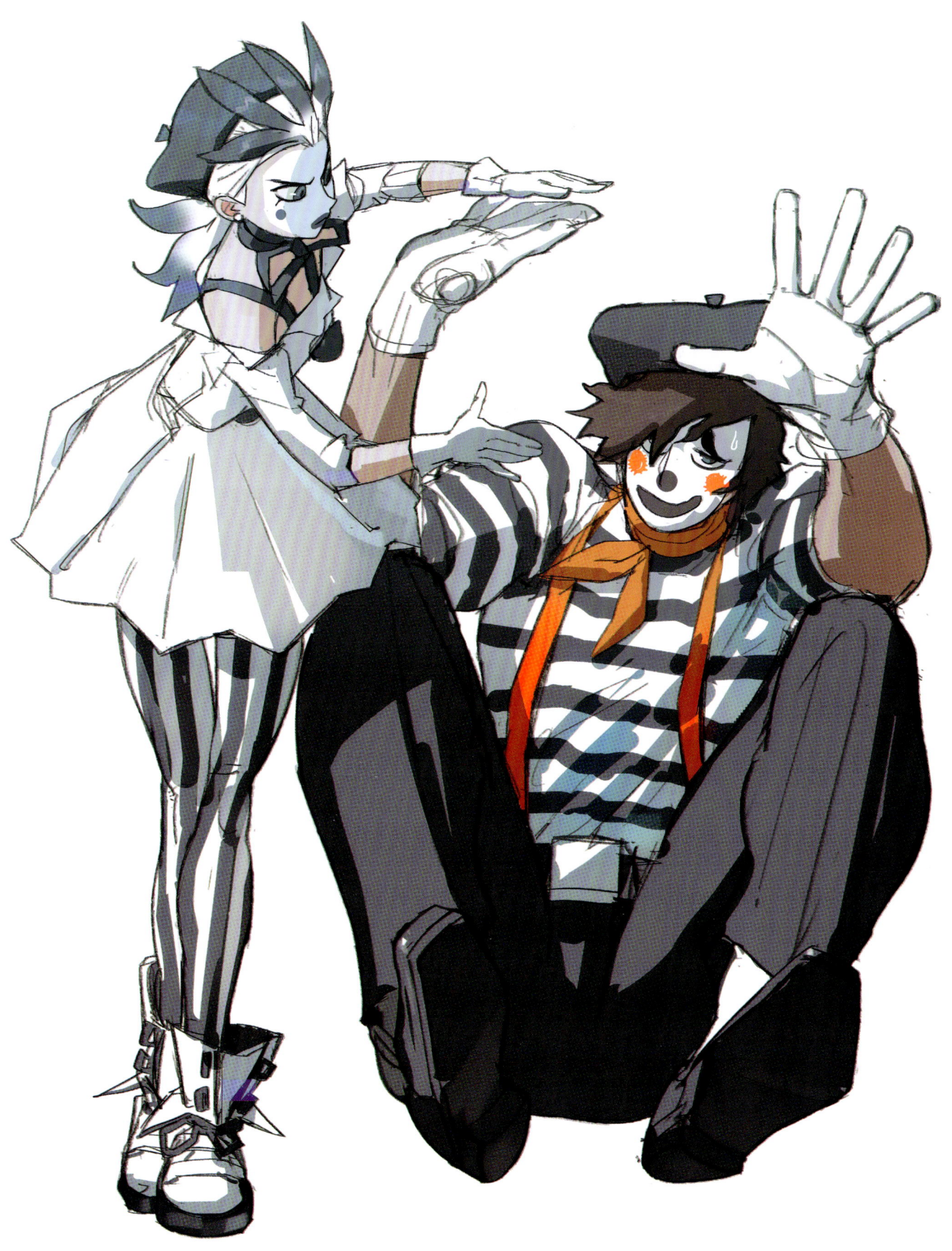

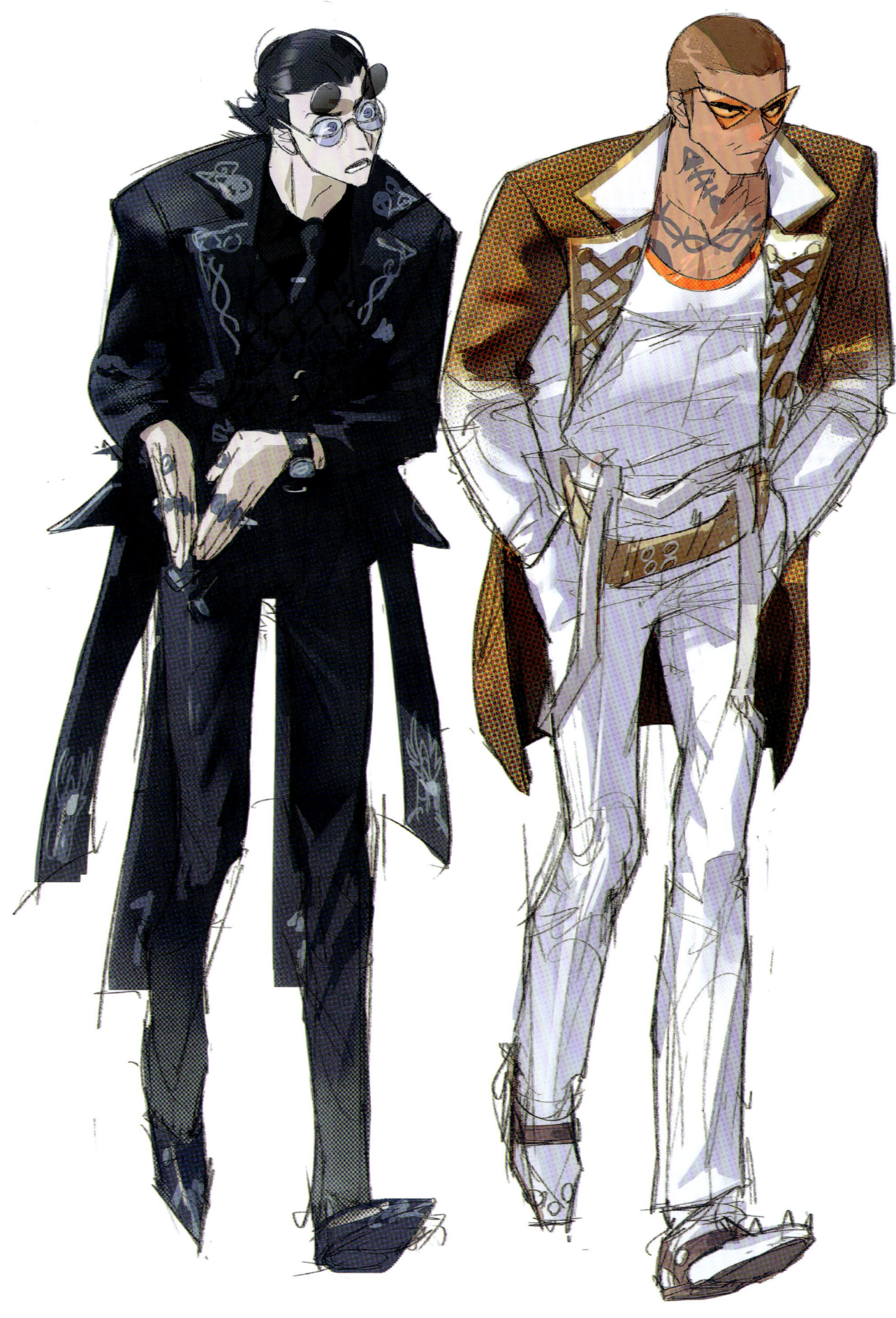

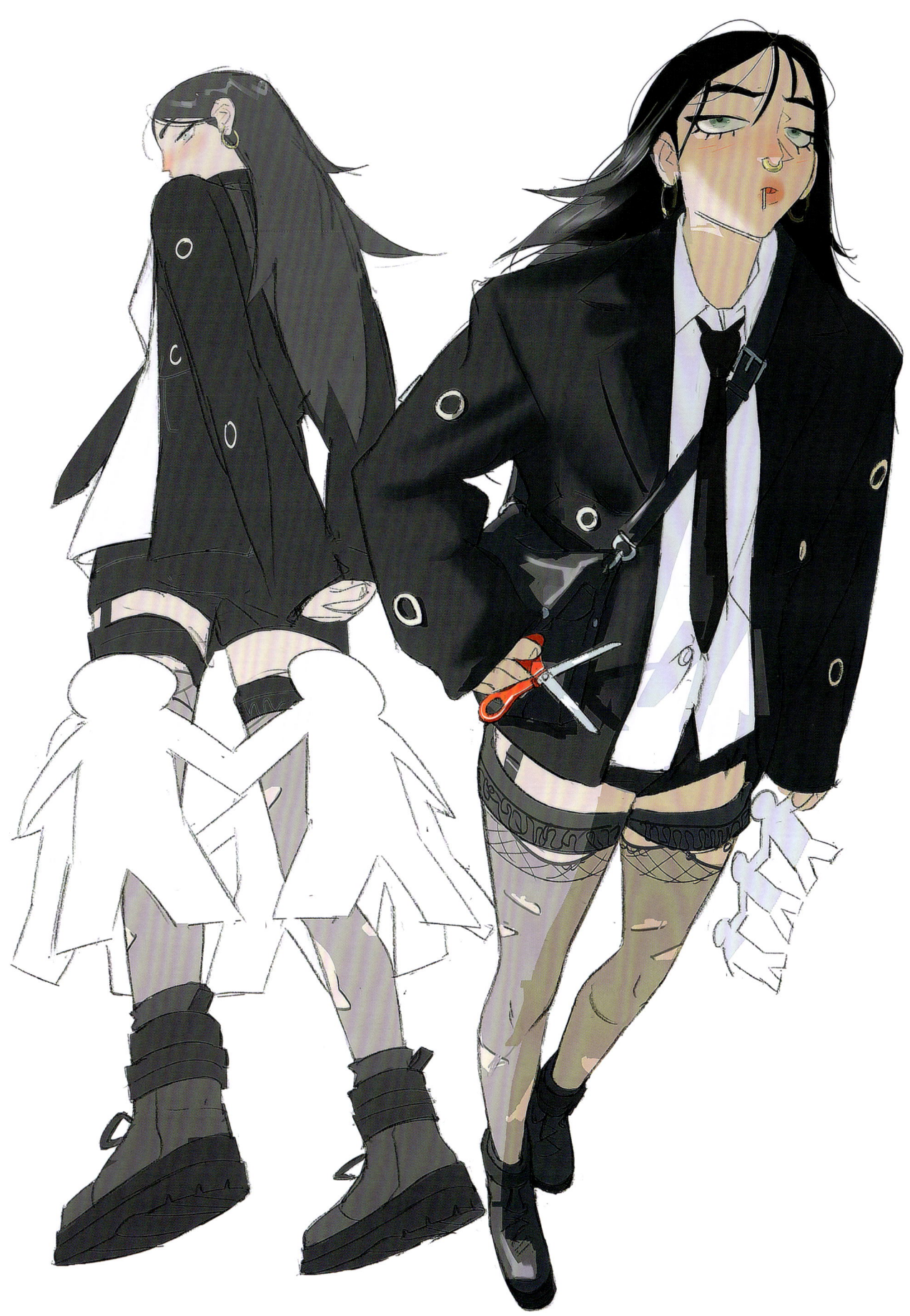

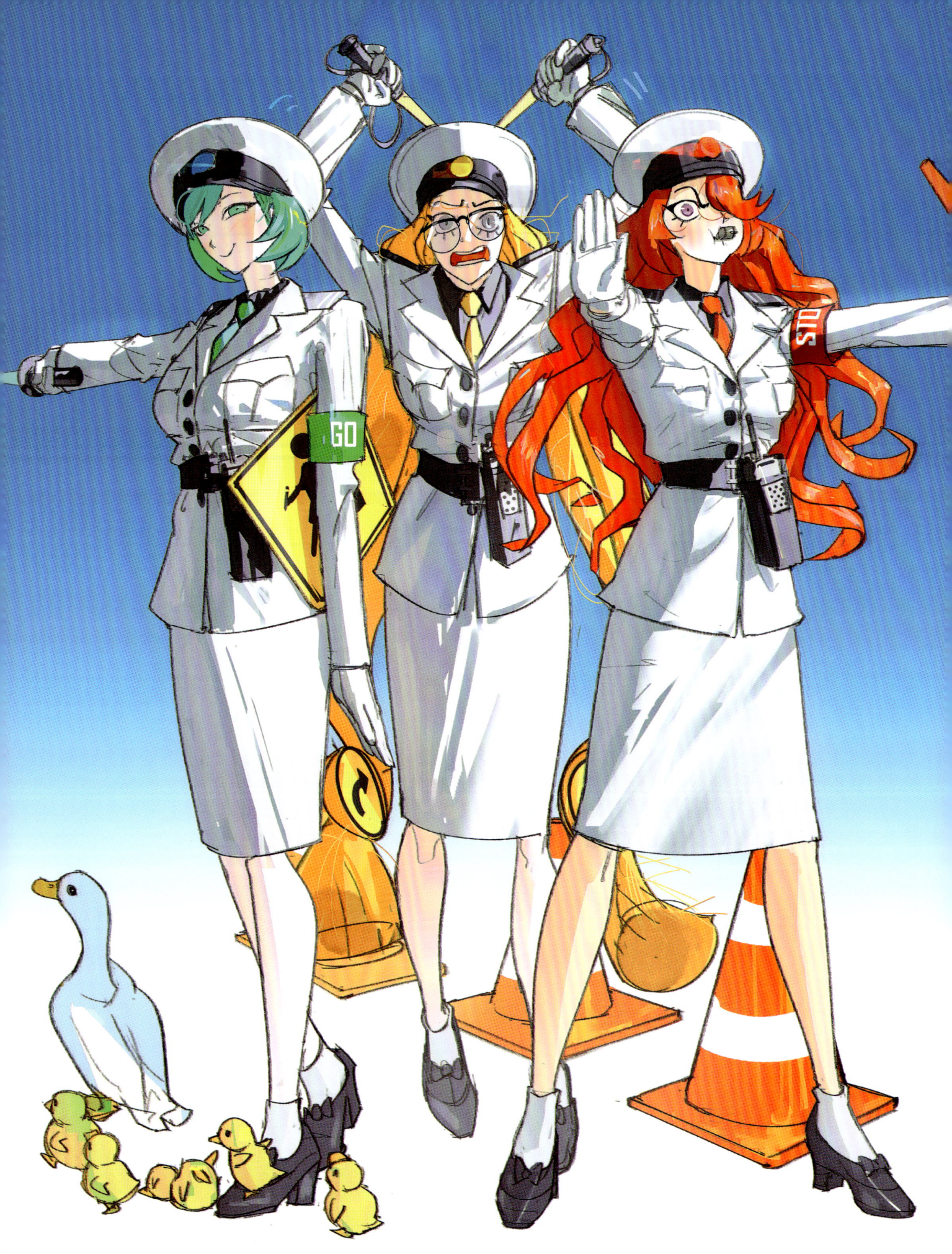

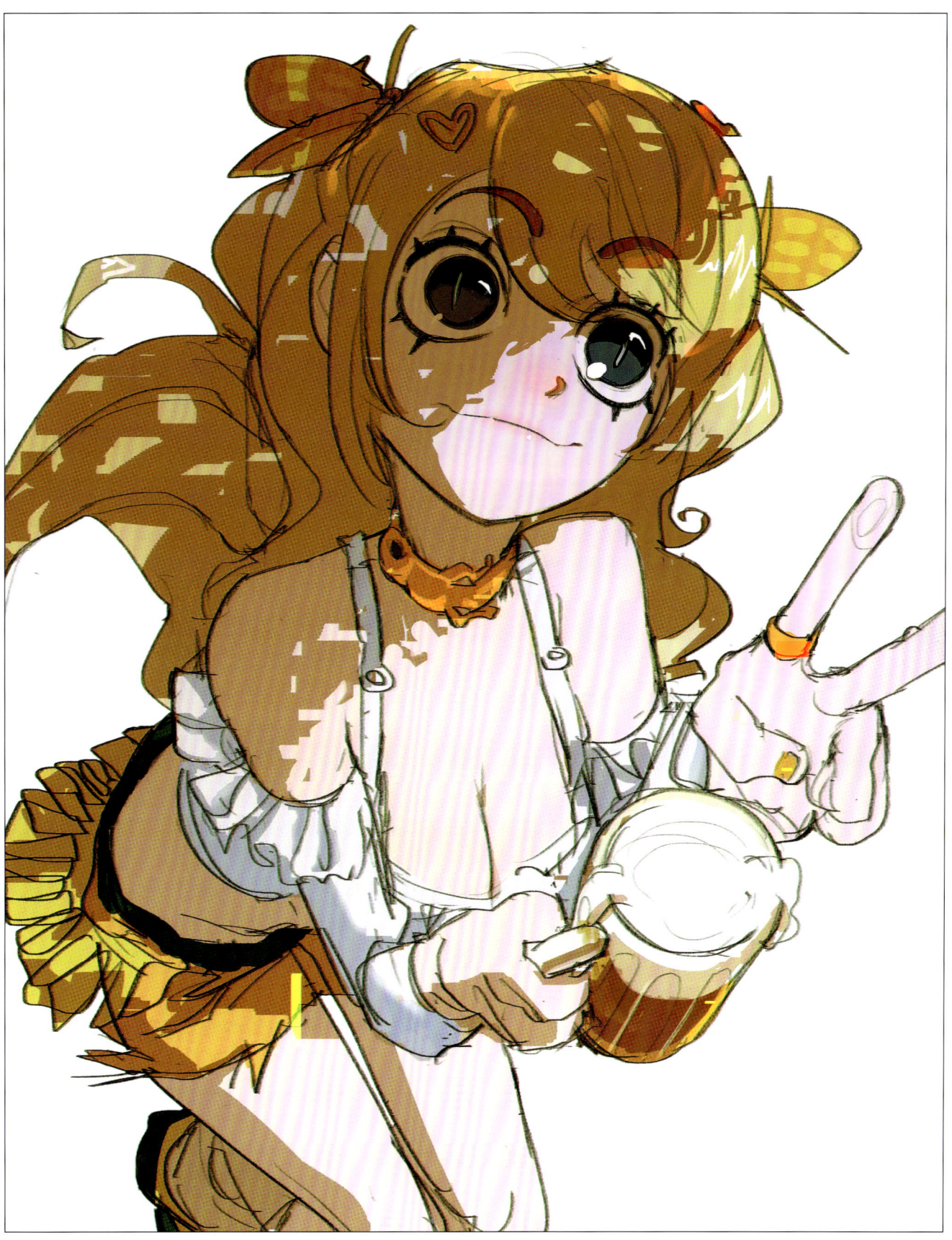

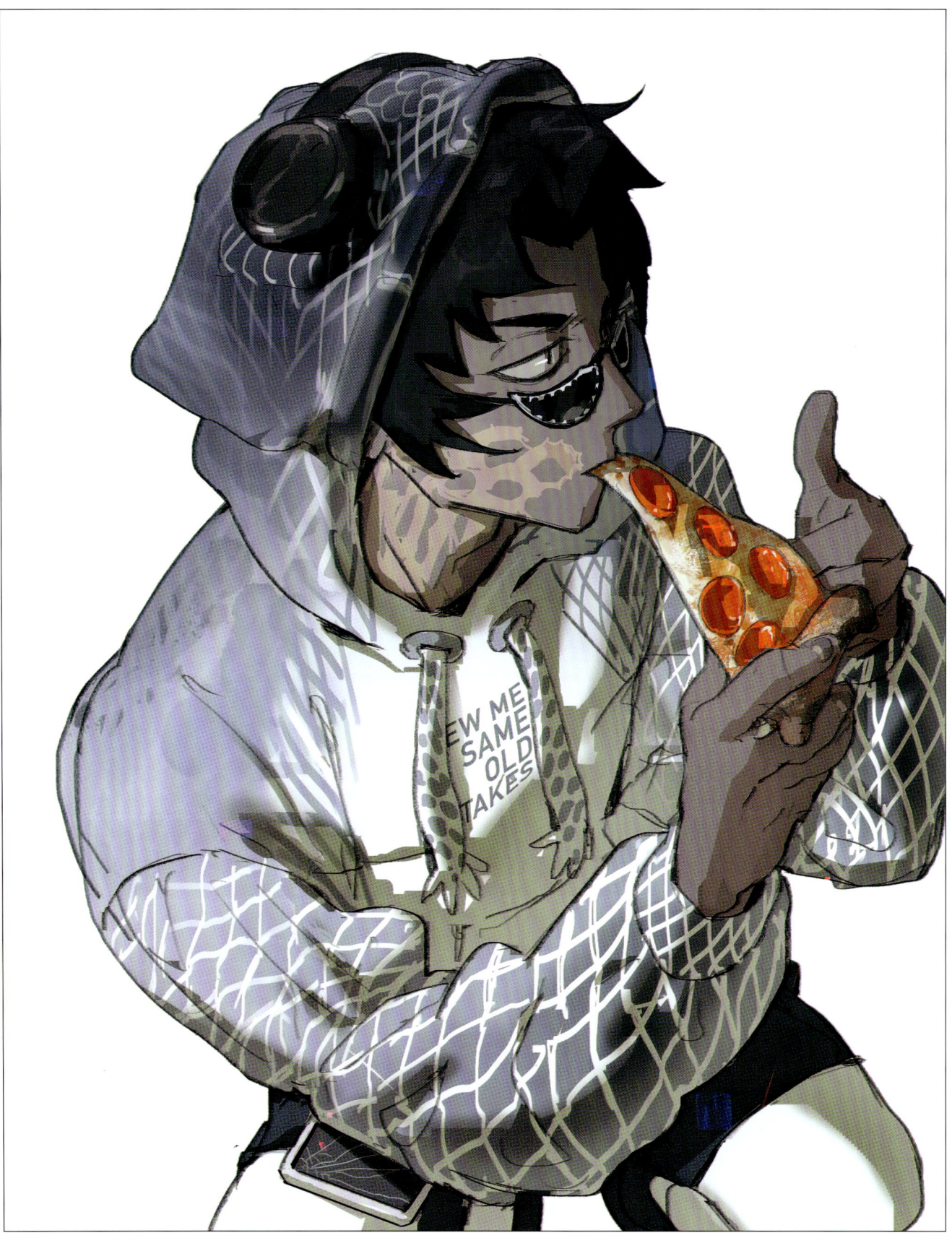

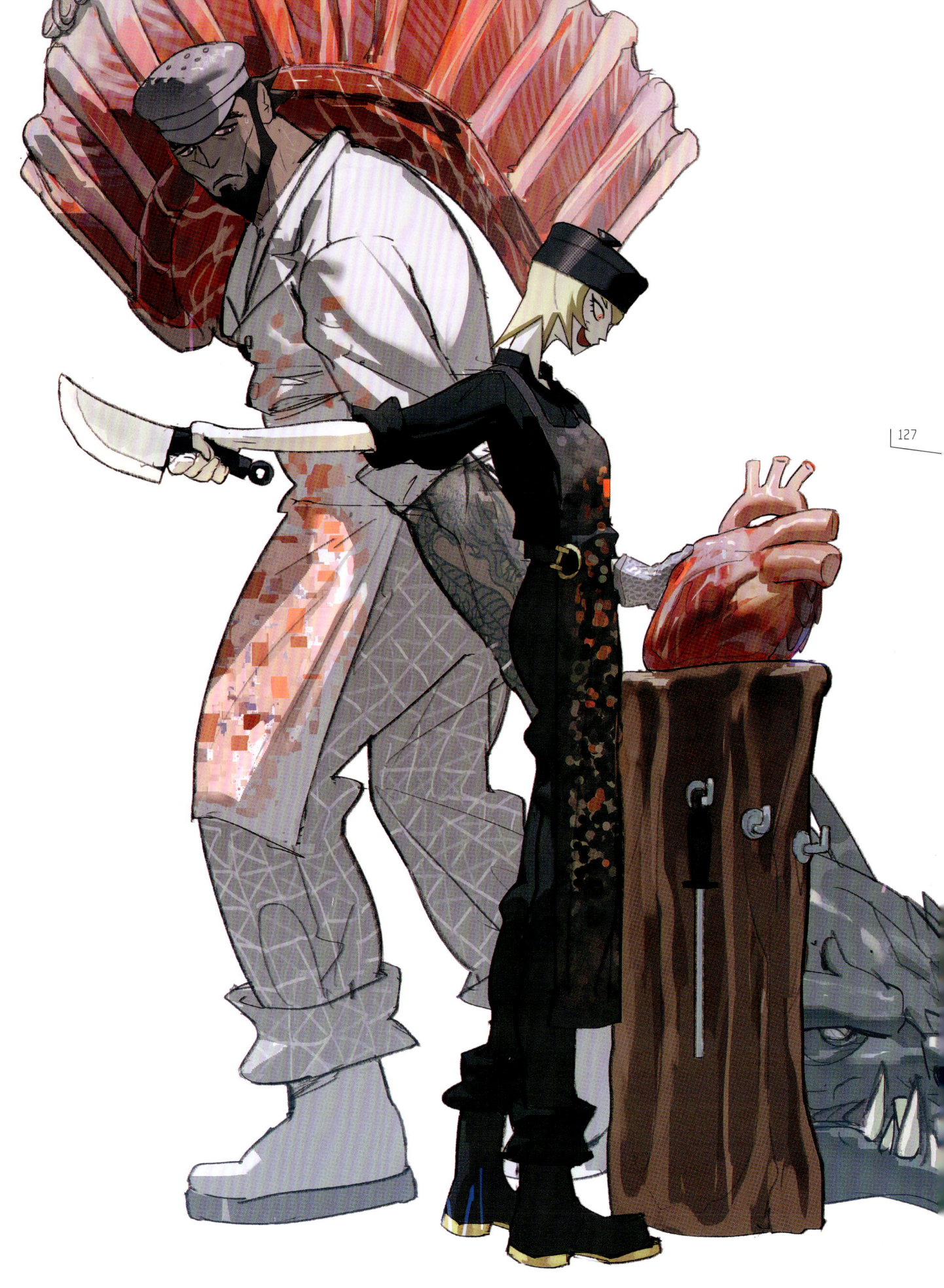

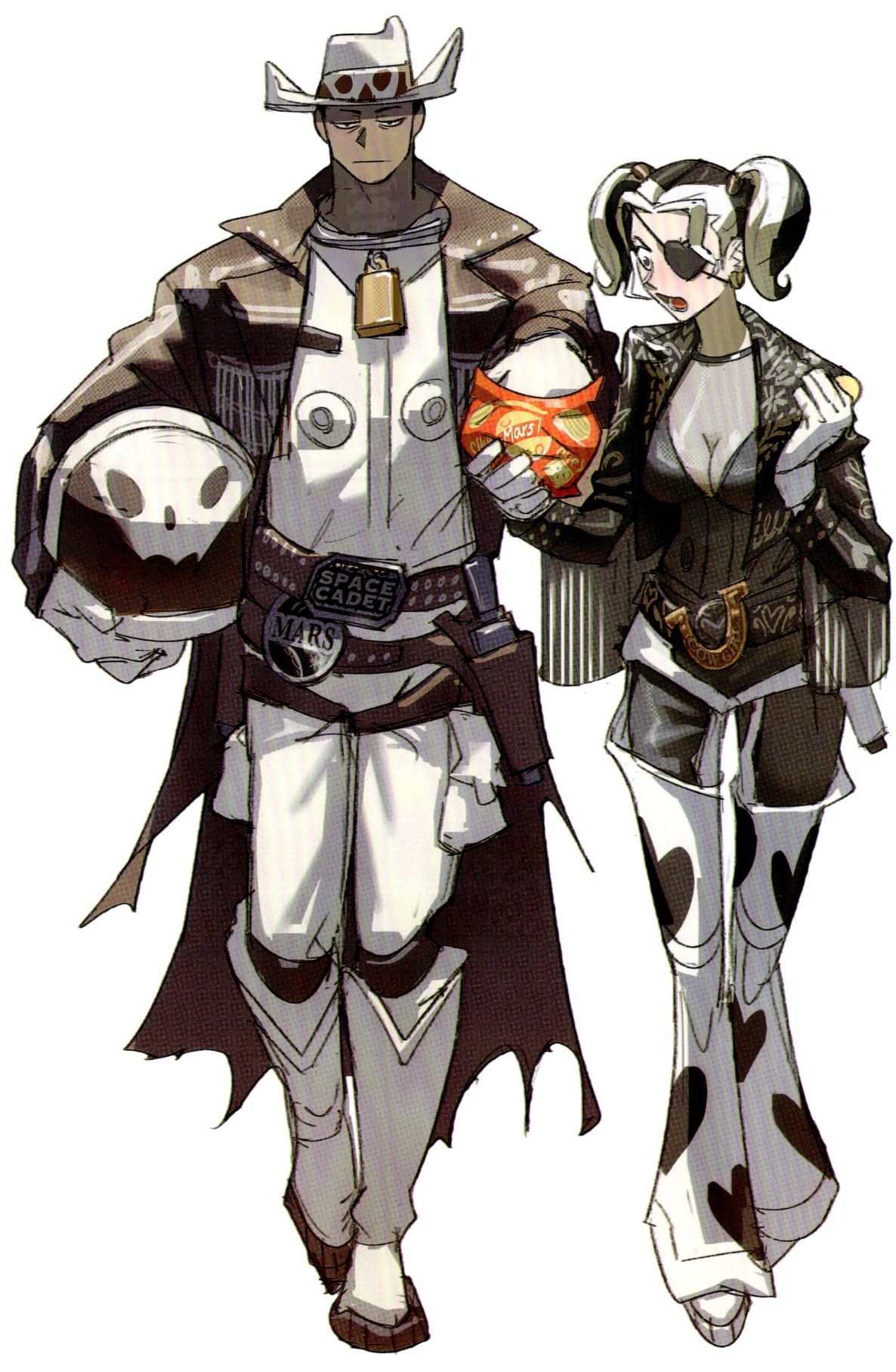

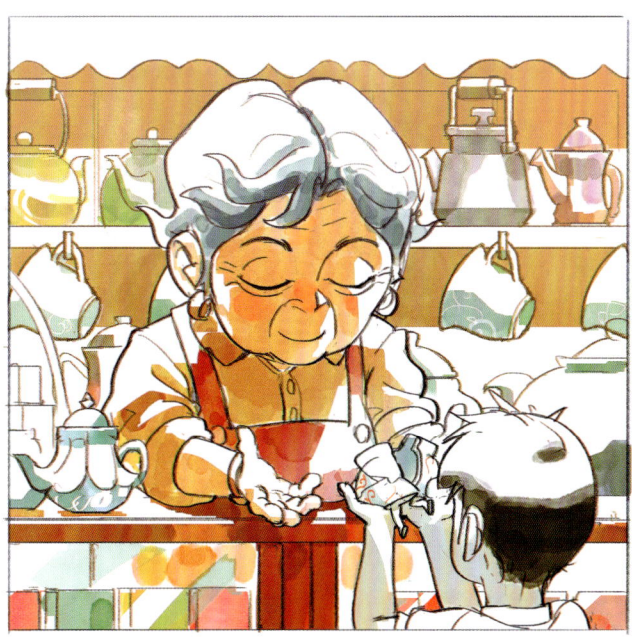

IS YOUR HEART BROKEN AGAIN?

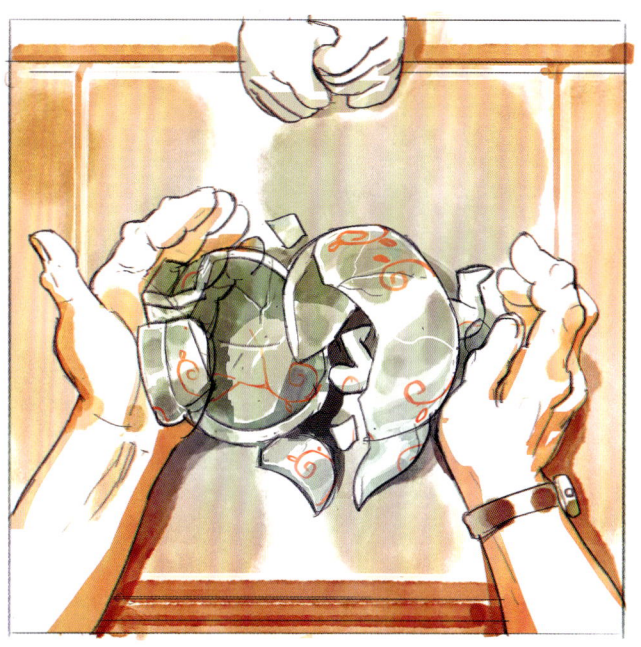

SOMETIMES IT FEELS LIKE WE'RE
IN LOVE WITH GRAVITY

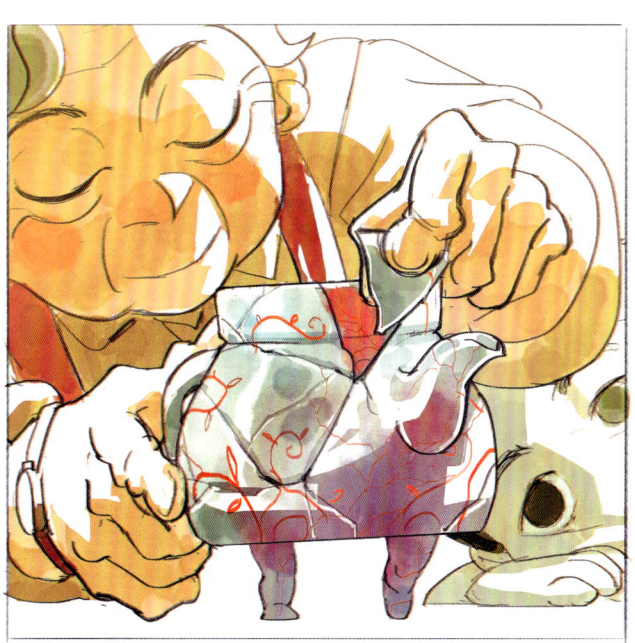

OH YES, WE WILL FALL AGAIN, BUT
FALLING ISN'T ALWAYS PAIN

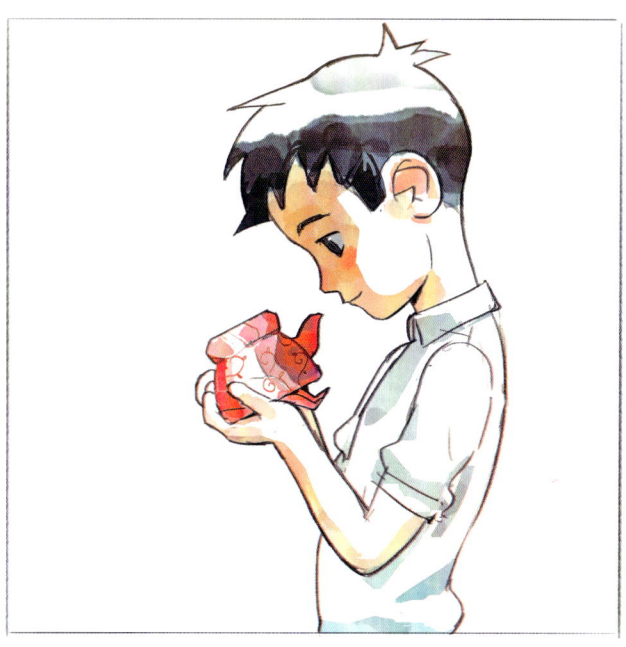

WE MUST FIX IT, AND ONE DAY,
SOMEONE MAY HOLD IT WITH US

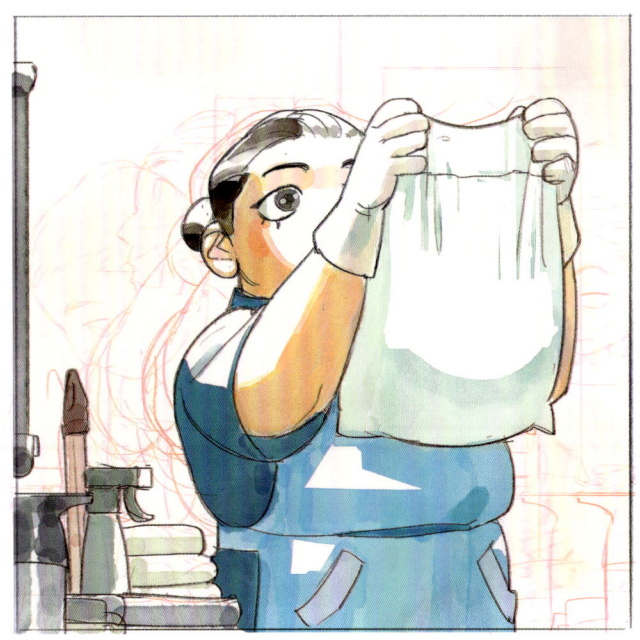

I'M HOMELESS WITH A HOME

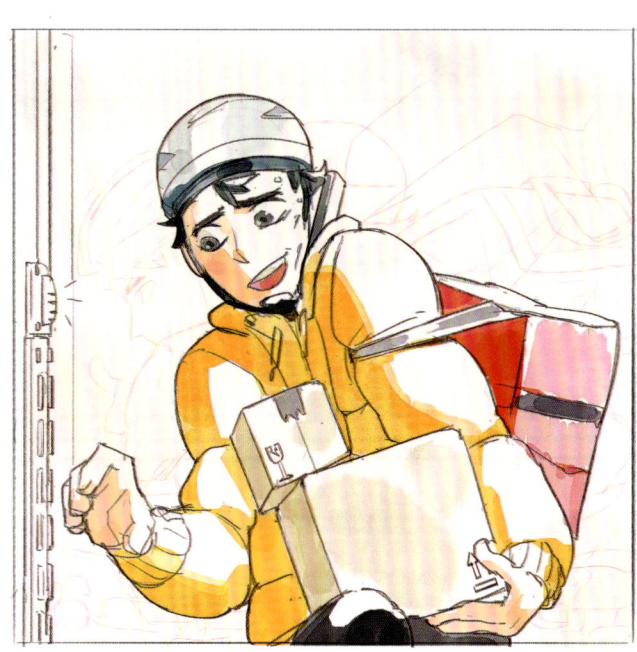

I HEAR LOVED ONES I CANNOT HOLD

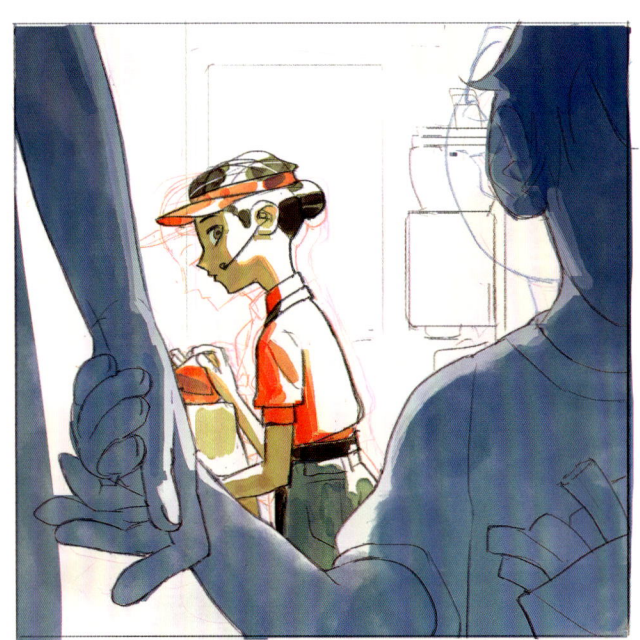

I'M AWAKE, YET I STILL DREAM

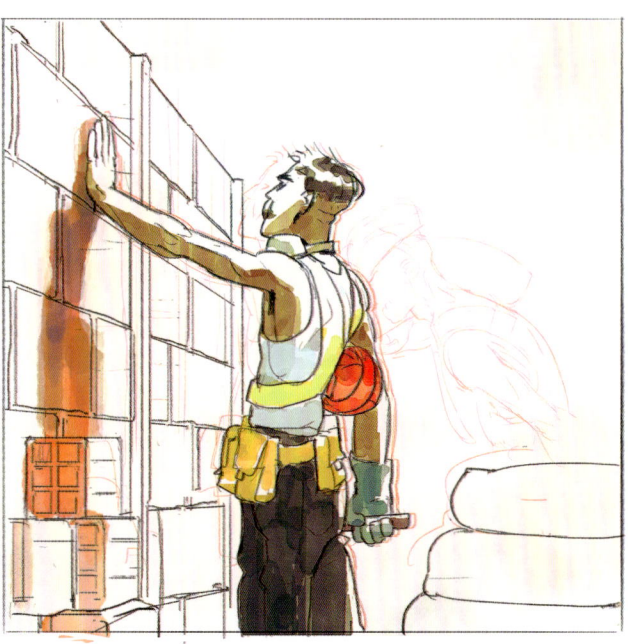

TO BUILD A PLACE WITH ALL WITHIN

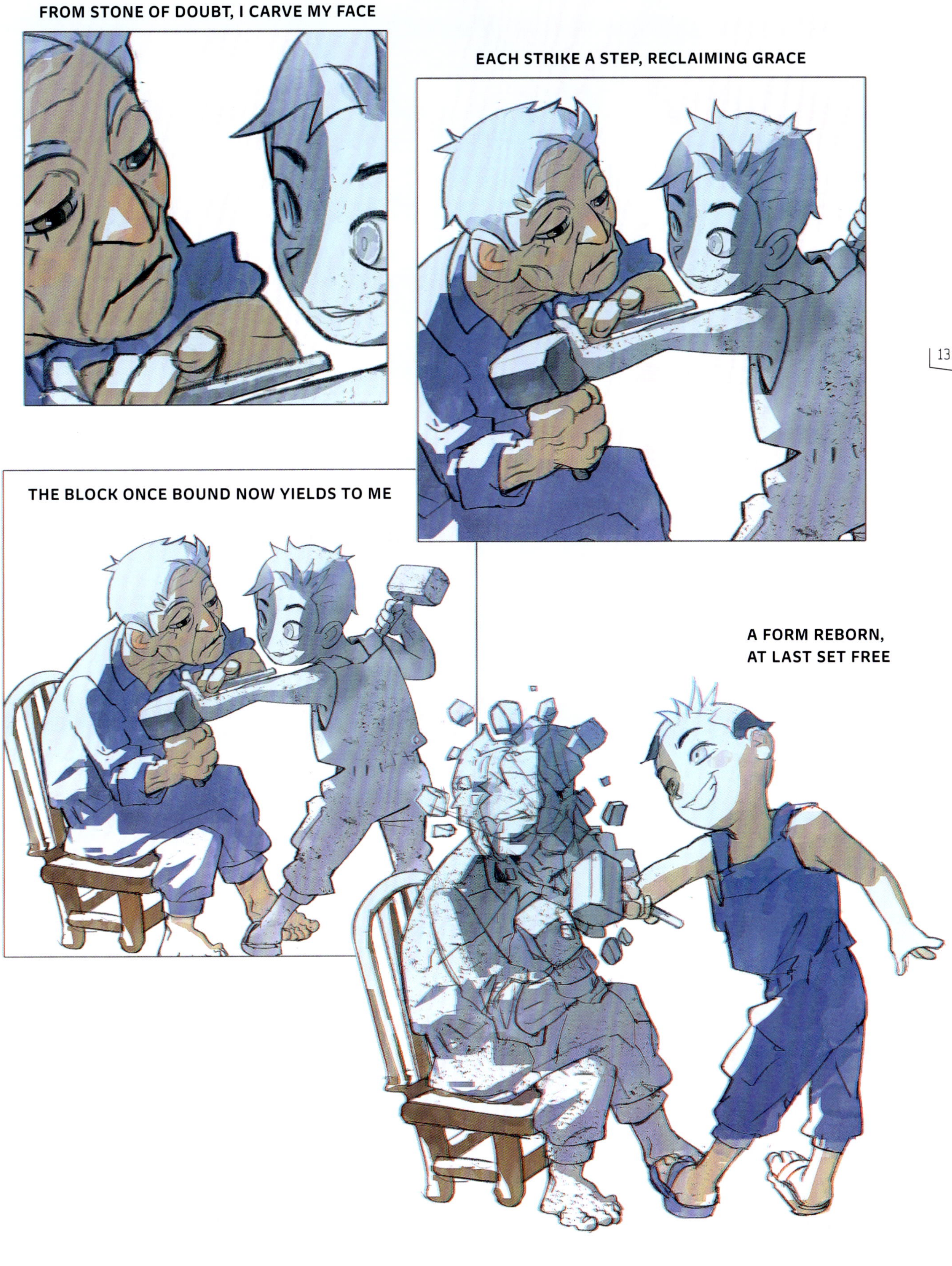

FROM STONE OF DOUBT, I CARVE MY FACE

EACH STRIKE A STEP, RECLAIMING GRACE

THE BLOCK ONCE BOUND NOW YIELDS TO ME

A FORM REBORN,
AT LAST SET FREE

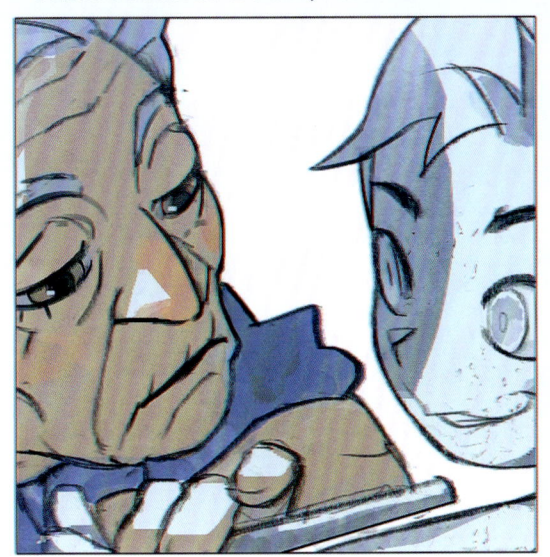

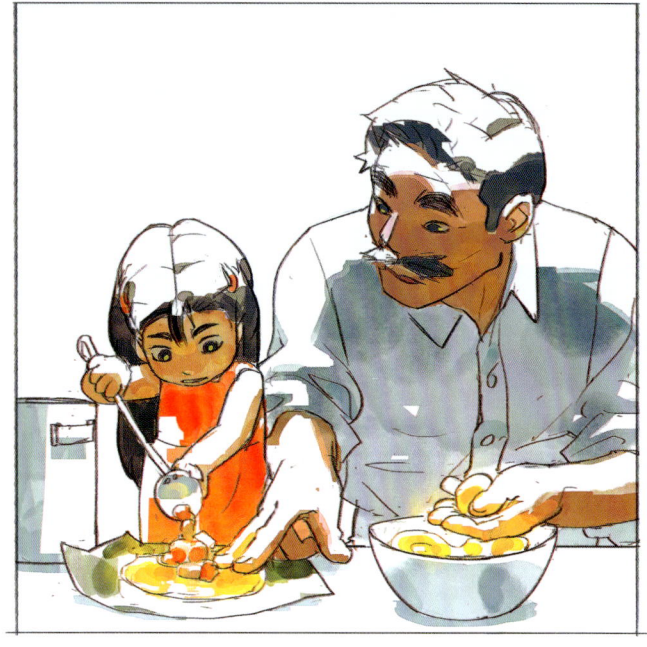

WE SHAPED IT SO IT WOULD NOT FADE

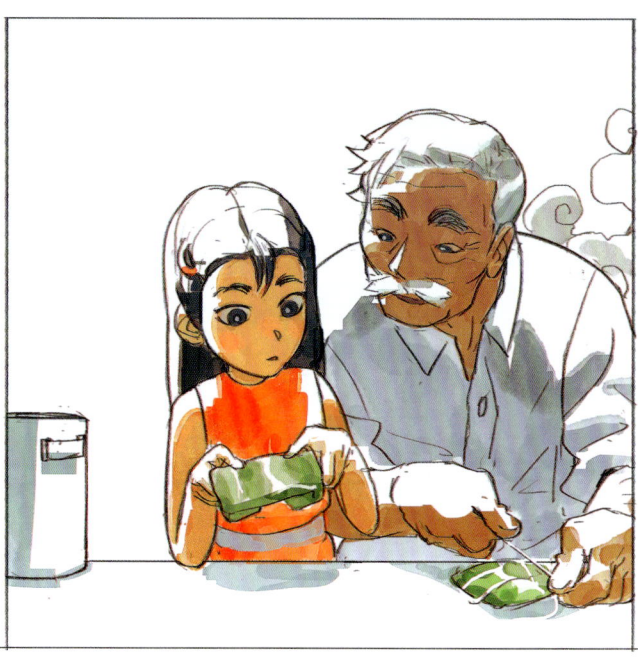

WE SEALED IT TO KEEP IT SAFE

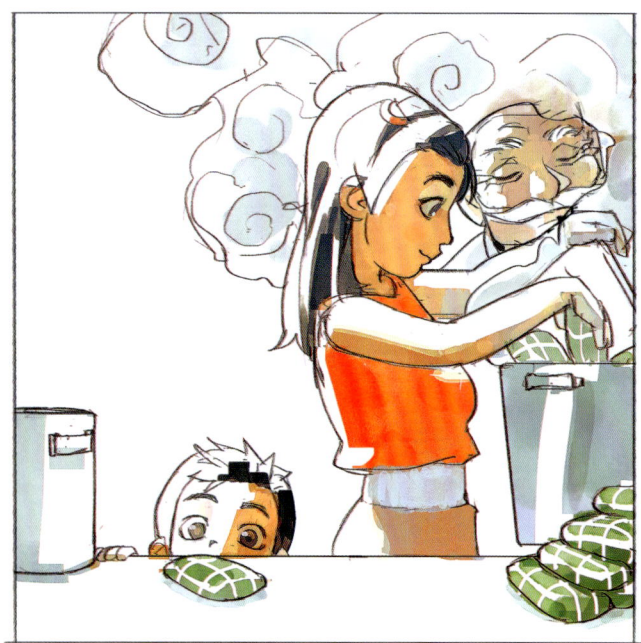

WE LET WARM MEMORIES TAKE HOLD

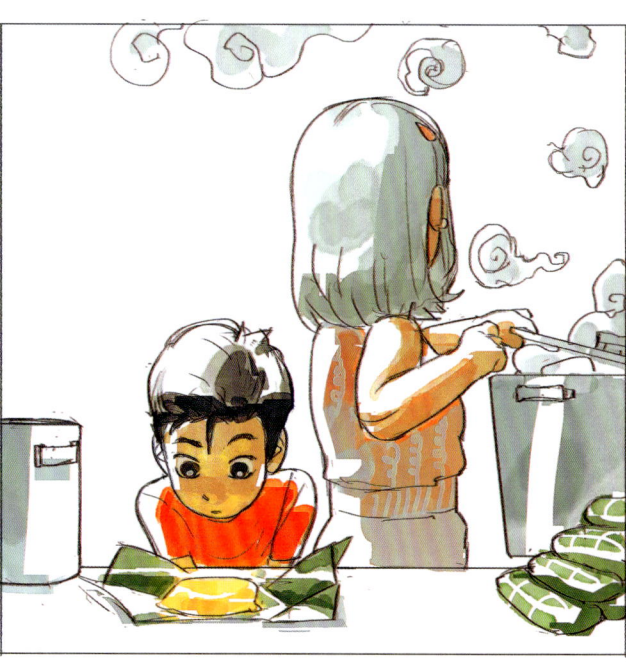

WE MADE IT A STORY FOREVER TOLD

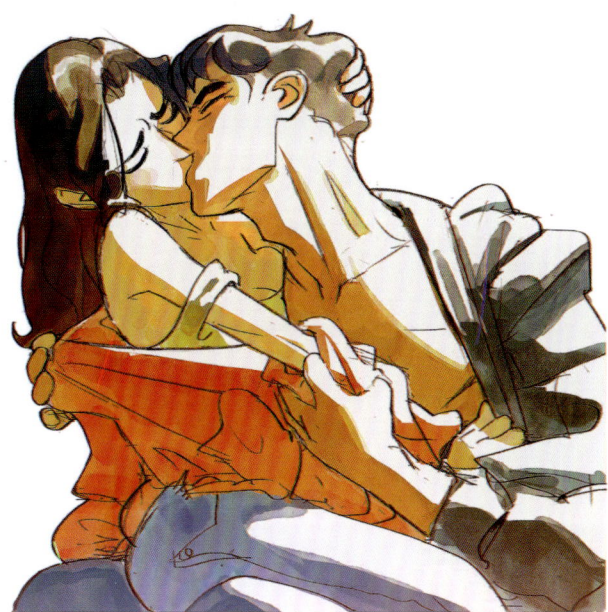

THEIR LIPS COLLIDE, THEIR BREATH RUNS DEEP

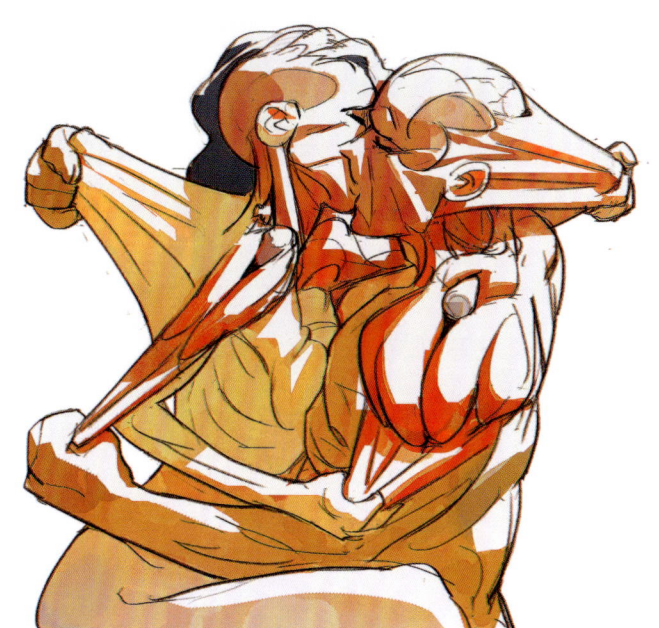

THEY STRIP THEIR FLESH IN LOVE'S FIERCE LEAP

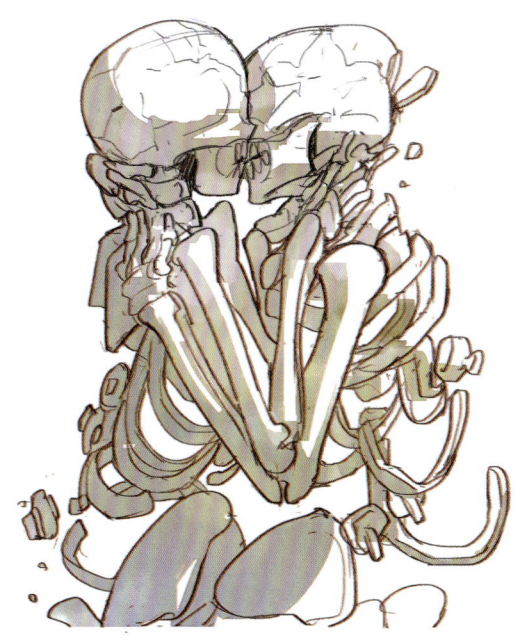

FROM BONE TO DUST, THEY SEEK TO BLEND

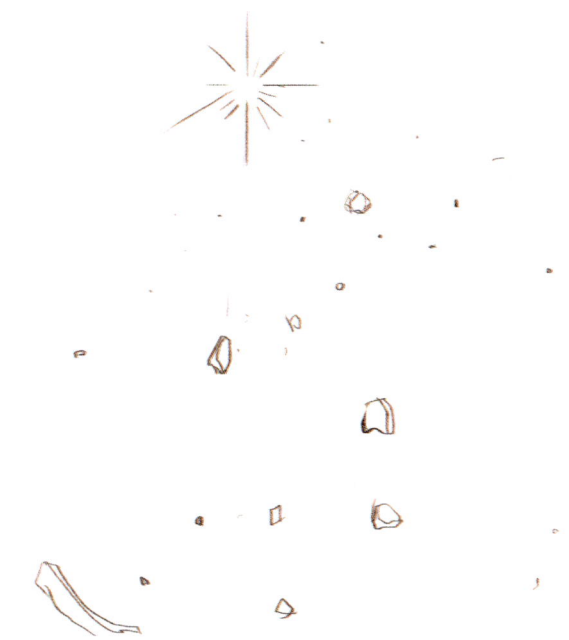

ONE SOUL REMAINS AS THEY TRANSCEND

TUTORIAL
Jellyfish

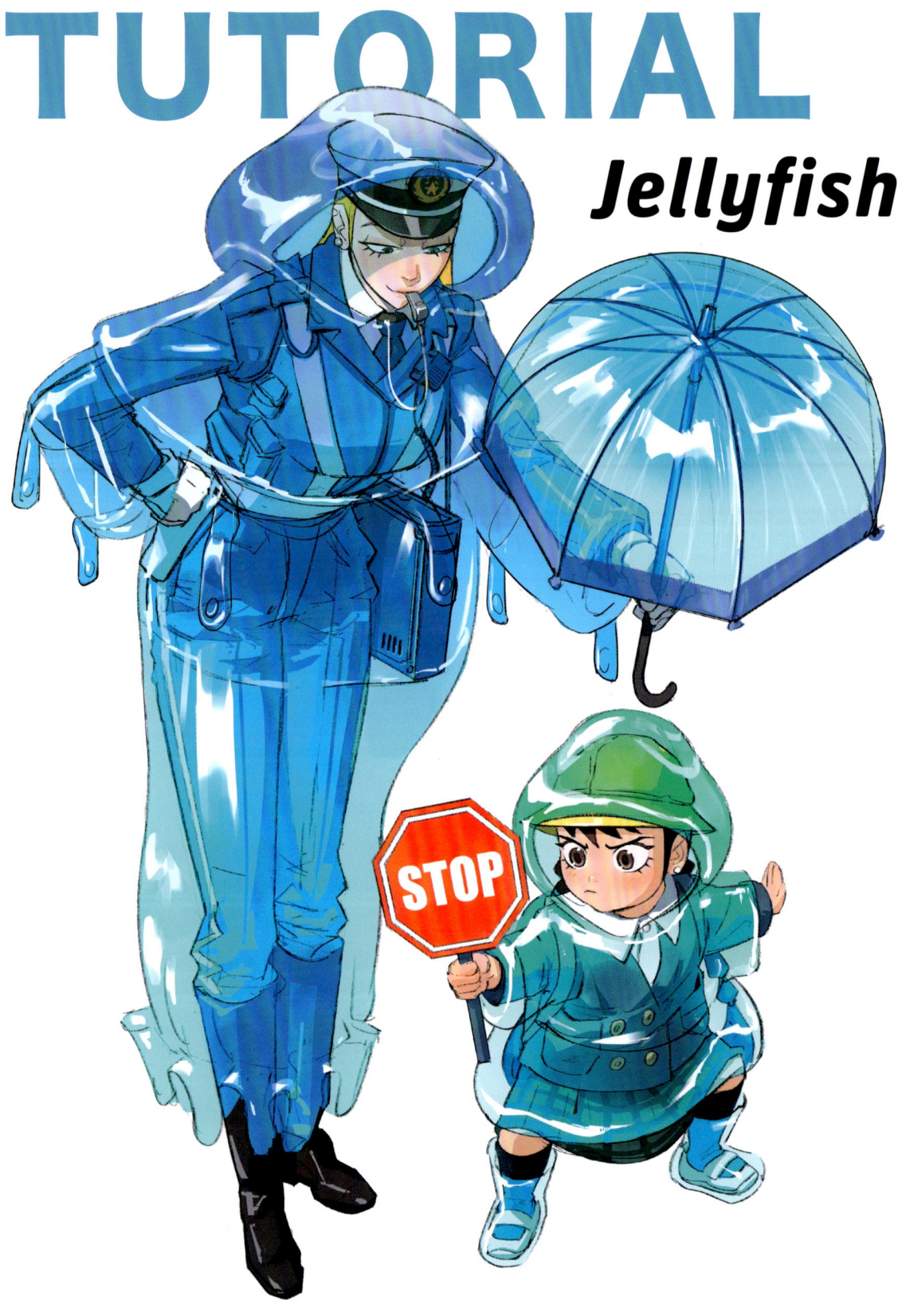

If you've been following along with the previous chapters, you already have a good idea of my process. Now, let's dive into a step-by-step tutorial where I'll break down how I created one of my favourite artworks, *Jellyfish*.

STEP 01: UNCONVENTIONAL IDEAS

First, I pick the theme. Sometimes, the idea comes from random thoughts, or I just see a picture online. In this case, I want to create something related to sea animals, which is why I choose a jellyfish. At this point, I am not entirely sure what I'm going to do with it, but I start imagining professions that might share visual characteristics with my main theme.

Initially, I think of a ballerina because the shape of the dress resembles a jellyfish, but I am not completely convinced, so I keep searching. Sometimes, when I can't decide, I choose random themes unrelated to the main subject and explore ways they might share similarities beyond the obvious.

That's exactly why I choose a traffic police officer. What truly captivates me is the fact that I have never designed this profession before – it seems like an interesting challenge. The visual matches, like the blue tones and the uniform, will become part of the process later.

What should your approach be for a process like this? Keep things simple. Choose one subject and mix it with something unconventional. It doesn't even need to belong to the same category. The challenge is to think of original ways they can relate through colour, shape, or even function.

For example, ask yourself: What does [insert subject] have in common with [insert another subject]? If you can find a connection, no matter how small, you'll be putting it into practice.

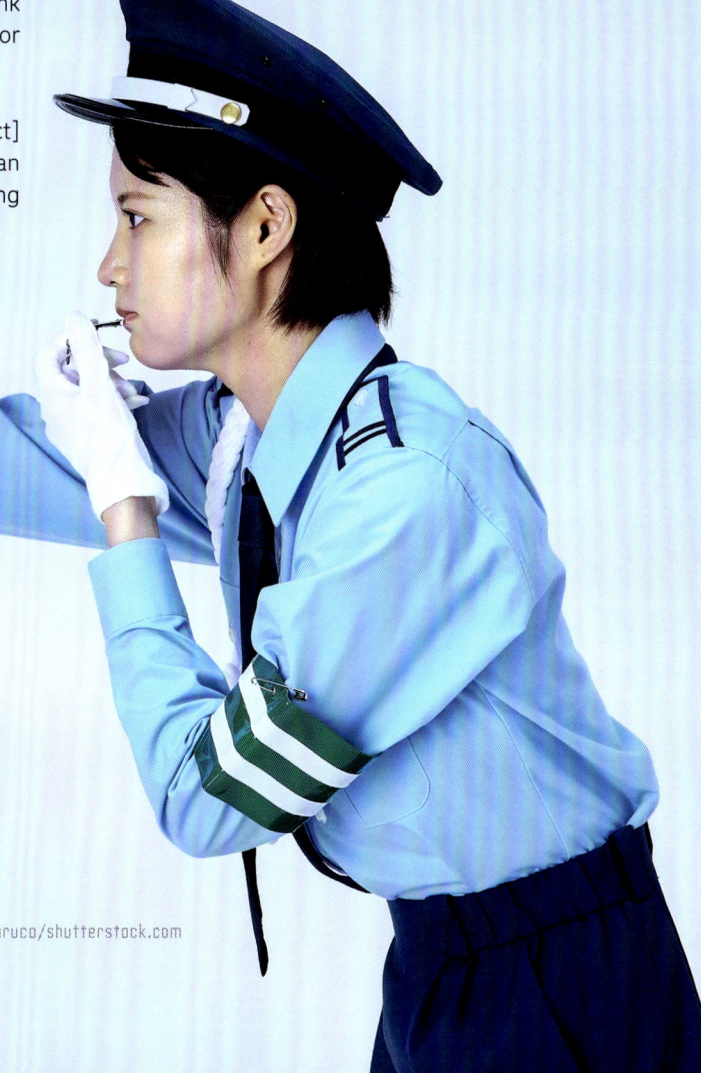

maruco/shutterstock.com

STEP 02: SKETCHING – BRING THAT LIFE!

This is probably the most important part of my process. Here, I use my technique to answer questions about the character and the emotions I want to evoke.

For this step, I start sketching in Photoshop on a canvas of 4688px width and 5864px height at 300 dpi. Why? I notice that the brush I use for drawing looks significantly better at this size.

When working on a smaller canvas with a lower resolution, I find that reducing the brush size too much disrupts the continuity of my strokes. The lines appear broken or inconsistent, likely due to the texture settings of the brush. Since I prefer a thin, textured line that resembles graphite, I need a larger canvas to maintain the visual consistency of the strokes without increasing the brush size.

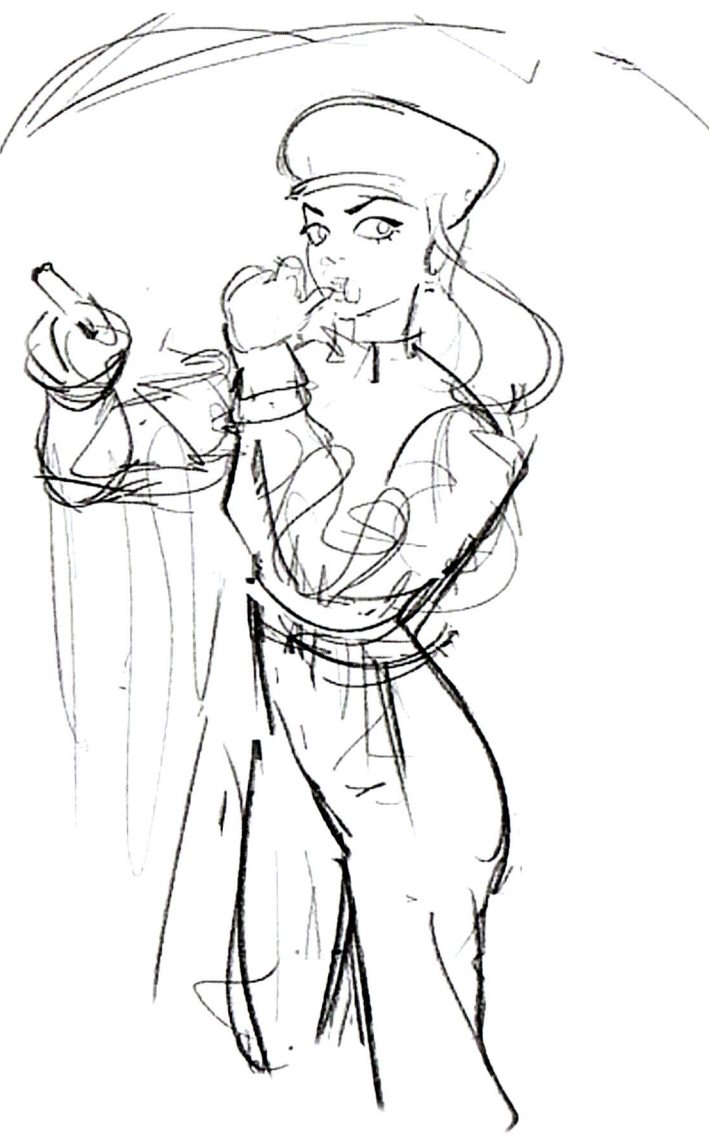

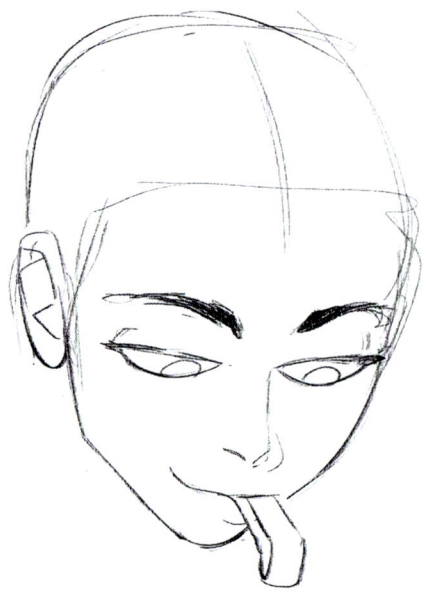

I begin by sketching a face that shares similar features with most of my characters – big eyes, a small nose, and some kind of expression. The key to lifelike characters lies mostly in their facial expression and body gestures. And when it comes to facial expressions, the most important elements are the eyes, eyebrows, and mouth. You'd be surprised how strong emotions can be conveyed just by adjusting these three elements.

FINDING THE RIGHT GESTURE

Your goal here is to capture the motivation of your character through facial expression or full-body gestures. Don't be afraid to *exaggerate*. Sometimes, in our attempt to maintain correct proportions, we end up with rigid, lifeless characters. My advice? Sacrifice perfect anatomy in favour of interesting gestures that truly reflect your character's personality – you can refine proportions in the next step.

Let's assume you manage to create an interesting sketch where your character's motivation is clear. Why is this important? Beyond making your character feel real, it's how you communicate ideas to the viewer. Expression evokes emotions – ones that the viewer can recognize, relate to, and respond to.

Lifelike characters are simply characters living a life, just like everyday people. They experience struggles, suffering, joy, and meaning. See yourself as the creator of a language – one that doesn't rely on letters or words, but on reflections of life, expressed through strokes, colours, and values; mirrors in which the audience can see themselves.

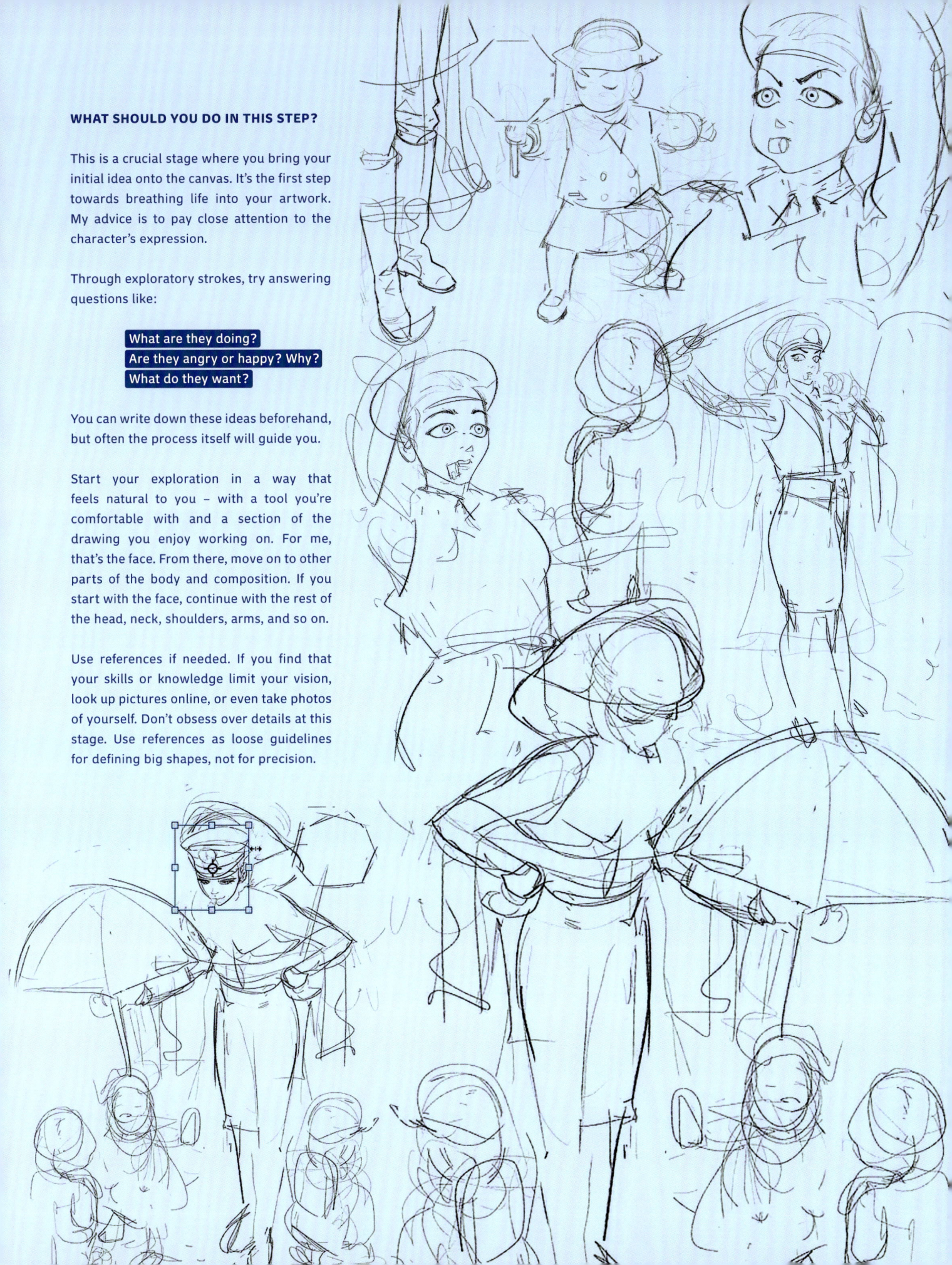

WHAT SHOULD YOU DO IN THIS STEP?

This is a crucial stage where you bring your initial idea onto the canvas. It's the first step towards breathing life into your artwork. My advice is to pay close attention to the character's expression.

Through exploratory strokes, try answering questions like:

> What are they doing?
> Are they angry or happy? Why?
> What do they want?

You can write down these ideas beforehand, but often the process itself will guide you.

Start your exploration in a way that feels natural to you – with a tool you're comfortable with and a section of the drawing you enjoy working on. For me, that's the face. From there, move on to other parts of the body and composition. If you start with the face, continue with the rest of the head, neck, shoulders, arms, and so on.

Use references if needed. If you find that your skills or knowledge limit your vision, look up pictures online, or even take photos of yourself. Don't obsess over details at this stage. Use references as loose guidelines for defining big shapes, not for precision.

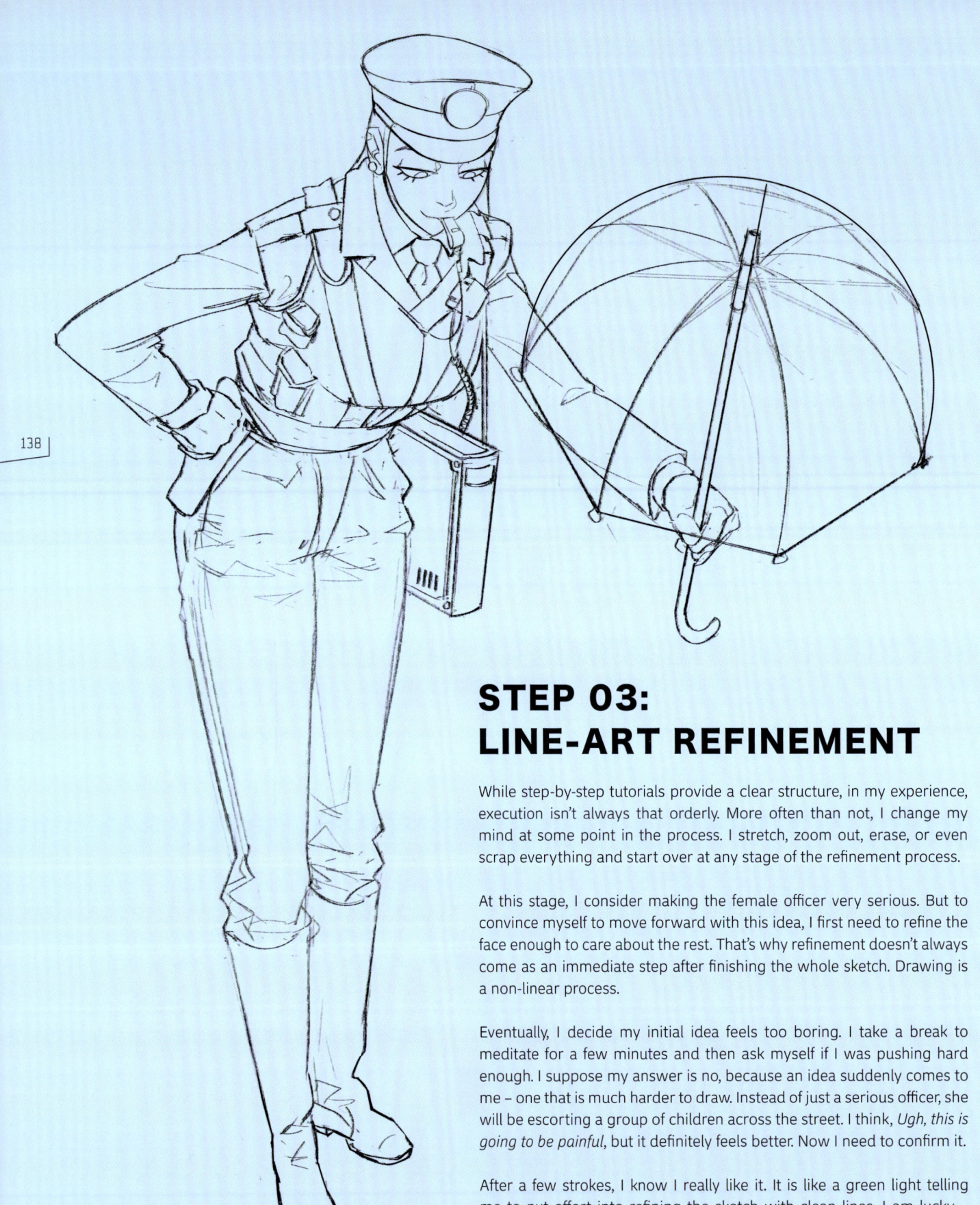

STEP 03: LINE-ART REFINEMENT

While step-by-step tutorials provide a clear structure, in my experience, execution isn't always that orderly. More often than not, I change my mind at some point in the process. I stretch, zoom out, erase, or even scrap everything and start over at any stage of the refinement process.

At this stage, I consider making the female officer very serious. But to convince myself to move forward with this idea, I first need to refine the face enough to care about the rest. That's why refinement doesn't always come as an immediate step after finishing the whole sketch. Drawing is a non-linear process.

Eventually, I decide my initial idea feels too boring. I take a break to meditate for a few minutes and then ask myself if I was pushing hard enough. I suppose my answer is no, because an idea suddenly comes to me – one that is much harder to draw. Instead of just a serious officer, she will be escorting a group of children across the street. I think, *Ugh, this is going to be painful*, but it definitely feels better. Now I need to confirm it.

After a few strokes, I know I really like it. It is like a green light telling me to put effort into refining the sketch with clean lines. I am lucky – often, I don't find enough reasons to move forward, but I have to anyway, making the struggle of drawing even more uphill.

I don't create a new layer for cleaning. Once I capture that life, that moment, I simply duplicate the sketch and refine it in the same layer.

Now, I start defining details in the character's proportions and outfit, sometimes from memory or imagination, though I find real-world references much more effective. In this case, I look up police-officer uniforms, profession-related tools, school uniforms for the children, and so on. I assume most artists create a reference board before reaching this stage – which is smart – but I'm more chaotic in that sense. Sometimes, I prepare references ahead of time, and other times I just start drawing and figure things out as I go. I guess it depends on how I feel and how the idea comes to me.

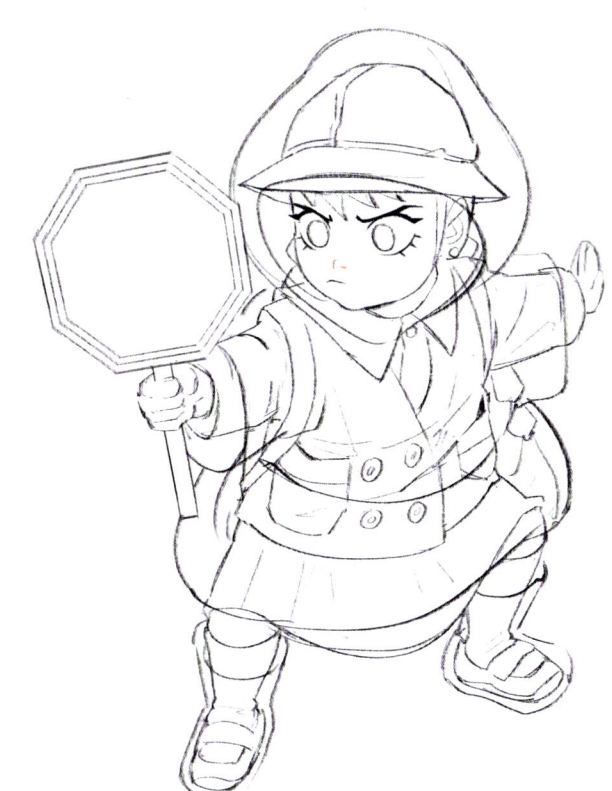

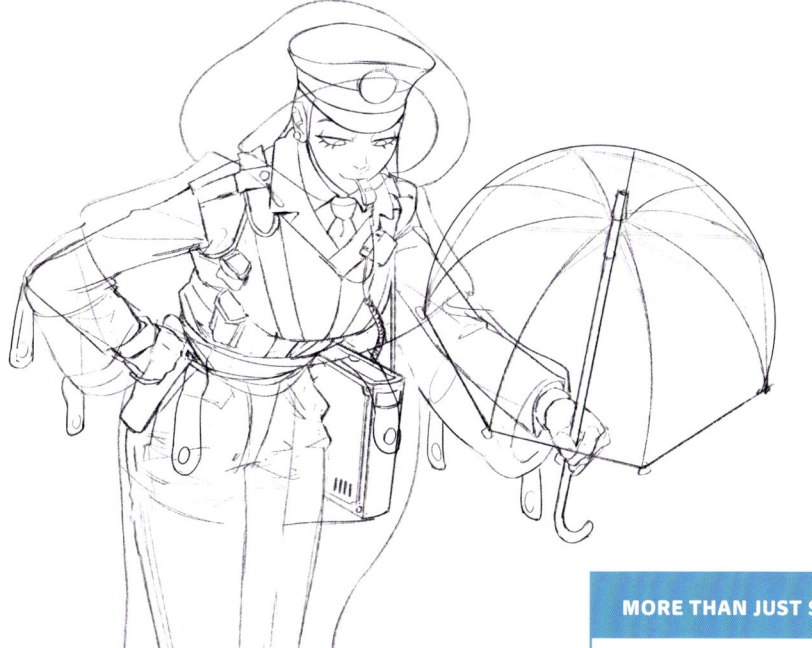

When I refine my line art, I like to keep curved lines because they feel more organic to me. In areas where I've used short, shaky lines, I erase parts while keeping the previous sketch as a guide. Then I make a quick curved stroke on top and erase the remaining sketchy lines, letting the clean stroke take the lead. It's not perfectly clean, but it clarifies the shape refinement. I use this approach for pretty much all the big shapes.

MORE THAN JUST SKILL

Drawing doesn't rely solely on skill. It also depends on your willingness to accept the results. In my opinion, this is influenced by multiple factors: your mental state, experience, and personal taste. If you're having a bad day, even a perfectly good sketch might not look right to you.

Not every day will be great, and you won't always be in the right mindset to judge your performance fairly. But be aware that your self-criticism might not always be as objective as you think – especially when you're tired. Let your ideas rest for at least a day before deciding to erase them or seal their fate.

Sounds dramatic, doesn't it?

STEP 04: COLOURS, COLOURS, COLOURS!

Once I refine the line art, I create a new layer beneath it and paint a grey shape within the character's silhouette. This grey shape helps separate the character from the background. Above the base layer, I add new layers for colours, values, and other details, all clipped to the grey silhouette using Photoshop's Clipping Mask feature. This method is commonly known as blocking, as it establishes a structured base.

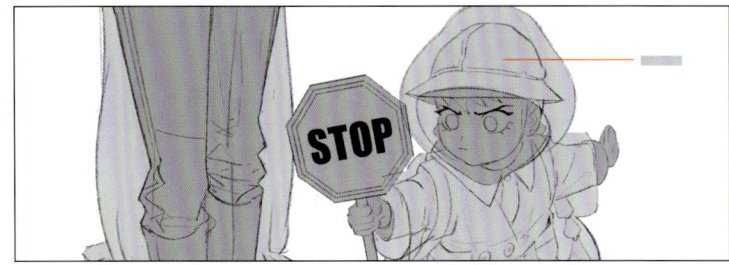

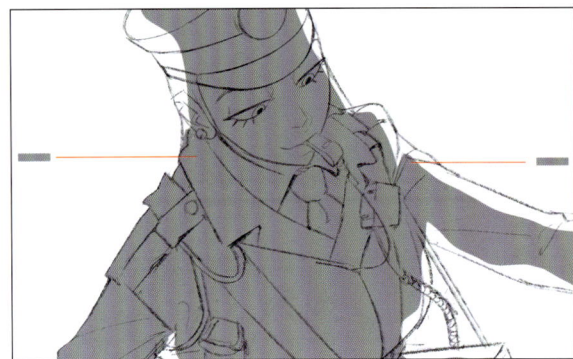

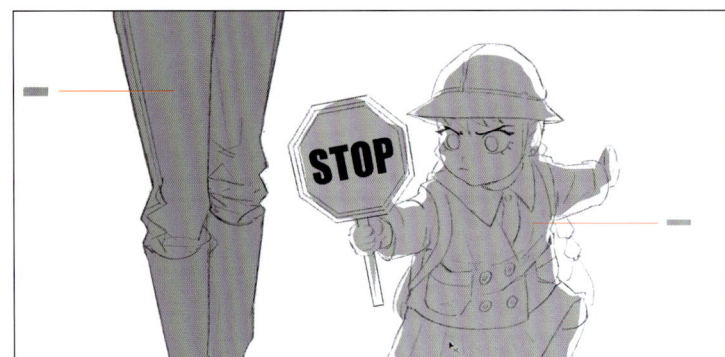

The colour palette for this piece is heavily inspired by the blue tones of the jellyfish reference. I want to keep things simple, using two or three variations of bright blue, contrasted with white and grey.

I prefer bright colour tones because they make the piece feel fresh and alive. However, that doesn't mean I always use saturated colours – on the contrary, I often use more saturated tones for shadows. In this step, I focus on laying down the base colours, which will later serve as the foundation for shadows and refinements. Saturation adjustments typically come at the end when I apply refinements using Photoshop filters.

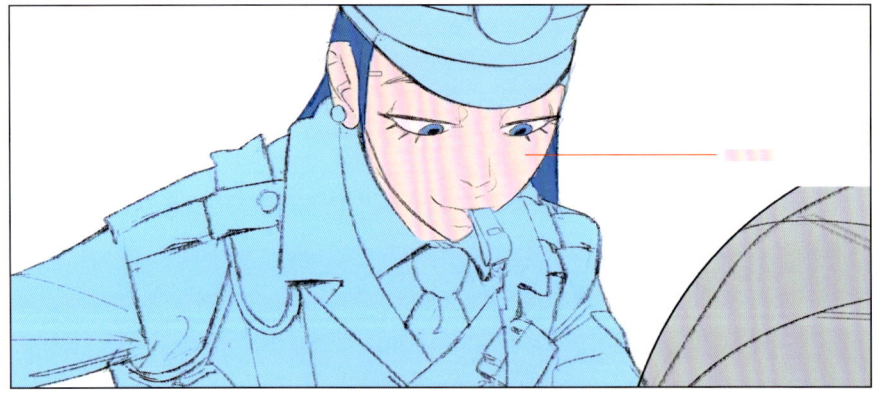

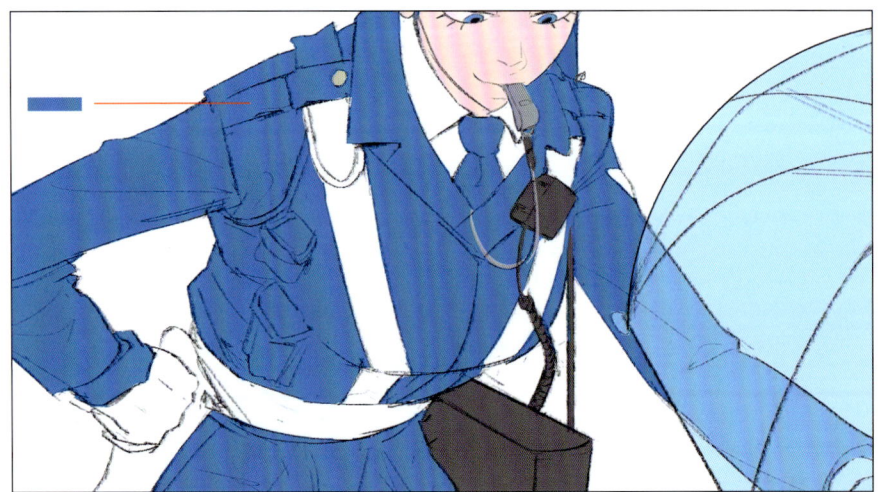

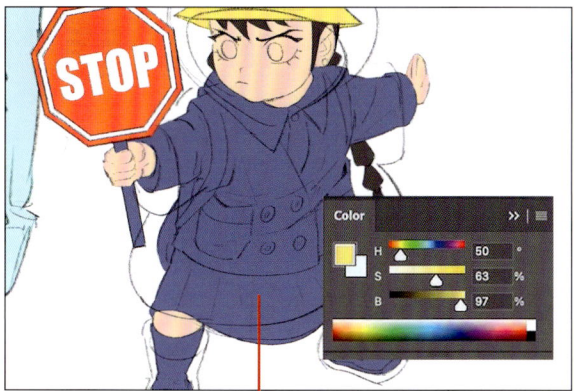

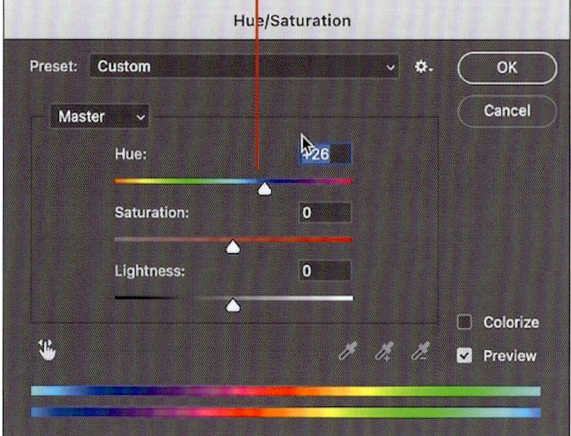

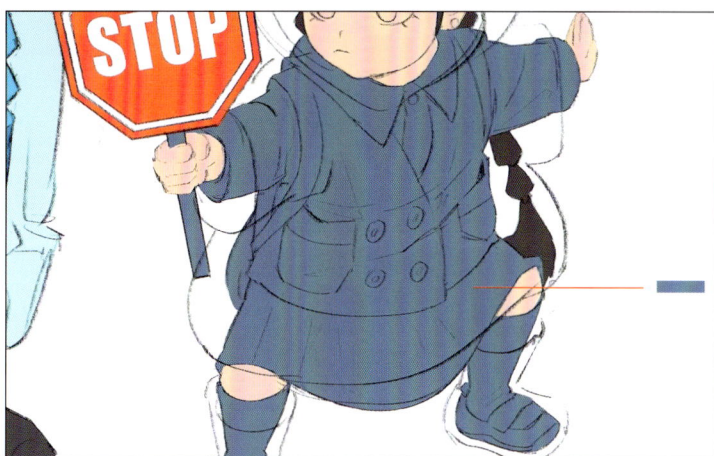

The problem I've found with starting with highly saturated colours is that they can be distracting. Instead, I prefer to begin with desaturated tones and sometimes add small spots of saturated colours, even in complementary hues, to create contrast.

WHERE TO START?

What should you do? What to paint? What colours to use? How? So many questions.

Start by choosing one base tone to paint the entire shape. Then, introduce one variation of that tone. It can be:

◊ More saturated
◊ More desaturated
◊ A bit darker
◊ A bit brighter

Once you choose a variation, apply it to specific elements of the character or shape. For example, if you're painting boots, make them slightly darker. If it's a shirt, make it a bit brighter. Work with the main colour and two variations to create contrast and make the composition more engaging.

To increase contrast, combine the base colour with white or darker grey. Avoid using black too early, as it can be overpowering before the shadowing phase. As a final touch, add small accents of the complementary colour to enhance the visual interest. For instance, if the main colour is blue, try incorporating small hints of orange or yellow in select areas of the character.

Why? Because contrast – between colour tones, values, and complementary colours – is what makes a composition visually compelling.

Balancing the Colour Composition

There is no universal formula that works every time, but for this *Jellyfish* example, I balanced the colour composition roughly as follows:

◊ 70% main colour (blue)
◊ 30% values (white or dark grey)
◊ 10% complementary accents (yellow)

While these percentages are subjective and difficult to measure precisely, I suggest ensuring that at least one predominant colour defines your composition. This dominant colour sets the mood, while the remaining values and complementary colours act as contrasting elements, making the piece visually interesting.

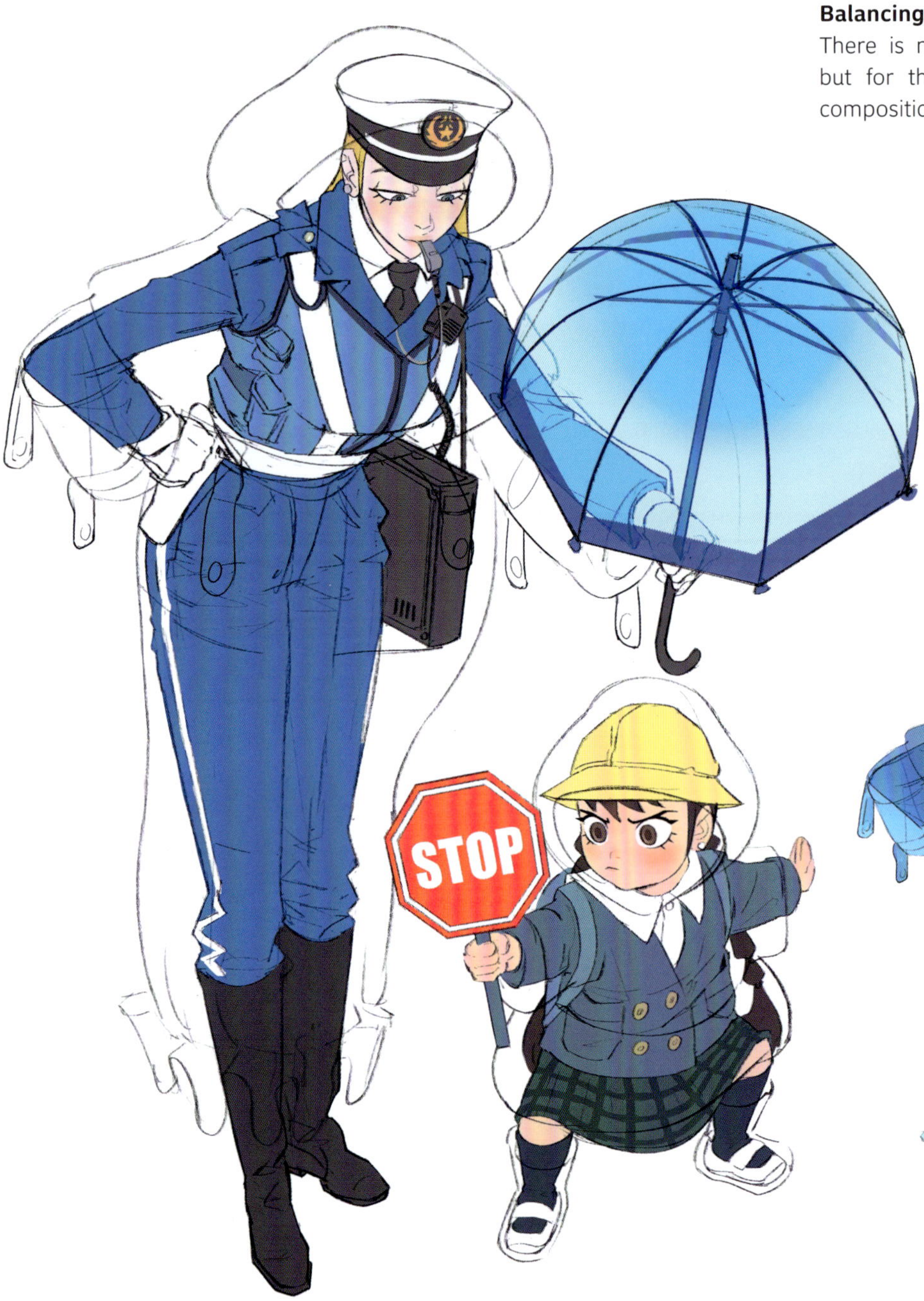

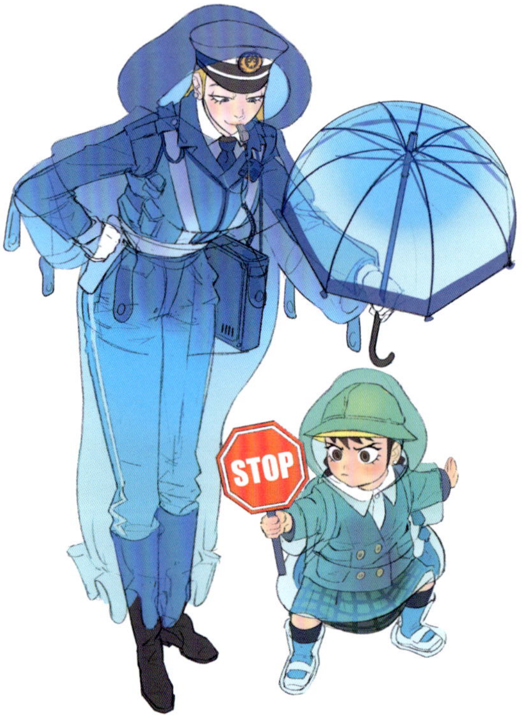

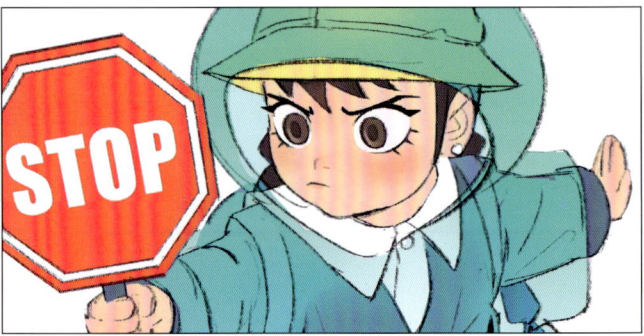

STEP 05: VALUES – LIGHT & SHADOW

As I mentioned earlier, values refer to the range of tones from white to black that create the illusion of volume. Some artists call it shading, others call it rendering or painting, but for me, it's simply 'values'.

Since I envisioned this composition outdoors in daylight, the primary light source comes from above, casting shadows beneath each form. These shadows follow the volumetric structure of the objects, expanding and distorting based on their three-dimensional shape.

I create a new layer on top of the colour layers (but still inside the grey blocking layer) using a clipping mask, and set the blending mode from Normal to Multiply. In this new layer, I use a hard-edge brush and an almost-grey tone to define the shadow shape silhouette.

Why a Hard-Edge Brush?
A hard-edge brush allows me to clearly see the contours of the shadow shapes, resembling the cel-shading style used in animation. Additionally, using a grey tone prevents the shadows from becoming oversaturated, which often happens when using the Multiply blending mode.

Besides, shadows aren't usually saturated, as they naturally lack light. Depending on the mood you want to create, you can choose:

◊ Desaturated brown tones for warm moods
◊ Desaturated bluish or green tones for cool moods

In this case, I choose warm tones.

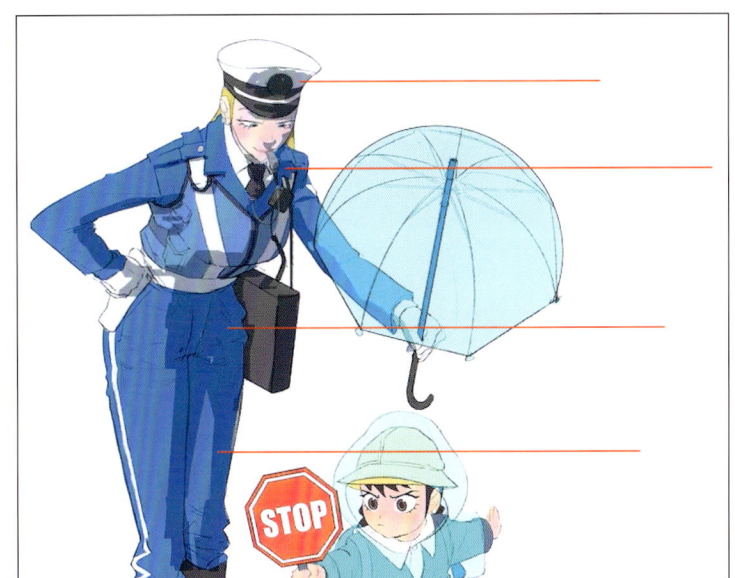

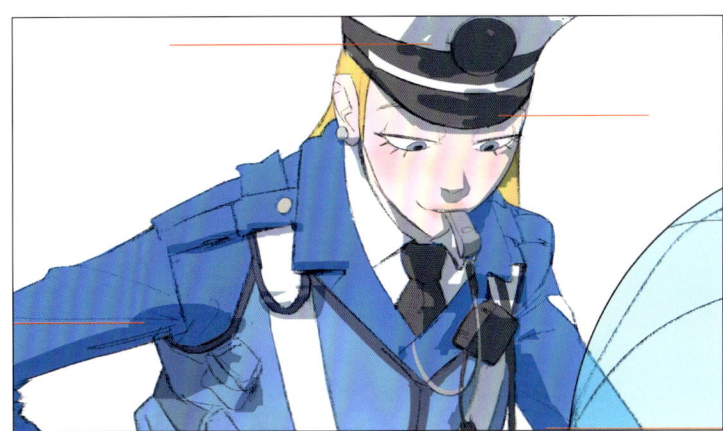

REFINING SHADOW TONES

Shadows in sunlight settings are usually cool, often shifting from purple to blue. However, I prefer to define the shadow shapes first and adjust the tones later. At the beginning, I always use a single tone – this prevents getting lost in unnecessary details when working with multiple shadow variations too soon.

For me, the key is to first build a three-dimensional look by carefully balancing soft and hard edges within the shadow shapes. Only after this structure is established do I fine-tune the shadow colours, adjusting them according to the surrounding tones.

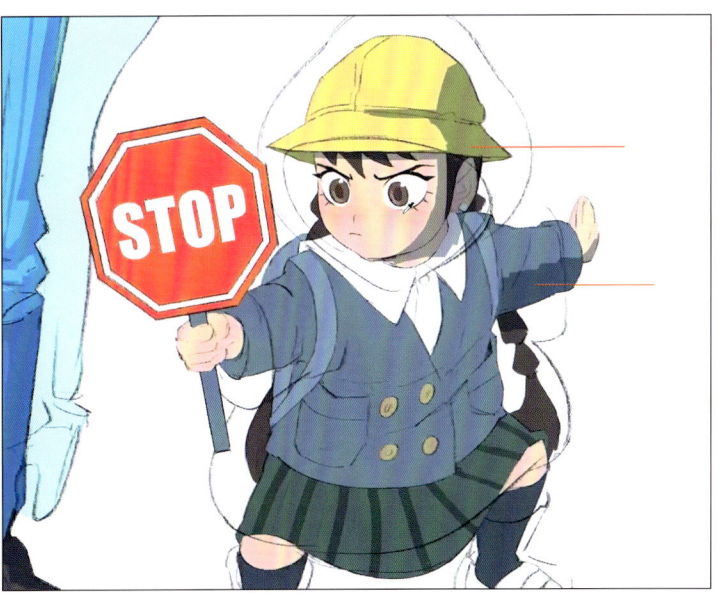

Adding Depth to Values

Once the shadow shape is roughly defined, I add new layers of value depth, painting highlights or darker variations of the existing shadow tone. These deeper shadows go in areas where light doesn't reach, and I usually paint them on smaller-sized layers so they don't compete with the larger shadow tones already in place.

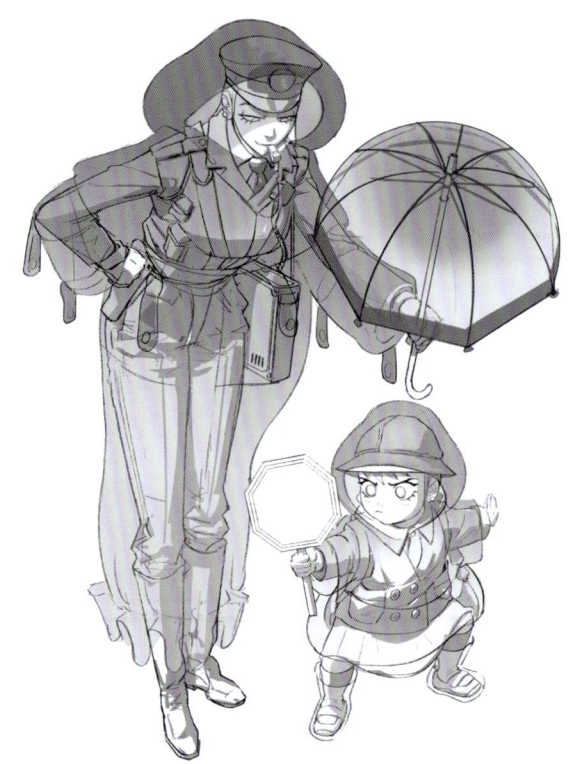

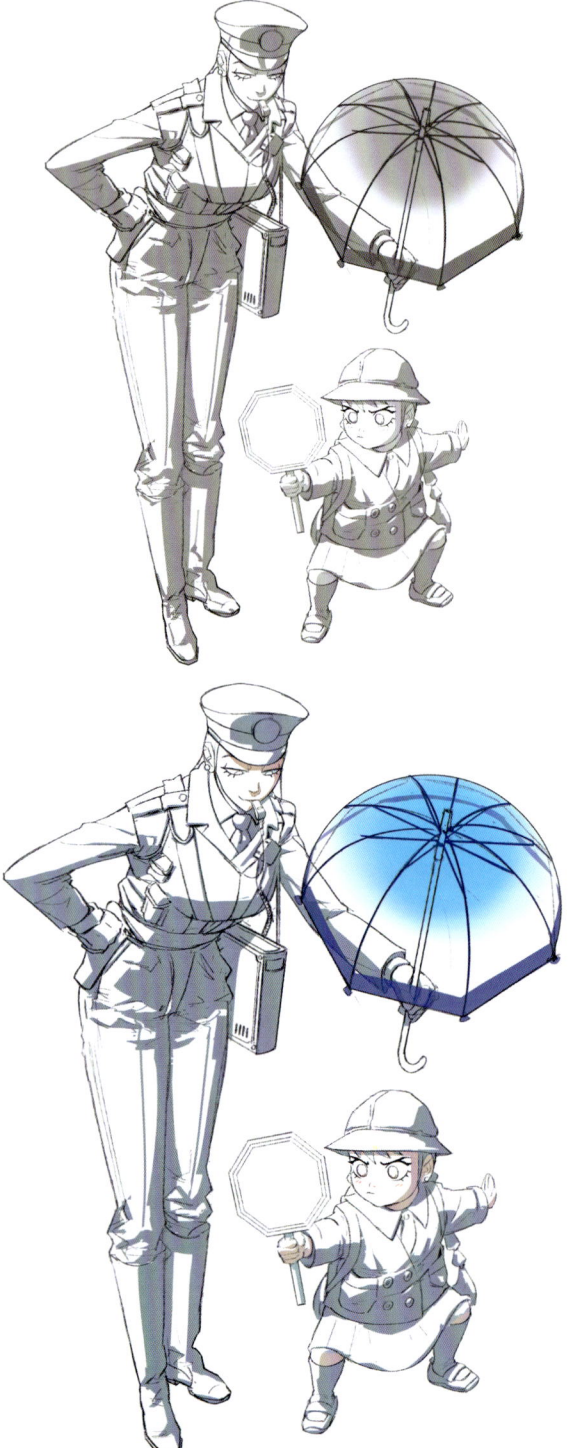

This process helps create value contrast in a balanced way, ensuring that one subject remains visually dominant over others. Hierarchies in value composition are important.

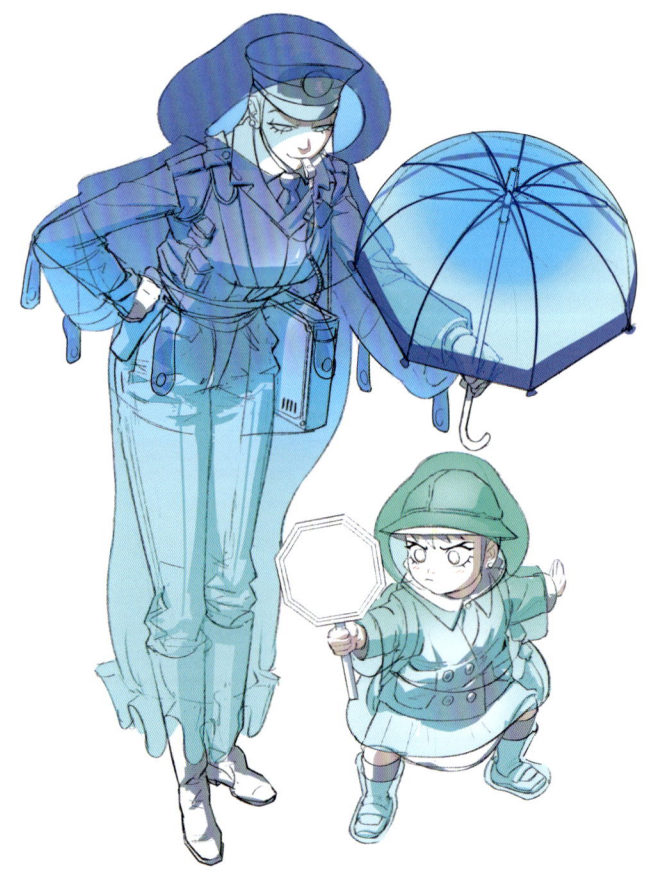

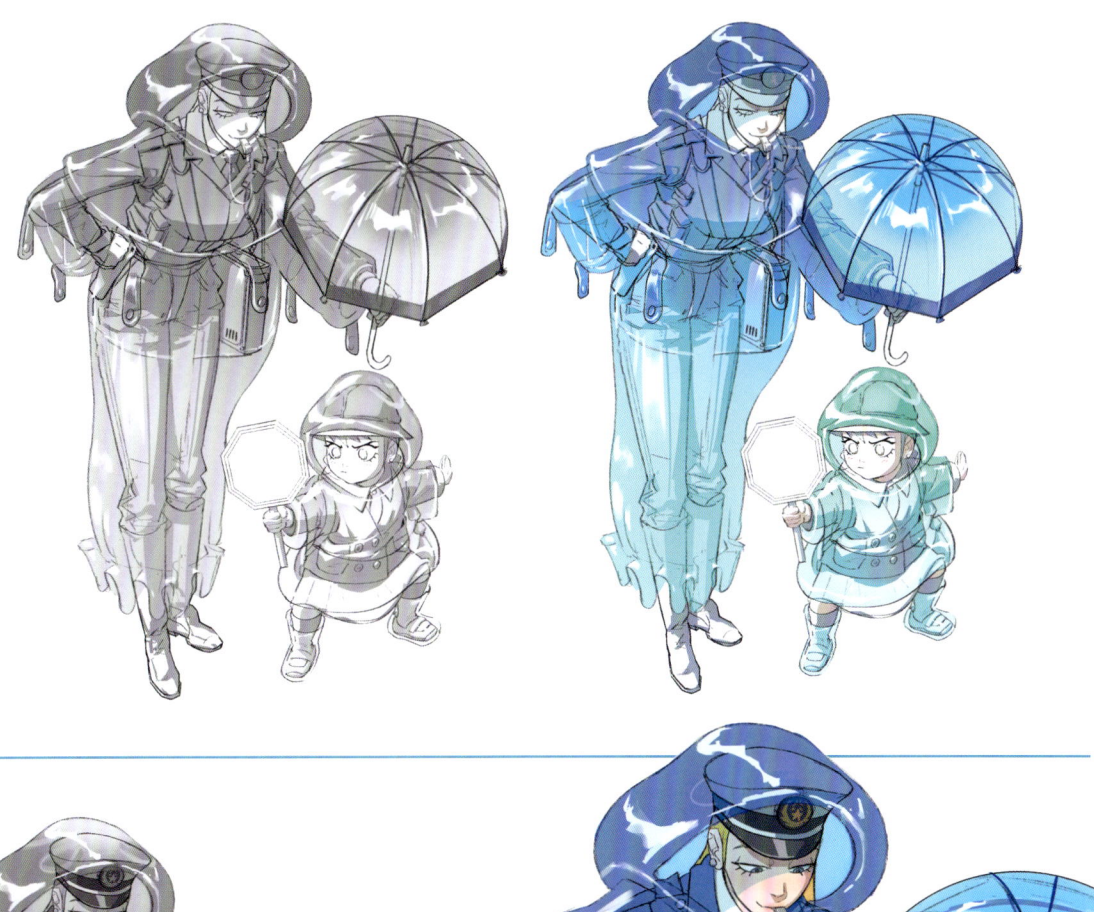

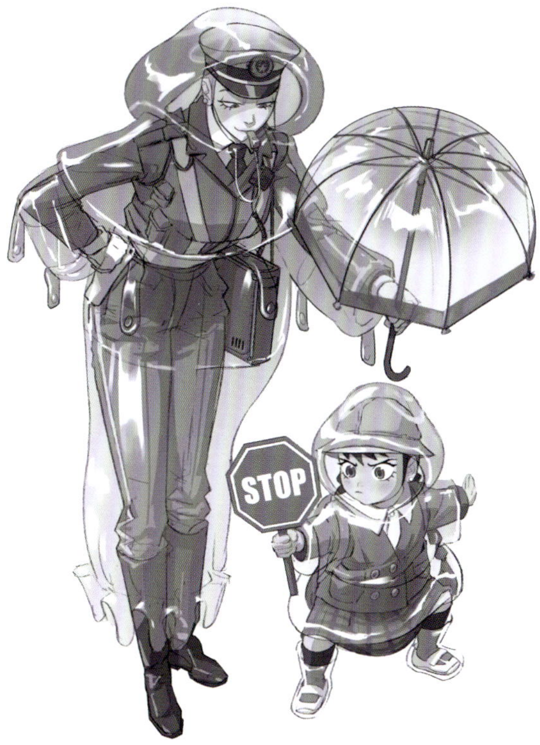

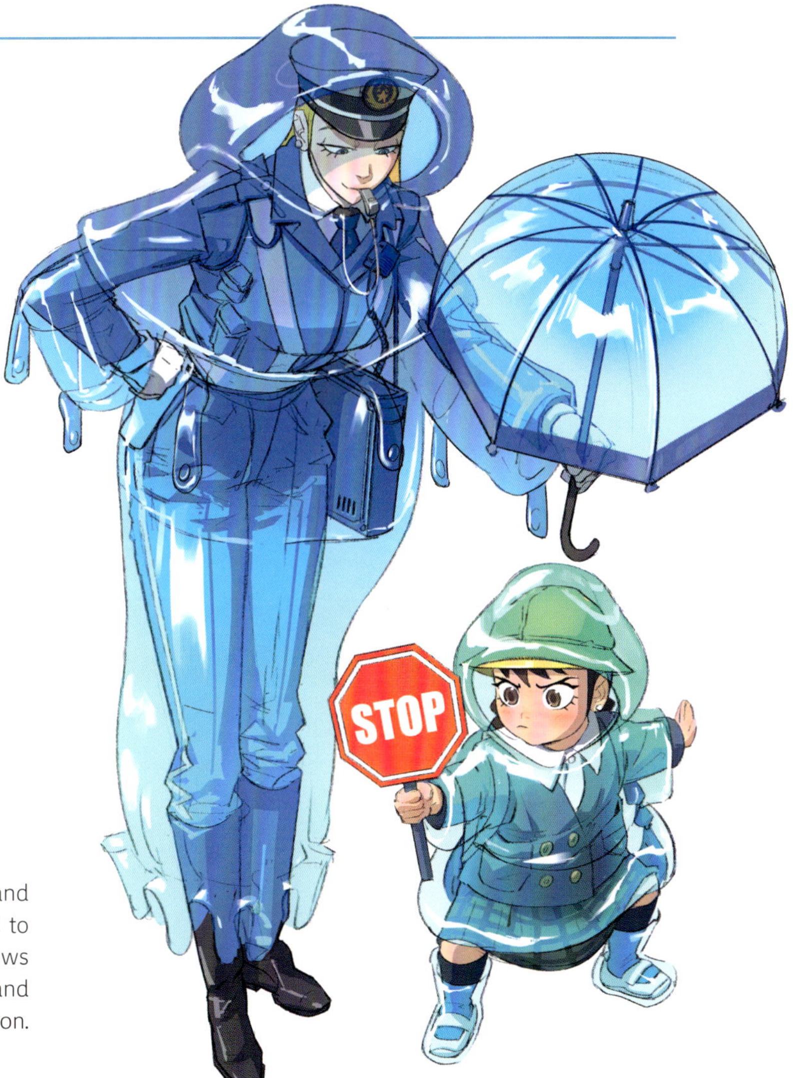

The presence of transparent materials, like raincoats and umbrellas, adds complexity. These materials allow light to pass through while still casting diffused, layered shadows that subtly reveal the forms beneath. This interplay of light and shadow enhances the realism and depth of the composition.

STEP 06: DETAILS

When refining details, I mainly focus on small adjustments from the previous steps, such as removing unnecessary sketchy lines, adjusting colours that don't match, and refining the shapes of shadows and highlights.

To enhance colour vibrancy, I often use Selective Color, adjusting the properties of whites, neutrals, blacks, and specific colours. However, in this particular case, I didn't. I felt the blues were already saturated enough for my taste.

I also tend to use effects like Smart Sharpen to sharpen line edges, along with other filters to add textures, as I mentioned in 'My Creative Process'.

Finally, I export the image using Photoshop's Export As option, reducing the scale so the height matches 1920 pixels. This resolution works well for HD screens, which is where most of my art is displayed. There's no need to export a larger size unless it's intended for printing.

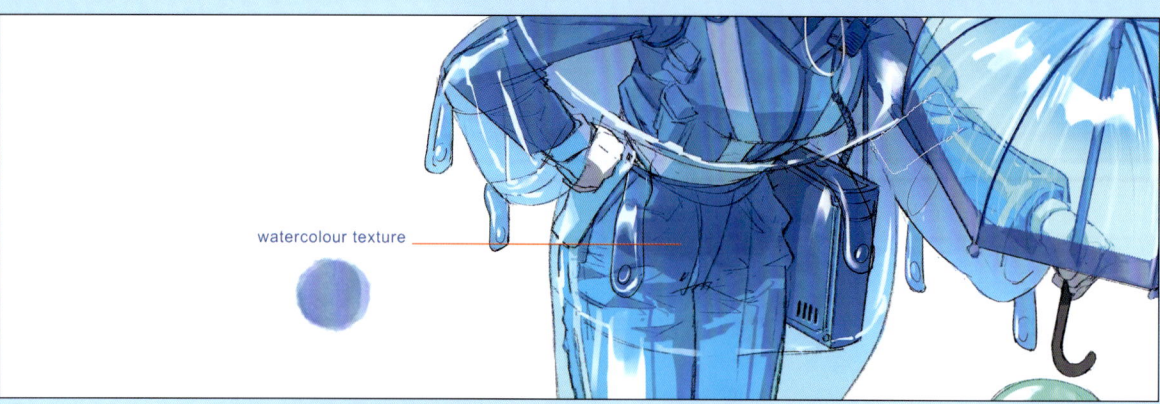

watercolour texture

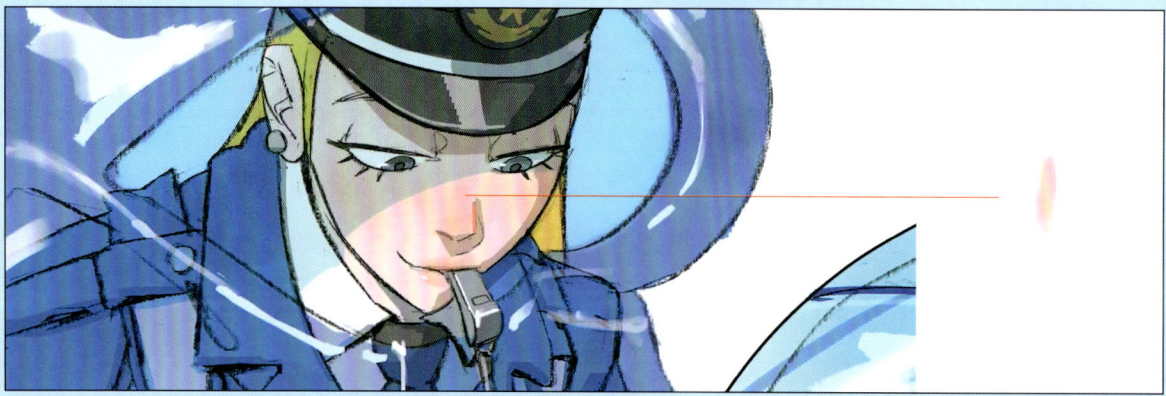

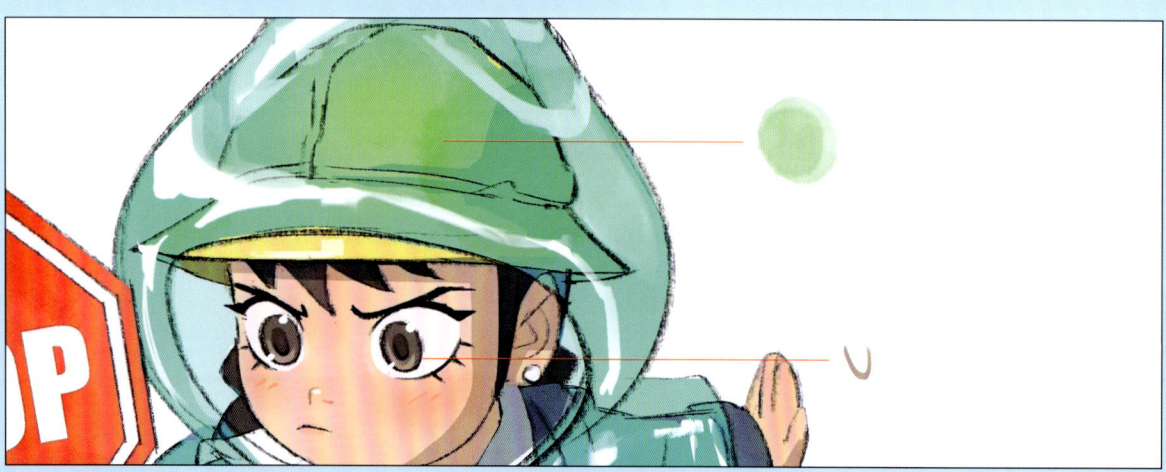

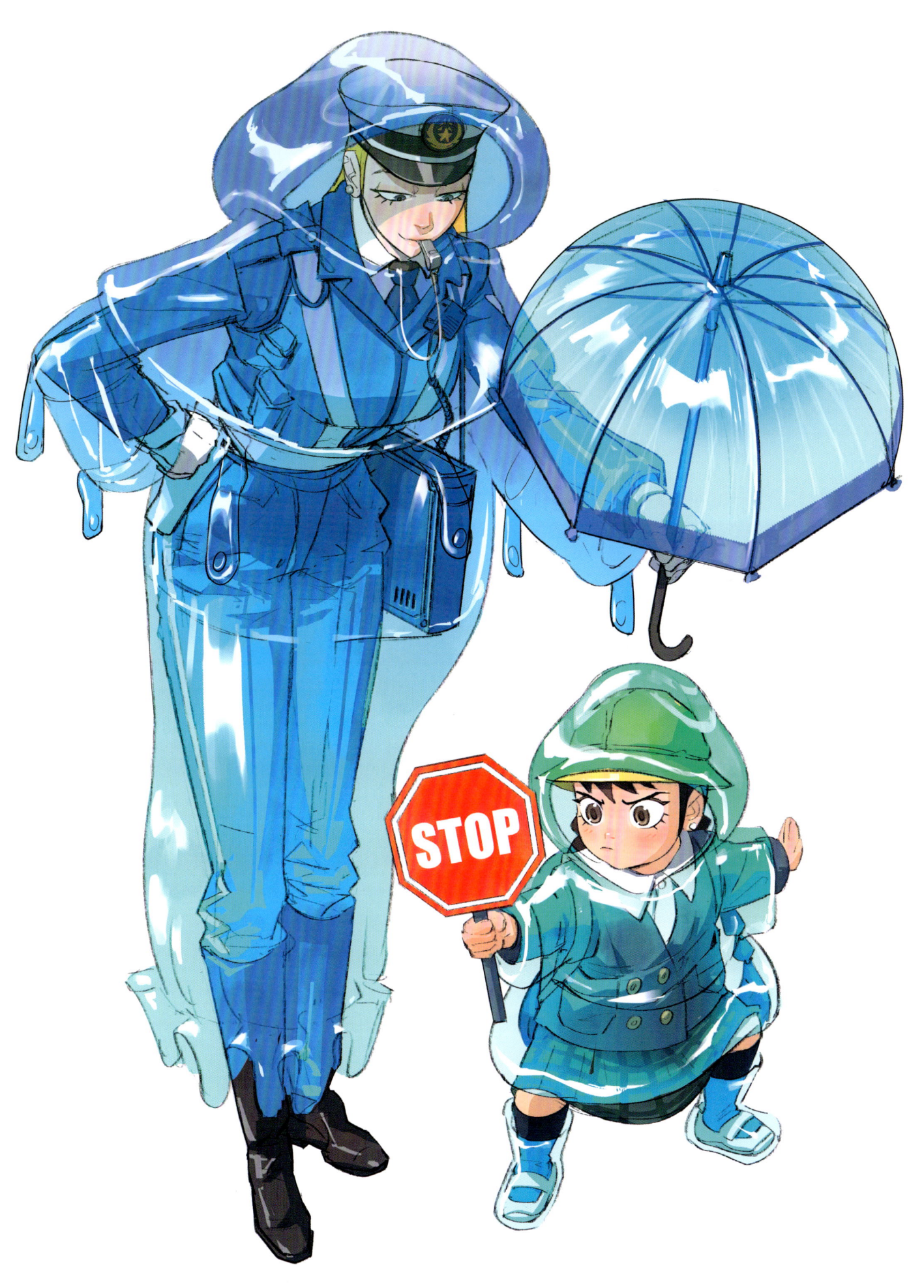

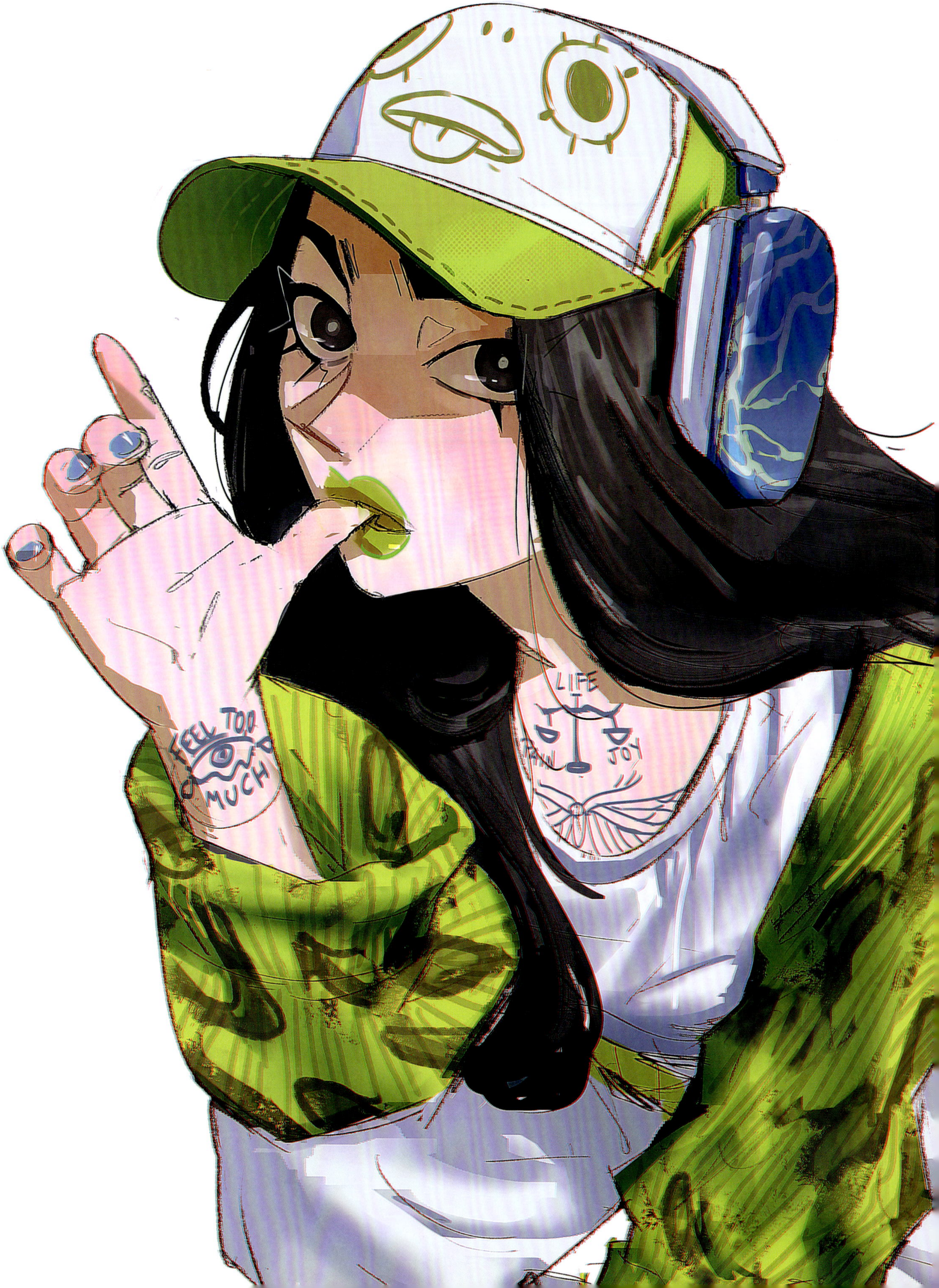
FEEL TOO
MUCH
LIFE
PAIN
JOY

THANK YOU

Thank you for buying this book. I'm deeply grateful that you consider my work worth exploring and supporting, whether you're an artist or simply someone who loves art. Your unexpected interest in my work intrigues and fascinates me, just as my art does for you.

Thanks to the 3dtotal team for making this book happen and for helping my sceptical self believe it was possible. They were very professional throughout the entire development process – such a smart way to bring value to artists and to those who appreciate art.

Thanks to my family – so much of what makes me the artist I am exists as a consequence of the experiences we shared. The work-in-progress that I am is driven by their well-being, which gives meaning to what I create.

Finally, thanks to God, because I could not have done any of this without Him.

FINAL THOUGHTS

What I'm sharing here is nothing but my experience – what I've discovered and found worthy of describing. I'm sure there's even more happening beyond my conscious decisions that I can't fully comprehend. Hopefully, some of these words serve as a tool in your journey, but keep in mind that a great part of your creative process escapes your control – and that's a good thing. It humbles you.

What should you do with that information? I'm not sure. I guess I just want to invite you to welcome that part of yourself, to let it create alongside your structured approach and goals. To become a child again and, maybe through that inexplicable but fascinating combination, bring life to every sketch.

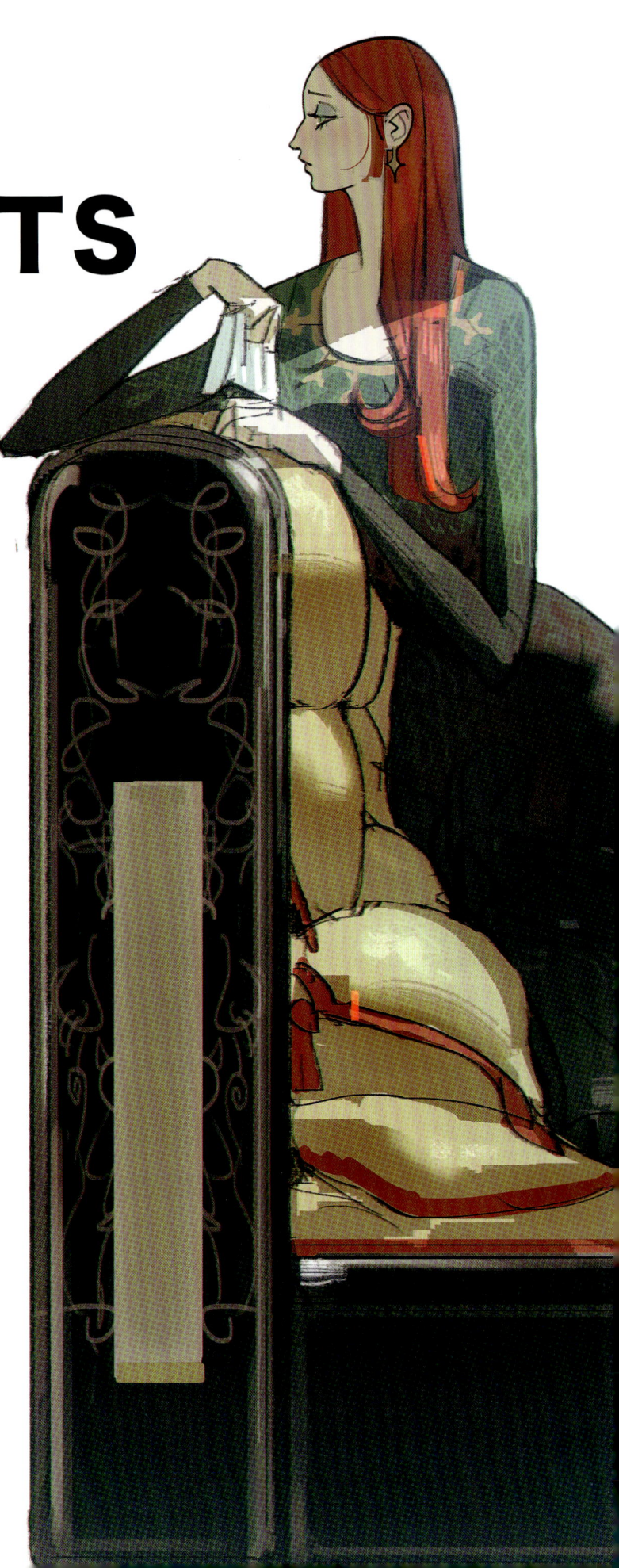

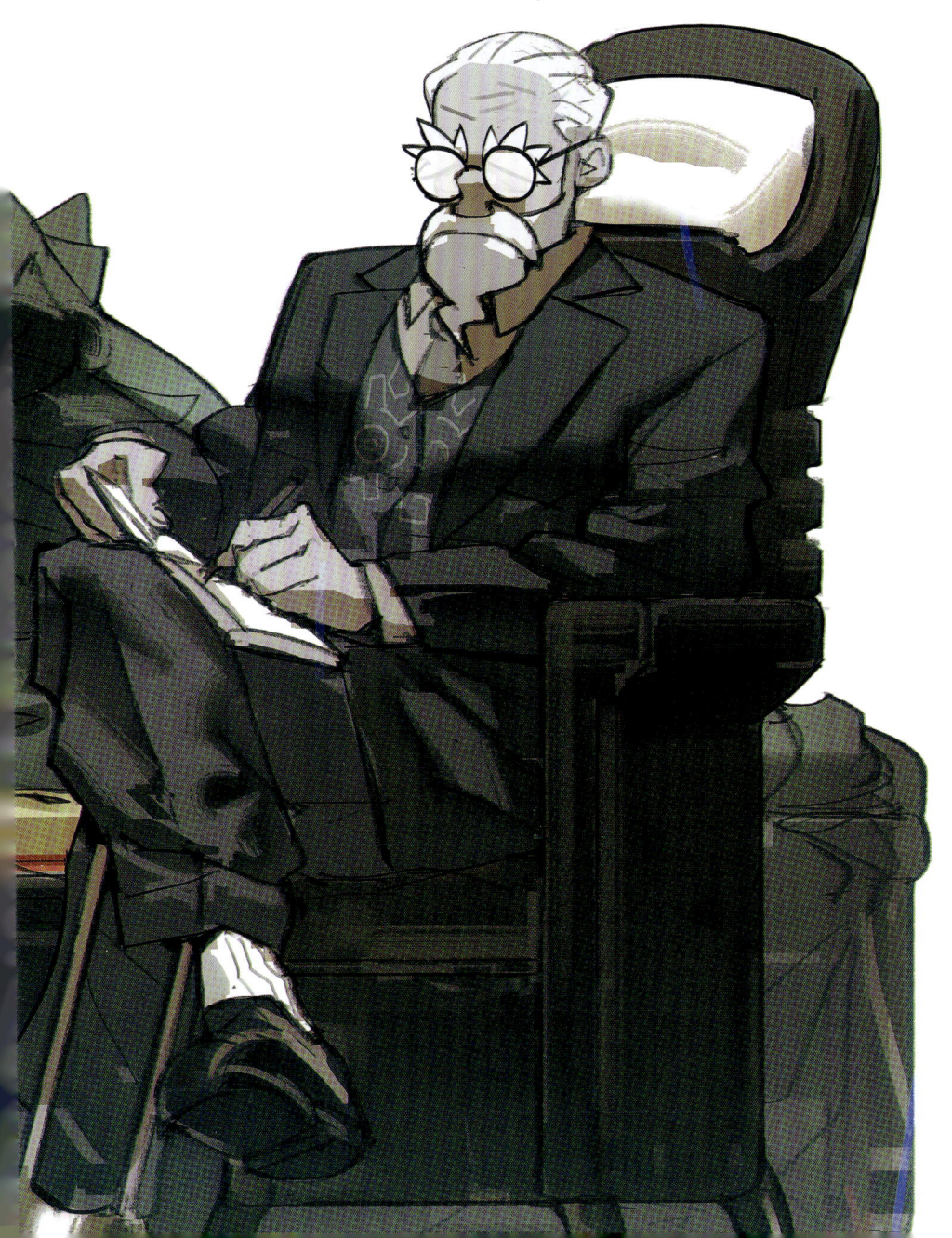

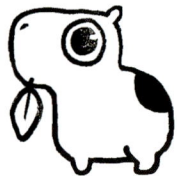

3dtotalPublishing

3dtotal Publishing is a trailblazing, creative publisher specializing in inspirational and educational resources for artists.

Our titles feature top industry professionals from around the globe who share their experience in skilfully written step-by-step tutorials and fascinating, detailed guides. Illustrated throughout with stunning artwork, these bestselling publications offer creative insight, expert advice, and essential motivation. Fans of digital art will enjoy our comprehensive volumes covering Adobe Photoshop, Procreate, and Blender, as well as our superb titles based around character design, including *Fundamentals of Character Design* and *Creating Characters for the Entertainment Industry*. The dedicated, high-quality blend of instruction and inspiration also extends to traditional art. Titles covering a range of techniques, genres, and abilities allow your creativity to flourish while building essential skills.

Well-established within the industry, we now offer over 100 titles and counting, many of which have been translated into multiple languages around the world. With something for every artist, we are proud to say that our books offer the 3dtotal package:

LEARN · CREATE · SHARE

Visit us at store.3dtotal.com

3dtotal Publishing is part of 3dtotal.com, a leading website for CG artists founded by Tom Greenway in 1999.

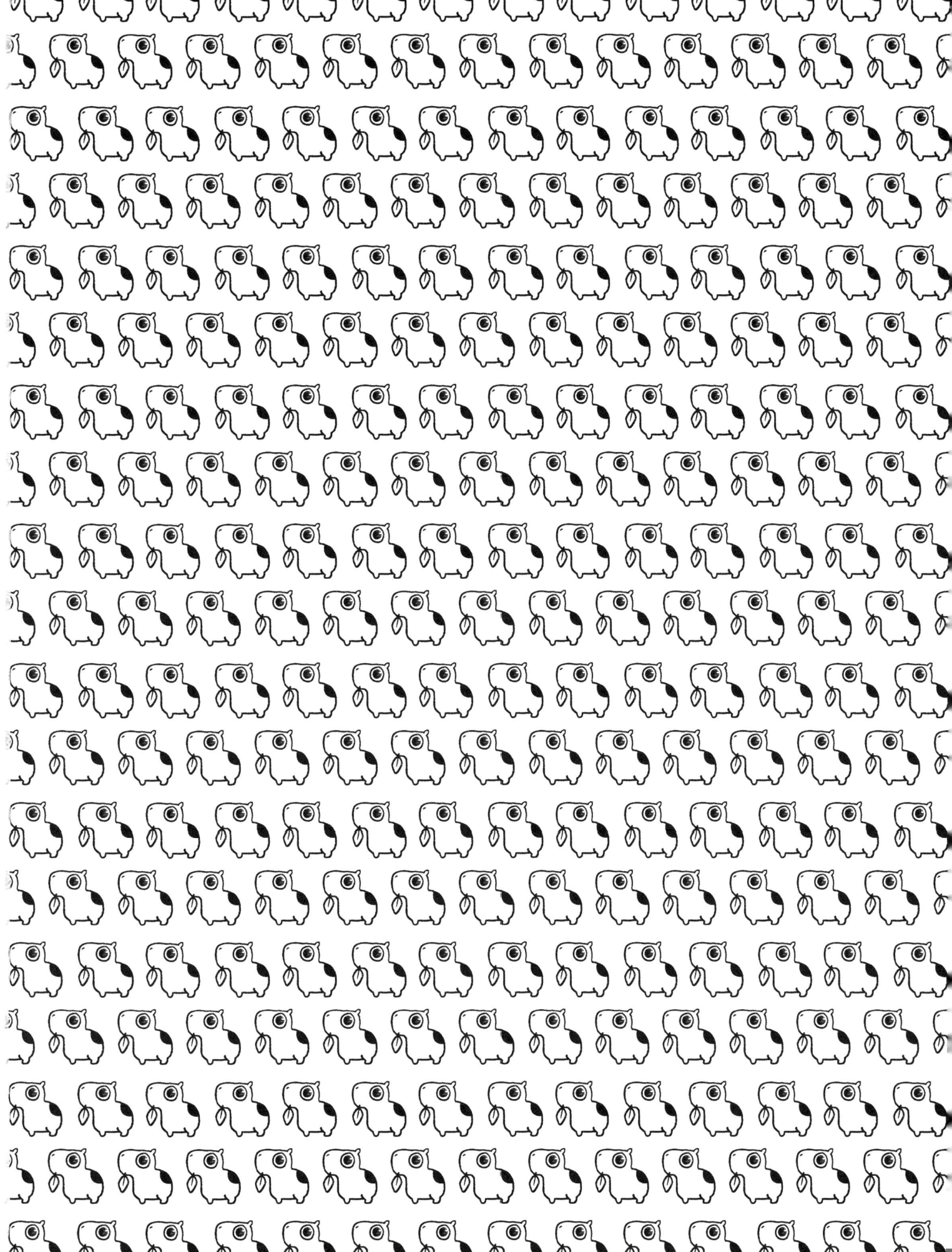

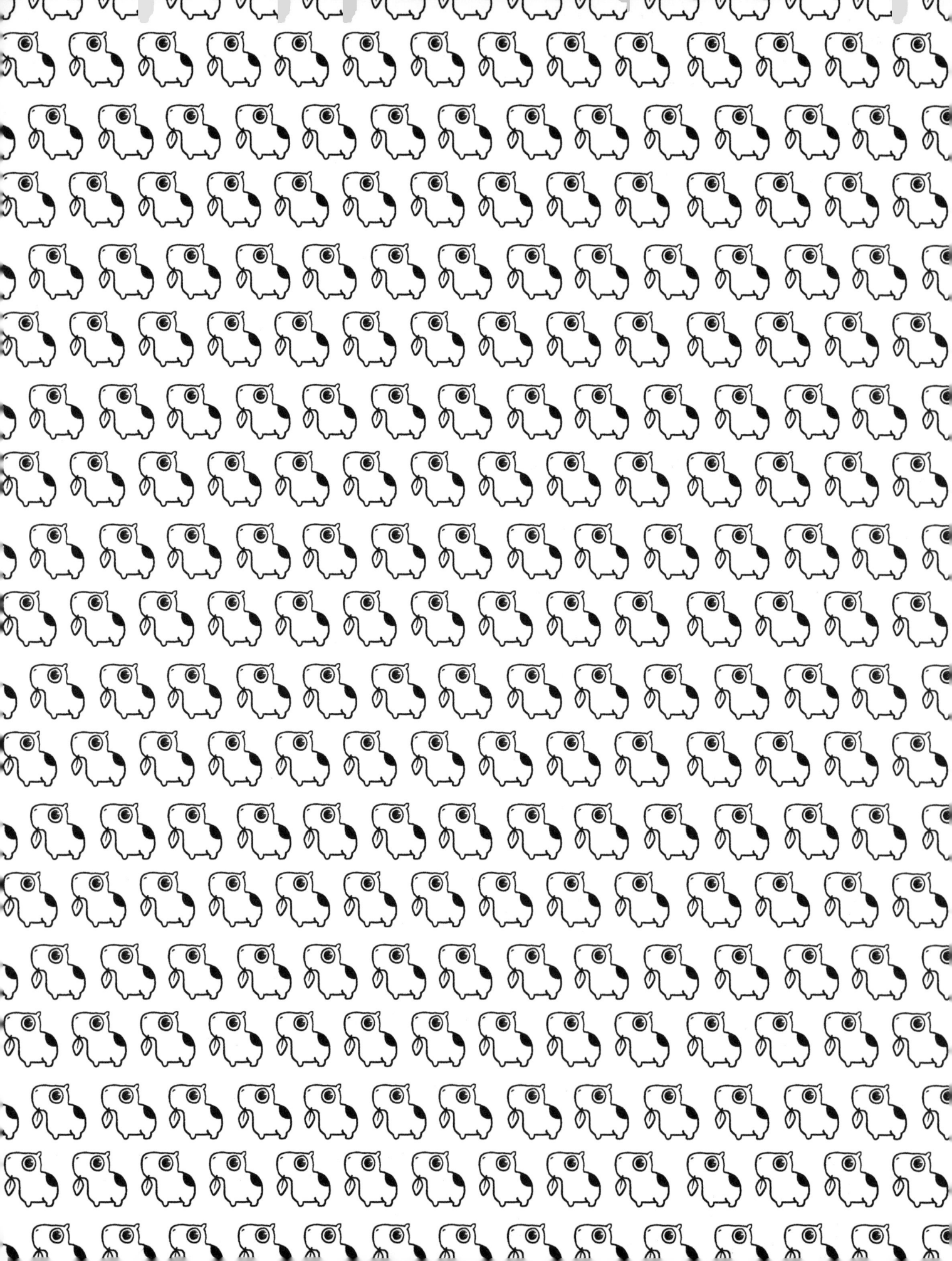